Robert P. Resch

Before Stalinism

To the memory of those killed in
Tlatelolco – Mexico City – October 1968
Tiananmen Square – Beijing – June 1989

Before Stalinism

The Rise and Fall
of Soviet Democracy

SAMUEL FARBER

V

VERSO

London · New York

First published in the United States by Verso 1990

© Samuel Farber 1990

Verso
UK: 6 Meard Street, London W1V 3HR
USA: 29 West 35th Street, New York, NY 10001-2291

Verso is the imprint of New Left Books

ISBN 0 86091 315 5
ISBN 0 86091 530 1 pbk

Library of Congress Cataloging-in-Publication Data
is available for this book from the Library of Congress

Typeset in 10 on 11½ pt Ehrhardt by Acorn Bookwork, Salisbury,
Wiltshire
Printed in Great Britain by Billing and Sons Ltd, Worcester

Contents

Contents

Acknowledgments

I am grateful to the staff of the Interlibrary Loan department of the Brooklyn College Library, particularly Professor William C. Parise, for their invaluable assistance in obtaining the materials necessary to carry out my research. I am also grateful to Liz Paton for her editorial assistance and to my editor at Polity Press, Anthony Giddens, for the trouble he has taken to bring this project to a successful conclusion.

I also want to thank the numerous people who read and commented on partial and complete drafts of the manuscript while it was in preparation: Johanna Brenner, Robert Brenner, Jane Burbank, Eric Chester, David Finkel, Samuel Friedman, Brent Garren, Adolfo Gilly, Nancy Holmstrom, Michael Letwin, T. H. Rigby, Michael Rogin, S. A. Smith, and Hillel Ticktin. I especially want to express my gratitude to Gerald Surh for his early intellectual guidance and encouragement, and to Selma Marks for many years of intellectual, moral, and spiritual support.

Major Events in Russian History
1917–1924

Dates in Old Style until 1 February 1918 when conversion was made to Gregorian Calendar (13 days ahead of Old Style).

1917

February 27	February Revolution. Overthrow of Tsarism.
March 2	Formation of Provisional Government.
April 3	Lenin returns to Petrograd and formulates 'April Theses.'
July 3–5	The 'July Days.'
July 26–August 3	Sixth Party Congress. Slogan 'All Power to the Soviets' is set aside.
August 23–27	Kornilov coup is defeated.
October 25	October Revolution. The Bolsheviks overthrow the Provisional Government.
November 12	Elections to the Constituent Assembly.
November 18	Left Socialist Revolutionary Party enters coalition government.
December 7	Organization of the Cheka – All-Russian Extraordinary Commission for Combatting Counterrevolution and Sabotage.
December 25– January 1	First All-Russian Congress of Trade Unions.

1918

January 5–6	Convocation and dissolution of Constituent Assembly.
February 1(Feb. 14)	Gregorian Calendar goes into effect.
March 3	Treaty of Brest-Litovsk is signed.
March 6–8	Seventh Party Congress. Bolsheviks adopt the name 'Communist.'
March 10–14	Capital moves to Moscow.
March 15	Left SR Party leaves government in protest against Treaty of Brest-Litovsk.
May 25	Beginning of major Civil War.
June 28	Large-scale nationalization is decreed. Beginning of War Communism.
July 6	Left SR uprising.
August 30	Assassination attempt against Lenin fails but attempt on Uritsky's life succeeds.

1919

January 16–25	Second All-Russian Congress of Trade Unions.
March 18–23	Eighth Party Congress. Establishment of Politburo, Orgburo, and Secretariat.
December 2–4	Eighth Party Conference.

1920

March 29–April 5	Ninth Party Congress.
September 22–25	Ninth Party Conference.
November	End of Civil War.
November 29	Decree nationalizing small industries.

1921

March 2–17	Kronstadt Uprising.
March 8–16	Tenth Party Congress. Trade Union debate. 'Temporary' ban on inner party factions. Beginning of NEP.

May 17–25   Fourth All-Russian Congress of Trade Unions.

June 22–July 12   Third Comintern Congress acknowledges revolutionary wave has receded in Europe.

1922

January–February   Lenin takes a six-week vacation owing to illness.

March 6–25   Lenin takes another vacation.

March 27–April 2   Eleventh Party Congress.

April 3   Stalin appointed General Secretary of the Communist Party.

May 25   Lenin partly paralyzed and unable to speak.

September–April 1923   Dispute over Georgia and policy towards nationalities.

December 13   Lenin suffers two strokes.

December 25   Lenin writes his political Testament.

1923

January–March   Lenin's last articles.

March 10   Lenin's third stroke and end of his political activity.

April 17–25   Twelfth Party Congress.

December 8   Trotsky calls for a 'New Course'.

1924

January 21   Death of Lenin.

Introduction

The Russian Revolution and its Impact on the Twentieth Century

The extent to which Lenin's rule in Russia was responsible for the rise of Stalinism has recently become a live public issue in the USSR. Gorbachev's policy of *glasnost* quickly opened the gates to a massive assault on Stalin's record, unheard of since the days of Khrushchev. Initially, Lenin's earlier rule was sacrosanct and not open to critical examination. Since then, however, the line has been crossed, and more than once. Starting in 1988, many articles have appeared in the publications *Sovetskaya Kultura, Novyi Mir, Znamya, Nash Sovremennik, Raduga*, and *Moscow News*, probing to varying degrees the connection between Lenin's rule and Stalinism.[1] While these contributions have tended to exempt Lenin from any personal political blame, they have at least legitimated the questioning of Stalin's *and* Lenin's rule. Moreover, the airing of this topic has significantly contributed to the excitement one senses in the Soviet press. The truly great questions concerning the relationship between revolution, democracy, and bureaucratic dictatorship have begun to be publicly discussed in that country. We do not of course know at this point how thorough these debates will be or how long they will be permitted to last.

If there is a deepening and extension of the process of *glasnost* in the Soviet Union, further democratic critiques of Lenin's political role may be formulated from a pro- or anti-revolutionary perspective. It is worth noting in this connection what happens to many former Communists when they give up on Stalinism and are attracted to democracy. In Eastern as well as in Western Europe, these people much more often than not abandon their previously more militant anti-capitalist perspectives for some variety of liberalism or social democracy, and sometimes even right-wing politics. In this context, it is important to point out that while, in the last few years, the democratic movement in the Soviet-type societies of Eastern Europe and Asia can be credited with great achievements, this has unfortunately been accompanied by a growing enthusiasm for the market – not even 'market socialism,' but the market pure and simple. This market fever has engulfed capitals as diverse as

Warsaw, Budapest, Moscow, and Beijing. At the same time, as in the case of Poland, the great deal of interest in the ideas and practices of worker self-management is no longer as evident as it was in the early years of the *Solidarność* movement. Some groups, such as the small 'Democratic Union' in the USSR, have not only repudiated the revolution of October 1917, but have also advocated that the private capitalist sector of the economy be placed 'on an equal footing' with the public sectors. Equally noteworthy are the developments that have taken place in the last 20 years among West European Communist parties such as the Spanish, the British, and the French. In that period, those parties have often developed factions and even central leaderships who criticize the anti-democratic practices of the Eastern bloc countries, while at the same time considerably moving to the Right on domestic questions. Missing inside the West European Communist parties are significant tendencies supporting both greater democracy *and* a more miltant, if not revolutionary orientation.[2]

The renewed Soviet interest in reexamining the sources of Stalinism in the very early years of the Bolshevik Revolution has implications far transcending their obvious importance for the Russian people. I am thinking in particular of countries such as South Africa, Brazil, South Korea, and Mexico, where dynamic industrial working classes have been growing in the context of explosive economic and political developments. Conditions such as these may, in a not too distant future, place workers' revolutions, and the role of democracy in the process of socialist transformation, on the political agenda of those countries.

In the light of this, it is important to recall that the Russian Revolution, besides being Russian, also became a *hegemonic model* establishing the terms of worldwide revolutionary discourse for most of the twentieth century. I am referring here of course to the model of the one-party state and the eventual Stalinist outcome of the revolution, not to the very strong working-class and substantially democratic Soviet orientation of the October 1917 upheaval. As the first government to maintain itself in power in the name of the working class and socialism, the Russian model preempted or at least greatly diminished the opportunities for consideration of other revolutionary choices and possibilities. This is one crucial reason why subsequent revolutions claiming to be socialist, e.g. in China, Cuba, and Vietnam, cannot, strictly speaking, be considered *independent* revolutionary experiments. Least of all can these revolutions be considered as independent experiments on the critical issue of the relationship between socialist revolution and democracy. The 'Marxist–Leninist' one-party state as interpreted and developed in Stalinist Russia was the common model upon which national Communist parties introduced, at most, some relatively minor variations in matters relevant to democracy. In any case, the essentials of the Russian model have been adopted by local revolutionary leaderships quite independently of their degree of organizational dependence or independence from the Soviet Union.

Moreover, neither can these twentieth-century revolutions claiming the mantle of socialism be considered to be independent experiments on the key question of whether or not, and the extent to which, there is a *necessary* causal relationship between economic underdevelopment and Stalinism, or between violent revolution and Stalinism. The existence of societies such as China, Cuba, and Vietnam does not at all prove that their Stalinist political systems are the necessary outcome of violent revolution and/or economic underdevelopment. One of the principal reasons for this is remarkably simple: nothing in the political upbringing of these revolutionary leaderships made them the least inclined to, or interested in, even attempting to establish pluralistic socialist democracies. Instead, they made conscious political and ideological choices favoring undemocratic political arrangements. Furthermore, these institutional arrangements were normatively regarded as good in themselves and not as lesser evils imposed on their respective countries by the *economic and other objective difficulties encountered at the time of, and subsequent to, the overthrow of the old order.*[3] I am not addressing here, of course, the issue of whether there is something about conditions of economic underdevelopment that encourages revolutionary leaders, long before they can even contemplate taking power, to choose 'Marxism–Leninism' as their preferred ideology and political program. While very important in its own right, this question is, however, irrelevant to the central concerns of this study.

The Political Dimension

These are some of the considerations that have prompted me to carry out this analytical survey of various aspects of democracy in the early years of the Russian Revolution. At the same time, I have tried to keep in mind the broader lessons and implications that can be drawn from a study of that period. Indeed, I would like to think of this book not as just one more reexamination of the Russian Revolution, but as an effort to begin the construction of a theory of the *politics* of the post-revolutionary transition to socialism in the light of that experience. Socialists, and Marxists in particular, have been prone to the development of numerous analyses of the economics of the transition to socialism. Yet, in the absence of a theory of revolutionary democracy, these analyses tend to deal with the question of democracy as if it was in some way derivative from the economics, if not altogether irrelevant.[4]

When I write about democracy, I have in mind a society where institutions based on majority rule control the principal sources of economic, social, and political power at the local and national levels. I am also thinking in terms of an authentic participatory democracy based on the self-mobilization and organization of the people. However, majority rule would need to be complemented by ample minority rights, and civil liberties. There can be no real socialist democracy, or for that matter full and genuine innovation and progress, with dissident individuals and minorities terrorized into silence and conformity, and forcefully prevented from attempting to become the new majorities. In any case, the ultimate guarantee of that democracy would be the reliance on the people's own efforts and struggles, and the institutions that resulted from such strivings, rather than the faith in well-intentioned leaders or elites.

The key question then becomes if, and to what degree and for how long, objective obstacles and crises confronting a successful revolutionary movement can justifiably be claimed as reasons to abridge democratic freedoms. In such a context, the politics and ideologies prevalent among the revolutionary leadership and rank-and-file are critical, since they shape the different perceptions of danger and of the appropriate responses to it. In addition, it is also important to examine how various responses to danger are compatible with the original short- and long-term goals of the revolution, and the way in which these responses are publicly justified. This in turn helps us to understand whether measures adopted in an emergency situation were just that, or whether, so to speak, necessity has been converted into virtue, thus actually and fundamentally altering the original revolutionary project.

Again, I want to stress the importance of *political* institutions and freedoms in the present context. Other authors, like myself supporters of the general goals of the October Revolution, have studied the development and fate of industrial democracy under the Bolsheviks. They have also shown how workers' control of production disappeared not long after the Bolshevik government made it official policy in late 1917. Yet it is troubling how many of these analyses tend to ignore or downplay *political* issues and institutions in the early days of the Soviet regime.[5] Perhaps the most striking example of this kind of political underestimation is Carmen Sirianni's *Workers' Control and Socialist Democracy. The Soviet Experience.*[6] Although a very good study written from an overall pro-October democratic socialist perspective, Sirianni nevertheless downplays the issue of political freedom. Furthermore, Sirianni briefly but positively refers to Mao's China, Tito's Yugoslavia, and Castro's Cuba.[7] He seems to suggest that there has been shopfloor democracy in those countries – actually it never existed in Cuba and is highly questionable in the cases of Yugoslavia and especially China. In any case, even if there had been a degree of shopfloor democracy in any of these places, it was not an acceptable substitute for the absence of democracy at the levels of local and national politics.

The past celebration of so-called workers' control in Yugoslavia and peasant communal government in Mao's China, without much concern for the elitist one-party rule and political repression in those countries, suggest that this has been a political ideology by no means limited to the few allusions to be found in Sirianni's work. This ideology often involves the notion of what Sheldon S. Wolin has aptly called 'groupism'. 'Groupism' maintains that human needs can and should be satisfied in some bodies smaller than and different from national political entities.[8] This approach unavoidably detracts attention from the society-wide context, which in the last anaysis decisively determines the nature of localized problems and their solutions. Wolin maintains that 'human existence is not going to be decided at the lesser level of small associations' since it is 'this political order that is making fateful decisions about man's survival.'[9] After a workers' and peasants' revolution, such questions as who decides on society-wide economic priorities, on how much is going to be invested, and what and how much is going to be consumed, cannot be avoided. If the majority of the population is really going to ultimately decide these matters, they will simply not be able to to do it without freedom of association and speech and other political freedoms. Under both capitalism and 'really existing socialism' local workers' control is ultimately an illusion given the powerful constraints of the market and/or the plan which lie beyond the reach of the workers in any given plant or firm. No matter how much local control there might be under socialism, the fact remains that a significant degree of centralization will still be required to successfully carry out the revolutionary economic and social program.

Moreover, the existence and survival of political freedom most definitely affect the ability of the working classes to maintain and protect shopfloor democracy itself. As the post-1917 degeneration of the Russian Revolution amply demonstrated, the loss of working-class power is not an overnight event but a process of deterioration that must be combatted long before it has come to its end result in the consolidation of a new bureaucratic class. After the revolutionary overthrow of the old order, the unavoidable existence of *hierarchies* based on the *division of labor* can act as a bureaucratic Trojan Horse inside the revolutionary ranks. As the anti-Stalinist Communist leader Christian Rakovsky noted in 1928:

> When a class takes power, one of its parts becomes the agent of that power. Thus arises bureaucracy. In a socialist state, when capitalist accumulation is forbidden by members of the directing party, this differentiation begins as a functional one; it later becomes a social one. I am thinking here of the social position of a communist who has at his disposal a car, a nice apartment, regular holidays, and is receiving a maximum salary authorized by the party; a position which differs from that of the communist working in the coal mines and receiving a salary of fifty to sixty roubles per month.... The function has modified the organism itself; that is to say, that the psychology of those who are charged with the diverse tasks of direction in the administration and the economy of the state, has changed to such a point that not only objectively, but subjectively, not only materially, but morally, they have ceased to be a part of this very same working class.[10]

It is true that favorable material conditions would facilitate the reversal or halting of bureaucratic trends. A shorter working day, for example, will certainly ease working-class participation in the political process. But it is equally certain that neither extended leisure nor an improved standard of living will automatically create, let alone restore, institutions of working-class democracy. With or without improved material conditions, the popular classes need political freedoms (i.e. the right to strike, organize, and agitate) to combat the process described by Rakovsky. Economic abundance will improve the chances that this combat will have a socialist outcome. Economic scarcity will reduce such possibilities, but the combat will be necessary in both cases in order to minimize, if not eliminate, the exploitation and oppression suffered by the people.

The Problem of Determinism

'Men make their own history, but they do not make it just as they please; they do not make it under circumstances chosen by themselves, but under circumstances directly found, given and transmitted from the past.' So wrote Karl Marx on the first page of *The Eighteenth Brumaire of Louis Bonaparte*. This is indeed a dialectically elegant and well-balanced formula on the respective roles of human agency and the objective limitations on that agency. However, many analysts of the Russian Revolution either have paid no attention to Marx's dictum or have had a great deal of difficulty in applying it. Let us take as an example the French economist Charles Bettelheim. He has made some specific and valuable criticisms in his writings on the early years of the Russian Revolution; for instance, pointing out the Bolshevik lack of any strategy for the transformation of work relations. Yet Bettelheim, going beyond such specific criticisms, has also more generally argued that the Bolsheviks were wrong in believing that the level of economic development limited the possibilities of socialism in Russia. However, what Bettelheim counterposed, in the last analysis, to this Bolshevik belief, which he defined as 'economism,' was in fact an extreme idealist voluntarism à la Mao Zedong. In this view of the world, if the masses believe in the correct ideology, they can indeed move mountains. Therefore, the propagation of the correct ideas among the population can become a substitute for the classical Marxist insistence, shared by all Mensheviks *and* Bolsheviks at least until 1921, that socialism cannot be developed without a sufficiently high material and economic base.[11]

On the other hand, some critics of Bettelheim have slipped into the opposite error of underestimating, if not totally neglecting, the important role played by political purposes and ideas, and the specific historic *choices* these may help to shape. Thus, the historian S. A. Smith, while making criticisms of Bettelheim similar to my own, nevertheless ends his otherwise excellent and non-determinist monograph *Red Petrograd* on a deterministic and misleading note:

> The depressing experience of socialist societies to date suggests that the imperatives of economic and social development in underdeveloped societies necessitate types of compulsion which ultimately conflict with the creation of free social relations. In other words, even if the Bolshevik government *had* been more percipient concerning the dangers to democratic socialism posed by the methods which it was forced to adopt, it seems probable that objective circumstances would ultimately have conspired to drain socialism of its democratic content. As it was, blind to the risks that it was running, the government was very quickly forced along a path which in October 1917 it had never dreamed of traversing. Already by 1921, the Bolsheviks no longer represented a socialism of liberty, but

one of scarcity, in which the needs of individual and human liberation were firmly subordinate to the exigencies of economic development.[12]

A good part of this book will in fact be an attempt to answer several of the important issues raised in the above quotation. However, at this time I merely want to underline how S. A. Smith seems to view the existence of compulsion in the 'socialist' countries in the underdeveloped world as a *necessity* resulting from 'the imperatives of economic and social development.' In other words, political ideologies, purposes, choices, and practices (e.g. Maoism, Castroism) that are not merely a passive reflection of objective circumstances apparently don't count at all. Secondly, while I would agree with Smith that, in broad terms, we cannot have a socialism of liberty while material scarcity prevails, he begs the question of whether something less than a democratic and libertarian socialism, yet better than Lenin's or Stalin's Russia, might have been a viable alternative for the Soviet people. I think that he might agree that only hardened and callous dogmatists would be indifferent to the consideration of such possibilities. I would further suggest, and attempt to show in this book, that the particular politics held by the revolutionary leaders made for very significant differences in terms of the specific form of society that eventually developed in that country.

In any case, as this study will attempt to show, Lenin's Russia, unlike subsequent 'socialist' revolutions, *was* a very good test of the relative weight of political choices and objective circumstances in causing the complete disappearance of democracy. This was so, in part because this was the first successful attempt on the part of revolutionary socialists at taking and holding power, and in part because, as S. A. Smith pointed out above, the path that was eventually traversed had not been anticipated. This, again, unlike subsequent 'socialist' revolutions, which, for the reasons I suggested earlier, were not appropriate independent tests of the causal impact of objective difficulties on the development of Stalinism.

Cultural Determinism and the Russian Revolution

The determinism contained in the above citation from S. A. Smith is materialist and is most commonly found within the broad confines of the Marxist intellectual and political tradition. Nevertheless, there is another kind of determinism, which derives from a quite different intellectual and political source. This is what I will call cultural determinism, an influential school of thought that in the present context goes back to early commentators on Soviet Russia such as Nicholas Berdyaev, Bernard Pares, and Sir John Maynard. This school or approach argues that much of contemporary Russian behavior can be accounted for by traditional Slavic character and institutions. In other words, Russia has not changed that much, since it was always rough and arbitrary, society always had precedence over the individual, and the government always prevailed over society. Even the party can be seen, according to some versions of this approach, as an equivalent of the ancient institution of the priesthood.

One of the major political implications of the cultural determinist approach is what the Chinese scientist and prominent dissident Fang Lizhi has critically referred to as 'The Law of Conservation of Democracy', by which he meant the notion that 'a society's total capacity for democracy is fixed. If there was no democracy to start with, there also will be none later.'[13]

Moreover, the anthropologist Marvin Harris, although himself a determinist of another kind, has strongly criticized the cultural school of thought of which the above-mentioned scholars of Russia are examples. Harris has particularly taken issue with those of his colleagues who have written about the immutability of national character (e.g. Ruth Benedict). He also argues 'that in principle, radical infrastructual and structural changes can lead to complete reversals of personality configurations in a very short time.'[14] He then proceeds to give some trenchant examples:

> When the Jews in Nazi Germany failed to organize an effective resistance against their own genocide, psychologists depicted them as having lost the capacity for forceful struggle. In a single generation, however, Jewish refugees created a militaristic state defended by one of the world's most formidable small armies.... Abram Kardiner once depicted the Afro-American male as a psychologically damaged individual whose aggressive impulses were turned inward, giving rise to feelings of worthlessness and inadequacy ... blacks allegedly exaggerated their own shortcomings by accepting the self-image of a slow-witted, affable, shuffling 'Sambo.' The black-power movement broke the Sambo stereotype. Haughtily self-confident black leaders fought the Sambo image in the courts and in the streets ...[15]

To be sure, there is a kernel of truth in the 'cultural determinist' approach. Furthermore, it can reasonably be argued that the establishment of post-revolutionary democratic institutions raises issues different and probably more complex than those involved in Harris's examples. Nevertheless, Harris's attack does call attention to the fact that whatever degree of truth is to be found in the 'cultural determinist' approach is more than compensated by its powerful and devastating fatalism, i.e. a view of reality that denies the ability of human actors to change reality through political and other means. This ability is particularly decisive in the context of successful revolutions, where the fluidity of social relations greatly facilitates important innovations and serious modifications, if not full reversals, of long-standing cultural and political patterns. It is at such critical junctures that concerted and massive efforts can be made to raise the cultural and political level of the mass of the population. This is why it is so important to understand the actual political aims of the revolutionaries, the nature and content of the institutions they attempt to build, and how they go about agitating and organizing for change, i.e. through empowerment and raising consciousness from below, or by imposition from above.

A variety of revolutionary currents, inside and outside the Bolshevik Party, disagreed on *and fought out*, during the early years of the revolution, a whole variety of issues relevant to the fate of socialist democracy in Russia (e.g. workers' management of production and the nature of freedom of the press). I will argue that, again, even though socialism might not have been possible in the Russia of the 1920s, the relative strength, impact, and political choices made by these conflicting political tendencies was not predetermined, but was at least in part an outcome of the political struggle itself. In addition, these political factors did make a difference to the particular variety of non-socialist order that was eventually established. This is in contrast to the after-the-fact view that all the negative features of 'Leninism in power' and Stalinism were predetermined by the cultural and material realities of Russian society. Besides, these contending revolutionary leaders and rank-and-filers were not disembodied exponents of 'objective historical forces' or of 'cultural patterns.' They were instead human actors with purposes, justifications, and political ideologies that critically impinged on what they did.

Thus, the severe post-revolutionary crises did not elicit a uniform and homogeneous response among the revolutionary leadership and rank-and-file, contrary to the expectations one might derive from cultural and materialist determinism. Equally unfounded are the expectations derived from the premises of voluntaristic idealism, whether those of Lenin in the 1920s or the later and much more extreme Maoist version. The objective reality of the critical economic situation in the 1920s set definite limits to what could have been accomplished in Soviet Russia. In other words, severe economic scarcities were not conducive to, or compatible with, authentic socialist institutions.

Yet, to say that the Soviet Russia of the early twenties was not likely to have witnessed a full-fledged revolutionary democratic socialism is not to say that whatever decisions the revolutionary leadership made were indifferent or of no consequence to the future prospects for democracy in that society. The taking of certain actions or the establishment of particular institutions may have helped to *open* or *close* off a *process* of democratization. That a society may not be 'ready' to enjoy a high degree of democracy does not at all mean that it is not 'ready' to enter the process of struggle and practical learning leading to that goal.

Historical Orthodoxy and Revisionism

My approach also differs from two of the more important and politically distinctive schools of thought among Western historians of the Russian Revolution. First, there is the orthodox, or so-called totalitarian, school, which maintained its hegemony for a considerable number of years. This school is associated with the works of such people as Zbigniew Brzezinski, Adam Ulam, and Leonard Schapiro. While there are of course significant differences of quality and content among the works of these various authors, it is nonetheless possible to outline a composite summary of the views that the orthodox have tended to hold in common. As their revisionist critic Stephen F. Cohen briefly, and I believe fairly, summarized the orthodox point of view insofar as the early years of the Russian Revolution and the Soviet state are concerned:

> In October 1917, the Bolsheviks (Communists), a small, unrepresenta-
> tive, and already or embryonically totalitarian party, usurped power and
> thus betrayed the Russian Revolution. From that moment on, as in 1917,
> Soviet history was determined by the totalitarian political dynamics of the
> Communist Party, as personified by its original leader, Lenin – monopo-
> listic politics, ruthless tactics, ideological orthodoxy, programmatic dog-
> matism, disciplined leadership, and centralized bureaucratic organization.
> Having quickly monopolized the new Soviet government and created a
> rudimentary totalitarian party-state, the Communists won the Russian
> civil war of 1918–1921 by discipline, organization, and ruthlessness.
> Exhausted and faced with the need to settle the Lenin succession, the
> party then retreated tactically in the 1920s from its totalitarian designs on
> society by temporarily adopting less authoritarian policies known as the
> New Economic Policy (NEP).[16]

The 'revisionist' response to this orthodox approach has been mixed. On one
hand, part of the revisionist literature has amply and convincingly demonstrated
that the presumed monolithism of the Bolshevik Party before and after the
October Revolution is a myth. Ironically, this myth has been fostered by both
Stalinist and Western orthodox historians. Similarly, the revisionist historians
have also shown that the October Revolution was not a coup, but the culmination of a social and political movement with a great deal of active involvement
and support among the Russian people, particularly the working class in the
industrial centers and soldiers and sailors in the garrisons. Lastly, revisionist
historians have also shown, among other things, how the Bolshevik Party only
began to acquire a significant bureaucratic apparatus several months after the
October Revolution, i.e. in the years of the Civil War and War Communism.[17]

On the other hand, several prominent revisionist, like many of their orthodox
opponents, have often engaged in the various forms of determinist analyses I
criticized above. Specifically, what could have been a reasonable skepticism
about the possibilities for authentic democratic institutions in post-
revolutionary Russia has been transformed by some revisionists into an almost
uncritical defense of Lenin's NEP and Bukharin's subsequent political line.
This, on the grounds that, in the light of Russia's economic situation and
cultural and historic background, no democracy from below was possible in the
1920s. Therefore, it is implied that nothing better could have been expected
than the concessions that were offered from above.[18] It is not surprising that
revisionists such as Stephen F. Cohen have found favor with Gorbachev and his
program of limited reforms from above.

Revisionism developed at least in part as a reaction to the apologetic pro-
Western Cold War politics of the orthodox school. However, in the course of
pursuing the goal of criticizing the work of the Cold Warriors, some revisionists
may have blunted their critical faculties and 'pulled their punches' in their own
analyses of present and past Soviet reality. These revisionists were perhaps too

exclusively focused on the implications of their work for East–West great power rivalries. What I mean is that they may have at least implicitly thought of the Western capitalist powers, and in particular their most aggressive right-wing elements, as the only parties that could possibly stand to gain from a thorough criticism of the Soviet bloc. Missing here was the perspective of the victims of exploitation and oppression on both sides of the East–West divide. Consequently, most revisionists did not consider that it was possible to combine an opposition to the Cold War and Western imperialism with a thorough criticism and rejection of the anti-democratic practices of the USSR and the Eastern bloc countries. This may have been inevitable given the limitations of the liberal politics generally inspiring revisionism. Perhaps only a completely revolutionary perspective would have made it possible to combine a strong critique of Stalinism and "Leninism in power' with a clear opposition to Western capitalism and imperialism. While such analyses have not been common or predominant, they have fortunately appeared in print as in the notable cases of important works by Victor Serge and Ante Ciliga.[19] These are precisely the kinds of works that have most influenced me.

Metaphysical Pathos, Democracy, and Revolution

Finally, it is important to note how the very idea of revolution, socialist or otherwise, has for many people become associated with repression and totalitarianism. The historian of ideas, Arthur O. Lovejoy, pointed out that theories are associated with, or generate, sentiments that those upholding the theory may sense only in part. He called this the 'metaphysical pathos' of ideas, a pathos that is 'exemplified in any description of the nature of things, any characterization of the world to which one belongs, in terms which, like the words of a poem, evoke through their associations and through a sort of empathy which they engender, a congenial mood or tone of feelings.' Alvin W. Gouldner, commenting further on Lovejoy's point, noted that a commitment to a theory may then occur because the theory is congruent with deep-lying sentiments of its adherents, rather than simply because the supporters of the theories analyzed them and found them intellectually valid.[20]

In the light of this, it is rather curious to find some agreements among people one would not normally expect to agree on anything at all. Thus, the contemporary exponents of 'Marxism–Leninism,' whether in or out of power, usually think of socialist revolution in totalitarian terms, i.e. necessitating an elitist, undemocratic, one-party state administering a nationalized economy in the name of the working class. Interestingly, the Polish oppositionist Adam Michnik would very likely agree. This is a man who, for more than two decades, has been imprisoned many times for courageously opposing the bureaucratic exploitation and oppression of his fellow Poles. Yet, confronted with the 1968 Polish and Czechoslovakian experiences and the overwhelming military power of the USSR, Michnik and others decided to explicitly reject any strategy leading to the eventual overthrow of the ruling class oppressing their country. Recently, the reform strategy of Michnik and his co-thinkers has become embodied in a power-sharing agreement with the Polish authorities. While it is very difficult to predict the eventual outcome of this compromise, it is evident that it has already provoked a split in the opposition, particularly along generational lines, with many younger militants refusing to support the agreement. Moreover, there is a serious danger that the mainstream Solidarity leadership may become compromised by participating in the implementation of a government program of economic rationalization that is likely to include the creation of unemployment, speedup, and a greater enforcement of labor discipline. Be that as it may, there are some signs already pointing to a growth of the political prestige of nationalist groups that oppose the compromise agreement and may thus come to represent, in the eyes of many Poles, an authentic alternative to the system.[21]

Furthermore, the elaboration and development of Michnik's political ideology has led to some perhaps unanticipated political conclusions. Thus, Michnik has broadened the concept of totalitarianism beyond that of a system consisting of specific socio-political institutions and practices, e.g. the one-party state, abolition of civil liberties, a secret police not subject to the rule of law, etc.; indeed, he has come to see radical political change itself as somehow totalitarian. In this spirit, he criticized the 'totalitarian temptation' of those activists in Polish Solidarity who wanted the movement to become an alternative to the authorities and struggle for state power. Going farther, he has even attributed a 'pre-totalitarian' tendency to the old Polish Socialist Party because it did not limit itself to what Michnik calls 'a clear-cut program of reform' and instead put forward a vision of a 'Socialism [that] promised total change, building this promise on the complete negation of a world based on the exploitation and oppression of nations and individuals.'[22]

In broader terms, Michnik's worldview seems to be ultimately rooted in a deep-lying Western sentiment that sees democracy as counterposed not only to the necessary use of violence but even to quick and decisive action as well. Thus, for example, Karl Kautsky on one hand praised the democratic institutions the European working class built in the late nineteenth and early twentieth centuries, but on the other hand lamely remarked that 'the conduct of war is not the proletariat's strongest point.'[23] In this fashion, Kautsky not only condemned the proletariat to irrelevance, but also made a damning concession to twentieth-century political bureaucracies. The latter could only be delighted with the opportunity to justify the elimination of democracy by claiming the very real need to act quickly and decisively. In this context, the early George Orwell at least intuitively understood well the relationship between the use of necessary violence and the maintenance of democratic institutions when he predicted an English working-class revolution that would shoot traitors and yet be able to preserve free speech.[24]

Of course, totalitarianism may originate and has sometimes originated from violent revolutionary situations. In order to establish the conditions under which revolution and violence do incline towards totalitarianism, one must find out about the objective situation facing the revolution *and* the kind of politics that guided the revolutionary leaders and rank-and-file. In any case, neither Michnik nor his 'Marxist–Leninist' opponents attempt to approach the relationship between revolution and democracy in an open, problem-solving manner. As far as both of these sides are concerned, this is not a matter of tendencies and probabilities but a closed and dead issue. Again, Alvin W. Gouldner's comments on the predominant 'pathos' among social scientists studying bureaucracy is very apropos here:

> Wrapping themselves in the shrouds of nineteenth-century political economy, some social scientists appear to be bent on resurrecting a dismal science. Instead of telling men how bureaucracy might be mitigated, they insist that it is inevitable. Instead of explaining how democratic patterns may, to some extent, be fortified and extended, they warn us that democracy cannot be perfect. Instead of controlling the disease, they suggest that we are deluded, or more politely, incurably romantic, for hoping to control it. Instead of assuming responsibilities as realistic clinicians, striving to further democratic potentialities wherever they can, many social scientists have become morticians, all too eager to bury men's hopes.[25]

Nature and Organization of this Study

I do not pretend to be writing history here, if by this we mean primary research leading to the discovery and interpretation of new data. For one thing, I do not read or speak Russian, nor have I ever visited the USSR. Yet I have been most fortunate in having had access to, and become familiar with, several hundred articles and book-length monographs dealing with a whole range of matters concerning early revolutionary Russia. The great majority of these works have been written since the 1960s. In part this reflects the availability of new Soviet materials, and the opportunity to conduct research in the USSR on academic exchange programs begun in 1958.[26]

Therefore, this study should be seen as an attempt at synthesis focusing on the theme of revolutionary democracy and its fate in the early years after the October Revolution. I also attempt, whenever I think it is appropriate and important, to draw the lessons and implications suggested by the Russian materials for revolutionary democratic politics in today's world. In other words, this book is an attempt at a political reflection on history, an inquiry into what alternatives existed and *might* have worked at the time, as well as what can we learn for today, particularly in light of recent developments in the Communist and Western capitalist worlds. In sum, my aim was to write a book that, to quote E. J. Hobsbawm, 'is not detailed narrative, but interpretation and what the French call *haute vulgarisation*. Its ideal reader is that theoretical construct, the intelligent and educated citizen, who is not merely curious about the past, but wishes to understand how and why the world has come to be what it is today and whither it is going.'[27]

There is an underlying chronology to the principal themes discussed in this study, which is significant not merely as a convenient way of organizing information, but also because of the substantive policy changes that these dates connote. There are four key periods to be considered here: (1) from the overthrow of Tsarism in February 1917 to the Bolshevik Revolution in November 1917; (2) from November 1917 to the beginning of the Civil War in the Summer of 1918; (3) the Civil War period and the policies of War Communism, lasting from the Summer of 1918 to the end of 1920; (4) from the strike waves in the big cities, the Kronstadt rebellion, and the establishment of the New Economic Policy in February–March 1921 to the death of Lenin in early 1924 and subsequent Interregum. These dates form a loose backdrop rather than the main organizing principle of the text. This, given that this book was organized thematically, and not as a chronologically detailed narrative.

As we shall see, it is indispensable to divide the early years of the Russian Revolution into these four historical stages in order to achieve a good understanding of the fate of the democratic features of the October upheaval. Thus, for example, many of the claims made by the 'orthodox' school about the nature of the Bolshevik Revolution and the Bolshevik Party will be shown to be quite unfounded, particularly during the first two of the four historical stages mentioned above. Likewise, I will try to demonstrate that the claims made by at least some of the revisionists are also unfounded insofar as the period of the New Economic Policy is concerned. Furthermore, the great *objective* difficulties confronted by the revolutionary government during the period of the Civil War will be shown to have combined and interacted with the *political* priorities of the policies of War Communism. This interaction resulted in the transformation of what up to that point had been some democratically flawed predispositions of the Boshevik mainstream leadership into a systematic political doctrine of a clear and marked anti-democratic character. In this context, I shall discuss, for example, the far worse fate suffered by the opposition political parties during NEP than during the period from October 1917 to June 1918, and even in comparison with the Civil War years. Last but not least, I will also discuss soviet democracy, workers' management and control, and trade union independence as they rose and declined in connection with the objective and political changes that took place during these four historical stages.

The book is divided into two parts. The first part, consisting of five chapters, takes up the following topics. Chapter 1 discusses the rise and decline of the democratic soviets. Chapter 2 attempts to accomplish the same task for workers' control and trade union independence. Chapter 3 discusses the fate of freedom of the press during the early years of the Bolshevik Revolution. Chapter 4 analyzes the nature of repression in these years, with particular emphasis on the role of the All-Russian Extraordinary Commission for Combatting Counterrevolution and Sabotage (Cheka). Chapter 5 deals with the status of legality in the post-revolutionary period. I also attempt to draw, whenever appropriate, the political lessons and implications for today, especially in chapters 3, 4, and 5.

The second part of the book analyzes the revolutionary alternatives that existed in the early years of the revolution, before the death of Lenin and the rise of Stalinism. Chapter 6 analyzes the political strengths and shortcomings of the Right and Left Bolshevik oppositions to the Leninist mainstream leadership. Finally, Chapter 7 takes a critical look at the alternative currently popular among some revisionist historians and the supporters of Gorbachev in the USSR, i.e. the New Economic Policy or NEP.

PART I

Soviet Democracy under Attack

Objective and Ideological Factors

1

The Rise and Decline of Democratic Soviets

The Origin of the Soviets

The soviets, or councils, originally became a major institution of the Russian working class during the 1905 Revolution. When the strike movement spread from Moscow to St Petersburg in October of that year, the workers in the old capital spontaneously attempted to develop joint action. Deputies (*starosti*) were elected in several factories, including the Putilov and Obukhov works. Eventually, about forty delegates founded the St Petersburg Soviet on 13 October. By the third meeting on 15 October, 226 representatives from ninety-six factories and workshops and five trade unions were present. Soon, this body turned into a general political organ representing all workers, and the revolutionary movement, in the city as a whole. In fact, the Petrograd Soviet had become a true workers' parliament acting and taking positions on a great number and variety of questions.[1]

The Resurgence of the Soviets in 1917

With the overthrow of Tsarism in February 1917, the soviets re-emerged in a fashion similar to that of 1905, with the elected delegates to these councils subject to immediate recall by their constituents. These 1917 soviets spread from Petrograd and took hold in other large cities, industrial towns, and cities housing large garrisons. Later, they also emerged in non-proletarian, smaller, and more remote locations. According to one conservative estimate, in May there may have been 400, and in August 600 soviets.[2] It did not take long before these soviets, representing not only industrial workers but also soldiers, sailors, and peasants, became a dual political and governmental power to that of the Provisional Government. At the same time, as we shall later see in greater detail, a number of political parties became very active and indeed dominant in the soviets. These included the Socialist Revolutionaries (SRs), Mensheviks, Bolsheviks, Anarchists, and a number of smaller socialist groups. However, the majority of these parties did not perceive the soviets as an alternative to the parliamentary form of government prevailing in the democracies of the capitalist countries of Western Europe. Indeed, for a while it appeared that even the Bolsheviks were themselves contemplating a 'composite state' combining a Constituent Assembly and the soviets.[3] Eventually, while Lenin and the Bolsheviks recognized the democratic republic as progressive and the highest form of capitalist political system, they also came to advocate soviet rule as an even higher form of democracy, and the only one they claimed to be compatible with the economic rule of the working class.

The Soviets after October 1917

By October 1917, the number of workers', soldiers', and peasants' soviets in existence had risen to 900.[4] Yet numbers alone cannot convey the enthusiasm and mass self-mobilization that accompanied the development of these institutions as authentic organs of popular participation and decision making, extending their powers into practically every area of Russian society. The successful October Revolution – which took place at a time when the Bolsheviks enjoyed enormous popular support and had obtained a majority in the soviets – gave a further impetus to these trends. Then, on 17 December 1917, the majoritarian character of the soviet system was confirmed when the Second All-Russian Peasant Congress split, and its left-wing majority elected an executive of 81 Left SRs and 20 Bolsheviks, which formally merged with the All-Russian Central Executive Committee (CEC) of the Workers' and Soldiers' Soviets.[5]

The minutes of the CEC of the soviets clearly show that this body was very far from being a rubber stamp for the wishes of the Bolshevik leaders.[6] In fact, these minutes record wider political differences than those to be found in many democratic parliaments in capitalist countries. Even after the Left SRs joined the government in late 1917, they remained a party with views substantially different from those of the Bolsheviks, as reflected in the important policy struggles that took place, for example, inside the Cheka and in the Left SR-led Commissariat of Justice (see Chapter 4 dealing with repression). Moreover, the Left SRs wielded considerable power in many regional and local soviets at least through the early months of 1918. This in turn fueled the open and sharp public debate on the Treaty of Brest-Litovsk that took place at that time in the soviets, as well as inside the Bolshevik Party, with the press keeping score of the local soviet votes cast for and against the proposed treaty.[7]

However, the CEC's power was not comparable to that of the Council of People's Commissars (Sovnarkom), which was the actual central government established shortly after the October Revolution. This, even though Sovnarkon was formally accountable to the CEC, and all of its legislative acts and regulations of major political significance had to be considered and approved by the CEC *after* they had been promulgated by Sovnarkom. Still, the very fact that a Sovnarkom had been created as a separate body from the CEC of the soviets clearly indicates that, Lenin's *State and Revolution* notwithstanding, the separation of at least the top bodies of the executive and the legislative wings of the government remained in effect in the new Soviet system. In any case, the actual subordination of the soviets to Sovnarkom, particularly after the beginning of the Civil War in mid-1918, did not fail to be noticed by party dissidents. Thus, for example, at a Moscow party conference held on 18 January 1919, a number of local Bolshevik leaders led by E. N. Ignatov introduced a motion that included a call for the abolition of Sovnarkom in order to increase the authority of the soviet CEC.[8]

Nevertheless, until the Communist Party bureaucratic apparatus acquired an ever-increasing degree of clout, beginning in the latter half of 1918, the soviet organizations enjoyed considerable power at the national and even more at the local level. As T. H. Rigby described the situation prevailing in the early period of revolutionary rule:

> the ability of the people's commissariats to implement Sovnarkom measures through the field organs inherited from the old [Tsarist] ministries was extremely limited and dependent on the cooperation of the soviets and their executive committees, in which effective power at the regional and local levels was now focused. It is true that the Bolsheviks quickly assumed control of most of these bodies, but the party had no machinery through which it could run things itself, as it was later to do, nor would this have been politically expedient at this period. The authority of the CEC, however, carried great weight with the lower-level soviets, since it was peculiarly 'their' organ at the centre. . .[9]

Moreover, in a case study of the first city district soviet in Petrograd from November 1917 to June 1918, Alexander Rabinowitch found little indication that the Bolshevik city-wide or lower party committees controlled or even attempted systematically to guide the district soviet's work. In fact, it was only in the Summer of 1918 that a Bolshevik group formally responsible to the party district committee was organized in the district soviet.[10] It is interesting to note that while at the time the Petersburg committee of the Bolshevik Party was itself divided on the question of soviet–party relations, virtually no Petersburg Bolsheviks proposed anything resembling a systematic party control of the soviet. One Bolshevik group emphasized the supreme importance of independent soviets and altogether minimized the significance of party work. The other, and presumably 'harder', Petrograd Bolshevik group, known as the 'preservers of old traditions,' in fact looked down on governmental work as somehow unclean and was preoccupied with governmental bureaucratization. This second group conceived of party work as limited to the fields of propaganda and agitation.[11] Another study of the soviet and party committees in the central provinces also found that the role and strength of the party had declined in the months subsequent to the October Revolution. This phenomenon had two major causes: first, full-time work in the soviet had consumed all the time and attention of Bolshevik Party members; second, a widespread sentiment developed among the party rank-and-file in the central provinces similar to that of the 'softer' Petrograd party group, i.e. the achievement of soviet power had made the party superfluous.[12]

The Bolshevik Losses in the Soviets – Spring of 1918

The Bolsheviks retained their electoral hegemony in the soviets for the first several months after the October Revolution. Nevertheless, that was not uniformly true in all areas of the country. For example, John L. H. Keep cites an incident in Kiev, as early as 29 November 1917, when the Bolsheviks swamped the regularly elected deputies to the soviets with members of factory committees in order to secure the adoption of pro-Bolshevik resolutions and the election of a pro-Bolshevik executive. However, Keep also points out that on other, although less frequent occasions, these types of tactics were also used against the Bolsheviks by other parties.[13]

The Bolshevik's soviet electoral hegemony began to significantly erode in the country as a whole by the Spring of 1918. This is the context in which the government continually postponed the new general elections to the Petrograd Soviet, the term of which had ended in March 1918. Apparently, the government feared that the opposition parties would show gains.[14] This fear was well founded since in the period immediately preceding 25 January, in those Petrograd factories where the workers had decided to hold new elections, the Mensheviks, SRs, and non-affiliated candidates had won about half the seats.[15] This approximate relationship of forces continued to hold when general elections were finally held in Petrograd factories from 18 June to 24 June 1918. This time the Bolsheviks obtained 48.5 per cent of the delegates, while the left SRs obtained 12.2 per cent, the SRs 17.6 per cent, the Mensheviks 11.1 per cent, and the remaining 10.7 per cent of the delegates were non-affiliated.[16] The opposition did well in printing establishments, railroad workshops, state metalworking factories, and municipal enterprises, and among the predominantly female labor force of Petrograd's four tobacco factories. On the other hand, the Bolsheviks did better in the traditionally militant, formerly private metalworking factories, among the predominantly unskilled and female textile workers, and at the Treugol'nik Rubber Factory.[17]

It is worth noting the perhaps unexpected strength of both Right and Left SRs and the relative weakness of the Mensheviks in Petrograd. This was particularly true of the Nevsky district, a traditional SR stronghold where much of the worker opposition to the Bolsheviks was centered.[18] Besides, populist appeals and terminology, e.g. the use of the term *trudovoi narod* or 'toiling people,' previously had a certain degree of currency among the Petrograd working class.[19] In any case, Petrograd was the home of working-class Bolshevism, and for this party to elect somewhat less than half of the soviet delegates was indeed a very serious setback. As discussed in greater detail in chapter 7, an even more critical decline in Bolshevik strength took place in the nearby radical city of Kronstadt. In the general soviet elections held there on 1 April, 1918 (i.e. before the outbreak of full-scale Civil War), the proportion of Bolshevik delegates declined from the previous 46 per cent elected in late January to 28.9 per cent, with the remaining delegates being apportioned as follows: SR Maximalists (who could be politically located somewhere between the Left SRs and the Anarchists), 22.4 per cent; Left SRs, 21.3 per cent; non-affiliated, 13.1 per cent; Menshevik Internationalists, 7.6 per cent; and finally the Anarchists with 5.4 per cent of the delegates.[20]

Moreover, as far as Russia as a whole was concerned, figures published in the Soviet Union by A. M. Spirin in 1968 show that the Bolshevik Party's representation in 100 county soviets declined from 66 per cent in mid-March 1918 to 44.8 per cent in the period from April to August 1918 – full-scale civil war began in late May and War Communism in late June of 1918.[21] The extensive data collected by Vladimir Brovkin fully agree with those of Spirin on the major loss of Bolshevik representation, and additionally also show big gains by the SRs and particularly by the Mensheviks. As Brovkin sums it up:

> The data presented here demonstrate that the Menshevik–SR bloc won the city soviet elections in 19 out of a total of 30 provincial capitals of European Russia where Soviet power actually existed.... I did not include the capitals [Petrograd and Moscow] in this survey. Pskov province was occupied by the Germans; in Simbirsk, the ruling party and the opposition had parity; in two provinces (Novorossiisk, Novgorod) there were no elections; and for six provinces (Voronezh, Ufa, Perm´, Astrakhan´, Petrozavodsk, Smolensk) there are no data. Therefore, in all provincial capitals of European Russia where elections were held on which there are data, the Mensheviks and the SRs won the majorities in the spring of 1918...[22]

While Spirin's data, as I indicated above, do concur with Brovkin's on what is the most important issue for us here, i.e. the great Bolshevik losses in the soviet elections, they diverge from Brovkin's in some other respects. According to Spirin, the Bolshevik loss was primarily due to big gains by non-party delegates (9.3 to 27.1 per cent) and a slight gain by the Left SRs (18.9 to 23.1 per cent) – the Left SRs had left the government by March 1918 in protest over the signing of the Treaty of Brest-Litovsk. One possible explanation for the divergence between Spirin's and Brovkin's data is that while the latter concerned 19 provincial capitals in European Russia, the former referred to 100 *uezd* (county) congresses of soviets. If we assume random representation, most of these would have been rural, since rural *uezdy* far outnumbered urban. Besides, at the time, urban 'congresses' of soviets wouldn't normally have been called *uezd* congresses.[23]

This interpretation is supported by data for 504 rural *volosti* (the next larger geographical unit above the village) of the Northern region concerning elections between December 1917 and May 1918. A total of 16,553 delegates were elected of whom 29 per cent corresponded to Bolsheviks and sympathizers, 5.8 per cent to Left Socialist Revolutionaries and sympathizers, 1.1 per cent were listed under the category of 'Other,' while no fewer than 64.1 per cent were non-party delegates.[24] Moreover, the fact that the Mensheviks had politically recovered and did well in the provincial cities of European Russia, but not in the countryside, would have been consistent with the party's historic social sources of support. Finally, it should also be noted that Brovkin's research showed that non-party delegates often voted with the Mensheviks and SRs, as was the case, for example, in Orekhovo-Zuevo, Orel, Saratov, and Rostov. In fact, research by other scholars suggests that many of these non-party delegates may have actually been members or supporters of the opposition parties.[25]

In light of the central concerns of this study, it is particularly important to note that, according to Brovkin, Bolshevik armed force usually overthrew the results of these provincial elections. He also indicates that the Bolsheviks who seized military control of the cities were not for the most part acting under instructions from Moscow, but were local party people who seized power for themselves. Indeed, they did this despite interference by the Moscow commissars in such cases as Tambov, Rostov, and Iaroslavl´. This leads Brovkin to conclude that 'it was not consolidation, but rather regionalism in local politics and fragmentation of central authority that prevailed in the spring and summer of 1918.'[26] A detailed case study of the city of Izhevsk in Viatka *guberniia* (province) in the valley of the Kama, the main tributary of the Volga, confirms Brovkin's findings. Thus, in the May 1918 election of deputies to the Izhevsk soviet, the Mensheviks and SRs won a majority (70 out of 135 seats). In June, these two parties also won a majority of the executive committee of the soviet. At this point, the local Bolshevik leadership refused to give up power and appealed for assistance to the Kazan´ Soviet of Soldiers' and Workers' Deputies. That soviet sent a detachment of sailors and soldiers to Izhevsk, who, together with the local Bolshevik-dominated Red Guard units, abrogated the results of the May and June elections and arrested the SR and Menshevik members of the soviet and its executive committee.[27]

It is also widely agreed that a severe economic crisis, which included serious unemployment and even famine, was a major cause of working-class and peasant discontent with the government, even before the Civil War broke out. There is little doubt that important sections of the working class and peasantry were withdrawing support from the Bolsheviks for their failure to deliver material improvements, just as a few months earlier they had withdrawn support from the Provisional Government for exactly the same reasons. Furthermore, as Marcel Liebman has reminded us, the signing of the unpopular treaty of Brest-Litovsk on 3 March 1918 was also a serious political setback for the Bolshevik government.[28]

In any case, the above-cited data and discussion provide the background to understand how Lenin and the Bolshevik mainstream reacted to their loss of working-class and popular support. In this period of March to June 1918, Lenin began to make frequent distinctions *within* the working class, singling out workers who could still be trusted, denouncing workers whom he accused of abandoning the working class and deserting to the side of the bourgeoisie, and complaining about how the working-class had become 'infected with the diseases of petty-bourgeois disintegration.'[29] These types of pronouncements laid the basis for what soon (i.e. in 1919) became Lenin's *fully explicit* revision of the concept of the dictatorship of the whole proletariat by changing it into the dictatorship of the most advanced workers, i.e. the party. In sum, the Bolsheviks were beginning to lose the hegemony they had acquired in the working class ever since the struggle against Kornilov in the late Summer of 1917. It seems that, at least in the case of Petrograd, the opposition to the Bolsheviks was strongest among those workers whose support for soviet power was a relatively recent phenomenon.[30] It goes without saying that the government was certainly doing no better among the bourgeoisie and other disenfranchised elements in the cities, and would soon earn the enmity of the bulk of the peasantry with the implementation of the policies of 'War Communism' beginning in the second half of 1918.

A recent debate has helped to elucidate the political meaning and consequences of the widespread working-class discontent with the Bolshevik government in the Spring and Summer of 1918. On one side, William G. Rosenberg has described in detail the severe economic conditions that the Russian working class endured in the early months of soviet rule, from December 1917 to April 1918.[31] In the case of Petrograd, these economic conditions led to the development of substantial worker protest, such as the convening of the Menshevik-inspired Conference of Factory Representatives in March of 1918. The Petrograd conference was attended by delegates from many printshops (traditional Menshevik strongholds) and from at least 15 major metalworking plants where many workers had been displaced owing to the end of defense production. According to Rosenberg, by April 1918 there were delegates to this conference in more than 40 Petrograd enterprises. Moreover, between May and July of 1918, working-class anti-Bolshevik activity in Petrograd had expressed itself in 18 strikes and 40 other instances of anti-government protest (e.g. demonstrations, factory meetings). The greatest number of these protests were directed against governmental acts of political repression such as shootings.[32] A case study by another historian has shown how at this time there was also considerable unrest among the working class in Moscow. There, the Mensheviks had significant influence, particularly among printers', railways', chemical, teachers', and employees' trade unions.[33]

However, Rosenberg has strongly argued that, unlike the Bolsheviks,

neither the Conference of Factory Representatives nor other opposition groups had a compelling explanation for the new disasters besetting the Russian workers or a clear and convincing vision of a viable alternative social order. The delegates called for a general strike in the name of the Constituent Assembly, civil liberties, a single, indivisble republic, and an end to repression, but these goals had little to do with solving the problems of food supply, unemployment, or production, or of constructing an effective state economic apparatus. Indeed, the disaster was beyond short-term relief. This was true as well before October, and one might argue that the promises of 1917 were false and illusory. But they nonetheless had political force, while in the aftermath of October promises of betterment were not persuasive.[34]

Vladimir Brovkin responded to Rosenberg and insisted that every social and economic demand reflecting popular discontent brought the workers into a political confrontation with the Bolshevik authorities, since certain economic policies were associated with certain parties. Specifically, Brovkin maintained that policies he attributed to the Bolsheviks (e.g. seizure of the banks and factories) had exacerbated rather than improved the economic situation. Brovkin further argued that, since the Mensheviks had strongly opposed these policies, their resurgence in the Spring of 1918 was very much connected with that fact.[35]

It is certainly disputable whether the growing Menshevik working-class vote meant that many workers sympathized with the Menshevik opposition to the seizure of banks and factories, i.e. opposition to a good part of what the revolution had been all about. However, there is no doubt that, as William G. Rosenberg himself points out, many workers had come to believe that confusion and anarchy at the top were a major cause of their difficulties. As Rosenberg describes it, scores of competitive and conflicting Bolshevik and soviet authorities issued contradictory orders, which were often brought to the factories by armed Chekists. In fact, it has even been suggested that this disorganization gave rise to a certain sympathy among the factory committee delegates for the Anarchists' criticisms of the government, if not for their proposed solutions.[36] In addition, scores of technicians were dismissed from above against the advice of workers' committees, and even of some commissars, that their skills were crucial to operations.[37] Nevertheless, it should be noted that the technicians' opposition to the Bolshevik regime had also brought about bitter clashes between them and blue-collar workers.[38] Or, again, it is not necessary to assume working-class sympathy for Menshevik politics to understand why in May 1918 a delegation of Putilov workers went to Smol'nyi to protest the delay in soviet elections and presented Zinoviev with an ultimatum: there must be immediate elections to the soviets or else the workers would hold revolutionary new elections.[39]

In the last analysis, both Rosenberg and Brovkin failed to directly confront the most fundamental and indeed normative questions raised by the Bolshevik refusal to acknowledge their soviet electoral losses. In the first place, given that the Bolsheviks had earlier proclaimed the superiority of the soviet system because of the rank-and-file's ability to recall its representatives, weren't then the workers entitled to remove the Bolsheviks from the government and find out if the opposition could do any better? If Rosenberg was right in maintaining that the opposition had no program to deal with the crises confronting the country, should the workers nonetheless have been entitled to find this out for themselves? On the other hand, were the Bolsheviks justified, and under what conditions, in resisting such an attempt?

A related, yet equally fundamental question raised by these events has to do with the evident fact that the Bolsheviks had risen to power on the basis of a very heterogeneous and even contradictory working-class and peasant support. At least some significant sections of the working class, let alone the peasantry, supported them on the basis of short-term expectations of material improvements, while other sections of the working class had become much more radicalized and also supported Lenin's party on a more long-range and radical programatic basis. I shall return to these difficult questions later in this volume. Meanwhile, I would like to note an irony concerning the great social upheaval that eventually degenerated into Stalinism. This has been the only twentieth-century radical social revolution that in its initial period allowed for electoral mechanisms that openly and clearly registered the amount of support for the government and the opposition among the working class and the peasantry.

The End of Multi-Party Soviet Democracy

The Red Terror and the Civil War that began in the Summer of 1918 brought about, among other things, the establishment of one-party rule in the soviets. Opposition parties were soon excluded from these institutions while at the same time they came close to being virtually outlawed from the larger society as well. On 14 June 1918, the Bolshevik-dominated Central Executive Committee of the soviets excluded Mensheviks and right-wing SRs from that body and instructed the local soviets to do likewise. In July, the Left SRs were also excluded after they took arms and engaged in terrorist acts against the government. By the middle of July, the Bolsheviks remained the only party in the soviets aside from some minor leftist groups that continued to be tolerated.[40] Yet, as we shall see in greater detail in chapter 4 on repression, for about a year and a half after this, opposition parties – including Mensheviks and Right SRs – were occasionally reinstated and allowed to have their representatives elected to soviet bodies. But, following a decree of 28 November 1919, a tiny number of appointed rather than elected non-Communist delegates were permitted to attend the Seventh Soviet Congress in December 1919 with a 'consultative voice' but no vote.[41] Thus, while the Fourth Congress of the Soviets in March 1918 had comprised 797 Bolsheviks and sympathizers (65 per cent), 275 Left SRs and sympathizers (22 per cent), 132 representaives of eight other parties (11 per cent), and 22 non-party delegates (27 per cent), by the time of the Seventh Congress in December 1919, 97 per cent of all delegates were members of the Communist Party.[42]

However, even the policy of allowing a token representation of appointed opposition delegates did not last very long. The Eighth Congress of Soviets in December of 1920 was the last to admit opposition party delegates without voting rights.[43] At the local level, however, opposition delegates continued to be elected to the soviets, in spite of great obstacles and difficulties, until 1921. In 1920, as a result of a brief revival of the local soviets, there were Menshevik delegates in the following provincial soviets: 205 in Kharkov, 120 in Ekaterinoslav, 78 in Kremenchug, 50 in Tula, and 30 each in Smolensk, Odessa, Poltava, Kiev, and Irkutsk.[44] In early 1921, massive working-class discontent in the cities, particularly in Petrograd and Moscow, produced a Menshevik resurgence that led to the election of many members of that party to local urban soviets. This development was met with severe governmental repression. By 1922, the Mensheviks still at large went underground and were thus no longer able to put up candidates for soviet office.[45]

Not only were opposition parties increasingly excluded from participation in the soviets, but the categories of citizens who had been disenfranchised from participation in soviet elections were also at least on one occasion considerably extended. In mid-march of 1920, a document signed by G. Petrovsky, chairman of the Central Executive Committee of the Ukrainian soviets, entitled 'Supplementary instruction on elections to the Soviets' included the following instructions:

> categories of people disfranchised shall now include anyone whose activities have discredited him in relation to the revolution, irrespective of whether he actually comes into a category of undisputed disfranchisement. Such people may include working-class elements who have branded themselves by overtly kulak-style activities or by active pronouncements against Soviet power ... betrayers of the Ukrainian peasantry, lackeys of the Polish gentry and gangsters of all kinds.[46]

The Elimination of Opposition Parties from Society at Large

By 1919, Lenin was proclaiming without any situational qualification whatsoever: 'Yes, the dictatorship of one party! We stand upon it and cannot depart from this ground, since this is the party which in the course of decades has won for itself the position of vanguard of the whole factory and industrial proletariat.'[47] Within less than a year after this pronouncement, Lenin described the attempt to distinguish between the dictatorship of the class and the dictatorship of the party as proof of 'an unbelievable and inextricable confusion of thought.'[48] Yet, and this is very much worth noting, *it was not during the Civil War, but during the period from 1921 to 1922*, as a political accompaniment to the economic 'retreat' of NEP, that the one-party state was completely and fully established. In the meantime, i.e. from 1918 to 1920, the opposition parties endured a semi-legal existence, very much harassed but also occasionally allowed to have public meetings, publish newspapers, and, as we just saw, even be reinstated in the soviets. During the actual Civil War period, the government apparently acted in a relatively 'pragmatic' fashion without a systematic approach to the question of the suppression of other parties. Sometimes, as we shall see in greater detail in chapter 4, the government's behavior suggested that those who had nothing to do with the White armies and were willing to conduct themselves as a loyal opposition would be allowed to function undisturbed. Nevertheless, these actions would quickly be negated by other policies leaving no room for anything but unconditional support for the ruling party. While it is certainly true that this 'pragmatism' did not yet indicate an unambiguous totalitarian vocation or direction, neither did it indicate even a verbal appreciation of the importance of political freedoms for the proper functioning of soviet democracy. In any case, the final elimination of the opposition parties was accomplished not through any state legal enactments,[49] but through the resolutions and actions of the Communist Party itself. Thus, in August 1922, a year and a half after the end of the Civil War and with a fully established New Economic Policy in existence, the Twelfth All-Russian Conference of the Communist Party passed a special resolution dealing with 'antisoviet parties and tendencies.' This resolution, approved at the last Conference in which Lenin actively participated before he ceased all political activity in 1923, opened the way for the consolidation and systematization of the one-party state. Specifically, it required that the Bolsheviks put an end to Menshevik and SR activities in trade unions, cooperatives, secondary schools, higher and auxiliary educational institutions, the youth movement, and the publishing world.[50]

The Final Decline of Democratic Soviets

Shortly after the Revolution, the soviets began to have problems related to their internal democratic functioning, with the development of significant bureaucratic tendencies at the local level. In Moscow, for example, the presidium and executive committees of the soviet had, before the Civil War, considerably reduced the powers of the soviet plenum and those of the collegia or committees running the various departments of the soviet. After the April 1918 elections, the attempts to 'deconcentrate' the soviet by taking powers away from the top-level presidium and strengthening the relatively lower-level functional departments failed. Furthermore, during the Civil War the collegia or committees of the departments were altogether abolished and replaced by one-person management.[51]

Moreover, once the Left SRs and other parties were virtually outlawed, the soviets lost most of their remaining raison d'être. A variety of logistical problems (e.g. masses of people going off to war, chaos, confusion) also negatively affected the soviets. Thus, these bodies began their final decline as independent and/or meaningful institutions of working-class and peasant power. The soviet congresses, which were supposed to meet every three months and actually met in January, March, July, and November of 1918, afterwards only met annually.[52] The Central Executive Committee of the soviets (CEC) – presumably a permanent body – did in fact up to the middle of 1918 meet, on average, once very four or five days. In the second half of 1918 it began to meet less frequently, and it did not meet at all in 1919.[53] In 1920, in what turned out to be a short-lived attempt to revive the soviets, the CEC became somewhat active again, having five sessions lasting 20 days in that year, while in 1921 and 1922 it had four sessions each with a duration of 10 and 24 days respectively. [54] It is true that the smaller Presidium, consisting of one-tenth of the members of the CEC, did acquire at least greater formal importance.

Meanwhile, while the soviets were declining, the previously small and weak party apparatus was reorganized and grew, particularly after the Eighth Party Congress held in March 1919. In fact, by 1922–3 the Soviet Presidium and even the Council of People's Commissars (Sovnarkom) itself had lost a good deal of their power to the party's Central Committee and especially to its inner bodies established in 1919, the Politburo and the Orgburo.[55] At the same time, party secretaries were replacing soviet and other officials as the key holders of power at the local level, although for some time the ties between the local party committee and the center remained tenuous.[56] Nevertheless, T. H. Rigby has estimated that by 1921 the party had come to exercise administative as well as political authority in the new society. Moreover, he has described in detail the 'gestation' of the nomenklatura system in the period 1919–23. Rigby traced the 'birth' of the system to 12 June 1923, as Lenin lay paralysed from his penultimate stroke. As Rigby graphically described it:

> On that day the Orgburo issued a resolution (*postanovlenie*) prescribing new procedures for the appointment and transfer of senior officials, which were to be based on two lists (*nomenklatury*), the first comprising posts which could change hands only by a decision (*postanovlenie*) of the CC (which in practice turned out to mean the Secretariat, Orgburo or Politburo), and the second comprising posts which had to be cleared (*soglasovany*) with the Orgburo. Just four months later, on 12 October, the baby cut its first tooth; a draft nomenklatura for the CC was presented to the Orgburo and duly approved. Well nursed and nourished by Stalin's faithful assistants and despite the inevitable childhood complaints and tumbles, it soon grew into a sturdy and formidable infant.[56]

At the same time, the Communist Party was rapidly losing its own internal democracy. What began, in August 1918, as organizational measures to increase party discipline developed into the loss of the rights and autonomy of local party committees, particularly after 1919. The Politburo and the Orgburo had begun to appoint officials to vacant posts in the provinces, both inside and outside the party, without prior consultation with the affected groups. Besides, the central leadership was willing and able to adopt far-reaching measures in order to maintain its control of the party. Thus, in March 1920, when the All-Ukrainian Party Conference elected a central committee composed predominantly of inner-party oppositionists, the Politburo simply disbanded it and replaced it with its own specially selected 'Temporary Bureau.'[57] The following month, at the Ninth Congress of the Communist Party, at least one delegate criticized the methods used by the Central Committee to suppress criticism, including the exile of the critics: 'One goes to Christiana, another sent to the Urals, a third – to Siberia.'[58] The Party Conference held in August of 1922 sanctioned the prevailing practice by which the secretaries of lower party organizations, while formally elected by the local membership, were in fact appointed by higher party organizations. Moreover, by 1922 party cells had degenerated to such an extent that rank-and-filers had great difficulty in expressing their opinions. In many places the agenda would not even be announced in advance of each cell meeting. Instead of a real discussion taking place, what usually happened was that the cell secretary would deliver a report, and the rest of the meeting would be spent in formally ratifying his proposals.[59]

The Structural Weaknesses of the Russian Soviets

There had always been important obstacles to the functioning of the soviets as fully effective and democratic organs. This, even at the peak of their power and influence in 1917–18, when they were still open institutions with considerable democratic achievements to their credit.

First of all, there were obstacles not inherent in the soviet system itself. Here I am referring to structural problems as they developed in the Russian context before the Bolsheviks came to power. One such problem seems to have been that, while right after the February Revolution parties were quite unimportant in the soviets,[60] eventually they came to play such a critical role that they even threatened the viability of the soviets themselves. As J. L. H. Keep explains it, delegates to the soviets

> increasingly ... found it necessary to identify themselves with one or other of the political caucuses or [party] 'fractions' (fraktsii). These held meetings to discuss tactics before those of the plenum, which inevitably deprived the latter of much of its interest. Before long cadre elements were complaining of 'apathy' and lack of attendance.[61]

This problem was aggravated by the soviet practice, already in existence before the October Revolution, of allowing various parties and other organizations to acquire voting representation in the soviet executive committees. The Petrograd Soviet, for example, permitted each of these groups to send two delegates, and that was often how high party leaders became voting delegates to that body. It should be underlined that these party delegates were selected by the leadership of each political organization, and not by the soviet assembly itself. In other words, these executive committee members were not directly elected by the representatives of the producers, be they from large or small plants. Moreover, the majority parties in the soviet began to control nominations from above to all important posts such as the departments in the ministries and the General Staff of the Workers' Militia. Marc Ferro cites the example of the Menshevik Anisimov. Through the influence of his party in the Petrograd Soviet of Deputies and in the Petrograd Committee of the Menshevik Party, he got himself appointed a member of a high-level representative body, in this case, the Presidium of the Soviet of *Raion* Committees (the *raion* was a geographical unit equivalent to a Tsarist police district). This presidium then elected him as their president. However, Anisimov had never previously even been a member of a local or lower-level *raion* committee, let alone been elected by these lower committees to the higher representative bodies of these organizations. This practice, initially developed by the Mensheviks and SRs, was later used to their own advantage by the Bolshevik organizational leaders Sverdlov and Stalin.[62]

While party competition in a soviet-type system is indispensable in order to make it possible for delegates and the people they represent to make choices among alternative general programs of government, there was obviously a problem here. The problem would have been considerably worsened to the extent that parties were internally disciplined, which was by and large not the case from 1917 to at least the latter part of 1918. Given the great weight of the parties, internal discipline would have virtually eliminated authentic soviet-wide debates of some critical issues; besides, internal discipline would have also allowed a bare majority of the principal party to convert itself into a soviet majority by forcing the minority in the ruling party either to vote against its own views or leave the party altogether. Still, the growing importance of the party fractions in comparison to the soviet plenums was a reflection of the political polarization prevalent in revolutionary Russia. As long as those conditions existed, there was not much that institutional reforms of the soviets could have accomplished to make the plenums more important than the fraction meetings. However, it might have been at least possible, if not probable, for the soviets to have eliminated the ex officio appointment of party representatives to leadership positions in the soviets.

In the second place, there were unavoidable imperfections of the developing soviet democracy that were to be expected in any truly popular revolutionary upheaval. These could have been at least partially remedied with the passage of time. Here, I include problems such as the following:

1 Disparities in representation, which meant that delegates to the soviets could not be said to represent roughly equal numbers of people. For example, small plants were usually favored over large ones. In Moscow, one deputy was elected for each 500 workers, but never more than three for a single factory, thus clearly discriminating against very large factories. Also, the variable ratios of representation in election of deputies created substantial differences among different soviets. For instance, the city of Voronezh had 140 deputies for 20,000 workers while Tver had 89 deputies for 35,000 workers.[63]

2 Potentially serious conflicts among multiple organs of representation (e.g. factory committees, unions, soviets, etc.) with ill-defined jurisdictional boundaries.[64]

3 In an admirable effort to ensure that workers in every sector would be heard, persons often attended or spoke who had no elected right to be there.[65]

One important cause of problems such as these was that the soviets were typically informal and loose bodies, but it should be noted that, at least until early in 1918, informality was usually inspired by the desire to broaden authentic mass participation rather than by the wish to increase the political discretion of leaders. The soviets also tended to be quite flexible in the definition and performance of their functions. One example of this flexible functioning was provided by the above-mentioned *raion* soviets. These committees, based on the geographically defined Tsarist police districts, were elected almost universally from the factories and barracks in the area. Thus, Marc Ferro is mistaken in claiming that these soviets represented all the supporters of the revolution in each district of the city and were elected according to the principle of residence.[66] Nevertheless, it is true that the *raion* soviets devoted a considerable amount of effort to community issues not immediately connected to the factory shopfloor or to life in the barracks. Among these were problems such as housing, rents, prices, and drunkenness, and social welfare activities such as the maintenance of orphanages, hospitals, and public dining halls for the poor. Moreover, the *raion* soviets also carried out cultural and educational activities: sponsoring lectures, clubs, and youth groups, and organizing libraries.[67] It is thus reasonable to conclude that the continuation of a flexible democratic spirit, such as the one just described, *could* have allowed the ironing out of many problems concerning appropriate mechanisms of democratic representation. This might have included difficulties not envisaged in the original soviet concept, e.g. the need for some forms of geographical representation that would not threaten the central position of the workplace in the soviets. In this context, it is interesting to note that the 1918 Soviet Constitution explicitly granted the right to vote to 'all who acquired the means of living through labor that is productive and useful to society, *and also persons engaged in housekeeping, which enables the former to do productive work.*[68]

One actual effect of uncontrolled participation, in spite of a well-meaning democratic motivation, was to worsen the soviets' tendency to become large and unwieldy. This had the unfortunate consequence of increasing the concentration of power in the hands of the more viable small executive bodies.[69] As it turned out, this informal feature of the soviet system eventually facilitated the Bolshevik Party's ability to pack local soviets once they could not longer count on an electoral majority. For example, Alexander Rabinowitch has pointed that, even though the elections to the Petrograd Soviet held in the second half of 1918 were still 'relatively free and intense, with all parties working to win adherents,' the Bolsheviks retained control because of '... the numerically quite significant representation now given to trade unions, [and] district soviets ... in which the Bolsheviks had overwhelming strength.'[70]

The weakness of the peasant soviets A major obstacle to the proper democratic functioning of the soviets in the nation as a whole was their great weakness among the Russian peasantry, no small problem for what was still a preponderantly rural country (approximately 80 per cent of the population in

1917). For one thing, the soviets in the rural areas did not play as central and unique a role as those in the cities in part because they competed with other forms of organizations and institutions at the village and regional levels. Moreover, in contrast to the urban soviets in which the working class had from the beginning become spontaneously and massively involved, the peasant soviets, unlike other peasant organizations, did not spring unaided from the villages. To a considerable extent, these peasant soviets depended on 'external' factors such as the presence of outside agitators. Soviets were not developed at the village and *volost* (the next larger geographical unit above the village) levels until after the Bolsheviks had come to power, and they made slow progress after that. It has been estimated that no more than 11 per cent of all *volosti* had soviets as of October 1917. The situation was considerably better at the next higher geographical units above the villages and *volosti*, namely the *uezd* (county) and *guberniia* (province) levels. By mid-July of 1917, 317 out of a total of 813 *uezdy* possessed soviets; by October this had risen to about 422. By October, *guberniia* peasant soviets existed in all *guberniia* of European Russia with the exception of Volynsk and Estland. It should therefore be hardly surprising that the *guberniia* and *uezd* soviets, being relatively removed from the villages, had less direct relevance to events in the countryside. Moreover, often the peasants were often represented, to a much greater extent than the working class, by outside intellectuals (e.g. SR party members), who did not necessarily fully understand or know the situation in the villages.[71] In addition, few women were involved in the activities of the peasant soviets, a very serious drawback rooted in the *mir* or peasant community where participation had traditionally been limited to the usually male heads of households.[72]

Nevertheless, the weaknesses of the peasant soviets were as political as structural in nature. In my view, the most serious of the political problems was the virtual absence of the Bolshevik Party from rural Russia, an issue that I shall explore in greater detail later in this chapter. Furthermore, Soviet peasant democracy was not helped, at least at the symbolic and ideological levels, when the 1918 Soviet Constitution set up a ratio of representation that was highly discriminatory against the rural population. Article 25 of the constitution established the number of delegates to the All-Russian Soviet Congress at one to each 25,000 voters for the urban soviets and one to each 125,000 inhabitants for the provincial (*guberniia*) soviet congresses, delegates to the latter being sent by soviets in the smaller geographical units. However, in practice, as Robert Abrams has shown in some detail, the average peasant smallholder did not turn out to be anywhere near as underrepresented as one might have expected from these constitutionally established ratios.[73] In any case, the peasant soviets soon became bureaucratized; thus, while the *volost* soviets of 1918 had been domin-ated by the open assembly of peasant elders, the *volost* soviets of 1920 were much more dominated by their executives, which in turn became much less peasant than in the earlier period of the Revolution.[74]

Ideological and Objective Background to the Decline of Democratic Soviets

Bolshevik politics and the Soviets

There is no doubt that the objective difficulties caused by economic crises and civil war constituted very major obstacles to the survival of democratic soviets and, as we shall see in the next few chapters, of workers' control of industry, press freedom, and socialist legality. Yet, these real objective difficulties cannot by themselves explain why Lenin and the mainstream Bolshevik leadership made, as we saw above, a virtue out of necessity, and did not seem to be particularly disturbed by the loss of the democratic achievements of the October Revolution. It is evident that, as a minimum, this leadership did not see these institutional democratic gains as *indispensable* characteristics of a workers' and peasants' state, or of socialism. In any case, the existence of working-class and peasant democratic institutions was not considered as important as the retention of the monopoly of foreign trade, the abolition or at least the severe restriction of the market, and the establishment of economic centralization and planning.

Indeed, in regard to the soviets, far from having been invented by the Bolsheviks, they spontaneously developed during the 1905 Revolution and were at the time resisted by Lenin's party. Thus, for example, at a conference of Bolshevik Party committees in the Moscow region in November 1905, the delegates agreed to accept the soviets' right to existence, but only where the party could not 'direct the proletariat's mass action in any other way.' Moreover, soviets were to be treated merely as 'the technical apparatus' for carrying the party's leadership to the working class.[75]

It is to Lenin's credit that at this time he tenaciously and successfully fought to have the party reverse its sectarian stand of abstaining from full participation in the work of the soviets.[76] Yet, while Lenin rejected the sectarianism of his comrades, he continued to view the party as a more important revolutionary vehicle than the soviets. By this I do not mean that at this time Lenin failed to understand the necessarily different functions of the soviets and the party, or that he refused to welcome and support the democratic role of the soviets. What I do mean is that Lenin had developed a point of view that represented a shift from the positions of classical Marxism. The *Communist Manifesto* had proclaimed that the Communists 'have no interests separate and apart from those of the proletariat as a whole,' and 'do not set up any sectarian principles of their own, by which to shape and mould the proletarian movement.' This was not intended to suggest a theory of 'spontaneity,' which implied that the Communists did not need to organize and push for their political point of view everywhere they could. Rather, it was a statement of priorities that indicated that the organizations of the *working class* took precedence over the sect-type organizations that Marx had to deal with in his time. Granted that Lenin's party was not an organization like the sects Marx knew, the fact remains that, at least in 1905, Lenin's theory still relegated class organizations to a supporting rather than a central role in the revolutionary process. In all fairness to Lenin, it must be pointed out that, contrary to a good deal of Cold War scholarship, he was neither the creator nor the inventor of this conception of the party's relationship to the working class. The Marxist scholar Hal Draper has shown how G. V. Plekhanov, the father of Russian social democracy, had already translated Marx's notion of the 'dictatorship of the proletariat' as a 'dictatorship of the party,' although originally, i.e. long before the 1920s, this was still taken to presage the introduction of complete democracy in government.[77]

Thus, it is not completely surprising that the outbreak of the 1905 Revolution found Mensheviks and Bolsheviks quite unprepared. As the historian Alan K. Wildman aptly put it, 'Bloody Sunday was a rude awakening for both wings of Russian Social Democracy and vividly demonstrated its failure to maintain leadership over the very social force [the proletarian movement born in the 1890s] which had been the product of its own vision.' While the Mensheviks reacted more quickly and flexibly to the new situation than did the Bolsheviks, the fact remains that the Mensheviks had few contacts with the workers until the general strikes of October 1905. As Wildman pointed out, this was the result of a Menshevik strategy that relied more on a radicalization of the intelligentsia and the liberals than on a rebirth of the workers' movement. On his part, Lenin, while criticizing the sectarianism of his Bolshevik comrades, failed to develop a consistent attitude towards the soviet phenomenon. Thus, at the beginning of November 1905, he was very positive about the St Petersburg soviet and urged it to become the broadest possible democratic organization. In addition, he also maintained that this soviet should not adhere to any one party and should proclaim itself the provisional revolutionary government.[79] Less than a month later, Lenin shifted course and argued, in the context of supporting the St Petersburg Soviet's decision not to accept the participation of the Anarchists, that the Anarchists had no right to demand admission to that body since this soviet was 'not a labour parliament and not an organ of proletarian self-government, nor an organ of self-government at all, but a fighting organization for the achievement of definite aims.'[79] Moreover, and most relevant for my present discussion concerning the primacy of the party, a few days later Lenin made it clear that,

> In the period of the democratic revolution, a refusal to participate in non-party organizations would in certain circumstances amount to a refusal to participate in the democratic revolution. But undoubtedly socialists should confine these 'certain circumstances' to narrow limits, and should permit of such participation only on strictly defined, restrictive conditions. For while non-party organisations, as we have already said, *arise as a result of the relatively undeveloped state of the class struggle*, strict adherence to the party principle, on the other hand, is one of the factors that make the class struggle conscious, clear, definite and principled ... Socialists may

participate in non-party organisations only by way of exception; and the very purpose, nature, conditions, etc., of this participation must be wholly subordinated to the fundamental task of preparing and organising the socialist proletariat for conscious leadership of the socialist revolution.[80]

Lenin was therefore clearly implying that the party could normally fulfill its revolutionary role without the existence of broad class organizations, and that a fully developed class struggle would no longer place non-party organizations at the center of future revolutionary outbreaks. Consequently, Lenin's and the party's eventual endorsement of the soviets in 1905 seems to have been tactical in character. That is, the Bolshevik support for the soviets did not at the time signify a theoretical and/or principled commitment to these institutions as revolutionary organs to overthrow the old society, let alone as key structural ingredients of the post-revolutionary order. Furthermore, it is again revealing that from 1905 to 1917 the concept of the soviets did not play an important role in the thinking of Lenin or of the Bolshevik Party. Moreover, while none of these strategies and tactics vis-à-vis the soviets can be taken to mean an endorsement of the notion of the one-party state, or of an authoritarian post-revolutionary order, they can be fairly seen as expressing a predisposition favoring the party and downgrading the soviets and other non-party class organizations, at least in relative terms.

After the February 1917 Revolution, Lenin was once again ahead of his party comrades in turning to the soviets as vehicles for workers' power. Thus, the Manifesto entitled 'To All Citizens of Russia' issued by the Bolshevik Party's Central Committee on 28 February (i.e. before Lenin's return to Russia) omitted any reference to the soviets, while it did demand a provisional revolutionary government that would enact a number of basic laws and call a constitutional convention.[81] However, in pronouncements made, and in letters sent from abroad, Lenin began to develop the perspective of a soviet seizure of power. Especially after Lenin's return to Russia during the Bolshevik All-Russian Party Conference in April 1917, he did, probably influenced by the popularity of the soviets, strongly advocate a soviet seizure of power in the famous 'April Theses'. These Theses signaled the beginning of a determined and successful struggle to win over the Bolshevik Party to his position.

It could be argued that in 1917 Lenin did come to endorse the soviets on something more than a strategic–tactical basis. It is true, for example, that, following Marx's defense of the Paris Commune in *The Civil War in France*, Lenin in his *State and Revolution* (begun in December of 1916 and finished in its present incomplete form in August/September of 1917) praised the most democratic features of the Paris Commune. These included the abolition of the distinction between the executive and legislative powers and the immediate recall of elected officials, who were paid no more than the prevailing working-class wages. Actually, neither the 1905 nor the 1917 soviets are mentioned at all in *State and Revolution*, although Lenin had planned to discuss them had the manuscript not been interrupted by the more pressing business of actually carrying out a revolution. Nevertheless, this is a peculiar document that, for example, virtually ignores the party and its function in the revolutionary transformation. Besides, I would argue that *State and Revolution* did not play a decisive role as a source of policy guidelines for 'Leninism in power.' For example, we saw earlier in this chapter how immediately after the Revolution the Bolsheviks established an executive power, i.e. the Council of People's Commissars (Sovnarkom), as a clearly separate body from the leading body of the legislature, i.e. the Central Executive Committee of the soviets. Therefore, some sections of the contemporary Left appear to have greatly overestimated the importance that *State and Revolution* had for Lenin's government. I would suggest that this document, which was, after all, written before the seizure of power, can be better understood as a distant, although doubtless sincere, socio-political vision. This as opposed to its having been a programmatic political statement, let alone a guide to action, for the period immediately after the successful seizure of power.

The Politics of Revolution and the Politics of Workers' Democracy

The relationship of mainstream Bolshevism to soviet democracy was further complicated by additional factors. I am referring in particular to the period before October 1917 when a *necessary* degree of tension existed between revolution, i.e. the need to overthrow the Provisional Government, and democracy, i.e. the still majoritarian sentiment expressed by the soviets supporting or at least not attempting to overthrow that same Provisional Government. It is obvious that a revolutionary movement cannot wait to be organized until it has obtained the support of the majority of the population. In addition, majorities and minorities are not merely static entities. Such an approach has more in common with the plebiscitarian assumptions of public opinions polls than with a view of democracy that sees it as a living process profoundly affected by ongoing social struggles. Furthermore, in a revolutionary situation the very nature of society is at stake. Many people will then support or follow those who, through their decisive leadership, actions, and programs, are perceived as the best defenders of the interests of the popular majorities and offer viable solutions to what has become an untenable situation. As Rosa Luxemburg put it not long after the Bolshevik Revolution:

> The Bolsheviks solved the famous problem of 'winning a majority of the people,' which problem has ever weighed on the German Social-Democracy like a nightmare. As bred-in-the-bone disciples of parliamentary cretinism, these German Social-Democrats have sought to apply to revolutions the home-made wisdom of the parliamentary nursery: in order to carry anything, you must first have a majority. The same, they say, applies to revolution: first let's become a 'majority.' The true dialectic of revolutions, however, stands this wisdom of parliamentary moles on its

head: not through a majority to revolutionary tactics, but through revolutionary tactics to a majority – that is the way the road runs.[82]

Moreover, one must confront the reality that the logic of *conflict*, and particularly of *revolutionary conflict*, is not in the short run necessarily compatible with the logic of democratic majority rule. Revolutionary situations, unstable by their very nature, tend to have an all-or-nothing power dynamic. In the light of this, revolutionaries may be forced to take power even without majority support. I would argue that there are situations where such a course of action could conceivably be justified from a democratic–revolutionary point of view. For one thing, revolutionaries may have to do this because, by the time they do have majority support, they may no longer be able to take power. Or, on an even more basic level of sheer survival, they may have to take power to protect themselves against annihilation.

This suggests, however, that there is at least a temporary lack of correspondence between an oppositional revolutionary movement that has not yet obtained majority support and a consolidated post-revolutionary democratic society. This is one major reason why authentic democratic revolutionary *institutions* (e.g. factory committees, soviets, trade unions) are indispensible if successful worker–peasant revolutions are to be and remain democratic. Furthermore, these institutions, rather than the ruling party, should be where power ultimately resides in a worker–peasant state. The existence of such institutions may compensate for, and bring to a successful end, the lack of correspondence between a pre-revolutionary movement that is initially (and inevitably) minoritarian and the post-revolutionary majoritarian goal.

In essence, the classical Marxist revolutionary approach implied a projection or wager that the class and economic structure of capitalist society established a realistic and objective basis for a working-class-led revolutionary movement winning a majority. However, the fact that the proletariat was far from being a majority in the Russia of 1917 obviously complicated the Marxist revolutionary approach. Nevertheless, it did not by any means fatally compromise such a perspective, if the proletarian revolution in Russia committed itself to an alliance with the peasantry through the policies of land redistribution. Moreover, the survival of the worker–peasant revolution in Russia was seen as dependent on its ability to act as a triggering or precipitating mechanism for a more general European workers' revolution that in turn would help Russia out of its economic backwardness. This was a plausible expectation in 1917, if we consider the widespread ferment and turmoil prevailing among the European working classes in the final stages of World War I. In any case, what I have just described was the explicit political perspective of the Bolshevik Party that led the revolution of October 1917.

Needless to add, this revolutinary strategy, like any other activist political strategy, *necessarily* entailed risks on the issue of democracy as well as in far more obvious matters such as loss of lives and general destruction. But it cannot be inferred from this that the *absence* of a revolutionary project or perspective would not have entailed equal or greater risks for the working class and the majority of the population in Russia. However, there is a far more serious problem that neither Luzemburg nor the Bolsheviks discussed or theorized about: namely, what should revolutionaries do if they succeed in taking *and* retaining power, but their wager or projection fails insofar as maintaining popular support and a democratic society are concerned?

It seems that, on the whole, the strategy and tactics followed by Lenin and the Bolshevik Party during the immediate pre-October period were defensible from a democratic–revolutinary point of view. The perspective of seizing power was more than justified by the undeniable fact that between February and October of 1917 the Mensheviks, the Socialist Revolutionaries, and the soviets led by these parties had failed to act decisively to bring the war to an end, redistribute the land among the peasantry, and carry out a necessary working-class radical program. The devastation caused by Russia's continuing participation in World War I, and the failures of the Provisional Government, and of the SR and Menshevik parties in particular, helped to radicalize the Russian masses. Specifically, this established the basis for the emergence of the Bolshevik Party as the only force capable of leading the struggle for a revolutionary solution to the crisis. Yet, while I believe Bolshevik strategy and tactics in this period were on the whole correct, it is also important to note that there were, within the Bolshevik Party, significantly different degrees of concern and understanding of the serious problems involved in taking and/or holding on to power without majority support. Moreover, at this time, Lenin seemed to have been on the side of those Bolsheviks less concerned with these problems.

This issue most clearly came to the surface in the inner-party debates that took place in the period immediately after the 'July Days', a failed uprising that the Bolsheviks decided to support, not without misgivings, after it had broken out in the open. At this time, the soviets and the SR and Menshevik parties failed to defend the Bolsheviks from the repression carried out by the Kerensky government. Moreover, it appeared that this government would increasingly move towards a repressive right-wing stance, and neither the soviets nor the other socialist parties were offering a clear alternative to this rightward drift. In other words, the dynamic of the political situation seemed to be definitely pointing in the direction of a right-wing dictatorial regime, unless the Left were to act decisively and take power.

Thus, while the Bolsheviks had very actively supported the soviets in the late Spring and early Summer of 1917, after the 'July Days' Lenin and the majority of the party leadership no longer saw the soviets as revolutionary, but rather as obstacles in the life-and-death struggle against the Provisional Government. However, it should be noted that at this time Lenin explained that the demand for soviet power had been 'a slogan for peaceful progress of the revolution' with 'full state power [passing] to the Soviets in good time.' Furthermore, that did not necessarily mean that in the absence of a peaceful transition there was no room for the soviets. Even then, Lenin continued to be, at least at an abstract level, 'in favour of building the whole state on the model of the soviets,' and also stated that 'Soviets may appear in this new revolution, and indeed are bound to, but *not* the present soviets, not organs collaborating with the bourgeoisie, but organs of revolutionary struggle against the bourgeoise.'[83]

This new orientation, sharply different from that of the pre-July period, was defended by Lenin at a secret two-day Bolshevik Conference held in Petrograd in mid-July. Lenin maintained that the counterrevolution, fully supported by the Mensheviks and the SRs, had managed to take full control of the government and the revolution. Both the soviets and the moderate socialist parties had become, according to Lenin, 'mere fig leaves of the counterrevolution,' as expressed, for example, by their failure to defend the revolutionaries from governmental persecution. The party now had to prepare for an armed uprising and transfer of power to the proletariat and poorer peasantry. The factory shop committees, rather than the soviets, would not become the insurrectionary organs.[84]

This Conference, and the subsequent Sixth Congress, clearly showed, as I earlier suggested, the varying degrees of awareness among the Bolshevik leaders of the tension between on one hand the need for a revolutionary seizure of power, and, on the other hand, the concern with whether a minority, and a relatively isolated minority at that, could or should attempt to do so. Lenin was opposed by M. M. Volodarskii who viewed the petty bourgeoisie as wavering between revolution and counterrevolution rather than having completely gone over to the Right. Volodarskii was seconded by M. Kharitonov, who predicted that the wavering petty bourgeoisie would, under the influence of events, inevitably move to the Left. Otherwise, according to both of these party leaders, the Bolsheviks would stand alone as an overwhelmed minority. Kharitonov also concluded that a dictatorship of the proletariat could not be declared under such circumstances.[85] As it happened, the mid-July Conference did not adopt Lenin's perspective as yet. The compromise resolution passed by the Conference did agree with Lenin that the Kerensky government was a dictatorship, but implied that it was not fully 'under the thumb of the counterrevolution.' The only other concessions that the resolution made to Lenin's views were to call for a government based on the proletariat and poorest peasantry, and to qualify the slogan 'All Power to the Soviets' by referring to the need to place power in the hands of *revolutionary* proletarian and peasant soviets.[86]

The Sixth Congress of the Bolshevik Party, meeting semilegally in Petrograd from 26 July to 3 August 1917, adopted a resolution put forward by Stalin, acting as party leader. He was replacing Lenin, Kamenev, Zinoviev, and the newly admitted Trotsky, who were all in hiding at this time. This resolution, which passed with only four abstentions,[87] went further in the direction of Lenin's position and substituted the slogan 'Complete Liquidation of the Dictatorship of the Counterrevolutionary Bourgeoisie' for the slogan 'All Power to the Soviets.' However, the party was to continue to make the soviets the central focus of its activities, and the possibility of working with other socialists in defense of the revolution was still left open. It is important to note that the adopted resolution made no reference to the likelihood that the seizure of power by the Bolsheviks might precede their acquisition of majority support in the country at large, nor did it specifically mention the factory committees or any other revolutionary group or institution as a replacement for the soviets.[88]

Although the vote on Stalin's resolution was virtualy unanimous, the discussion preceding the vote revealed important differences of opinion within the party, many of these relevant to the matter of obtaining popular majority support. The existence of these differences also helps to explain the somewhat conciliatory character of the text finally approved. K. Iurenev, a member of Trotsky's group that had just joined the Bolshevik Party, defended the transfer of power to the soviets, arguing that they still represented a revolutionary force. He was also particularly concerned that one effect of Stalin's resolution might be to isolate the proletariat from the peasantry and the masses. V. P. Nogin argued for retaining the pro-soviet slogan on the grounds that a new revolutionary upsurge could be expected soon, which would strengthen Bolshevik influence in the soviets. Several provincial delegates advocated the retention of the soviet slogan for the provinces, since the soviets in their areas continued to be revolutionary. In opposition to these delegates, others contended that the July events had conclusively proven the counterrevolutionary nature of the soviets, given that the soviets had refused to take power. In this group were G. Y. Sokolnikov and A. S. Bubnov, the latter also supporting the factory committees as a replacement for the soviets. Bubnov further maintained that the dictatorship of the proletariat and peasantry was no longer possible and instead put forward the notion of a dictatorship of the proletariat supported by the poorer peasantry. A third group, Bukharin among them, was taken aback by those denying any value to the soviets and stated that the soviets should be retained, although transformed by new elections into Bolshevik organs. This third group also indicated that, if necessary, more soviets should be organized.[89]

Moreover, in spite of the strong vote to drop the slogan of soviet power, the Sixth Party Congress did not change the views of a very large part of the workers in Petrograd or of many Bolsheviks. Thus, calls for soviet power continued to be made by various factories and working-class organizations such as the Textile Workers' Union. More remarkable in this regard was the Second Petrograd Conference of Factory Committees, i.e. the very organizations that in Lenin's view should have replaced the soviets. Meeting from 12 to 14 August, this conference first endorsed the position adopted by the Sixth Congress, but then was persuaded by the recent converts and minority voices within Bolshevism, I. Larin and A. V. Lunacharsky, to reverse itself and call for power for the 'revolutionary democracy' (i.e. soviet power). The Petrograd factory committees were evidently very concerned about obtaining the support of the majority of the population. As David Mandel has pointed out, these committees were worried not only about becoming isolated from the peasantry, but also about their isolation from the democratic and non-Bolshevik socialist intelligentsia as well. This was quite likely reflected in the grave concern with which the Conference discussed the scarcity of technical and administrative skills among the workers themselves.[90]

The decision of the Sixth Party Congress to publicly withdraw the slogan 'All Power to the Soviets' only remained in force for a short period of time until the end of August 1917. At that time, and as a result of the Kornilov military coup and the crucial role that the Bolshevik Party played in defeating this attempt to overthrow the Provisional Government from the Right, the masses once again moved to the Left, and increasingly swung behind the party of Lenin. It was in this context that the Bolsheviks formally resurrected the old pro-soviet slogan.[91] Thus, as it happened, the indispensability of Bolshevik initiatives *independent* of the soviets in defeating Kornilov's coup in August 1917 proved Lenin to be right on the main actionable issue at stake, although not necessarily on the various related questions that were raised during the inner-party deliberations. This victory in turn was crucial in reversing the drift to the Right and revived the soviets as revolutionary organizations. Last but not least, Bolshevik tactics at this time showed that the radicalization of the masses was a process not independent from, but instead dialectically related to, the existence of a courageous and shrewd revolutionary leadership. Indeed, the Bolsheviks turned out to be quite fortunate because, in fact, the party of Lenin came into power riding the crest of a groundswell of enormous popular support. Finally, not long after the Sixth Congress, Trotsky and Lenin disagreed as to whether the Bolsheviks should call for an insurrection before the Second Congress of Soviets took place. Lenin, probably fearing that the best moment to strike from a military point of view might be lost, argued for immediate insurrection. Trotsky, in this instance more attuned to the political and symbolic issues involved, argued for delay until the Congress was about to convene. As it happened, Trotsky got his way because, owing to changes in the schedule for the opening of the Congress, the uprising turned out to have been synchronized with it. In this situation, and unlike the period after the 'July Days,' formal Bolshevik support for the sovereignty of the soviets was not in dispute, except of course in the limited sense that the Bolsheviks did not wait to act until the votes were counted at the actual Congress itself.[92]

Thus, as I indicated in the Introduction, the October Revolution was not a mere coup, but the culmination of an authentic mass movement, notwithstanding the ideology and scholarship inspired by the Cold War. In this context, Jerry F. Hough has made the interesting observation that, while the contemporary 'educated public' has thought of the October Revolution as a coup brought about through the Bolshevik's monolithic 'organizational weapon,' recent work by specialists has instead depicted a divided Bolshevik Party whose program attracted mass support particularly in the cities and among soldiers stationed near urban centers.[93]

Civil War and War Communism

Full-scale civil war against the counterrevolutionary White armies began in late May of 1918. In their reaction to this very grave danger to the revolution, Lenin and the Bolshevik Party did not merely maintain an instrumental social and

economic orientation dedicated to winning the war while attempting to preserve, as much as possible, the worker–peasant alliance. Instead, the government committed itself to a maximum-type program referred to as 'War
Communism' accompanied by the Red Terror (see chapter 4). The Bolsheviks
at this time also ended up adopting a political posture that often seemed to
imply that 'whoever was not a friend of the revolution was an enemy.' Indeed,
during 'War Communism' (1918–20), Lenin seems to have acted without the
benefit of his usual tactical flexibility and conjunctural political insight. This
was the case not only in regards to economic policy, but also vis-à-vis such
critical political issues as the invasion of Poland (see chapter 6). In fact, Robert
C. Tucker has referred to this period as 'Stalinist Leninism' by which he meant
not just the hegemony of certain general ideas and systems of political belief,
but the

> ingrained habits of mind, ways of defining and responding to situations,
> styles of action, common memories, mystique, etc., that collectively
> constitute the culture of a political movement in so far as a given age
> cohort of its membership (and leadership) is concerned ... The heritage
> of that formative time in the history of Soviet culture was martial zeal,
> revolutionary voluntarism and *elan*, readiness to resort to coercion, rule by
> administrative fiat (*administrirovanie*), centralized administration, sum-
> mary justice, and no small dose of that Communist arrogance (*komchvan-
> stvo*) that Lenin later inveighed against.[94]

It is worth pondering whether and how the development of the desperate
political spirit of 'War Communism' was also in part a reaction to the loss of
popular support for the Bolshevik Party as expressed, for example, by the
serious losses it suffered in the Spring 1918 soviet elections. The governmental
euphoria with War Communism also implicitly revealed the political and
ideological priorities of mainstream Bolshevism. Thus, while this set of policies
greatly expanded the powers of the central state and vigorously attempted to
reduce the role of the market, at the same time it not only consolidated the Red
Terror but for all intents and purposes eliminated workers' control of industry
and democracy in the soviets. Again, there is no evidence indicating that Lenin
or any of the mainstream Bolshevik leaders lamented the loss of workers'
control or of democracy in the soviets, or at least referred to these losses as a
retreat, as Lenin declared in connection with the replacement of War Communism by NEP in 1921. In fact, as we shall see in the next chapter, the very
opposite is the case, e.g. Lenin defended one-man management as perfectly
compatible with socialism.

Specifically, the main features of War Communism consisted of the following: First of all, grain was forcibly confiscated from the peasantry by a variety of
often extreme and ruthless means, with grain frequently being classified as
surplus that in fact was part of the peasant's own meager diet or was being
stored as part of the normal and ancient practice of equalizing seasonal
variations in the availability of supplies. The most important groups carrying out

'surplus' extractions were the armed 'food detachments' of townsmen sent into the countryside.[95] However, it should be noted that this policy, and Lenin's advocacy of mass searches of all storehouses, had a precedent in practices carried out under the Provisional Government, and earlier in 1918 as soon as the food crisis had become acute in big cities such as Petrograd and Moscow.[96]

Furthermore, at the beginning of War Communism, and for a few months afterwards, the government established committees of poor peasants who were supposed to distribute grain and manufactured consumer goods, and to cooperate in taking surplus grain away from the kulaks. In return, the activists of these poor peasant committees were to receive a share of the grain and other requisitioned goods, an arrangement that *structurally* invited the numerous abuses that did take place. Although the middle peasants were supposed to be included in these committees, in fact the arbitrary power and sweeping requisitions carried out by the committees elicited the bitter hatred of both kulaks and middle peasants, i.e. a clear majority of the rural population after the revolutionary land redistribution had taken place. Besides, both the committees of the poor and the workers' food detachments attracted into their ranks a significant number of criminals and bandits, a predictable development given their informal and arbitrary methods of operation. Moreover, the 'poor peasant' policy had been based on Lenin's very questionable sociological assumptions concerning the size of this group and its weight and significance in the rural communities. For example, it has been estimated that in 1917 there were only 1.7 million landless wage laborers in Russian agriculture, out of a population of approximately 100 million rural dwellers.[97] In addition, as Marc Ferro has informed us, the documentary evidence indicates that, contrary to Lenin's expectations, the villages displayed a great deal of solidarity in 1917 and that, after October, 'the rural laborer who belonged to the 'committee of the poor' was generally as disliked as the *kulak* when he failed to unite with the other peasants; and the hostility of the peasantry overall towards townsmen and delegates of the machinery of the state (whatever its nature) counted for more than the conflicts among the peasants.'[98] Indeed, this is the conclusion that one would have expected from a Marxist analysis of the Russian peasantry, particularly when one considers that, by the time of the Civil War, small farms had become the norm in the Russian countryside.[99]

Before the October Revolution, at the Sixth Party Congress in August 1917, Bolshevik critics of Lenin had indeed argued that the 'poor peasantry' was neither a political entity nor a Marxist category, and that instead it suggested a lumpen element.[100] Shortly after this, at the Factory Committees' Conference in Petrograd, Lunacharsky had also claimed that there was no clear boundary line separating the poor from the non-poor peasantry.[101] It is also worth noting that, when considerable rural ferment was taking place in the months preceding the October Revolution, the special organizations of farm workers and the poor peasantry that Lenin's agrarian policy had long advocated played a very limited role. According to Graeme J. Gill, 'although such bodies did develop, they were not very widespread. The only areas in which they appeared on anything but a negligible scale as independent entities were in the Baltic region and in parts of the Ukraine, and even here they were an insignificant factor in rural unrest.'[102] Therefore, it should not surprise us that at the time the War Communist activities against the peasantry were being carried out, the Commissariat of Internal Affairs recorded 26 peasant uprisings in July, 47 in August and 35 in September of 1918.[103] The short-lived 'poor peasant' policy turned out to be a clumsy and artificial 'from-the-outside' attempt to split the peasantry.[104] Besides, there can be no doubt that, as in the case of the weak rural soviets, the Bolshevik Party's virtual absence from the countryside was an important reason for the party's ignorance of peasant realities, and consequently for their developing such ill-founded policies.

However, the contemporary Russian economic historian Vasili Seliunin is greatly exaggerating when he claims that the 'mass liquidation of kulaks took place precisely in the years of "war communism," and not in the early 1930s.' For one thing, collectivization of agriculture was not a significant phenomenon during the years of War Communism. Although there were some instances of peasant protests against overzealous local authorities who had attempted to force peasants into collective farms, nevertheless the fact remains that only about 625,000 out of the rural population of 100 million had joined collective farms of any kind before 1921. Moreover, according to the census of 1920, collective farming accounted for less than 1 percent of the total sown area.[105]

A second and extremely important characteristic of War Communism was the widespread nationalization of the industrial sector of the economy. This was accompanied by the elimination of workers' control and the introduction of one-man management, state control of the labor of every citizen (i.e. forced allocation of labor), and the attempt to implement extreme economic centralization.[106] I shall discuss these features of War Communism in some detail in chapter 2 on workers' control and the trade unions.

The third main feature of War Communism was the attempt to abolish money and trade by going over to a system of natural economy, in which all transactions were to be carried out in kind.[107]

Why 'War Communism'?

Some authors such as Maurice Dobb have argued that War Communism was merely a pragmatic and temporary response to the extreme economic conditions brought about by the Civil War, and not an integral part of Bolshevik theory and politics.[108] Other authors such as Paul Craig Roberts have argued for the diametrically opposite point of view and have maintained that it was a conscious and deliberate policy primarily designed to establish a full-fledged socialist organization of industry and society.[109]

The available historical research supports neither Dobb's nor Roberts' interpretation. It is clear, for example, that one critically important measure associated with War Communism, namely, the widespread nationalization of industry, was *initially* neither preplanned nor carried out by the government as a matter of high principle. In part, these nationalizations were carried out spontaneously by rank-and-file workers beginning at the end of 1917, more often than not as defensive actions against employer sabotage and lockouts. Then, when the central government issued the nationalization decree on 28 June 1918, this was done primarily as a response to the actions of Russian industrialists who had begun to transfer, through real or fictitious sales, banks, industries, and other properties to German firms and citizens. Had these transfers been successful, the Bolshevik government would have been forced to honor and respect German property claims under the provisions of the just-approved Treaty of Brest-Litovsk.[110] Similarly, the attempt to abolish money and trade may have been at least in part a governmental reaction to its inability to control inflation and deal with a serious crisis in the distribution of goods.

Yet it is no less true that soon after War Communism was established it ceased to be a mere 'situational' response to Civil War imperatives, and also came to represent a political and ideological urge among the majority of Bolsheviks to establish what they considered to be communist (in my view, state socialist) institutions regardless of objective economic and social conditions. As Stephen F. Cohen has commented:

> The notion (promoted by the Bolsheviks themselves after 1921) that only a few dreamers and fanatics accepted war communism as an enduring policy, as a direct route to socialism is incorrect. It was the sentiment of the party majority; few resisted the general euphoria. Most notably, Lenin, despite his fabled pragmatism and subsequent deprecation of the follies of war communism, was no exception. 'Now the organization of the proletariat's communist activities, and the entire policy of the Communists,' he said in 1919, 'has fully acquired a final, stable form; and I am convinced that we stand on the right road. . .'[111]

Bukharin, who years later would move to the opposite extreme and become a supporter of the most cautious version of the New Economic Policy – in contrast to Trotsky's more daring version of the NEP – sang the praises and became the foremost theoretical apologist for War Communism in his *The Economics of the Transition Period*, a study of nothing less than 'the process of the transformation of capitalist society into communist society.'[112]

This ideological inebriation of the majority of the Bolshevik Party negates the claim that War Communism, and the abandonment of the institutions of workers' democracy, was simply imposed on the government by objective necessity. I rather tend to agree with Alec Nové who suggests that a variety of factors played a role in bringing about War Communism: namely, 'revolutionary emergency, ideological preconceptions, political tactics, and just harsh overriding necessity, all of which tended to interact.'[113] It really is not difficult to visualize how the very real pressures of economic crises may have lured the Bolshevik government into measures that they had originally been *against* proposing, let alone implementing, in the period immediately after the revolutionary seizure of power. Yet War Communism, *unlike* the later New Economic

Policy, had a special attraction for the Bolsheviks, because once it came into being it appeared to bring the final goal closer to reality. Thus, while Lenin would call NEP a 'retreat' *at the time it was put into effect*, he regretted the prematurity of War Communism only *after* it had been superseded or abolished.

Was 'War Communism' Justified?

The 'situational,' as distinct from the political and ideological, arguments justifying the overall policies of War Communism claim that the Communist Party did not have the forces to administer an NEP-type peasant policy in 1918 (i.e. free trade and a fixed agricultural tax in kind to feed the workers and the army). Furthermore, the argument goes, uncontrolled free trade would have overwhelmed the still weak proletarian dictatorship. Thus, it was easier to ban free trade than to regulate it.[114] On the opposite side of this dispute, one scholar has pointed out that 'the total effort required to raise a tax in kind [a key aspect of the NEP] would hardly have equaled that involved in the requisitioning and might have established a clearer line of authority in the village. It might have required more effort at the center and less locally, but the total effort would perhaps have been no greater.'[115] Along the same lines, Roy Medvedev has maintained that, precisely because the party lacked forces, it was in no position to nationalize all enterprises, including the smallest workshops, and organize the direct product exchange between town and country in place of trade. In the meantime, the Soviet government's attempt to maintain a monopoly in grain, and most other basic necessities, turned the bulk of the peasants and former soldiers, as well as Cossacks and petty bourgeois, against the Bolsheviks. This provided the counterrevolution with a mass base.[116] In fact, Medvedev further argues, the illegal continuation of free trade during War Communism is what actually saved the urban and rural populations, and thus kept the revolutionary government in power.[117]

We do know, in support of Medvedev's thesis, that a contemporary study of three central Russian provinces for the months between September 1919 and January 1920 showed that, of all products acquired by peasants, only 11.1 per cent were acquired at fixed prices through state and cooperative outlets; 53.9 per cent came through the free market, and 35 per cent through in-kind exchange, presumably with state organs.[118] Moreover, groups of 'bagmen' moved from village to village, buying bread and vegetables that they would then sell or barter to the famished city dwellers. In fact, the countryside was affected by the sphere of state monopoly only as a source of requisitioned grain. By the end of 1920, illicit trade had become much more important than, and had largely supplanted, the official channels of distribution. In the process, inflation had also gone out of control.[119] Nonetheless, at this very time (i.e. the end of 1920), the Supreme Council of National Economy was still taking steps to extend nationalization even more widely.[120]

While also addressing himself to a number of issues not treated here, Lars T.

Lih's recent and detailed study of food supply policies in the period 1914–21 reached conclusions relevant to this discussion. According to Lih, a key reason the peasants had no incentive to sow more than they needed for their own consumption was not so much that the Bolshevik government took the entire surplus, but the absence of industrial items for which to exchange the grain. Yet, while the lack of industrial items was of course a very major obstacle and objective result of the Civil War for which the government could not be held responsible, this study also discussed the effect of specific Bolshevik policies that were clearly detrimental in their effects. Chief among these was the attempt to prohibit private trading through the use of devices such as the infamous roadblock detachments. As Lars T. Lih pointed out, 'the free market could have mobilized industrial items that the state could not otherwise get its hands on. But more important, the Bolsheviks had not yet learned that allowing a private market need not be a loophole through which escaped all the grain desired by the state, but could be an incentive for the peasant to *fulfill* state obligations in order to be able to trade without harassment.'[121] Again, policies such as the prohibition of trading and the administrative lawlessness with which requisitions were conducted were not objectively inevitable, and considerably aggravated an already quite unfavorable situation. It is worth noting in this context that two of the most important features of the post-Civil War NEP food supply reforms were the institution of greater predictability and definiteness in state demands, and the granting of freedom of disposal over private surpluses after the state obligation was met.[122]

Some leading Bolsheviks had apparently not always shared the party majority's enthusiasm for the various aspects of War Communism. As early as the end of 1918, a former Menshevik, Larin, had advocated a modified form of free trading with the villages, but with little support. Far more interesting is that none other than Trotsky, at the beginning of 1920 (that is, *a full year* before the adoption of the NEP), proposed to the Central Committee a limited form of free trade. Trotsky's proposal was defeated by 11 votes to 4.[123] After all, War Communism had achieved some results – the food detachments succeeded by 1920 in extracting supplies from the peasantry that were almost half of the average supplies for the years 1914–17.[124] Nevertheless, Trotsky became aware, as his biographer Isaac Deutscher put it, 'that the nation's energy and vitality was drying up at its very source – on the farmstead.'[125] Lenin, on the other hand, resisted the abolition of War Communism for as long as he possibly could, i.e. until after the 'Green' peasant revolts in Tambov and the Ukraine and the rebellion in Kronstadt. It should be emphasized that all of these truly tragic outbreaks took place *after* Trotsky's proposals to modify War Communism had been rejected. Far from acting to curb War Communism, Lenin's interventions, even as late as the Eighth Congress of Soviets in December 1920, led to a Congress resolution calling for the continuation of a War Communist policy consisting of a 'statewide plan of compulsory sowing,' under the general direction of the Commissariat of Agriculture.[126]

The Bolsheviks and the Peasantry

The endurance of War Communism and the Bolshevik majority's ideological enthusiasm for that policy can in part be explained by that party's attitude to the peasantry. Compared to the indifference if not hostility of the Mensheviks, Lenin and the Bolsheviks demonstrated a great deal of interest in the revolutionary potential of Russia's rural population, particularly the poor peasantry and farm workers. Lenin's pre-revolutionary attitude to the peasantry as a whole could be characterized as ambivalent. On one hand, and unlike the Mensheviks, he appreciated the revolutionary potential of the peasantry in its struggles against the landlords and the state power that supported them. On the other hand, he saw the peasants as inevitably becoming reactionary once they obtained their land. Thus, as Esther Kingston-Mann has pointed out, 'Lenin's "principled" rejection of the possibility that peasants might be anti-capitalist (much less socialist) prevented him from making a convincing case that peasants were an appropriate political constituency for revolutionary socialists.'[127] In this context, left-wing Russian populism tended to be more discriminating. For example, left-wing populists were more likely to see the small landowning peasant hiring no labor as constituting a progressive political force.

No wonder, then, that the Bolshevik Party hardly existed in the Russian countryside before the October Revolution and even for some time after that.[128] Thus, 80 per cent of the population had little if any contact with what, after all, became the principal revolutionary organization in the soviets and in the country. This important trait of the Bolshevik Party is clearly shown by a wealth of data going back to as early as 1905. In that year, only 4.8 per cent of party members were peasants. Twelve years later, in January 1917, this proportion had only slightly increased to 7.6 per cent. In 1916, only four rural party cells were in existence, and this remained a problem through October 1917, particularly for cells below the level of the *uezd* town. One source estimates that, between February and October of 1917, 343 Bolshevik organizations were established at the regional and sub-regional levels, but this was practically 'a drop in the ocean' if we consider that there were 10,000 *volosti* in European Russia alone. In any case, no peasant delegates were actually listed at the Sixth Party Congress in July–August 1917. Almost two months after the Revolution, in December of 1917, there were still only 4,122 rural Communists in a population of approximately 100 million rural dwellers. As late as 1918, one-third of all *volosti* had no Communist Party organizations, and many of the remaining two-thirds had only very small cells. Two years later, in 1920, the majority of *volosti* still had no party organizers.[129]

Equally remarkable was the Communist membership's apparent ignorance of and perhaps even lack of interest in the problems of the peasantry. Thus, on 26 October 1917, when Bolshevik delegates to the Second Congress of Soviets were asked to fill out a questionnaire, 50 out of 140 delegates answering left question 19 blank or didn't know the answer to it. Question 19 read as follows:

'Have there been agrarian disorders in your region? What is the soviet's influence over the peasantry, and what part does it play in the rural movement?' In the remaining 90 questionnaires, the answer was given with a single word without further elaboration. Many party leaders remained uninvolved in rural work even when confronted with the disaster of the Civil War. Thus, a Central Committee survey of 17 gubkoms (*guberniia* committees) and bureaus in the second half of 1919 found that only 2.1 per cent of the 3,211 questions discussed at their meetings concerned rural problems.[130] All of these facts point to at least two rather obvious conclusions:

1 The Bolshevik Party had utterly failed to recruit even among those elements of the rural population that its political theory saw in a favorable light, i.e. the poor peasantry and farm workers. Indeed, it is worth noting that much of the impact that the Bolshevik Party did eventually have on the rural population at the time of the revolution was indirect, i.e. through returning soldiers and sailors who had been exposed to Bolshevik ideas and activities while serving in the Tsarist armed forces.
2 An alliance between the Bolsheviks and a party or parties representing the peasantry was not only desirable but indeed nothing less than an objective necessity.

Of course, sooner or later a ruling party *had* to recruit peasants if it was to administer a country as big and diverse as Russia. However, it is hardly surprising that, if careerism had become a problem among urban recruits to the party, it should have become an even greater problem among its recruits in areas where the party had virtually no pre-revolutionary roots. Thus, among the new post-revolutionary rural Communists were to be found priests, former Tsarist policemen, and government employees interested in advancing their careers. So low was the quality of these rural recruits that, while in 1921 peasants comprised 28.2 per cent of the party membership, they constituted 44.8 per cent of those purged.[131]

Needless to add, there were strong economic and political considerations supporting a prioritizing of policial work among the industrial working class. First of all, this prioritizing, which did not necessarily imply *ignoring* the peasantry, was a corollary of the Marxist projection that the working class would be the leading class in a revolutionary movement based on an alliance with the peasantry and other oppressed groups. Second, most peasant families individually worked the land and thus lacked any built-in incentive for sustained collective action. Workers, of course, did not individually own the places or machines with which they labored and were furthermore collectivized by their very conditions of work, i.e. the factory shopfloor. Third, capitalism as an expanding and dynamic system had brought about huge means of production and national working classes that were increasingly interdependent. This laid the basis for the forging of international political organization and solidarity among these working classes. They would thus become, at least in the long run, potentially capable of creating a new revolutionary and international socio-economic order. In turn, such an order would abolish the objective need for exploitation and oppression. In applying these Marxist assumptions to the particular context of Russian society, Lenin and the Bolshevik Party as a whole additionally concluded that the town dominated the country and that the capitals would therefore lead the rest of the Russian population. Furthermore, they also thought that the strategic concentration of the proletariat assured it command over the capitals. There, the most politically advanced, organized in the Bolshevik Party, would lead the rest of the proletariat and behind them the rest of the masses into struggle, thus raising the general level of organization and consciousness.[132]

Lenin's formulation of a 'dictatorship of the working class and the peasantry' did not explicitly state that Lenin conceived of this as an unequal coalition, with the working class as the senior partner. However, in all fairness to Lenin, he was as a rule quite clear on this point. Nevertheless, many of the Lenin's formulations on this matter were generally quite unobjectionable either from a democratic revolutionary socialist point of view, or from a universalistic and, if you will, humanist perspective on the social and political role of the urban proletariat. (By this, I mean an approach that sees the liberation of the proletariat as providing positive solutions to the problems, and leading to the liberation of all the oppressed and exploited groups in society as a whole.) Thus, even at the height of War Communism in December of 1919, Lenin was still able to formulate the question in these terms:

> The town cannot be equal to the country. The country cannot be equal to the town under the historical conditions of this epoch. The town inevitably *leads* the country. The country inevitably *follows the town*. The only question is *which class*, of the 'urban classes,' will succeed in leading the country, will cope with this task, and what forms will *leadership by the town assume?*[133]

This was a sociological characterization with a political conclusion concerning leadership. As far as this formulation goes, it is both universalistic and certainly unobjectionable from a revolutionary democratic point of view. Moreover, the Bolsheviks' initial actions after the October Revolution – e.g. the nationalization and division of the land and the majoritarian coalition with the Left SR Party – were consistent with this interpretation of the formula.

Far more problematic, and in fact largely inconsistent with the notion of working-class leadership as distinct from party dictation over the peasantry and most of the working class, were some of the other theses that Lenin subscribed to several months after the seizure of power. Neil Harding has summarized them as follows: 'The advanced, class conscious detachment of the urban proletariat [i.e. the party] alone expresses the essential interests of the proletariat as a whole. The proletariat expresses the real interests of all the exploited and toiling masses.'[134]

Thus, the lack of equality between town and country, and the consequent need for leadership by the town, turned out to be remarkably slippery and ambiguous concepts, just like the equally slippery and ambiguous notion of the lack of equality between the 'advanced' party members and the more 'backward' elements in the working class. 'Leadership' could subtly and not so subtly be transformed into dictation, imposition, and even discrimination. This was never truer than under War Communism. Thus, the head of the revolutionary Russian state could in a public speech disrespectfully refer to the peasant, who as a class constituted the overwhelming majority of the population, as 'half worker and half huckster.'[135] Lenin maintained the same tone in May of 1919 when he claimed that 'the workers and peasants are equal as working people, but the well-fed grain profiteer is not the equal of the hungry worker. This is the only reason why our Constitution says that the workers and peasants are not equal.'[136] More important, when confronted with the tremendous problems created by the very real scarcity of food, the language of proletarian universalism often gave way to the language of proletarian particularism. How could the mass of the peasantry feel any loyalty or be attracted to a regime that sometimes spoke, and seemed to act, as if Marxist sociological considerations could replace the more pertinent criteria (vis-à-vis starvation) of elementary equity and degree of need. In fact, Lenin later admitted that 'the essence of "War Communism" was that we actually took from the peasant all his surpluses and sometimes not only the surpluses but part of the grain the peasant needed for food.'[137] Last but not least, for those who had the temerity to suggest that it was necessary to grant freedom to trade in food products in order to encourage peasant production, Lenin answered:

> ... what is [Kolchak's] economic basis? His basis is freedom of trade. This is what he stands for; and *this is why* all the capitalists support him. ... This is the answer we give ... without casting any slur on the honour of the Socialist-Revolutionaries and the Mensheviks who deserted Kolchak when they realized that he is a tyrant. But if such people, in a country which is fighting a desperate struggle against Kolchak, continue to fight for the 'equality of labour democracy', for freedom to trade in grain, they are still supporting Kolchak, the only trouble being that they do not understand this and cannot reason logically.[138]

Apparently, it was first necessary that the rebellions in the Ukraine, Tambov, and Kronstadt take place before Lenin also became a supporter of Kolchak in 1921!

In any case, it was striking that a major and original contributor to the Marxist tradition such as Lenin had a difficult time reconciling himself to the unavoidable reality that allowing the existence of petty trade was, in the last analysis, not a matter of a voluntaristic choice of government policy. Instead, petty trade was a reflection of a material reality, i.e. a very backward development of the still non-collective, petty commodity means of production, and similarly of the means of distribution. After all, Marx and Engels had assumed that the abolition of the market as the principal regulator of economic activity would take place in the context of an extended factory system where production was already conducted on a collective rather than an individual basis. Indeed, in the pamphlet *Socialism: Utopian and Scientific*, Friedrich Engels underlined the importance of a key contradiction of capitalism, namely the 'contradiction between socialised organisation in the individual factory and social anarchy in production as a whole.' This key contradiction would only be solved, according to Engels, when the proletariat 'seizes the public power, and by means of this transforms the socialised means of production . . . into public property, . . . and gives their socialised character complete freedom to work itself out. Socialised production upon a predetermined plan becomes henceforth possible.'[139] These are the crucial considerations ignored by Lars T. Lih,[140] in an interesting article discussing the various policy components of War Communism and the NEP. In this contribution, Lih suggested that it would have been possible to eliminate the hated War Communism policy of *Razverstka*, i.e. the compulsory requisitioning of food goods from the peasantry, without at the same time establishing a policy of free trade in agricultural products. According to Lih, this could have been achieved by the central government's willingness to exchange an equitable amount of industrial products for the agricultural goods produced by the peasantry. Leaving aside the key question of whether the government might have been able to manufacture and deliver such a quantity of industrial products, Lih is again ignoring the built-in structural links between petty production and petty private trade, particularly in a huge country like Russia with the relatively undeveloped means of communication it had in the 1920s.

Now, it is certainly true that part of Lenin's anti-peasant sentiments can be accounted for not by his original political theories but as a result of the contingencies of the post-revolutionary situation in Russia. Yet I would insist on the inadequacy of Leninist and Bolshevik policies on the peasantry, with the exception of the short period immediately preceding and subsequent to the October Revolution when Lenin adopted the SR land program. At least since the 1890s, Lenin had reasonably assumed that, as Russia became increasingly integrated into the world capitalist system, its own economy would dramatically change. One key aspect of this change would be a growth in the specific social weight of the working class and a corresponding decline in the specific weight of the peasantry. Furthermore, the countryside itself would change, with the peasantry becoming increasingly proletarianized owing to the introduction of capitalist agriculture and the breakup and decline of traditional rural society. This might have been sound reasoning as far as very long-term socio-economic *trends* were concerned.[141] What is very questionable is whether the speed and tempo of this economic process could have been great enough, particularly when matched with the much faster social and political disintegration of the Tsarist regime already suggested by the 1905 Revolution.

Could capitalist economic development have conceivably produced, at least within the lifetime of Lenin and his fellow revolutionaries, the rural and/or urban proletarianization of the great peasant majorities? If that was not possible, then even an entirely peaceful revolution would not have eliminated the unfavorable objective situation confronting the working-class revolutionary movement. This would have surely been the case, unless we make the completely unrealistic, and unMarxist, assumption that a society with a large peasant majority could somehow have avoided facing serious questions of economic priorities and conflicts between the agricultural and industrial sectors. A successful socialist revolution in Germany would have naturally helped a lot; for example, it might have shortened the period of scarcities and lack of capital for infrastructural investments, but it could in no way have eliminated it. This becomes all the more evident when we consider the damage suffered by the German economy during World War I, and the urgent needs and priorities of the German working class and peasantry themselves.

In other words, there was perhaps no conceivable set of conditions, including that of socialist revolution in the West, that would have allowed for the short-term development of authentic proletarian socialism in the *whole* of Russia. In that case, one must ask whether the New Economic Policy, or something very much like it, rather than being the 'retreat' that Lenin called it, was actually the only conceivable democratic policy that could have been implemented. This may have been the only possible *type* of policy even if there had been a peaceful transfer of power to the Bolshevik-led soviets, no civil war, and a successful revolution in Germany. Again, given a huge mass of petty commodity producers, only the use of severe police methods can attempt – and then with only rather limited success – to suppress private trade.

Moreover, even if post-revolutionary economic development had proceeded at a rapid pace, the voluntary rather than the forced disappearance of petty commodity producers would have occurred in a gradual manner. This post-revolutionary society would then have been a sort of 'muddling-through,' more or less democratic workers' and peasants' state attempting to crawl its way to socialism with the help of more developed socialist states to the West. In such a situation, an aggressive policy vis-à-vis the peasantry would presumably have meant, at the very best, the creation of full-fledged proletarian democratic communes in the cities confronting a politically disenfranchised and economically exploited peasantry in the countryside. Needless to add, such a system of urban proletarian 'kibbutzim' could not have remained democratic for very long in the face of the overwhelming hostility of the surrounding majority of peasant second-class citizens.

The Bolsheviks and the Constituent Assembly

The soviet system established by the successful October Revolution led by the Bolshevik Party has been criticized as an undemocratic form of representation. This criticism has been leveled, in particular, by those who supported the Constituent Assembly as the key institution of an alternative democratic system representing *all* classes and sectors of Russian society.

As a matter of fact, the Bolshevik Party had, after the February Revolution, supported the convening of a Constituent Assembly, to be elected under the principle of universal suffrage. They continued to do so even after they had taken power in the October Revolution. Lenin did argue for a postponement of the elections,[142] but they were still held as scheduled on 12–14 November in most of the country, although in some areas the elections were held over a period of many weeks and, in some cases, never took place at all. As it turned out, the Bolshevik Party obtained about one-fourth of the *national* popular vote. However, Lenin's party won the elections in the big cities, in the industrial towns, and in the rearguard garrisons. They also obtained strong support among peasants in the central, White Russian, and northwestern regions. Nevertheless, the SR party emerged as the big winners. In spite of defections, the SRs were still the peasants' party, and they did especially well in the black-earth zone, the valley of the Volga, and in Siberia. The Mensheviks did very poorly, except in Georgia and the general area of the Transcaucasus. Similarly, the Constitutional Democrats (Kadets) obtained very little support except among the relatively numerous middle and upper classes in Petrograd and Moscow. Finally, after the Bolshevik government unsuccessfully attempted to have the Constituent Assembly endorse the outcome of the October Revolution, they dissolved it after a single session on 5 January 1918.[143]

The Bolshevik rationale for the dissolution of the Constituent Assembly would have been justified from a democratic–revolutionary point of view *only if we assume* that their arguments in defense of the soviet system, particularly after the formal merger with the majority of the Peasant Congress in late 1917, represented a genuine and long-term commitment to that alternative form of democratic government. Moreover, the Bolsheviks were justified in their claim that, since the Socialist Revolutionary Party split into Left and Right wings *after* the electoral lists were prepared but *before* the elections, the SR Party delegation at the Constituent Assembly was not representative of that current of opinion as it existed at the time the ballots were cast. As Oliver H. Radkey, the historian of the SR Party, has shown in considerable detail, the official party lists had been prepared in September and October of 1917, before the Left SRs had split, and the Left SRs were therefore unable to run their own slate.[144] Radkey further showed that the Right SRs had been greatly overrepresented in the electoral lists because of their effective control of the nominating mechanisms at the time the slates were prepared. He also speculated on what would have happened had there been a lengthy interval between the SR schism and the elections, and thus the opportunity for the Left SRs to nominate their own slate and campaign extensively. Radkey thought that if the Left SRs had in such a case conducted a lengthy campaign of exposure to show the peasantry that the Right SRs were no longer representative of the old SR Party with its old revolutionary ideals but, as Radkey put it, instead 'consisted of burnt-out revolutionaries who were Kadets in everything except in name,'[145] then the election might have had substantially different results. According to Radkey's calculations, those hypothetical elections would have then produced an Assembly with many more Left SRs and many fewer Right SRs. However, such a hypothetical Assembly would have also had somewhat fewer Bolsheviks than the Assembly that was actually elected. This would have been because, in the absence of a separate Left SR slate, many peasants sympathetic to that party voted for the Bolsheviks instead of the single SR slate.[146]

Turning to other matters related to the Constituent Assembly, it seems that the Bolsheviks had been consistent in supporting the call for a Constituent Assembly before they came to power. After all, there is no contradiction between advocating what that party believed to be a higher form of democracy while, in the meantime, accepting a lower form. But the Bolsheviks were inconsistent when they continued to support holding the elections and convening the Constituent Assembly *after* they had won a majority in the soviets and justified the October Revolution on that basis. This inconsistency is particularly striking in light of the fact that the Bolsheviks knew well that the Left SRs would not be able to run their own slate. Many Bolsheviks might have expected that the impact of the revolution was going to be sufficient to swing the election in their favor. This would not have been an unreasonable expectation, but perhaps a little more time would have been needed for the benefits of the revolution to make themselves felt, and this certainly constitutes an argument in support of Lenin's stand for a postponement of the elections. The Right Bolsheviks and Left SRs, given their strong support for the notion of an all-socialist government, supported holding elections for the Constituent Assembly. Others, such as Bukharin, supported the elections on the grounds that 'constitutional illusions' were still strong among the masses.[147]

Rosa Luxemburg's Criticisms

One of Rosa Luxemburg's criticisms of the Bolshevik revolution involved her concern with the dissolution of the Constituent Assembly. Basically, her arguments were based on the following grounds: First, a general defense of the parliamentary system of representation. Specifically opposing the argument, which she attributed to Trotsky, that bourgeois parliamentarism discourages 'any living mental connection between the representatives, once they have been elected, and the electorate, any permanent interaction between one and the other,'[148] Rosa Luxemburg claimed that experience demonstrated quite the opposite:

> namely, that the living fluid of the popular mood continuously flows around the representative bodies, penetrates them, guides them. How else would it be possible to witness, as we do at times in every bourgeois parliament, the amusing capers of the 'people's representatives,' who are suddenly inspired by a new 'spirit' and give forth quite unexpected sounds; or to find the most dried-out mummies comporting themselves like youngsters . . . whenever there is rumbling in factories and workshops and on the streets.[149]

Second, while defending the parliamentary system, Rosa Luxemburg accepted the Bolshevik argument that the Constituent Assembly actually elected reflected not the new state of affairs but the vanished past. In the light of this, Luxemburg proposed that the 'still-born Constituent Assembly should have been annulled, and without delay, new elections to a new Constituent Assembly should have been arranged.'[150]

As a democratic critique of the Bolsheviks, Luxemburg's reasoning was in this instance, unlike her arguments in the same pamphlet in defense of free speech and other political freedoms, rather unimpressive. Luxemburg's critique could have been convincingly refuted in practice by what I earlier referred to as a genuine long-term commitment to the soviet system as an alternative and presumably higher democratic form of government. Furthermore, the view of the Bolsheviks as a vanguard party could have been reconciled with the principle of the joint dictatorship of the working class and peasantry *only* if those classes ultimately had the right to replace the current party in power. Lenin did not, before 1918, say much concerning this question; for example, as I previously indicated, parties are barely mentioned in *State and Revolution*. However, at one point, when Bolshevik fortunes were on the upswing shortly before the October Revolution, Lenin did affirm that, if the soviets quickly seized power, they could ensure a peaceful development of the revolution and 'a peaceful struggle of parties inside the Soviets where the programs of the various parties could be tested in practice and 'power could pass peacefully from one party to another.'[151] Luxemburg did, however, make one powerful point in this context; namely, her contention that, if the objection to the Constituent Assembly was that it no longer represented the state of opinion in the country, then new elections should have been called by the Bolshevik government.

Surprisingly, Luxemburg's other arguments in defense of the Constituent Assembly flew in the face of what is practically the ABC of revolutionary Marxism. Her pamphlet did not even bother to discuss the question of whether soviet workplace representation was more compatible with working-class rule, and superior or inferior to the geographic representation commonly utilized in bourgeois democratic systems. Moreover, there is no doubt that radicalized masses often find an echo in parliamentary bodies. But what Luxemburg seems to have missed in this instance is that the function of parliament has been to deflect rather than reflect, or at best to act as the rearguard rather than the vanguard of mass movements. This happens not because parliamentary representatives are necessarily 'bad people' but because of institutional and structural constraints. The rules of the parliamentary game, based *on the absence of recall mechanisms*, structurally tend to separate left-wing and workers' representatives from their frequently more militant mass base. In addition, the very structure of parliaments tends to foster a variety of obligations among representatives of all political colors, which are very often incompatible with what are presumably the representatives' obligations to their own constituents. Rosa Luxemburg had noticed in her own party, the German Social Democratic

Party, how the parliamentary representatives had become a conservative controlling force and commented how 'it is laughable how being [a member of the Reichstag] goes to all those good people's heads.'[152] The mechanism of immediate recall established first by the Paris Commune and then by the soviets, but typically absent from bourgeois parliaments, could have been at least one powerful tool to check this oligarchical tendency. Yet, in spite of her critique of the Bolsheviks, when in late 1918 Rosa Luxemburg faced the prospects of socialist revolution in her own Germany she rejected the proposals for a German Constituent Assembly and proclaimed the 'Constituent Assembly as the bourgeois solution, Councils of Workers and Soldiers as the Socialist one.'[153]

The Problem of Disenfranchisement

Rosa Luxemburg also directed her criticisms to the Bolshevik government's disenfranchisement of the bourgeoisie and allied strata. It is very revealing of her own particular kind of 'workerism' that in this context she said nothing about the constitutional discrimination against peasant electoral representation, which I discussed earlier in this chapter.[154] Luxemburg was specifically referring to the provisions contained in Chapters 5 and 13 of the Soviet Constitution promulgated in July 1918. These chapters established, respectively, the obligation of all citizens to work and confined the franchise to those who earned their living by production or socially useful labor, to soldiers, and to disabled persons, and specifically excluded persons who employed hired labor, rentiers, private traders, monks and priests, and officials and agents of the former police.[155] It should be noted in this context that Lenin explicitly indicated that he regarded these exclusions not as matters of principle regarding the general nature of the dictatorship of the proletariat, but as the result of specific Russian conditions, i.e. the extreme resistance offered by bourgeois and petty bourgeois circles to the October Revolution and the radical social changes introduced by it.[156] While Luxemburg clearly realized this, there was a sense in which she really missed the issues at stake here. Thus, a good part of her criticism dealt with the fact that the Russian economy was in no condition to offer gainful employment to all who requested it.[157] This was of course true, but a point of marginal significance in this historical context. The aim of the Bolsheviks was not the disenfranchisement of the idle or the unemployed in general, but to *punish* the bourgeoisie and allied elements even if they requested state employment after being thrown out of their confiscated businesses, factories, and churches.

My own view on this issue may at first seem paradoxical but closer inspection will reveal otherwise. On one hand, I find Chapter 13 of the 1918 Constitution to be on the whole acceptable, *if* it had been primarily an approximation or first attempt to establish the legal and political basis for a toilers' democracy. One can certainly make a democratic argument for a workers' and peasants' revolution disenfranchising those who are physically able but refuse to carry out their share of socially productive activity. I am assuming, of course, that there is work available when people offer their services (this could have been an hypothetical amendment to satisfy Luxemburg's criticism). The general exclusion of those who refuse to work would have been logically no different from, say, the bourgeois democratic exclusion of felons. Unfortunately, however, the real problem here was quite different – again, the government was using this aspect of the 1918 Constitution not as a place to legislate into effect Bolshevik democratic theory, but rather as a vehicle for *categorial* class punishments of acts that were necessarily committed by *individuals* or by *groups* specifically organized to carry out counterrevolutionary deeds. The fact that a disproportionate number of these individuals and groups actually belonged to the bourgeoisie and allied strata in no way changed the potentially dire legal and political consequences of collective or categorical punishments for *all* classes and groups in the population. Luxemburg seemed to have touched on this point when she remarked that the suffrage law in Russia 'involves a deprivation of rights not as a concrete measure for a concrete purpose but as a general rule of long-standing effect,'[158] although she did not make this a central element of her critique. At a more abstract level, I am trying to suggest that there is no reason why a workers' and peasants' state should not be perfectly compatible with the principle of universal and equal citizenship. In reality, I am not proposing anything new. Equal citizenship has been for centuries perfectly compatible with the class rule of the bourgeoisie. As a matter of fact, when this matter is examined from both a logical and a historical perspective, one cannot but conclude that a majoritarian worker–peasant revolution should be even more compatible with equal citizenship than a revolution carried out on behalf of, and benefiting, a small minority of the population, i.e. the bourgeoisie.

Conclusion

I referred earlier in this chapter to Rosa Luxemburg's notion that, for revolutionaries, the 'road runs' not 'through a majority to revolutionary tactics, but through revolutionary tactics to a majority.' This is indeed sound advice for a revolutionary party out of power or immediately after seizing power. However, the situation changes quite significantly when such a party has consolidated its power – especially in a society where relative material abundance cannot be attained in a short period of time. Holding the monopoly of the means of violence in a whole society, particularly if this is accompanied by control of the most important forms of economic activity, is a far cry from what a revolutionary party is in opposition, i.e. a voluntary association. A revolutionary party out of power presumably represents the most advanced elements trying to lead and persuade the less advanced among the oppressed and exploited. The same party in power must of course continue to do this, but it has also acquired a tremendous power of coercion over these other elements in the population which can easily become a new form of exploitation and oppression.

But what about the possible objection that War Communism, 'excesses' and all, was a desperate gamble to fight counterrevolution and help bring about the international revolution that would break the vicious cycle of underdevelopment and allow Russia the opportunity to construct socialism? The answer to that is that there are very different kinds of gambling. The October Revolution was itself a gamble of course, but it was a gamble based on a revolutionary but still objectively plausible program for economically backward Russia: namely, a quick end to the war, denunciation of all imperialist treaties and annexionist claims, self-determination for the victims of the Tsarist 'prison-house of nations,' radical redistribution of the land, and, last but not least, workers' control of large-scale industry. This was a worker-led majoritarian program that could expect to and did win the support of the broad masses of the exploited and oppressed. Furthermore, this program could and did become a beacon and call for the radical wing of the international workers' movement to make an even more advanced revolution in their own countries. Had this revolution succeeded in the more developed countries, then and not before, the material possibilities might have been developed for truly socialist institutions in Soviet Russia. What is politically not acceptable from a revolutionary democratic point of view is the kind of gambling that involves highly voluntaristic social and economic policies. Given the economic backwardness of Russian society, such policies could not possibly have been carried out without the systematic mass coercion and oppression of at least a major part of the exploited and oppressed classes (e.g. the peasantry). Again, the notion that democratic working-class rule could survive in such a situation is surely utopian.

2

Workers' Control and Trade Union Independence

The Rise and Fall of Industrial Democracy

The Russian Revolution witnessed the development of workers' democracy at the point of production along similar and roughly parallel lines to those of soviet democracy. The powerful shopfloor democratic and libertarian currents in the Russian working class were supported by the Bolshevik Party in the period between February and October of 1917. Moreover, the successful October Revolution initially encouraged the further expansion and growth of these tendencies; but the original thrust from below was reversed only a few months after October. At this point, the still developing institutions of workers' democracy sharply declined, never to recover again.

Workers' Control

The demand for, and the reality of, workers' control in the Russian Revolution was not based on any precise or rigorous ideas and programs. From 1917 to 1918, workers' control took various forms and underwent important changes. Yet it is possible to maintain that the *core* element of workers' control related to encroachments on management rights and control of work processes and conditions rather than to the degree of exploitation (i.e. wages and hours). As we shall see, the very development of the class struggle and of economic crisis in the Russian Revolution determined that the principal struggles and activities of the workers' factory committees would take place over the issues of capitalist control of the production process and over the procurement and distribution of such items as food and fuel.[1]

The revolution that took place in February 1917 opened the gates to the free organization of the working class. Workers began to demand better treatment by the employers, an 8 hour day, higher wages, and protection against industrial accidents and old age. One result of the frequently strong employer resistance to these claims was the establishment of factory committees in most plants. These were *locally* elected by the assembly of workers, and sometimes partly by the works administration. The extension of the workers' encroachment on management rights was, as a rule, also purely defensive and certainly not attributable to the strength of revolutionary ideologies among the working class. Workers' demands were often met by employer sabotage and lock-outs, leaving the workers little choice other than an enlargement of their control, sometimes up to outright occupation of the plants themselves. Based on these developments, a dual power developed in the factories. This was parallel to what had taken place with the soviets in the country as a whole. However, soviets typically had jurisdiction over a certain geographic area, were composed of delegates elected by all the work centers and military garrisons within those boundaries, and were more likely to deal with general political questions than was the case with the factory committees.

On 23 April 1917 the Provisional Government legally recognized the existence of the factory committees, defining their methods of election and their representative rights.[2] Meanwhile, a serious crisis had also developed in the means of transportation and in the supply of food and coal, causing the factory committees to attempt to remedy the situation through their own efforts. Moreover, the Provisional Government was also becoming increasingly discredited and provided one disappointment after another – for example, it had not even signed the 8 hour day law.[3] It was in this context that the great majority of the working class came to reject capitalist rule both inside and outside the plant. As the institutions closest to the proletarian rank-and-file, the factory committees were the first to respond to the shift to the Left that took place in mass attitudes, often coming into conflict with the soviets, then under the more conservative leadership of the Socialist Revolutionary and Menshevik parties.[4] Another result of this radicalizing process was the establishment of the Red Guard defense groups. These were created by and remained under the control of the factory committees until the committees put them at the disposal of the trade unions and the soviets in late 1917.[5]

In May 1917, the Bolsheviks began to agitate for the slogan of workers' control and to pay attention to the factory committees. In a fundamental way, Bolshevik support for 'workers' control' had been a weapon against the Menshevik insistence on 'state control' by the Provisional Government.[6] However, as we shall see below, the party of Lenin did not have a clear and unified view, let alone a theory, of the role of workers' control before and/or after the socialist revolution. Although the many Bolsheviks involved in the work of the factory committees saw them as being primarily responsible for workers' control of production, remarkably little attention was paid to these institutions in the party's general propaganda and theory. In fact, through a variety of pronouncements, the Bolsheviks seemed to be making the vague and unfocused suggestion that workers' control was the responsibility of all labor organizations. In the pre-October period, Lenin and the Bolshevik Party, far more concerned with the problem of smashing the Provisional Government than with issues affecting the point of production, paid a great deal more attention to the soviets and even to the unions than to the factory committees.

As we saw in chapter 1, this changed in the brief period between the July Days and the Kornilov coup in late August. At that time, Lenin, sorely disappointed with the soviets, considerd a *tactical* turn towards the factory committees as potential agencies for a revolutionary overthrow of the Provisional Government.[7]

However, in its daily grassroots agitation, the Bolshevik Party rank-and-file propagated the slogan of workers' control and encouraged the factory committees' encroachment on management prerogatives, sometimes to the extent of taking over capitalist enterprises and declaring them nationalized. This, even though Lenin's conception of workers' control tended to emphasize solely the inspection of the company's books and accounts at the local factory level, and worker representation on the state organs of economic regulation at the regional and national level. In the last analysis, workers' control by the factory committees was, for Lenin and mainstream Bolshevism, a crucial part of the struggle to overthrow capitalism. Nevertheless, the committees had not been much thought about as important working-class institutions in their own right, let alone as an important structural element of the post-revolutionary society. Yet, some working-class Bolsheviks active in the factory committee movement preceding the October Revolution, such as N. A. Skrypnik, greatly emphasized the centrality of workers' control. Others, primarily intellectuals such as Osinsky, Sergeev, and Savel'ev, were more skeptical about the presumed accomplishments of the factory committees. This latter group also defended the need for centralization and argued that the working class needed first to take political power and *then* to organize the regulation and management of production. Characteristically, Lenin took a more pragmatic attitude and did not side with any of these more clearcut, polarized positions. Thus, for example, when towards the end of the party's April 1917 Conference, a delegate asked him whether workers' control meant state-centered or enterprise-centered power, Lenin replied that the question had not yet been settled and that 'living practice' would provide the answer. However, while Lenin approved of the workers' initiatives, he also expressed the concern that the workers might lose their revolutionary temper as they became involved in the administration of economic activities before they had actually taken political power.[8]

After October, 1917: Workers' Control and Workers' Self-Management

A few days after the seizure of power, the Bolshevik government approved a Decree on Workers' Control which legalized the workers' power that had already been accomplished in most large Russian factories. According to a survey of industry conducted in 1918, at the time of the October Revolution, 22.5 per cent of all factories, and 68.7 per cent of all factories employing over 200 workers, had factory committees. The survey also showed that nearly two-thirds of the committees, and 79 per cent of those in enterprises of over 200 workers, had taken an active part in management.[9] The Decree on Workers'

Control recognized the right of workers in all industrial enterprises to control all aspects of production and to have complete access to the financial and all other spheres of administration, and the right of the lower organs of workers' control to bind employers by their decisions.[10] However, the decree simply stipulated general matters of principle and still needed to be operationalized by specific instructions on how to implement workers' control in practice.

As it happened, two substantially different sets of instructions were promulgated. One set, elaborated by the Petrograd Central Council of Factory Committees and first published by *Izvestiya* on 7 December, was quite radical. These instructions recommended the active intervention of the workers in the employers' disposal of capital, stocks, raw materials, and finished goods in the factory, and active supervision of the fulfillment of orders and use of energy and labor power. Moreover, public control (*obschchestvennyi kontrol*) was seen as replacing the existing forms of management and administration. The Council also stated that 'control must be regarded as a *transition stage* in organizing the entire economic life of the country on a social footing, as the first necessary step in that direction, taken from below and in parallel with the work of the central economic organs above.'[11] In truth, what was being proposed here was no longer the usually limited pre-October conception of workers' control, but a thoroughgoing workers' management. Thus, these instructions indicated a different view of the relations between workers' control bodies and the state from that of Lenin. By the end of 1917, Lenin and other Bolshevik leaders, in the face of the developing economic crisis and the radicalism of the factory committees, had defined control as a function of the state, and the organs of workers' control as subordinate and accountable to state bodies. On the other hand, as Thomas F. Remington has pointed out,

> the factory committee leaders understood control as a power exercised by the new proletarian society, through which workers gained genuine responsibility, not merely 'experience.' This view of participatory democracy was broader than any syndicalist perspectives on industrial and social organization, for which the committees had picked up a certain notoriety.[12]

At about the same time, a much more moderate set of instructions was developed by the All-Russian Countil of Workers' Control (ARCWC) which was shortly after absorbed into the government's principal economic institution, the Supreme Council of National Economy (VSNKh or Vesenkha). This second set of instructions promulgated a centralized system of control in which local factory committees would be subordinated to the control–distribution commission of the trade union of that particular branch of industry. These in turn would be subordinated to regional councils of workers' control and ultimately to the VSNKh. Even more important was the stipulation that management functions remain in the hands of the employer. Therefore, it is not surprising that, out of more than 40 members, the ARCWC included only 5 representatives from the factory committees. The rest were representatives from the soviets, the trade unions, and the cooperatives.

Many workers, particularly the majority of metalworkers in Petrograd, seem to have supported the radical interpretation of workers' control. In some other industries and regions there was support for the more moderate instructions – this was the case among textile and needle workers and for the Councils of People's Commissars in Moscow (Mensheviks were closely involved in drafting the local instructions in this city), and in a smaller city such as Kostroma.[13] There is little doubt, however, that the October Revolution gave a powerful impetus to the drive for workers' management. Before October, as I indicated earlier, workers' control had generally been limited in scope and to a considerable degree had been a response to threats of cutbacks or lock-outs. After October, workers in an increasing number of factories had moved towards control without justifying their actions in terms of specific grievances against management.[14] Furthermore, although the factory committees seldom used the term 'self-management' (*samoupravlenie*), when workers often referred to a 'democratic' factory, or of taking the factory 'into their own hands,' they meant very much the same thing.[15]

Yet, many workers were still acting against employers for primarily reactive, defensive reasons. For example, on 12 December 1917, the committee of the Robert Krug factory in Petrograd reported that the administration had rejected workers' control and had announced that it would stop operations. The meeting voted in favor of taking over the factory and removing the top five administrators. The workers were compelled to act on this immediately, since that very day the entire administrative staff disappeared taking with it the plant's current operating funds.[16]

The Decline of the Factory Committees and the Erosion of Workers' Management and Control

Towards the end of 1917, Lenin decided to centralize in reaction to the increasing radicalism of workers' control and the worsening of the economic crisis. To this end, he also began to turn away from the factory committees and towards the trade unions as better suited to the task of centralized state economic regulation to be implemented under the direction of the Supreme Council of National Economy. As a general rule, the unions had been supporters of the more moderate version of workers' control. Furthermore, unlike the factory committees, the unions had originally been organized with close ties to the socialist political parties and on an industry-wide basis. This is why Larin, representative of the Bolshevik fraction in the unions, claimed in November of 1917 that 'the trade unions represent the interests of the class as a whole whereas the Factory Committees only represent particular interests.'[17] Moreover, although from the point of view of the ruling party's leadership the committees had shown more vigorous political support for Bolshevik tactics than the unions had earlier in 1917, their organizational links to the party were weaker than those of the older trade union organizers. As might be expected, the latter group had a stronger tradition of cooperation with and tutelage by the party leadership.[18] This was the context in which the Bolshevik majority at the First Congress of Trade Unions, which took place in December 1917 to January 1918, voted to transform the factory committees into local union organs.[19] However, it should be noted that both the subordination of the local committees to the unions and the statization of the unions remained more of a wish than a reality for a considerable period of time.[20]

At this time, a large majority of the nationalizations had been carried out by factory committees and by other local economic organs such as trade unions, local soviets, and local economic councils. However, the smaller proportion of nationalizations carried out by the central government helped to undermine workers' control and management. Thus it is worth noting that when, on 14 December 1917, Lenin signed the first decree *officially* nationalizing 81 businesses, a large majority of which employed over 1,000 persons, the government clearly distinguished management from control of industry. While the government appointed new boards in which the former management and the factory committees were represented, it also made it very clear that decisions concerning management belonged exclusively to this new board. Workers' control organizations were not to participate in or take responsibility for the management of the enterprises.[21] These early nationalizations by the center affected places where there had been strong working-class pressure but little motion toward self-management (there were 48 nationalizations in the Urals, 14 in Moscow, 8 in the Ukraine, and only 11 in Petrograd). Nonetheless, it must be stressed that, at the very least until March 1918, the center's attempt to control the nature and pace of nationalization, or more generally the economic life of the country, was not fully carried out in practice.[22]

With the beginning of War Communism in the early Summer of 1918, large-scale nationalizations were officially decreed for Russian industry. Yet, many of the firms that were officially nationalized at this time remained under the old management because the government was simply unable to send out new administrators. At the same time, a large number of crafts and small industries were locally taken over without the knowledge or approval of the center.[23] Nevertheless, the War Communism Decree on Nationalization of 28 June 1918 clearly indicated the direction of the government's policy vis-à-vis the relationship of workers' control to the state. With the national factory committee movement in the process of dissolution by March 1918,[24] the government now gave one-third of the places in management to the elected representatives of the workers, while giving effective control to the two-thirds appointed by the Council of People's Commissars (Sovnarkom). Moreover, by this Decree, workers' control itself was supposed to return to the conception of monitoring and inspection rather than management.[25]

It is worth emphasizing that it was not the localism of the supposedly Anarcho-Syndicalist factory committees that created or helped to create the economic chaos that encouraged Lenin to establish one-man management in the economy. While the Anarcho-Syndicalists did support and participate in the factory committees, they were only a minority, and were certainly far less significant than the Bolshevik membership of those bodies. In any case, the real problem of localism was not due to Anarcho-Syndicalist ideological and political influence but was instead a response to objective economic conditions. In the face of shortages and overall scarcity, it was to be expected that workers in each factory would tend to 'look out for themselves,' e.g. hoard supplies for their own use even at the expense of other factories.[26] The scarcity of skilled personnel and proficient organizers was also a problem, and this justified, if not centralization properly speaking, at least a consolidation of leadership functions.

It is therefore important to distinguish two kinds of localism: namely, structural and ideological. While the factory committees had, of course, been active primarily at the local level and their functioning was thus structurally biased by their position in the economy, this did not at all mean that they were politically or ideologically averse to regional or central coordination. In fact, as S. A. Smith has noted, at the time the original Decree on Workers' Control was being discussed during the days of the October Revolution, the All-Russian Council of Factory Committees (ARCFC) submitted a draft of a decree that dealt entirely with the creation of a central apparatus to regulate the economy. Ironically, it was Lenin who at the time criticized this draft of the decree because it said nothing about workers' control.[27] Furthermore, a proposal was made towards the end of 1917 to call a national congress of factory committees. This did not take place precisely because, as I mentioned before, at the time the Bolshevik Party leadership made a *political* turn towards the trade union leadership. Again, the trade union leadership was not at all committed to workers' management and this is a major reason why the First Trade Union Congress was called into session at the end of 1917.

Given the absence of important political or ideological obstacles, it is reasonable to expect that a congress of factory committees, had it been held, might have seriously attempted to coordinate the activities of the local committees in order to minimize the compensate for structurally induced localism. This congress might have perhaps taken steps to work out a functional differentiation among the various organs of working-class power (soviets, unions, factory committees, etc.)[28] After all, the All-Russian Congress of Factory Committees held on the eve of the October Revolution had also made proposals aiming at the regulation of the entire economy. Later, after the revolution, the leadership of the committee movement opposed factory parochialism and on three separate occasions attempted to carry out their plans for the coordination of the entire economy, but were in each instance overruled by the central political leadership. In fact, shortly after October, the leadership of the factory committee movement had proposed the implementation of the aims of the draft decree concerning national regulation of the economy. Specifically, they had proposed the creation of a working-class Supreme Economic Council which would coordinate four areas of work: workers' control, management, the distribution of consumer goods, and general economic policy.[29] Moreover, it should also be pointed out that every previous conference of factory committees had called for close cooperation with the unions and even for an eventual merger with them.[30]

In March 1918, Lenin took another step away from workers' control and began to campaign in favor of one-man management of industry. These managers were to replace the collegiate boards that had been established beginning with the early nationalization decrees in late 1917. Not surprisingly, Lenin later reacted with outrage on learning that a comission of the First Congress of Councils of People's Commissars, which met from 25 May to 4 June of the same year, had prepared a resolution going in precisely the opposite direction, since it proposed that two-thirds of the management boards of enterprises be elected by the workers themselves.[31] In 1919, only 10.8 per cent of enterprises in the country were under one-man management, but a dramatic increase took place by 1920.[32] By December of that year, according to official estimates, the number of plants run without collective management rose to 2,183 out of 2,483, and by 1922 the change away from collegiality had been fully implemented. In fact, the Ninth Congress of the Party, which had taken place in March–April of 1920, confirmed the establishment of one-man management. At this Congress, Bukharin used a familiar type of schematic argument that was already becoming the stock in trade of the opponents of soviet democracy. If the Soviet state was a proletarian dictatorship, argued Bukharin, there was no intrinsic merit to collegiality, since there were no conflicting class interests to be mediated by this form of representation.[33]

However, it is worth noting the workers' considerable resistance to one-man management, which was at least partly motivated by the fact that the single person who became the manager was often a bourgeois specialist. The workers' resistance was particularly strong in Petrograd, the bastion of workers' self-management. Thus, in March 1920, 69 per cent of Petrograd factories employing more than 200 workers were still run by a collegial board.[34] Nevertheless, one cannot conclude from this that these factories were as democratically run as they had been two years earlier. As early as the beginning of 1918, labor organizations were becoming less democratic in relation to their own members. The majority of factory committee activists were caught in a dilemma when they were unable to convince the people they represented that the policies of the government these activists supported were in the interests of the working class. Neither did these factory committee activites endear themselves to the ranks when they tried to improve labor discipline among a working-class population ravaged by hunger and growing unemployment. It is no wonder, then, that many factory committees began to dispense with democratic practices, as attested, for example, by complaints in early 1918 that factory committees at the Pipe, Nobel, Old Lessner, Langenzippen, and Cartridge plants in Petrograd had paid no attention to demands from general worker assemblies that they submit to re-election.[35]

Objective and Ideological Background to the Decline of Workers' Control and Management

By mid-1918 the situation in Petrograd had become truly desperate. The number of employed industrial workers had drastically declined as a result of the lack of fuel and materials, the breakdown in transport, the shutting down of war industry (by far the single most important form of economic activity in the period immediately preceding the October Revolution), and the evacuation in February due to the German offensive. Thus, while on 1 January 1918 the Petrograd industrial labor force was 83.5 per cent of what it had been on 1 January 1917, this proportion further declined to 35.1 per cent on 1 May 1918 and 29.7 per cent on 1 September 1918.[36] Earlier, shortly after the October Revolution, the demobilization of war industry had been carried out in a chaotic fashion. This situation was not helped by Lenin's underestimation of the technical problems involved in the demobilization of industry. The government did eventually implement a recommendation that Lenin made in mid-December of 1917 and established a 'commission of technicians' to find and distribute orders to factories. However, much less order was restored to Petrograd's industry by the work of this commission than by the factory committees' plans, which had been prepared even before October.[37] In fact, the situation eventually became so hopeless that, in July 1918, Lenin exhorted the workers to leave Petrograd altogether. As he put it:

> To sit in Piter [Petrograd], to go hungry, hang around empty factories, divert oneself with the ridiculous dream of resurrecting Piter's industry or saving Piter – that is *stupid* and *criminal*. The workers of Piter must break with this stupidity, kick out the fools who defend it, and go in their tens of thousands to the Urals, the Volga and the South, where there is much grain, where one can feed oneself and one's family, where they must help to organise the poor, where the Piter worker is necessary as an organiser, leader, commander.[38]

In Moscow, the working class also shrank. In 1917, there had been 190,000 workers in that city, but by August 1918 there were 140,000, and by January 1921 only 81,000. By 1920, the majority of the remaining industrial working class in Moscow was composed of former peasants and the spouses and children of workers who had left production.[39]

It is clear that the post-1918 conditions of virtual industrial and economic collapse in cities such as Petrograd did not, to put it mildly, encourage the maintenance of workers' management, workers' control, or even trade union independence. Yet these very negative conditions evoked significantly different political responses among various revolutionary currents, both inside and outside the new government. This suggests, among other things, that if we are trying to understand why these gains of the Russian working class were lost, *and were never even partially recovered*, then we have to take into account not only objective material conditions but also the previously existing purposes, ideas, and motivations of the political actors involved. It may very well be that if objective conditions are highly unfavorable, as they were in the years subsequent to 1918, even the most democratic and proletarian political leadership would have been unable to maintain the achievements of workers' control, workers' management, and union independence. Indeed, we just saw above how the degree of democracy in working-class rank-and-file institutions did decline during the severe economic crisis in 1918.

Yet a national leadership strongly oriented towards rank-and-file control would not have *permanently* committed itself to the elimination of democracy. At the same time, it would probably have been more modulated and sensitive to the *degree* of despotism, harshness, alien class content, and political dangers of the various specific measures introduced. Such a hypothetical leadership might also have been highly alert to any improvement in objective conditions with a view to the earliest, even if partial, reintroduction of the original institutional gains of the revolution. Another way of looking at this issue would be to suggest that, even in the presence of highly favorable economic conditions, a weak or nonexistent commitment to working-class democratic institutions would have still brought about, if not the extremes of Stalinism, at least a very problematic future for these institutions. Indeed, what did take place, as we already saw in chapter 1, was something else again; namely, the rationalization of the harsh and undemocratic measures that might have originally been justified as necessary into the very embodiment of virtue. Moreover, I would further suggest that one can point to certain rationalizations and show how they were rooted in previously held political positions, inclinations, and ideologies.

Bolshevik Politics and Workers' Management and Control

Prior to 1917, the concern with workers' power at the point of production was by and large alien to the social democratic tradition in Russia, among revolutionaries as well as among reformists. Nevertheless, it should be noted that A. A. Bogdanov and the Left Bolshevik faction he led in opposition to Lenin during the 1908–9 period were sympathetic to syndicalism.[40] Moreover, even during the revolutionary process preceding the October Revolution, Bolsheviks and Mensheviks tended to agree that centralized, statist solutions to economic problems were both necessary and sufficient. Of course, these two parties disagreed on the kind of central state that should control the economy – the Mensheviks opted for a bourgeois state and the Bolsheviks for a workers' and peasants' state.[41] The Mensheviks also opposed the slogan of workers' control, a slogan that was initially raised by the factory committees quite independently of the central leadership of the Bolshevik Party. The Mensheviks claimed that workers' control, given that it consisted of decentralized, spontaneous initiatives, would only exacerbate the economic problems affecting the country. In fact, as the historian Jane Burbank has pointed out, the Menshevik leader

Martov had in 1917 blamed the Bolsheviks for creating the local, particularistic attitudes prevailing among the masses. Later, in January 1918, he reversed his earlier point of view and maintained that it was the localized consciousness of at least part of the laboring population that preceded and thus explained the popularity of what Martov saw as a Bolshevik program in support of factory acivism.[42]

The fact remains that neither Lenin nor the mainstream of the Bolshevik Party ever attempted to work out a theory of the relationship among soviets, factory committees, and unions, and of their respective roles in the strategy for the achievement of socialism. This was true even of Lenin's most visionary writings concerning the post-revolutionary society, such as *State and Revolution*. It is important to note that, when in that pamphlet he predicted that under socialism every cook would govern, Lenin, beyond praising the Paris Commune, barely hinted at the institutional mechanisms through which the cook would be able to do so. This theoretical and political neglect of *institutions* may in part have been due to the Leninist quasi-Jacobinism that I will discuss later in this volume. In addition, this might have also party resulted from an unfortunate application of the traditional Marxist aversion to utopianism. However, it is hard to see how the clarification of the role and meaning of those critical institutions of workers' power could have been interpreted as being equivalent to the making of detailed blueprints that Marxists have traditionally opposed. Last but not least, this 'deficiency' was likely reinforced by the fact that the Bolsheviks, with the exception of their recent convert Trotsky, had not, before 1917, discussed on a systematic basis the likelihood of a workers' and peasants' revolution placing socialism on the immediate agenda.

After October, as we saw earlier, Lenin's perspective for the growing self-management movement in Russian factories never went beyond his views on the earlier and more limited movement for workers' control – that is, beyond his usual emphasis on accounting and inspection. Lenin then became primarily concerned with avoiding chaos and bureaucratization of the economy, and by the end of 1917 he had abandoned his earlier emphasis on the spontaneous initiatives of the working class,[43] even though these may have turned out to be more useful precisely because of the worsening economic situation. Besides, it was one thing to see the factory committees as important institutions in helping to bring about the overthrow of capitalism; it was quite a different matter to define and build them as crucial elements of the new society's institutional power structure. The underlying issue here was not, as some have claimed, that Lenin and the Bolsheviks were cynically manipulating the factory committees and that once the party leaders 'got power' they had no more use for them. In the last analysis, the key political problem was that Lenin and the mainstream of the Bolshevik Party, or for that matter the Mensheviks, paid little if any attention to the need for a transformation and democratization of the daily life of the working class on the shopfloor and in the community. These political traditions were even less likely to see this transformation and democratization as an essential part of the *process* by which that class could indeed become the ruling class.

In any case, for Lenin the central problem and concern continued to be the revolutionary transformation of the central state; what happened at the point of production was derivative. In fact, Lenin had been most impressed with the trustification of German industry during World War I, and this become the central element of his initial vision of what would be the first, necessary 'state-capitalist' stage of the Russian revolution. Again, in *State and Revolution*, the capitalist state's Post Office is accepted as a sound organizational and economic model for socialism. It is revealing that, in his view, the additions or changes that needed to be made in the Post Office did not affect its existing organizational and hierarchical systems, except in the matter of monetary rewards. In Lenin's own words:

> At present the postal service is a business organized on the lines of a state-*capitalist* monopoly. Imperialism is gradually transforming all trusts into organisations of a similar type, in which, standing over the 'common' people, who are overworked and starved, one has the same bourgeois bureaucracy. But the mechanism of social management is here already to hand. Once we have overthrown the capitalists, crushed the resistance of these exploiters with the iron hand of the armed workers, and smashed the bureaucratic machine of the modern state, we shall have a splendidly-equipped mechanism, freed from the 'parasite', a mechanism which can very well be set going by the united workers themselves, who will hire technicians, foremen and accountants, and pay them *all*, as indeed all state officials in general, workmen's wages ... To organise the *whole* economy on the lines of the postal service so that the technicians, foremen and accountants, as well as *all* officials, shall receive salaries no higher than 'a workman's wage', all under the control and leadership of the armed proletariat – this is our immediate aim.[44]

Moreover, Lenin shared with many Russian social democrats, of both reformist and revolutionary persuasions, the prejudice that organizational efficiency was directly proportional to the degree of centralization in the economy of society. This approach became especially evident even before the beginning of the Civil War in mid-1918.[45] However, in practice, hypercentralization turned into infighting and scrambles for control among competing bureaucracies. Thomas F. Remington cites the not untypical example of a small condensed milk plant with fewer than 15 workers that became the object of a drawn-out competition among six organizations including the Supreme Council of National Economy, the Council of People's Commissars of the Northern Region, the Vologda Council of People's Commissars, and the Petrograd Food Commissariat.[46] Ironically, the ultimate outcome of this kind of organizational struggle was a *reduction* of central control, and the running of the state in what the Bolshevik trade union leader Alexander Shliapnikov described in mid-1919 as a homemade or handicrafted fashion (*kustarno*). This was the unavoidable result of what he complained was the government's response to chaos; namely, to use the cudgel (*dubinushka*) or brute force to eliminate the obstacles to the carrying out of the government's will. According to Shliapnikov, this approach increased the haphazardness of results and personalized authority, thus corresponding to the old world of petty bourgeois individualism. To the model of the cudgel, Shliapnikov (who after the revolution behaved in a more libertarian and democratic fashion than Lenin but was by no means immune to the intellectual currents that had influenced the principal Bolshevik leader) counterposed the model of the *mashinushka* or little machine, which he saw embodied in the Ford Motor Company. There, the Bolshevik trade unionist thought that each worker performed a built-in specialized function in the collective effort independent of the personal whims of the industrial authorities.[47]

As I suggested in chapter 1, the political priorities of mainstream Bolshevism implicitly revealed themselves in War Communism when the exigencies of the Civil War also came to be seen as a great opportunity to implement a maximum socialist program. In this regard, the period of War Communism turned out to be uniquely different from the first several months after the revolution and from the post-Civil War NEP. During War Communism, the government placed its main emphasis on the establishment of centralized state ownership and control of the economy with an ever-decreasing element of soviet and shopfloor worker control and ever-increasing element of labor compulsion. This was, of course, accompanied by an attempt to eliminate private trade. As we also saw in chapter 1, these measures eventually came to be defended not as unfortunate necessities imposed by the needs of the war but as part of the essence of socialism itself. During the debate over one-man management at the time of the Ninth Congress of the Communist Party in 1920, Lenin in fact argued that whether there was collegial management or individual management on the shopfloor was irrelevant to the question of 'how a class governs and what class domination actually is,' since 'the victorious proletariat has abolished property, has completely annulled it – and *therein* lies its domination as a class. The prime thing is the question of property. As soon as the question of property was settled practically, the domination of the class was assured.' Furthermore, Lenin claimed that there was 'absolutely *no* contradiction in principle between Soviet (that is, socialist) democracy and the existence of dictatorial power by individuals.'[48] The closest that Lenin got in the post-revolutionary period to an affirmation of the need for actual, day-by-day worker involvement in running the affairs of the society was in his persistent emphasis on worker staffing of leadership positions in state and party institutions. This was, of course, a democratic measure to the extent that it abolished the monopoly that the old ruling classes had acquired over the important positions in the economy and polity. Yet it must be stressed that an emphasis on the social class background of the leaders, rather than on whether they were elected democratically by the workers and peasants and were thus *institutionally* responsible to these class groupings, could do very little for an overall democratization of the sources of power and control in Soviet Russia.

Lenin was indeed presenting a highly schematic view of the nature of socialism and its possible internal contradictions and problems (or, speaking more precisely, the lack of them). Therefore, it should not surprise us that many Bolsheviks, as we shall later see in this chapter, concluded that there was no need for workers to have independent trade unions to defend themselves against 'their own state.' Likewise, as long as the workers presumably controlled the state because the Communist Party was in power, Lenin felt that such developments as his support for a modified form of Taylorism or the reestablishment of piece rates could not be thought to be a threat to the survival and development of socialism in Russia.[49] Presumably, neither could many other measures be considered a threat to socialism: for example, the evolution of the voluntary donation of labor (*subbotnik*, after the word Saturday) from what was originally, in 1919, a movement restricted to party members, to what by late 1920 had become a regular and decreasingly voluntary occurrence involving the calling out of virtually the entire population. Even the sympathetic historian William Chase, while stressing the voluntary aspect of the *subbotnik* movement, has acknowledged that by early 1921 the line between normal work and *subbotnik* labor had beceome significantly blurred.[50]

Moreover, by 1920, compulsory labor was increasingly being used as punishment, in contrast to the earlier conception that it was the social obligation of all citizens.[51] In sum, as Silvana Malle, a scholar of War Communism, has pointed out, labor conscription may have been originally justified since it 'was imposed on the industrial sector only when absenteeism, mainly due to the food crisis, reached 40–50 per cent of the employed.' Yet she also noted how this policy 'was accompanied by ideological rationalizations within that framework of militarized culture which affected deeply some of the leaders.'[52]

Bolshevik Dissidence and Workers' Democracy

While mainstream Leninist Bolshevism proved itself to be a temporary and ultimately unreliable ally of workers' democracy at the point of production, that was not the case for many of the early dissident Bolshevik factions (1917–23). It is interesting and important to note that several dissidents on the Left of the party strongly defended the ideas and practices of workers' control and/or management, as did of course numerous Anarcho-Syndicalists outside the party's ranks. In fact, Lenin had a point when he accused some of these Left factions (e.g. the Workers' Opposition) of being Anarcho-Syndicalists in Communist 'disguise.' At the same time, many dissidents on the right wing of the party, who were no friends of workers' management, equally strongly defended the ideas and practices of trade union autonomy. Among the Left factions were such party opposition groups as the Workers' Opposition, the

Democratic Centralists, and the smaller Workers' Group and Workers' Truth.[53] Among the right-wing dissidents, there were in this period no organized factions as such, but rather the significant influence of prominent trade union leaders such as A. L. Lozovsky and D. K. Riazanov.

The Left Bolshevik Position

Some of the Left oppositionists in the Communist Party demonstrated an awareness of and sensitivity to issues related to workers' control and management that are not to be found in Lenin's thoughts and actions, even in his most democratic and libertarian moments. One of these was V. V. Osinsky (V. V. Obolensky), who was later to become a principal leader of the Democratic Centralist party faction. He had originally been a strong centralizer and critic of the factory committee movement. Nevertheless, by mid-1918 his actual experience as a provincial administrator made him an advocate of greater local autonomy and what he called 'a more balanced centralism.'[54] In the Spring of 1918, Osinsky had already put forward a critique of Lenin, which was published as a two-part article in one of the few issues of the Left Communist theoretical journal *Kommunist*. Osinsky pointed out that nationalization by itself was not 'in any sense, equivalent to socialism.' He was also concerned with the working class becoming 'a passive element, the object rather than the subject of the organisation of labour in production.'[55] Furthermore, Osinsky claimed that such management devices as Taylorism and piece wages would tend to destroy the solidarity of the working class, for the same reasons that they did so under capitalism. While he sympathized with Lenin's efforts to raise productivity, he accused Lenin of confusing labor productivity with labor intensity. In any case, Osinsky argued, labor intensity was a much less important component of productivity than other factors such as the condition and organization of the means of production, and the skills of the labor force. Problems with these objective factors, in his estimation, accounted for two-thirds to three-quarters of general labor productivity. Not only that, but the existence of these types of problems also demoralized the workers and encouraged carelessness. Any attempt to compensate for the objective difficulties by increasing labor intensity would lead nowhere but to the exhaustion of the working class itself.[56] Osinsky was also a critic of the extreme militarization of labor, although he was not opposed to labor discipline provided that it was established and administered by the workers themselves. For example, production norms must be set by the workers' organizations, and workmates and 'comradely courts of justice' should deal with the violations of those norms. He was also not opposed to the hiring of bourgeois technicians and specialists and payment of higher salaries to them, while workers should attempt to learn from them in the process.[57]

Most interesting from my point of view were Osinsky's proposals for workers' management and democratic planning on a nationwide basis. He proposed an extensive network of democratically organized people's economic councils (PECs), all the way from the local level to the national Supreme Economic Council (SEC), with strong intermediate regional councils as an explicit alternative to hypercentralization. Osinsky criticized the then existing Supreme Council of National Economy for being an ineffective and top-heavy organization dominated by the trade union bureaucracy and representatives of the state. He praised the Kharkov regional council, which until its destruction by the German occupation had been an example of the type of institution he had in mind. Basing himself on the experiences of this council and rejecting syndicalist ideas (meaning the notion that the means of production belong to the workers of each factory instead of to the working class as a whole), Osinksy also proposed an alternative system of industrial organization. According to his proposed system, workers would have a decisive two-thirds majority in the management of each factory, but only half of these would come from within the particular factory, the other half coming from the PECs, the workers' soviets, and the trade unions. While each particular factory management was to have a significant degree of independence, it had to strictly subordinate itself to the democratically elected regional economic council, whose task was to exmaine the factory's production plans and cost estimates and to make sure that it was operating within the boundaries of the approved plans.[58] Osinsky was alarmed by many of Lenin's notions on 'state capitalism' and the possibility that nationalized industry would be penetrated by foreign capital. Finally, he warned that 'Socialism and the socialist organization of work will either by built by the proletariat itself, or it will not be built at all; but then something else will be erected, namely state capitalism.'[59]

Lenin, for his part, dismissed these and similar arguments as '*absolutely nothing but* the same petty-bourgeois waverings' of other enemies of the revolution from Martov on the Left to Miliukov on the Right.[60] Lenin also claimed that the vanguard of the proletariat supported the regime's introduction of labor discipline and had confidence in the workers' state's ability to control the industrial managers. It was the petty bourgeoisie, and not the workers, who opposed labor discipline. Otherwise, he had no comment to make on the merits or demerits of the substantive proposals made by Osinsky and other like-minded Communists.[61] It may very well be, as I previously suggested, that any attempt to implement Osinsky's or similar ideas might have failed given the disastrous economic situation facing the country, particularly in working-class strongholds such as Petrograd. Yet the fact is that these notions were not seriously entertained, let alone tried, by Lenin and the mainstream of the Bolshevik Party. Thus, whether or not, and the *extent* to which, they might have worked remains a matter of historic speculation. Besides, the lack of mainstream Bolshevik consideration of and/or support for Osinsky's type of orientation could not but have negatively affected the possibilities for workers' democracy in subsequent years as the economy gradually improved.

The Right Bolshevik Position

Dissidents on the right wing of the party (the Bolshevik right wing will be discussed in more detail in chapter 6) tended to be opponents of full-scale workers' management and were willing to support only a limited version of workers' control. However, it is important to consider that their position on workers' control and management was rooted not only, or even primarily, in the organizational and technical possibility of workers' control and management, but, more fundamentally, in the general question of whether or not Russia was economically ripe for socialism. A. Lozovsky, perhaps the most important Right Bolshevik trade union leader, in a pamphlet published on 8 January 1918, argued against the more radical instructions on workers' control on the grounds that they dispersed control of production instead of centralizing it, and thus made no connection with the planned regulation of the economy. This was, of course, the type of argument that to a considerable extent was shared by the Rightists and Lenin himself after late 1917. However, Lozovsky also maintained that the radical instructions were illogical because, while on the one hand they allowed for the survival of employers and profit, on the other hand they effectively abolished the old management in practice. This in reality meant workers' self-management and the complete socialist reorganization of the economy.[62] Interestingly, in this pamphlet Lozovsky seemed to have agreed with people like Osinsky that socialism meant to 'socialize all enterprises and hand the whole apparatus into the hands of the workers.'[63] Of course, the difference was that Lozovsky did not think that socialism was on the practical agenda of the day in Russia. Instead, he thought that what was possible in Russia was a lengthy transitional period of state capitalism or state socialism until a socialist revolution took place in the more advanced countries of Western Europe. Until then, the working class would in the meantime acquire greater organizational experience and would have to act 'against the state-employer in selling its labor power.' Therefore, what was required at this point was the transitional measure of workers' control that did not affect the foundations of the capitalist system, and the *regulation* rather than the *organization* of production. In sum, the proletariat could 'reduce the appetites of the ruling classes with a rough hand and force them to submit to its control – but more than this it cannot do.'[64]

Right-wing Bolsheviks like Lozovsky and David K. Riazanov represented a significant force among the party's trade union leaders. As such they opposed the shopfloor democracy of the factory committees. Accordingly, they were no more likely than Lenin to share the insights of Osinsky and other Left oppositionists who saw rank-and-file decision making as an antidote to working-class powerlessness and the resulting passivity and demoralization. Yet, unlike Lenin, these Right Bolsheviks were generally quite sensitive to state and party violations of trade union autonomy and very often to issues of political freedom as well. Thus, for example, on 20 December 1917 the official trade union journal published a piece by Lozovsky protesting against the government's violent suppression of strikes. As he put it:

> The task of the trade unions and of the Soviet power is the isolation of the bourgeois elements who lead strikes and sabotage, but this isolation should not be achieved merely by mechanical means, by arrests, by

shipping to the front or by deprivation of bread cards ... Preliminary censorship, the destruction of newspapers, the annihilation of freedom of agitation for the socialist and democratic parties is for us absolutely inadmissible. The closing of the newspapers, violence against strikers, etc., irritated open wounds. There has been too much of this type of 'action' recently in the memory of the Russian toiling masses and this can lead to an analogy deadly to the Soviet power.[65]

In sum, one can say that both the early Left and Right oppositionists often defended democratic ideas and practices against Lenin and the central party leadership. The Leftists were more likely to be strong proponents (in the terminology of the American 1960s) of participatory democracy, while the Rightists were more likely to be defenders of the more traditional democratic rights and civil liberties against state and party interference. I shall discuss in a later chapter the serious and perhaps tragic limitations of both the Right and Left's political conceptions on this and other matters.

It should also be pointed out that sometimes the trade union politics of the right-wing Bolsheviks made them coincide on specific issues with the position of the Left oppositionists. Thus, for instance, in January 1918, the Petrograd Council of Trade Unions, under the influence of Riazanov, resisted the establishment of piece rates as incompatible with socialism.[66] Later, at the First Congress of Councils of People's Commissars (*Sovnarkhozy*) held in mid-1918, Lozovsky opposed the proposals of Alexei Gastev, the principal Bolshevik exponent of 'Taylorism.' Lozovsky then wondered where Russia would find the model worker whose output would be taken as the norm and expressed concern about the large number of starving and exhausted workers in the country. In this context, he even warned of the creation of a Russian Asiatic despotism.[67] Earlier, the metalworkers, usually close to the Bolsheviks, had rejected the Taylor system and piece rates at their First Moscow *Oblast* Conference (19–22 April 1918), as had the Menshevik-led printers' union (the *oblast* was a geographical unit within the union republics).[68] Along the same lines, at the meeting of the All-Russian Council of Trade Unions on 12 January 1920, the Bolshevik fraction rejected, by a vote of 58 to 2, Trotsky's and Lenin's pleas for the militarization of labor.[69] Clearly, such a lopsided margin could have only come about through the agreement or coincidence of Right and Left Bolshevik trade unionists against the party's central leadership. It even happened on occasion that the logic of a consistent trade unionist orientation placed the unionists to the Left of the factory committees. Thus, in the Spring of 1917, both Lenin and Riazanov criticized the factory committees because they were in fact functioning as agents of capital in their efforts to obtain fuel and new orders for their factories. Lenin accused the committees of acting as 'errand boys' of capital in the absence of a soviet power and workers' control at the national level that would ensure that the actions of the committees would be to the benefit of the working class as a whole. Similarly, Riazanov pointed out at the time that 'the union movement does not bear the stain of the entrepreneur, and it is the bad luck of the committees that they seem to be component parts of the administration. The union opposes itself to capital, while the factory committee involuntarily turns into an agent of the entrepreneur.'[70]

The Fate of the Trade Unions

The majority of Russian unions were formed after the February Revolution. They were relatively slow in organizing, but by July 1917 there were about half a million union members in Moscow and Petrograd and 145 trade unions in the provinces with a membership of 150,000–160,000. As I earlier indicated, Russian trade unions were organized on an industry-wide basis rather than at the enterprise level; besides, the unions were closely tied to political parties – mostly, but not exclusively, to the various wings of social democracy. However, the Bolsheviks had gained most of their supporters among the factory committees and that helps to explain why the unions played a less important role in the pre-October revolutionary process. Nevertheless, the increased Bolshevik strength in the working class eventually spread to the unions. Thus, in the summer of 1917, the central administration of the Moscow Textile Workers' Union and of the Metal Unions of Petrograd, Moscow, Samara, Kharkov, and some Urals towns had passed into Bolsehvik hands.[71]

The first national Congress of Trade Unions, which met at the end of 1917, besides formally converting the factory committees into the local units of the trade unions, dealt at considerable length with the question of the relationship of the unions to the state. In fact, the trade union debates at this and at the Second Trade Union Congress in 1919 were much more consequential and revealing than the generally better known debate on the unions at the 1921 Tenth Congress of the Communist Party. In the first place, at the First, and even at the Second, Trade Union Congress, the mainstream Bolshevik trade unionists had to confront the arguments put forward by vocal minorities within their own party *and* by trade unionists belonging to the still legal opposition parties. Approximately 500 delegates attended the first Congress, 428 of whom had voting rights, representing 19 national unions with a membership of 2.5 million. Of the voting delegates, 281 were Bolsheviks (66 per cent), 67 Mensheviks (16 per cent), 21 Left SRs (5 per cent), 10 Right SRs (2 per cent), 6 SR Maximalists (a group somewhere in between the Left SRs and the Anarchists with 1 per cent), 6 Anarcho-Syndicalists (1 per cent), and 37 belonged to no political party (9 per cent).[72] The report of the mandate commission of the First Congress revealed that the Bolshevik weakness in the *national* union organizations dating back to the days before October had not been eliminated even though they had been in power for a couple of months. Thus, at the All-Russian level Menshevik representatives outnumbered the Bolsheviks 12 to 9; while at the lower *oblast* level it was exactly the reverse. Moreover, at the local council level the Bolsheviks outnumbered the Mensheviks 28 to 12, and at the local union level the Bolsheviks had an overwhelming lead of 232 to the Mensheviks' 34.[73] This was apparently an expression of the fact that the relatively recent Bolshevik upsurge at the local rank-and-file union level had not yet been able to make itself fully felt in the national union hierarchies.

Second, it must be emphasized that, at the time of the First Congress, Bolshevik politics on the trade union question had obviously not been affected by the harsh and bitter experiences of the Civil War and War Communism. Furthermore, although the country was already experiencing an economic crisis, it was less important in comparison to the economic debacle of the subsequent months and years. Yet, M. P. Tomsky, one of the most important Bolshevik trade unionists, argued for the subordination of the unions to the state by asking whether 'the trade unions should tie their fortunes to those of the Soviet government or whether they should remain independent organs of economic class struggle.'[74] Apparently, it did not then occur to Tomsky that the trade unions could conceivably support the Bolshevik government in general terms *and* retain their independent economic role vis-à-vis the workers' and peasants' state. It is not surprising that Tomsky and others failed to make this crucial distinction given the tendency of the Bolshevik delegates at this Congress to confuse the concept of union organizational independence with the quite different notion of union political 'neutrality.'[75] More ominously, Zinoviev, while speaking on behalf of the Bolshevik Party argued: 'I ask you, why and from whom do you need independence: from your own government. . .?' and also explictly rejected the right to strike, arguing along the same lines that 'the strike would be directed against the workers themselves.'[76] A motion put forward by Tsyperovich, an important Bolshevik trade unionist, recommending that the unions should continue to use strike action in defense of its members was rejected, although at the same time the Congress left the question in abeyance by not explicitly coming out against strikes.[77]

Mensheviks such as Ivan Maisky responded to the Bolshevik arguments with a strong defense of the independence of the unions, although it should be carefully noted that he and other Mensheviks did this on the basis that the revolution could only be bourgeois democratic, not socialist, and that consequently the workers would still need to defend themselves against the *capitalist* employers.[78] Not surprisingly, it was the highly sophisticated Left Menshevik leader Martov who added a more subtle argument to the Menshevik case for trade union independence; namely, that the revolutionary government could not represent the working class alone, and thus could not help but be connected with a diverse mass of people consisting of both proletarian and non-proletarian elements. Consequently, the trade unions as representatives of the working class had to retain their autonomy vis-à-vis the government. Martov's resolution, supporting trade union independence on the basis of the usual Menshevik arguments against the economically premature Bolshevik socialism, received 84 votes, against 182 for the Bolshevik majority motion.[79]

However, it seems to me that the most interesting objections to the position of the Bolshevik Party's majority at the Congress came from right-wing

Bolsheviks Riazanov and Lozovsky. Lozovsky objected, as did the Moscow party organization, to Zinoviev's characterization of trade unions as 'organs of state power' and pointed out that 'this would mean that the decisions of the Trade Unions would be carried out by compulsion . . . that they would not be connected with the activity of the mass of productive workers,' and went on to predict that in that case coercion would replace spontaneous class solidarity. Lozovsky allowed that perhaps under full socialism the statification of the unions would be justified, but Russia could not become socialist until after the revolution had been won in the West; until then the trade unions should remain separate from the state.[80]

At the end of this important debate, the Congress stopped short of recommending that the unions become part of the formal governmental machine. For the time being, the unions would retain a certain degree of independence but would continue to fulfill a variety of state functions such as the administration of a variety of social welfare institutions. Nevertheless, the Congress left little doubt about the longer-term fate of the unions:

> As they develop the Trade Unions should, in the process of the present socialist revolution, become organs of socialist power, and as such they should work in co-ordination with, and subordination to other bodies in order to carry into effect the new principles. . .
>
> The Congress is convinced that in consequence of the foreshadowed process, the Trade Unions will inevitably become transformed into organs of the socialist state, and the participation in the Trade Unions will for all people employed in any industry be their duty vis-a-vis the state.[81]

Furthermore, the Congress recommended that, as the unions became instruments of the socialist state, 'membership in [the unions] of all persons employed in a given industry will be enforced by the government.'[82]

The Civil War and War Communism resulted in a great expansion of the governmental role of the trade unions (e.g. they played an important role in the mobilization of manpower). Accordingly, the Second All-Russian Congress of Trade Unions held in January 1919 placed much greater stress than the First Congress on opposing the independence and favoring the statification of the unions. At this Second Congress, the Menshevik leader Martov continued to support union independence. So did Lozovsky, now a member of the small group called United Social Democratic Internationalists, after his expulsion from the Bolshevik Party in early 1918. Lozovsky predicted that unions transformed into agencies of the state would rest on force, substitute coercion for consent, and become objects of hatred among the masses. He also cited the example of the executive board of the railwaymen's union, which had been taken over by the government. This had produced a serious conflict of interest for the union officers, who were torn between their commitments to the state and to their membership, and had also alienated the union rank-and-file from their organization. Finally, Lozovsky at least implicitly showed that union organizational independence was not the same thing as union political neutrality when he explained that, when he spoke of independent unions, he did not in any way mean by this that unions were to be 'independent of socialism, independent of the socialist struggle.'[83]

During the Second Congress, Boshevik trade union leader Tomsky also flatly declared that no strikes could take place in Soviet Russia. Lenin spoke about the inevitability of the statification of the unions. He also pointed out that the Supreme Council of National Economy, the body put in charge of directing the country's economy, was primarily staffed by the trade unions. This was yet another instance where Lenin implied that *staffing* of state institutions by people of working-class background was in some way a vehicle for working-class control of the state. Yet, the final resolutions adopted by the Congress retained a certain ambiguity. While the majority of the delegates rejected union neutrality and independence, they did not make it clear whether the unions were to be subordinate to the state.[84] Moreover, the delegates also approved a number of motions strengthening the power of the unions in the economy. As Jay B. Sorenson has pointed out, 'the delegates – all basically committed to the principle of strong labor unions – proved themselves to be either unwilling to cut union powers or unable to resolve the question of union–state relations. Thus, although union independence was further narrowed, the question of union power remained fluid.'[85]

The government's attempt to limit and control working-class resistance exacerbated the previously existing theoretical and political confusion over the very role of the unions in the post-revolutionary society. There was, after all, a kernel of truth in Zinoviev's arguments at the First Trade Union Congress, in that there *is* some validity to the notion that unions, factory committees, and other working-class organizations must and should encourage rank-and-file workers to produce more and better, *if* indeed a revolution has brought the working class and its allies to power. Given such a situation, workers could truly be said to be working for themselves. The point is, however, that this 'encouragement' can easily be a thinly veiled rationalization for what is in fact compulsion by an outside, distant, even hostile, state. Moreover, even a state run by a government based on strong majority popular support (and the Bolsheviks were losing a lot of that support in 1918) could not immediately eliminate the hierarchical division of labor. As I will argue later in this chapter, there is thus the need for workers to be able to defend themselves against their state (or remaining private) managers and employers. The two congresses did not fully clarify this issue nor did they produce any clear, much less definitive, answers to the following two questions: Should the unions be defensive organizations or institutions for economic administration, or should they attempt to be both? What should have been the relationship of the unions to the factory committee movement when the latter was still in existence?

Shortly after the Second Trade Union Congress in January 1919, the Communist Party held its Eighth Congress in March 1919 and adopted a new Program. Point V of this Program promised, rather surprisingly considering the then dramatically increasing emphasis on one-man management, a very large self-managing role to the trade unions. In the words of the Party Program, 'the organizational apparatus of socialized industry ought to be based, in the first instance, on the Trade Unions ... the Trade Unions ought in the end actually to concentrate in their hands all the administration of the entire national economy...'[86] According to Isaac Deutscher, Point V was a 'syndicalist' slip of the Bolshevik leadership written into the Party Program as an expression of the leadership's gratitude to the trade unions for their work in the Civil War.[87] Whether this was a 'syndicalist slip' or the expression of a political compromise, as other scholars have maintained,[88] this promise was never put into practice. Point V did become an important symbol around which future Bolshevik dissident factions were to rally.

Instead of trade union control of the economy, what did take place was a tremendous growth in the power of the Communist Party, just as we saw happened in the context of the soviets. This power was reinforced by the gradual outlawing of the opposition parties and by the efforts of the ruling party to assert its control over a variety of bodies that overlapped and conflicted with each other, such as the unions, the soviets, the Supreme Council of National Economy, and the Commissariat of Labor.[89] Furthermore, the Eighth Conference of the party, held on 2–4 December 1919, established a system of internal organization that was bound to sharply curtail, if not eliminate, the considerable freedom of action that party members had hitherto enjoyed. In the case of the trade unions, for example, it was decided that party members were to belong to a 'fraction' (*fraktsya*), which was supposed to enjoy autonomy on internal union matters vis-à-vis the party as a whole, but which had to submit to party discipline in case of conflict. However, the party could easily prevent conflict from occuring in the first place, since it had the power to appoint members of the fraction even if these people were not union members at all. Thus, if a pocket of dissidence developed in any individual union, the situation could quickly be changed through the literal flooding of the fraction with new members willing to do the bidding of the central party leadership. Furthermore, the party could force a member to resign an office to which he or she had been elected by the union as a whole. Along the same lines, the fraction also proposed candidates to union office in agreement with outside party bodies at the relevant local, regional, and national levels. Last but by no means least, trade unionists belonging to the party were obliged to argue and vote for the same positions at general union meetings. Discussion and disagreement were permitted inside the fraction, but, once the fraction decided, the individual member was not permitted to disagree with, let alone vote against, the previously adopted fraction position.[90] In fact, this measure meant that factional differences, or even the mere airing of internal party disagreements, on substantive institutional policy matters had for all practical purposes been abolished *insofar as the non-party public was concerned*. It is worth emphasizing that the consequences of such fraction discipline for a party in power, particularly if opposition parties have been outlawed, are *qualitatively* different from those for a party out of power. In the former case, we are really speaking about the end of any significant policy debates within the trade union or in whichever organization the ruling party's fractional discipline is being invoked. The Bolshevik leadership's apparent indifference to such a critical distinction, and its consequent lack of self-restraint, turned out to be truly devastating in its consequences.

Two dramatic examples of this unrestrained new disciplinary setup took place at the Fourth All-Russian Congress of Trade Unions (17–25 May 1921) and at the Congress of the Metalworkers' Union, which also met in May 1921. At the All-Russian Congress of Trade Unions, Riazanov, with the support of the party fraction, presented an amendment to fill an omission in the main resolution. The crucial part of the amendment, which was adopted by a vote of 1,500 to 30, staed that 'the leading personnel of the trade union movement must be chosen under the general guidance of the Party, but the Party must make a special effort to allow normal methods of proletarian democracy, particularly in the trade unions, where the choice of leaders should be left to the trade unionists themselves'[91] On hearing of this motion, the Central Committee of the party, probably sensing a potential if not an actual threat to its hegemony, was completely outraged. Tomsky, who thought Riazanov's amendment was in accordance with the official party line, had his credentials as representative of the Central Committee of the party to the Congress withdrawn. He was replaced by Lenin, Stalin, and Bukharin. Eventually, a special commission headed by Stalin investigated Tomsky's behavior and reprimanded him for his 'criminal negligence.' Tomsky was for some time to come relieved of all his functions on the All-Russian Council of Trade Unions and in the meantime sent on a party mission to Turkestan. Riazanov was barred from any future trade union work, and the party fraction was 'persuaded' to reverse its previous position.[92]

In the case of the Congress of the Metalworkers' Union, a stronghold of the Workers Opposition (an opposition group in the Communist Party), both the Communist Party fraction and the union delegates as a whole rejected (by a vote of 120 to 40) the list of candidates for union leadership that the Central Committee of the party had prepared. In the end, the Central Committee disregarded the votes of the Congress and appointed a metalworkers' committee of its own. A. Shliapnikov, the Bolshevik leader of the Metalworkers' Union, was not even allowed to resign from the Central Committee to express his outrage at this action.[93] Later, in August 1921, after Shliapnikov continued to criticize the party leadership, Lenin demanded that he be expelled from the Central Committee. Short of the necessary two-thirds vote to carry out this expulsion, Shliapnikov was instead censured by that body.[94]

Earlier, a number of women's unions that are known to have existed in 1919 and 1920 were also suppressed. These unions had been formed independently of the Communist Party by working-class women who felt that they were not treated fairly by the male-led unions. The representative of one such union in the city of Tsivilsk, Kazan province, explained to a soviet congress in 1919 that, although the revolution had declared female equality, 'we don't have the strength [as individuals] to throw off such views of men and the habit of some women to humiliate us and consider us untalented creatures ... And now, we organize our union to protect the interests of women with out common strength. Its goal is the unity of all the women of the city.' Although the strength and number of these unions is unknown, we do know that in 1919 Inessa Armand, then head of the Women's Bureau in Moscow, ordered the groups disbanded. *Pravda* also published three different announcements declaring these unions abolished in June and October of 1919, and in June of 1921. Apparently, some of these organizations had survived party pressure for as long as two years.[95] At least part of the opposition to the women's unions was due to the hostility that many Bolsheviks felt towards what they considered 'separatism,' an accusation often levelled against the official Women's Bureau itself.

In light of all I have just described, the position taken by Lenin during the sharp debates on the unions at the March 1921 Tenth Party Congress appears to be far less consequential than many have thought. At this Congress, Trotsky and Bukharin argued for the complete statification of the trade unions, while the Workers' Opposition, led by A. Shliapnikov and A. Kollontai, supported the practical implementation of Point V of the 1919 Party Program, i.e. trade union administration of the entire economy.[96] Lenin, while opposing the Workers' Opposition much more strongly than he opposed Trotsky and Bukharin, nonetheless dismissed the latter's notion that the trade unions had nothing to defend against the workers' state. Repeating some of Martov's 1918 arguments, Lenin pointed out that the Soviet state was not a workers' state but a state of workers and peasants, and furthermore it was also a 'bureaucratically deformed' state. The workers and their unions were, of course, obliged to defend and not systematically oppose this state; but, since the workers still had to defend themselves against their government for the reasons outlined above, it followed that the unions should retain a degree of autonomy.[97]

However, it seems to me that the degree of autonomy that Lenin spoke about was rather meaningless considering that, on the one hand, at that very time – the early twenties – opposition parties were being barred from the unions, and that, on the other hand, Communist Party fraction discipline was, as we have just seen, beginning to be implemented in a ruthless fashion. Besides, Lenin's resolution at the 1921 Congress made it clear that the thrust of his policies was not the strengthening of the defensive character of the unions. At this time, Lenin thought that the unions should be instruments of persuasion or 'schools of communism.' He pointed out that the unions had 7 million members and the Communist Party only half a million, and that the members of the party should not attempt to impose themselves, but try to be accepted by the non-party unionists on the basis of their own merits. The trade unions were also asked to participate in the tasks of economic planning and administration, e.g. by recommending people for responsible administrative positions and by developing production norms. Last but not least, the unions were also supposed to function as 'schools of labor discipline,' e.g. by establishing comradely disciplinary courts.[98] At the same time, by 1921, the unons had lost their earlier prerogatives to approve decrees dealing with labor questions, fix minimum wages, control labor distribution, settle disputes, administer social insurance, etc.[99] Thus, while the unions could not be said to have lost all of their previous power, it was clear that they were increasingly becoming 'transmission belts' for the party rather than defensive institutions and/or powerful social and economic policy makers.

At any rate, in January 1922 (i.e. less than a year after the Tenth Party Congress held in March 1921), the Central Committee of the Communist Party dotted the i's and crossed the t's when it declared that,

> just as the very best factory, with the very best motors and first-class machines, will be forced to remain idle if the transmission belts from the motors to the machines are damaged, so our work of socialist construction must meet with inevitable disaster if the trade unions – the transmission belts from the Communist Party to the massess – are badly fitted or function badly. It is not sufficient to explain, to reiterate and corroborate this truth; it must be backed organisationally by the whole structure of the trade unions and by their everyday activities.[100]

Having declared this, the Central Committee then recognized the contradictory position in which it had placed the unions. On one hand, they were supposed to defend the interests of the workers, but on the other hand they were 'participants in the exercise of state power;' 'on the one hand . . . [they] must operate in military fashion, for the dictatorship of the proletariat is the fiercest, most dogged and most desperate class war; [but] on the other hand, specifically military methods of operation are least of all applicable to the trade unions.'[101] In the face of this, the Central Committee *in fact* ruled out any semblance of union independence as a solution to these contradictions, thus demonstrating the misleading nature of Lenin's pronouncements at the March 1921 Party Congress. Moreover, the party saw the predicament in which it had placed the unions not as a response to an immediate and relatively short-term crisis, but indeed as lasting a whole epoch since 'these contradictions are no accident, and they will persist for several decades; for as long as survivals of capitalism and small production remain, contradictions between them and the young shoots of socialism are inevitable throughout the social system.'[102]

Moreover, the Eleventh Congress of the Communist Party (27 March–2 April 1922), the last at which Lenin actively participated, left even less doubt about the meaninglessness of Lenin's proposed union autonomy. This Congress resolved that the secretaries and chairmen of the central committees of the unions must be party members of long standing, i.e. since before the revolution, and that the chairmen, secretaries, and members of the leading regional trade union bodies had to be party members of at least three years' standing. Furthermore, the Congress decided that party members could be co-opted rather than elected to union office. Finally, it was agreed that all conflicts and frictions on union questions would be resolved by the party and the Comintern rather than by the unions themselves.[103] Later, in 1922, the unions were largely bypassed in the preparation and implementation of a new Labor Code to accompany the New Economic Policy. On the positive side, this Labor Code established the 8 hour day and a weekly rest period of no less than 42 continuous hours, limited the amount and established fixed rates of pay for hours of overtime work, forbade the employment of children under 14, and limited the workday of juveniles. Yet again it was left to perennial dissidents Riazanov and Larin to object to new provisions of the Labor Code that were clearly unfavorable to the working class. Among these were the following stipulations: collective agreements were not mandatory nor was management compelled to sign them; while all hiring had to be done through state employment offices, the employer had the right to refuse the employees sent to him; a lengthening of the workday in dangerous jobs; a reduction in unemployment insurance; and the expansion of the number of grounds upon which management might dismiss a worker without compensation.[104]

In spite of all of these developments, it still took some time before the independent initiatives of the working class were completely crushed, under Stalin's regime. Many workers had expressed their discontent by dropping out of the unions, at least through late 1923. Yet, strikes had not been outlawed. Thus, and even though the unions pursued a no-strike policy, there were reports of 102 strikes involving 43,000 workers in 1921–2, and 267 strikes involving 42,000 workers, mostly in state industries, in 1924. In 1925 no strikes were sanctioned by the unions but there were still 186 strikes involving 43,000 workers. In 1926 there were 327 strikes involving 32,900 strikers in state industries. Finally, the figures for 1927 and the first half of 1928 were 396 strikes involving 20,100 state employees and 90 strikes involving 8,900 state employees, respectively.[105]

Conclusion

The role that trade unions and factory committees should play in the post-revolutionary transition toward socialism has been inadequately theorized in the socialist and Marxist traditions. The issues involved here go beyond the necessary workers' defense against state bureaucratic distortions or deformations, although these tendencies would almost inevitably affect the new society and would need urgent attention. However, even a highly democratic and egalitarian society that fell short of suffering significant bureaucratic deformations would still have a hierarchical division of labor. Marx claimed that the material conditions of existence powerfully contribute to the creation of particular ideologies and outlooks. If he was correct, and I believe he was, then there cannot be but the slightest doubt that rank-and-file workers need to defend themselves against the effects of the hierarchical division of labor even among those they have democratically elected to represent them. The historian David Mandel has written about how many revolutionary leaders developed an 'administrative outlook,' changed their attitude and tone, and acquired a certain condescension and impatience towards the masses just a few months after the October Revolution; that is, long before one could really speak of hardened bureaucracies. Mandel cites Shelavin, a leading Bolshevik, to the effect that, at this early time,

> a whole series of responsible, highly skilled comrades who had gone through the school of the underground became infected with an exclusively 'soviet' mood, not to speak of the young contingent... They felt that now the real thing was to organise, for example, the district soviet of the national economy, but not by any means to 'ferment' in the district party committee.[106]

It is also relevant to note here that, as the Civil War encouraged the growth of a large number of organizations, local and national Communist Party bodies fast acquired human and material resources similar to those already possessed by state institutions. Soon, party functionaries began to be preoccupied with the status and prerogatives of their offices, e.g. the need to receive higher wages to match those given to their state counterparts.[107]

The power of immediate recall of elected representatives is certainly an important weapon of the rank-and-file, but by its very nature can be used only as a last resort against office holders. This needs to be supplemented by other permanent, ongoing institutional arrangements that may even obviate the need for recall. This is also the context in which the different kinds of organizations will probably have to fulfill different functions. Thus, it may very well be that unions will concern themselves only with such issues as the defense of wages and working conditions, including the defense of individuals and groups not only against leaders but sometimes, if necessary, even against majority decisions of the factory committees themselves. These committees, perhaps in a 'non-syndicalist' manner similar to that suggested by Osinsky in 1918, would be properly speaking the governing bodies of the factories and offices in all matters regarding production policies. Thus, these institutions would become the principal vehicles for the workers' active and democratic involvement in the administration of the firm. These democratic committees would also constitute an important weapon against the worker apathy and alienation that contribute to the development of a variety of social ills ranging from alcoholism to the production of shoddy goods. The councils or soviets could then become, according to such an arrangement, the political bodies establishing the most general social, political, and economic policies for society as a whole.

3

Freedom of the Press

The Bolsheviks and Freedom of the Press before the October Revolution

Before the seizure of power, the Bolsheviks did not have a well worked out view of the role of the press in the transitional period immediately following the triumph of the revolution, let alone under socialism. However, we know that Lenin and the Bolshevik leadership took the role of the press very seriously insofar as the struggle against Tsarism and capitalism was concerned. Specifically, this leadership saw the party press as a key unifying and organizing tool.

Undoubtedly, the importance that Lenin and the Bolsheviks attached to the press was in part related to the considerable growth in literacy during the 20-year period preceding the two 1917 revolutions. Besides, the working class benefited in this context from its relatively advantageous urban location, particularly in the case of the two biggest cities, Petrograd and Moscow. Thus, the 1897 census revealed that, while only 21 per cent of the total population of European Russia was literate, this figure comprised two rather different situations, i.e. 17 per cent literacy in the countryside compared to 45 per cent in the towns. By 1918, while in the country as a whole the literacy rate was 79 per cent and 44 per cent for male and female workers, respectively, in Petrograd the equivalent rates were 89 per cent for male workers and 65 per cent for females, with younger women more likely to be literate than older women workers.[1] It is therefore not surprising that by 1917 more than 150 newspapers and different kinds of sheets and 450 journals were published in Petrograd, while 100 newspapers and 270 journals were issued in Moscow. The Russian press, already fairly diverse by 1917, became qualitatively more heterogeneous when Tsarist censorship was abolished after the February Revolution, and an untrammeled socialist press was able to flourish at the time.[2]

Lenin's views on issues of press freedom *before* the October Revolution were by and large democratic. Unquestionably, this was closely connected to Lenin's vigorous support for democratic demands as a keystone of the struggle against Tsarism. Thus, in 1905, Lenin argued for the specific democratic demand of freedom of the press, while at the same time pointing out that this in no way contradicted a party's right to include or exclude people on the basis of political agreement or disagreement. As Lenin put it:

Everyone is free to write and say whatever he likes, without any restrictions. But every voluntary association (including a party) is also free to expel members who use the name of the party to advocate anti-party views. Freedom of speech and the press must be complete. But then freedom of association must be complete too. I am bound to accord you, in the name of free speech, the full right to shout, lie and write to your heart's content. But you are bound to grant me, in the name of freedom of association, the right to enter into, or withdraw from, association with people advocating this or that view.[3]

Lenin's views on freedom of the press further evolved in the period between the February and October revolutions in 1917. After the 'July Days,' already discussed in chapter 1, *Pravda* was shut down by the Provisional Government. At the time, Lenin and other Bolshevik leaders went into hiding, and the press described Lenin as a German agent. Lenin, feeling that the press had failed to expose the real reasons for the government's crackdown on the Bolsheviks, announced that a revolutionary government would, at the appropriate moment, close down the bourgeois press.[4] Lenin did not at this point clarify whether this was a temporary measure to be adopted as part of a state of emergency, or, if it was meant as a general statement of social policy, what kind of press regime would replace the previous capitalist arrangement.

However, in September 1917, Lenin presented his most democratic and fairly detailed vision of how a post-revolutionary press system could be organized. This proposal was presented in 'good times;' i.e. during the Bolshevik upswing that followed on the heels of the defeat of Kornilov's coup, and less than two weeks before Lenin proclaimed that Soviet power could have as one of its features 'the testing of the various programs in practice and the peaceful passing of power from one party to another.'[5] Setting for himself the goals of making sure that every village in Russia got plenty of copies of newspapers from all the big parties, and of eliminating the power of the censor as well as the power of money over the press, Lenin proposed a state monopoly of commercial advertising. He further proposed that,

State power in the shape of the Soviets takes *all* the printing presses and *all* the newsprint and distributes them *equitably*: the state should come first – in the interests of the majority of the people, the majority of the poor, particularly the majority of the peasants, who for centuries have been tormented, crushed and stultified by the landowners and capitalists.

The big parties should come second – say, those that have polled one or two hundred thousand votes in both capitals. The smaller parties should come third, and then any group of citizens which has a certain number of members or has collected a certain number of signatures.[6]

In early November, a few days after the triumph of the revolution, Lenin suggested 10,000 as the number of citizens forming a group entitled to press facilities.[7]

Nevertheless, there were problems with Lenin's views on press freedom even when he was proposing his most democratic policies. Thus, while Lenin's new proposals clearly indicated the end of the capitalist press system, he did not spell out whether groups of present or former bourgeois would be entitled to have access to the press in strict proportion to their numbers in the population, or whether they would be disenfranchised. Far more worrisome was the extreme statification implied in his support for a state monopoly of advertising. Of course, in practice, this measure was only relevant to a society where total nationalization had not been carried out. Given such conditions, Lenin's proposal would have, for example, prevented political organizations from supporting their publishing activities by *directly* obtaining advertising funds from small industry, shopkeepers, or independent professionals. Moreover, while there is certainly a democratic case to be made for *equalizing* advertising funds and thus avoiding the inequities of the bourgeois press system, Lenin's remedy was at least potentially worse than the illness it was supposed to cure. It would not have been at all difficult to conceive of alternative ways of equalizing advertising funds, e.g. through a progressive system of taxation of advertisements in the more commercially successful publications. Such a policy, if carried out on a local and national level, could have provided the funds for a considerable equalization of publishing opportunities without at the same time creating a dangerous government monopoly.

The Soviet Press after the October Revolution

There were significant changes in the Soviet press regime between the October Revolution and the consolidation of a fully monolithic Stalinist press in the late 1920s. These changes can be best described and analyzed if, following the chronology I suggested in the Introduction, we divide the years from 1917 to 1925 into three distinct sub-periods: (1) from the October Revolution to the beginning of the Civil War in mid-1918, (2) the Civil War period from mid-1918 to late 1920, (3) from the end of the Civil War in late 1920 to the Interregnum (i.e. late 1923 to 1925).

From the October Revolution to the Beginning of the Civil War in mid-1918

A mixed press regime prevailed at this time. The press was still relatively open, but the government acted in a confused and arbitrary manner, while at the same time being comparatively mild in its repressive activities – unlike the situation after 1921, let alone under Stalin.

From the early days after the Bolsheviks came to power some very important debates took place and decisions were carried out that deeply influenced the future development of the Soviet press. One of the first actions of the Council of People's Commissars (Sovnarkom) on taking power was to issue an order closing all hostile newspapers. This included not only the bourgeois press but newspapers close to other socialist parties such as *Golos Soldata*. At this time, the government also attempted to close down *Rabochaia gazeta*, the newspaper of the Menshevik Central Committee; the *Den* edited by Potresov; and *Edinstvo* edited by Plekhanov.[8] On the other hand, the first closing order, dated 27 October 1917, was highly instructive in that it explicitly stated that these were 'temporary and special measures' and further cited the specific grounds for closing a newspaper. In the language of the order, 'those organs of the press will be closed which (a) call for open opposition or disobedience to the Workers' and Peasants' Government; (b) sow sedition by a frankly slanderous perversion of facts; (c) encourage deeds of a manifestly criminal character. . .'[9] This was a 'retreat' from the Military Revolutionary Committee position, which had ordered a blanket ban on the 'bourgeois press' without any further qualifications.[10] In any case, the order was not fully enforced since at least some of the supposedly banned papers continued to appear through the use of such devices as changing their names. Moreover, the government's first press order was met with strong protests lodged by writers and by the Menshevik-led printers' union. It was in response to these protests and to settle what was after all the provisional character of the original decree, that the matter was referred to the Central Executive Committee (CEC) elected by the Second Congress of Soviets.

On 4 November, the CEC of the soviets met to arrive at a more definitive resolution of the press question. Two positions confronted each other in what turned out to be a most interesting debate between the majority of the Bolshevik Party, represented by Lenin and Trotsky among others, and an alliance of the Left Socialist Revolutionaries (Left SRs) with Bolshevik dissidents such as Riazanov and Larin, at the time associated with the right wing of that party. Larin argued that 'the press should be free so long as it does not incite subversion or insurrection. Censorship of every kind must be completely eliminated.'[11] He presented a resolution revoking the original press decree and establishing a special tribunal, to be chosen by the CEC in proportion to the strength of each party fraction, and empowered to authorize acts of political repression as well as repeal acts of repression that might have already occurred.[12] The implication of Larin's motion was that this tribunal would have jurisdiction over all acts of repression, whether or not they specifically concerned the press. V. A. Avanesov, for the majority of the Bolshevik Party, moved a resolution which stated that the closure of bourgeois newspapers was not motivated simply by military considerations but was also an essential transitional measure in establishing a new press regime. The next measure, according to Avanesov's resolution, was to confiscate private printing presses and stocks of newsprint and transfer them to the soviets in the provinces and the center, 'so that parties and groups may have the technical means to publish in proportion to the number of their adherents.'[13] However, it is important to note that Avanesov's resolution, unlike Larin's, did not state how the resolution would be carried out. In other words, it did not name any committee or body that would actually carry out the position of the majority of the Bolshevik Party, particularly in its declared intention to distribute press facilities among many different kinds of groups and parties. This vagueness by the Bolshevik majority could not but lend some credibility to Kalegayev's charge when, speaking for the Left SRs, he argued that it was not possible 'to carve up freedom of the press like a loaf of bread, allocating so much freedom to each group according to the influence exerted by its ideas,'[14] although Kalegayev himself did not propose any alternative to capitalist control of the media.

Trotsky indicated that newspapers controlled by the banks should not be allowed to publish and, responding to the Left SRs, stated that indeed the Bolsheviks had demanded freedom of the press for *Pravda* before the revolution, '... but then we were living under conditions which were apposite to our programme-minimum; now we are putting forward the demands in our programme-maximum,'[15] at best, an ambiguous formulation that clearly opened itself to the charge of cynicism and duplicity. Karelin, a Left SR leader, echoed Kalegayev's earlier objection to the Bolshevik majority proposal and stressed that he found them to be impractical and made a general pronouncement extolling the virtues of freedom of the press.[16] This type of praise was primarily expressed by the Bolshevik dissident-Left SR side of this debate. Malkin, another Left SR leader, spoke in the same vein as Karelin in defense of freedom of the press and argued that 'the lies of the bourgeois press do not represent an authentic danger to the socialist movement. The toiling masses have a reliable compass to guide them: the support of overwhelming numbers of people, who will sooner or later win over the remaining, more backward strata of democracy.'[17]

Lenin suggested that a commission be established to investigate the connection between the bourgeois newspapers and the banks and reiterated Trotsky's earlier argument on the banks, specifically suggesting that, before anyone started a newspaper, they should be required to prove their independence from them. Furthermore, Lenin repeated his earlier positions that private advertisements should be declared a state monopoly and that press facilities should be apportioned to parties according to the number of votes they had received. It is worth noting that Lenin, as on other occasions, drew an analogy between the government seizing the bourgeois press after the October Revolution and the closure of the Tsarist press after the overthrow of the monarchy.[18] Indeed, the Bolsheviks had earlier supported the efforts of the Petrograd Soviet to close down the reactionary monarchist papers shortly after the February Revolution.[19] Yet Lenin's analogy was very misleading since vastly different consequences were involved in suppressing what represented no more than a defeated and quite narrow *specific political group* in the case of the successful *political* revolution against Tsarism. Compared to this, Lenin's proposal, in the aftermath of the *social* revolution in October, meant the suppression of a class that was not only much larger and heterogeneous, but whose newspapers constituted a very large part of the then existing and far more diverse press system. This seems to be another instance where Lenin's penchant for drawing parallels between socialist and bourgeois revolutions missed critical differences between them. Needless to add, the above analogy was not only misleading, but in fact, became positively dangerous, when the term 'bourgeois' was used to describe not only the real thing but opponents within the working class, peasantry, and the Left.

When the resolutions came to a vote at this important meeting of the CEC of the soviets, Larin's motion failed by a vote of 22 to 31 while Avanesov's Bolshevik majority motion passed by a vote of 34 to 24, with 1 abstention. After the vote, Riazanov, a Right Bolshevik representing the trade unions, explained his vote against the Bolshevik majority by stating that he couldn't 'vote for any limitation on press freedom since I believe that even the Anarchists should have the right to express their views.'[20] As a result of this vote, the Left SRs, who had not yet joined the government, withdrew their representatives from the Military Revolutionary Committee and all responsible posts while remaining in the CEC of the soviets.[21] The vote also contributed to the decision by the Right Bolsheviks to resign as People's Commissars and from the Central Committee of the Bolshevik Party[22] on the question of the formation of an all-socialist coalition government. Some time later, the Council of People's Commissars declared advertising a state monopoly, warning the 'publications inserting advertisements without authority are to be closed.'[23]

In retrospect, I cannot help but conclude that while, abstractly speaking, the Bolshevik majority was right in advocating the seizure of all private printing presses and stocks of newsprint to be distributed to groups and parties according to their size, the lack of any proposals for specific mechanisms to bring this about made this a dangerous motion. In reality, the Bolshevik government for the most part utilized the confiscated paper supply, machinery, and buildings of the bourgeois papers to increase the circulation of their own newspapers and establish new ones such as *Bednota* (Village Poor), *Rabotnitsa* (Worker Woman), and *Voennoe delo* (Military Affairs). Thus, by the end of 1918, the overall circulation of Bolshevik papers had increased approximately tenfold since the October Revolution.[24] Furthermore, only a fraction of the suppressed newspapers were actually turned over, for a short time, to parties and organizations other than the Bolsheviks. Gorky's paper *Novaia Zhizn'* and the Left SRs were allocated some printing facilities and the Anarchists obtained access to the press in part through their own expropriations and in part through the largess of the Military Revolutionary Committee in Petrograd.[25] On the other hand, the Left SR paper *Znamia Truda* could not appear shortly after the revolution because the press had been commandeered for use by the new authorities.[26] Of course, many of the above actions were, in practice, almost as much the result of post-revolutionary chaos and fragmentation as of the fully worked-out designs of the central government.

The Right Bolshevik–Left SR position, while of course offering no answers to the longer-term problem of providing a socialist alternative to the control of the press by those with money, did provide a short-term solution to the most urgent problem; namely, how to deal with bourgeois or other newspapers that might have used their facilities in order to incite and/or assist uprisings against the revolutionary government. In the light of this, perhaps the best solution, at least from a 'parliamentary' point of view, would have been to pass the Larin resolution and table the motion prepared by the majority of the Bolsheviks until they spelled out how it was going to be actually implemented. Otherwise, the approval of the Avanesov motion as it stood sanctioned the establishment of a government monopoly over the means of communication without doing anything concrete to implement what remained a paper commitment to an authentic democratization of the press. In any case, it remains an open question what practical difference it would have made for the CEC of the soviets to have approved a different kind of resolution.

The full implications of the press debate in the CEC of the soviets and of the early measures decreed by the government were not immediately evident. First of all, during the period between the October Revolution and the beginning of the Civil War, censorship was first established, then abolished, and then reestablished. In any case, the repression of newspapers varied from place to place; for example, after the central government moved to Moscow in March 1918, the suppression of the anti-Bolshevik press softened in Petrograd.[27] This type of repression also varied from time to time; for example, during the process of negotiation to form an all-socialist coalition government in 1917, and from February to March of 1918, the non-Bolshevik socialist press was allowed considerable freedom.[28] Furthermore, according to E. H. Carr, the Constitutional Democrat (Kadet) newspaper *Svoboda Rossii* was still being published in Moscow in the Summer of 1918,[29] and Leonard Schapiro has noted how, until the middle of 1918, there existed an extensive Menshevik party press.[30] Some measures, such as the ban on private advertising, were, as we saw above, originally decreed in late 1917. Yet, the ban was abolished shortly afterward. In any case, this issue became totally moot after the government seized almost all of private industry during the period of War Communism.[31] However, even before the decree banning private advertisements had been abolished, there was a great deal of resistance to its implementation. Many local soviets had refused to carry it out, and the non-Bolshevik socialist press, which had usually not carried advertisements, started to do so as a gesture of solidarity with the bourgeois newspapers. Ironically, advertisements had even then ceased to be important as a result of the serious economic crisis facing the country.[32]

In fact, the struggle between the Left SR–Right Bolsheviks and the Bolshevik majority on the issue of press freedom did not come to an end with the defeat of the former in the soviet CEC debate. On 18 December 1917, Left SR leader I. Z. Steinberg, now acting as People's Commissar of Justice, inaugurated the Revolutionary Tribunals of the Press. Clearly following the spirit of Larin's defeated motion, Steinberg's decree allowed these tribunals to penalize offending newspapers, not persons.[33] But a little more than a month later (28 January 1918), the Council of People's Commissars changed the letter and spirit of Steinberg's decree by also empowering the tribunals to sentence offending journalists to prison, banishment to remote areas, deportation from the Russian Republic, and deprivation of political rights.[34] Significantly, while Steinberg had intended to punish only those who printed factual falsehoods, the new regulations were aimed against those who printed 'anti-Soviet material,' a much broader and vaguer category.

Some of the cases adjudicated by the Revolutionary Press Tribunals under the Sovnarkom's instructions are instructive. One newspaper, *Novyi vechernyi chas* (New Evening Times), was shut down because it was accused of frightening the people by suggesting the possibility of a Japanese intervention.[35] Yet, at the same time, it was possible in those days for a newspapers to win a case against the government. This happened in Petrograd on 18 April 1918, when a Revolutionary Tribunal there dismissed a case brought by the Cheka against the newspaper *Petrogradskoe Ekho*. Interestingly, this newspaper had accused a Cheka commissar of using his position for personal gain. As Gorky's *Novaia Zhizn'* explained, *Ekho* was then shut down and brought before the tribunal for violating the order of the Cheka prohibiting the publication of news relating to activities of that Commission not released under the signature of one of the members of the Cheka's presidium.[36] However, one particular case seems to have played an important role in sealing the fate of the Press Tribunals. This concerned the bringing to trial of Menshevik leader Martov in April 1918. On 31 March, he had accused Stalin, in the Menshevik newspaper *Vpered*, of having participated in armed hold-ups in Baku before the revolution. Stalin then accused Martov of slander. As it turned out, the Council of People's Commissars abolished the Revolutionary Tribunal of the Press less than a week after the case had begun. Since the trial did not turn out the way Stalin expected, there is reason to believe he had a hand in the suppression of this Court. Stalin's complaint was then sent on to the Moscow Revolutionary Tribunal, which was not supposed to have jurisdiction over the press. This, and the Revolutionary Tribunal's subsequent censure of Martov, only increased the volume of criticism directed against the government's handling of the matter. Eventually, the case was brought to the Bolshevik-dominated soviet Central Executive Committee (CEC). The verdict against Martov was quickly annulled, with Chairman Sverdlov refusing to allow a debate on any of the substantive and procedural issues at stake.[37]

This was not the only press case where the CEC was called upon to intervene during this period. In later years, it would have been inconceivable for the editor of *Izvestiya* to have taken the trouble to make clear that the Communist Party had no special rights to have its views endorsed in the soviets' newspaper. But this is precisely what happened when a Left SR delegate to the CEC of the soviets complained that *Izvestiya* had published the list of Bolshevik candidates for the elections to the Constituent Assembly. I. Steklov, for the editorial board of that paper, responded that *Izvestiya* was

the central organ [of the soviets] and in accordance with established convention has not printed any party lists or agitated on behalf of any party. This convention should be maintained in the future. The Bolshevik list was printed fortuitously. However, *Izvestiya* has been placed in a very difficult situation. The elections to the Constituent Assembly are due to be held in a few days, and it must tell its readers whom they should vote for. The Left SR's do not have their own list of candidates, but a joint list with the Right SR's. *Izvestiya* cannot call on people to vote for Right SR's, the most ferocious enemies of the revolution. Some way out has to be found, since one can't keep silent about the elections.[38]

Five days, later, during the Tenth Session of the CEC of the soviets meeting on 14 November 1917, this dispute was finally brought to a close when the CEC approved a resolution submitted by G. Y. Sokolnikov, a Bolshevik leader, stating that 'since the Left SR fraction, while protesting against the publication of the Bolshevik list in *Izvestiya*, did not introduce a list of its own, the CEC considers the matter closed.'[39]

The historian Marc Ferro has attributed the encroachments on press freedom, particularly during this period, to rebellious popular elements who acted in pogrom fashion to suppress the views of those they viewed as their enemies. As he put it, 'In Russia, society both at the top and the bottom had never known tolerance or practised liberty.' Thus, according to Ferro's 'cultural determinist' interpretation, which sees mass sentiments as unchangeable, the Bolshevik leadership should be held responsible for failing, 'in their anxiety to identify with the people,' to stop or restrain such popular acts, thus abandoning 'the traditional role of politicians, that of arbitrating and interceding for the popular will, and thus neutralizing it irreversibly.'[40] If we ignore for a moment its pronounced elitism, it would be foolish to deny that there is a kernel of truth to Ferro's thesis. Indeed, viewed from a democratic and revolutionary socialist vantage point in the 1980s, none of the parties supporting the October Revolution, including the Anarchists and Left SRs, could be said to have worked out fully satisfactory views on the appropriate and inappropriate limitations on press freedom in the context of a revolutionary upheaval. Moreover, there were in fact occasions when rank-and-file revolutionary workers spontaneously censored or threatened to take over newspapers that had offended or displeased them. Thus, for example, the printers of Gorky's newspaper *Novaia Zhizn'* refused to put out an edition of the paper on 12 January 1918. On another occasion, workers at the Cannon Department of the Putilov Factory threatened to shut down and stop the sale of the same newspaper when it criticized a demonstration in support of the ceasefire and the beginning of the Brest-Litovsk negotiations.[41]

However, I believe that Ferro's analysis is based on one more fatally flawed assumption. While it is certainly true that the workers at Putilov and elsewhere may have been far from having a full civil libertarian worldview, we are not entitled to assume that these workers shared a worldview *systematically and permanently hostile* to the idea of a free press. Moreover, there is a world of difference between, on the one hand, specific and sometimes even relatively isolated reactions that develop in the heat of struggle, and, on the other hand, a fully conscious support for the establishment of a systematic, institutionalized, long-term policy against press freedom. As we shall see, it was this latter type of policy that the mainstream Bolshevik leadership implemented right after the end of the Civil War.

The Civil War Period

The Civil War that began in mid-1918 considerably accelerated the process of the disappearance of press freedom. Almost all of the opposition press was shut down, especially after the Left SR uprising of 6 July 1918. Several days after this, some newspapers attempted to resume publication in the expectation that the prohibitions were not final. But this time the Cheka acted far more harshly, raiding printing shops and editorial offices and confiscating previously issued publication permits.

Yet, the government was still somewhat tentative about this new press policy, and was later occasionally willing to permit opposition newspapers to reopen for publication. This was specially true for groups and parties that coincided with the government in opposing the White counterrevolutionaries. Thus, the newspaper of the Menshevik Central Committee, *Vsegda Vpered*, resumed publication on 22 January 1919 under the editorship of Martov. This paper was so successful – it printed 100,000 copies – that after the fourth issue it came out daily. However, it was closed down again on 26 February of the same year.[42] Likewise, two different groups of Right SRs were briefly allowed to publish newspapers in 1919, and some, though not all, Anarchist periodicals continued to appear until the last ones were closed down after the Kronstadt uprising in March 1921. Lastly, a group of Left SRs under the leadership of Steinberg were permitted to publish nine issues of their periodical in 1920 and during the first five months of 1921.[43] It was thus only when the Civil War was already over that the one-party press was firmly established in revolutionary Russia. However, a few oppositional publications of a non-popular charcter were allowed to publish as late as 1922, e.g. the theoretical economic journal *Ekonomist*.[44]

From the End of the Civil War to the Interregnum

Thus, it was only after the end of the Civil War that Lenin and the Bolsheviks firmly adopted policies that moved them a considerable distance towards what later became the Stalinist totalitarian model. It is also interesting to examine how Lenin's views on freedom of the press had evolved by the time he discussed this question at some length in his letter to G. I. Miasnikov in August 1921 (i.e. several months after the end of the Civil War and the beginning of the New Economic Policy).

Gavriil I. Miasnikov, a metalworker from the Urals and a veteran Bolshevik – he had joined the party in 1906 – had by 1921 become a Left oppositionist as leader of the Workers' Group.[45] He wrote a memorandum to the Central

Committee of the Communist Party in May 1921 calling for such sweeping changes as the transfer of industrial administration to producers' soviets, the elimination of bureaucratic forms of organization, abolition of the death penalty, and, most striking of all, unrestricted freedom of the press for everyone 'from monarchists to anarchists inclusive.'[46] In Miasnikov's view, freedom of the press was the only effective means of checking power abuses and of maintaining an honest and efficient party. He maintained that no government could avoid error and corruption when critical voices were silenced.[47] Miasnikov's criticisms helped to create a revolt within the Urals party organization and he refused to abide by an order of the Perm' Provincial Party Committee to cease propagating his views at party meetings. He even published a pamphlet entitled 'Vexed Questions' in which he repeated the demands of the memorandum, especially in relation to freedom of criticism, and maintained that 'the Soviet government should maintain detractors at its own expense, as did the Roman emperors.'[48]

Miasnikov was a party member of some importance. Besides being an Old Bolshevik, he had also played a role in the liquidation of the imperial family, having been personally responsible for the killing of Grand Duke Michael, the Tsar's younger brother. He then became chairman of the Perm' Provincial Party Committee, where he was known to have a substantial working-class following. All of this caused Lenin to take him seriously. He first sent Miasnikov a brief note inviting him to the Kremlin for a talk. Then he wrote him a long letter.[49] Lenin's letter,[50] precisely because it was a detailed argument written in a friendly and calm manner, constitutes a very useful statement of his post-Civil War thinking on freedom of the press and, by implication, on other democratic questions. Let us look closely at the elements of Lenin's arguments in 1921:

1   A relativization of freedom of the press: 'every Marxist and every worker who ponders over the four years' experience of our revolution will say, "Let's look into this – *what sort* of freedom of the press? What *for*? For *which class*? We do not believe in 'absolutes'. We laugh at 'pure democracy'."'[51]

2   A historicization of freedom of the press: 'The "freedom of the press" slogan became a great world slogan at the close of the Middle Ages and remained so up to the nineteenth century. Why? because it expressed the ideas of the progressive bourgeoisie, i.e., its struggles against kings and priests, feudal lords and landowners.'[52]

3   A reiteration of the nature of what freedom of the press means 'wherever there are capitalists: it means to buy up newspapers and writers, to bribe, buy, and fake "public opinion" for the benefit of the bourgeoisie.'[53]

4   The 'falling dominoes' argument. Freedom of the press means freedom of political organization, 'for the press is the core and foundation of political organization.'[54] This, in turn, means to facilitate the enemy's task; it means helping the class enemy.

5   The enemy is now the international bourgeoisie – little mention is made of

whatever remains of the domestic bourgeoisie. Soviet Russia is surrounded 'by the bourgeois "enemies" of the whole world,' and they are stronger than the soviets are. Freedom of the press means in practice that the international bourgeoisie will buy up hundreds and thousands of Kadet, Socialist Revolutionary, and Menshevik writers, newspapers, and centers of political organization.[55] While it is certainly true that the international bourgeoisie were trying to overthrow the Soviet regime, it is worth noting that Lenin did not even bother to consider how his 1917 proposals on distributing press facilities to the population at large might have been an effective antidote to the international bourgeoisie buying up newspapers and writers.

6 Miasnikov should work from the inside; e.g. he should denounce abuses through the Central Control Commission of the party, or through the party press, *Pravda*.[56]

7 Appointments to important positions should be used as an instrument of reform; as Lenin put it, 'promote non-Party people, let non-Party people verify the work of party members.'[57]

In this document, Lenin's shift in position since his 1917 press proposals was remarkable. In 1917 he had also underscored the true meaning of freedom of the press under capitalism. But, at the same time, he had then in effect counterposed a popular version of freedom of the press in which the means of communication would become far more accessible to the mass of the population. Those proposals were now totally forgotten – all the more remarkable since this long letter was written in order to win over a libertarian revolutionary to Lenin's side. One also looks in vain here for even a slight suggestion on Lenin's part that his undemocratic views on the press, including the omission of his 1917 proposals, were a *conjunctural* response to the crises facing Soviet Russia at the time. This, plus Lenin's historicization and relativization of freedom of the press, brought his 1921 position dangerously close to what eventually became the standard Stalinist party line on this question.

Much of the tone and content of Lenin's 1921 arguments were cut from the same cloth as Trotsky's polemic against Karl Kautsky in *Terrorism and Communism* in 1920. There, Trotsky had failed to see that, even in a time of civil war, there was still a difference between ideological and other forms of struggle. Thus, Trotsky told us that

. . .we are fighting a life-and-death struggle. The Press is a weapon not of an abstract society, but of two irreconcilable, armed and contending sides. We are destroying the Press of the conter-revolution, just as we destroyed its fortified positions, its stores, its communications, and its intelligence system.[58]

Moreover, this argument ignored the sticky problem of differences *within* the revolutionary camp. No wonder then that Trotsky had earlier in the same pamphlet grossly amalgamated the various and qualitatively different types of opposition to the Bolshevik government and reduced all possible objections and criticisms to a purely military dimension:

> can it be seriously demanded that, during a civil war with the White Guards of Denikin, the publications of parties supporting Denikin should come out unhindered in Moscow and Petrograd? To propose this in the name of the 'freedom' of the Press is just the same as, in the name of open dealing, to demand the publication of military secrets.[59]

As I shall argue in greater detail below, Trotsky's and Lenin's views and actions, as exemplified by Lenin's letter to Miasnikov, necessarily led to an elite proclaiming itself as a vanguard with the correct workers' point of view. This elite would then have to forcefully suppress diverging views within the working class, let alone the rest of the population. And this is also why, from the point of view of maintaining working-class power, Miasnikov was absolutely right in demanding freedom for all, 'from monarchists to anarchists inclusive.' As Miasnikov later pointed out in his response to Lenin's lengthy letter:

> You say that I want freedom of the press for the bourgeoisie. On the contrary, I want freedom of the press for myself, a proletarian, a member of the party for fifteen years. . . . The trouble is that, while you raise your hand against the capitalist, you deal a blow to the worker. You know very well that for such words as I am now uttering hundreds, perhaps thousands, of workers are languishing in prison. That I myself remain at liberty is only because I am a veteran Communist, have suffered for my beliefs, and am known among the mass of the workers. Were it not for this, were I just an ordinary mechanic from the same factory, where would I be now? In a Cheka prison or, more likely made to 'escape,' just as I made Mikhail Romanov 'escape.' Once more I say: You raise your hand against the bourgeoisie, but it is I who am spitting blood, and it is we, the workers, whose jaws are being cracked.[60]

Even though Miasnikov later modified his views to demand freedom of speech for manual workers alone,[61] the inexorable logic of his earlier demand for freedom of speech for all still remained unassailable. While it was, of course, theoretically possible to limit the rights of free speech to persons who were workers (but how about former bourgeois, or their children, who had become workers in order to survive – should a rule of descent have been established for them?) or peasants, that would hardly have resolved the issue from the government's point of view. The problem for the government was not as much *who* was saying certain things, as *what* was being said and *how*. The fact remains that real and/or putative bourgeois ideas would have continued to be expressed by the non-bourgeois, and thus the government's ideological monopoly would have been seriously challenged anyway.

In reality, the main issue in 1921 was not, as Lenin would have had us believe in his letter to Miasnikov, what the international bourgeoisie might or might not have done in order to subsidize a hostile opposition press in Russia. As we shall see later, the main issue was that of a divided Communist Party that had just agreed to ban factions. Moreover, this party was desperately trying to hold on to power without a social base outside of its own bureaucracy, or much popular support. In addition, the government had just confronted the Krondstadt uprising in March of 1921 and the workers' strikes in Petrograd and Moscow – in the midst of a serious economic crisis. In order to hold on to its monopoly of power, that party could not tolerate an open political life in *any* class or stratum of the population. Needless to say, the decrease in the size and considerable dispersal of the working class only exacerbated the isolation and lack of popularity of the government. What Lenin could and should have done regarding the press is, of course, part and parcel of the overall political strategy he could and should have pursued at that time. I shall discuss this general question in some detail in a later chapter.

Finally, and this is indeed a supreme irony, it was not the international bourgeoisie, but Lenin's Soviet government itself, that from 1921 to 1922 partially broke the state's press monopoly and allowed the opening of private publishing houses and printing presses. By 1921, the government had acquired control of all material printing assets; but by 1922 there were already more than 200 private presses in Moscow alone.[62] A significant number of these enterprises were engaged in the production of 'gutter literature' appealing especially to wayward youth.[63] Similarly, in the years before 1921, as we saw above, commercial advertisements had virtually disappeared. But under NEP, in 1922 and 1923, advertisements in the major national newspapers took up from one-eighth to one-quarter of their space, although it is worth noting that much of this was advertising for state-owned enterprises, theaters, and cinemas in the big cities. At the same time, little advertising of any kind was available to newspapers in small towns and villages.[64] Furthermore, Lenin supported the creation of the journal *Red Virgin Soil*, the task of which was to bring together different literary trends from proletarian to bourgeois.[65] There was in fact at this time a veritable flourishing of non-party literary fellow-traveling.[66] Of course, there was a catch: none of these works and publications were allowed to politically challenge or oppose the Communist Party. This proves my earlier contention that the issue was not who published, but what was being published and how. In the last analysis, that was Lenin's real agenda in his reply to Miasnikov, notwithstanding all of his expressed concern for capitalist freedom of the press and snide remarks about 'pure democracy' to cover up what was in fact a defense of no democracy at all.

Although the opposition press was completely eliminated while Lenin was still functioning as the head of the revolutionary government, the government press had yet to become completely monolithic. This only came to pass years later with the full consolidation of Stalinism. However, the process of decline of press pluralism continued to develop in the Interregnum; that is, the period after Lenin's retirement in 1923 and before the beginning of the process of the consolidation of Stalin's power in 1925–6. The historian Jeffrey Brooks has pointed out how by 1924, although some remaining pre-revolutionary editors were still daring to include much information about government and politics in their papers, the main Soviet newspapers continued to be affected by a process where boredom, lack of criticism, and reluctance to unmask abuses were increasingly predominant. He has also shown that, while real people had continued to send letters and reports to the newspapers during the 1920s, the quality of these communications declined and increasingly showed the hall-marks of letters being sent to a boss. Brooks also cites an article written by Trotsky, and published in *Pravda* on 1 July 1923, in which the revolutionary leader complained about the general unwillingness of journalists to write about difficulties and the seamy side of life. Trotsky pointed out that if the Soviet press turned its back on popular curiosity, the people would get their informa-tion from less reliable sources on the street.[67]

The Establishment of Book Censorship

The Bolshevik government was, from the very beginning, less inclined to control book publishing than the press. In January 1918, for example, while its newspapers were being closed down, the Kadet Party was still able to print the full party program.[68] This governmental tendency prevailed through the early 1920s. At that time there continued to be a greater degree of openness in the publication of books, under Lunacharsky's ultimate authority, than in the much more restricted press. For instance, the works of authors such as Berdaev and Bulgakov were still printed in this period. Anti-Marxist philosophical, artistic, and socio-economic approaches could still be openly published as late as 1922 as long as these did not, like the press, concern themselves with immediate political issues.[69]

On the other hand, a quite disturbing process had begun to take place with a serious impact on the less educated popular majority; namely, the purging of popular libraries, an activity in which Lenin's wife, Nadezhda Krupskaya, played an important role. While it is quite clear that there were economic and pedagogical considerations at stake in the adoption of the policies concerning popular libraries, there can be no doubt that political censorship played a central role in these decisions. Krupskaya defended these purges from a storm of criticism abroad, including the protest of Maxim Gorky, who on this account even considered renouncing his Russian citizenship. Krupskaya argued her case in an article she wrote for *Pravda* on 9 April 1924 entitled 'Defects of the Bureau of Political Education.' Specifically. Krupskaya claimed in this article that 'the unfortunate list of books' to be purged was added to a 1923 decree 'without my knowledge.' At the same time, she made clear her preference for authors such as Tolstoi and Kropotkin and maintained that to make Plato, Kant, and Mach available to the masses was not harmful, but senseless, since 'a man of the masses will not read Kant.' While Krupskaya was of course correct in supposing that these were not authors with a mass appeal, it apparently did not occur to her that *some* self-taught peasants or workers might indeed be interested in reading those types of books. Thus, regardless of her conscious intentions, her policy had the elitist effect of depriving workers and peasants of access to authors and books that would be available to students and intellectuals. Unfortunately, this does not seem to have been an isolated or idiosyncratic attitude on the part of Krupskaya. Thus, for example, in September 1919, the editors of the Moscow journal for party propagandists seem to have anticipated the later institutionalization of Marxist manuals when they claimed that,

> we have no time at present to work out a 'complete world view' out of the inexhaustible treasure house of Marxism. We must receive precisely that ration of learning that is necessary for today's struggle, and no more. The worker, because of the lack of supplies, receives from the state a portion of bread not in those quantities that a man in general needs, but as much as he requires so that he can work and not collapse from exhaustion; it is the same with Marxism: it must be released in such doses as are necessary so that each of us can be a fighting political force. Anything more, and academism begins, knowledge for the sake of knowledge, refusal of practical work with the excuse of deepening one's understanding of the world.'[70]

Moreover, in the same article, Krupskaya also made it quite clear that the 1923 decree had not been tough enough on religious books. This, in spite of the fact that, as I point out in chapter 5 on socialist legality, the 1918 Soviet Constitution granted every citizen 'the *right* of religious and anti-religious propaganda.' Moreover, she asserted that other books had to be removed 'to protect the interests' of the mass reader and shield him from the 'destructive' influence of undesirable works. In this context, she explicitly mentioned 'books of pro-Black Hundred slant, monarchist rubbish, patriotic literature of the war period' and 'agitation literature written on current issues in the year 1917 in favor of a constituent assembly.' This latter item would have obviously included the propaganda published by her own Bolshevik Party, which at the time supported the convening of the Assembly. Furthermore, Krupskaya's article registered no other objections to the rest of the 1923 decree, which gave instructions to remove books under the following additional categories: Tsarist books used to spread literacy among the people, books and pamphlets by other socialist parties dealing with the war and the October Revolution, legal documents of the Tsarist and Provisional governments, and decrees of the soviets issued before the Bolsheviks had gained control. The most brazen attempt to rewrite the *government's own history* was contained in the order to remove the agitational and reference literature of the soviets for the years 1918, 1919, and 1920 on matters that since then the Soviet power had decided differently (e.g. the land question, tax system, free trade, policies of food distribution, etc.). This was, of course, the same type of prohibition as that regarding the 1917 propaganda in favor of the Constituent Assembly.

The detailed instructions regarding philosophical and religious books were a little more complicated. There were to be no philosophical books in the smaller, mass libraries but all philosophical books, including those by non-Marxists, would be available in the larger libraries. The smaller libraries for the masses would contain only anti-ecclesiastical and anti-religious literature, except for such fundamental texts as the Gospels, the Bible, and the Koran, perhaps because these were regarded as great literature. In all cases, provisions were made for two samples of those books regarded as harmful to be sent to central libraries for restricted use. Incidentally, these censorship policies did not completely escape censure within Russia itself, as witness the strong criticism and ridicule expressed in an article published in *Izvestiya* by a G. Ryklin writing under the pen-name of Amok.[71]

The newly established censorship, directed primarily at the cultural products consumed by the popular masses, in effect created a two-track cultural policy during the 1920s, i.e. one policy for the masses and another policy for the intelligentsia. This appears to have been the case since, during the NEP period, as the contemporary left-wing Soviet dissident Boris Kagarlitsky has aptly summed it up,

> there was . . . also a certain revival of the Russian intelligentsia: a cultural upsurge. Nobody can deny that for Russian literature, painting, art criticism and spiritual life generally, the twenties were an extremely fruitful epoch. Under the NEP a neutral position towards Bolshevism and the revolution was quite tenable: it entailed no personal catastrophes or inevitable repressions, at any rate so long as only the sphere of culture and science was affected.[72]

One can parenthetically note that this cultural model could conceivably become very attractive as a possible 'solution' to the dilemmas that Mikhail Gorbachev is likely to face in the 1990s. In other words, providing enough freedom to stimulate scientific, technical, and organizational innovation among the intelligentsia while at the same time attempting to prevent mass popular unrest and turmoil.

Implications and Conclusions

The Left has on the whole failed to develop a conception of freedom of the press that is neither liberal capitalist, nor authoritarian, nor Stalinist in inspiration.

By the liberal capitalist conception I am referring to the view that generally opposes the state's monopoly of or interference with the dissemination of news and views wherever this occurs. Those holding this view would also oppose actions of private or non-state groups (e.g. political parties) that would interfere with or impede press freedom.

However, while liberal capitalism is usually forthright in its opposition to state control or other types of interference with freedom of communication, it has no answers to, and is structurally incapable of posing an alternative to, the problems created by capitalist control of the media. In other words, liberal capitalism offers no real solution to the concentration of the means of communication, an extreme example of which is Rupert Murdoch, one man who controls a significant part of the media in four countries – the USA, Britain, Canada, and Australia. The problem of capitalist press power that is not subject to democratic accountability is further aggravated by the existence of international news agencies such as the Associated Press, United Press International, Reuters, and others, which are indispensable to those smaller newspapers and electronic media that can afford only a few, if any, reporters of their own. Besides, these agencies are a principal source of foreign news for hundreds of newspapers and radio and television stations in the Third World, in which case the question of capitalist control of the means of communication is compounded by its foreign character. In a more fundamental sense, and going beyond the issues of concentration and monopoly, liberal capitalism does not and cannot establish institutional changes through which freedom of the press and of other means of communication may become an effective reality for the majority of the population and not simply for a monied elite.

The logic underlying the US government regulations that have permitted a token degree of popular access to radio and television (through, for example, the right of editorial reply) clearly underlines the capitalist boundary lines that limit the extension of democracy in the means of communication. As Thomas I. Emerson has pointed out:

> There can be no doubt that the scarcity of facilities is a consideration in the application of the First Amendment to radio and television regulation. The essential point is that the scarcity is physical, rather than economic. This condition takes radio and television out of the traditional laissez-faire system that is the basis of the First Amendment's application to the press, publishing, and other types of media. . . . In radio and television, however, the open market condition brings only physical chaos. Not everybody can be accommodated. The government, therefore, has a different function, and that function is to bring initial order into the system by regulating access to limited facilities.[73]

Therefore, American capitalist society recognizes *natural* limitations, i.e. the shortage of airwaves, and that it is legitimate to do something about that – although what it does still leaves capitalist control of radio and television essentially unaltered. However, socio-economic limitations, i.e. the great deal of capital that it takes to establish a newspaper or radio or television station, are simply ignored.

Since the 1960s, a number of minor press reforms, influenced by the existing rules of token access in radio and television, have been proposed in the USA. Nevertheless, these reforms have been implemented only to the very limited degree that the press owners have *volunteered* to put them into practice. These proposed changes include the following: newspapers should be required to accept paid non-commercial advertisements on the same basis as commercial advertisements, to grant roughly equal space for reply to any person who has been libeled or personally attacked, and to make space available for issues and views that they do not normally present, and they should be compelled to observe a 'fairness doctrine' similar to that employed in radio and television. According to this last proposals, newspapers would provide on their own initiative for coverage of all 'newsworthy' subject matter and for the expression of all 'responsible' viewpoints.[74] Even if all these changes were carried out in the event of a liberal resurgence in the USA, the editors appointed by the owners and publishers would still, under such a reformed press system, retain overwhelming editorial control. The news columns, the decision as to which story goes on what page, and, of course, the editorials would again remain a matter of the judgment of the paper's owners and publisher, or their appointees.[75]

On the other hand, neo-conservatives (including the Reaganite Federal Communications Commission) have in the 1980s challenged the scarcity of airwaves argument by pointing to the decline in the number of daily newspapers – 1,650 as of mid-1987, most of them in one-paper towns, as compared to 10,000 radio stations, 1,800 television stations, and the 74 per cent of those households with cable that can get more than 10 signals. Needless to add, these neo-conservatives do not therefore conclude that there should be an extension of the 'fairness doctrine' to the greatly reduced number of newspapers. Instead, they propose the complete repeal of the existing 'fairness doctrine' for the airwaves on the grounds that there is more availability of radio, cable, and regular television than of newspapers! In accordance with these views, former President Reagan vetoed congressional attempts to make the 'fairness doctrine' the law of the land, thus taking this doctrine out of the discretionary powers of the FCC.[76] Therefore, neo-conservatives, even more than liberal reformers, accept and do not question the basic reality that, in capitalist society, freedom of access to the mass media is for those who have the capital to buy themselves a newspaper, a radio station, or a regular or cable television station.

Lastly, traditional liberalism is unable to understand the revolutionary takeovers of media organs when these takeovers are aimed not at establishing a single monolithic one-party media but, in fact, at providing access for hitherto unrepresented groups. The workers' takeover of the newspaper *La Republica* during the revolutionary upheavals in Portugal in the mid 1970s is a case in point.[77] Similarly, traditional liberalism also has a great deal of difficulty approaching civil war situations, where, as I will argue at some length in chapter 4 on repression, temporary and military defense-related restrictions on freedom of the press may well be warranted.

As might be expected, the Stalinist conception rejects liberal views on freedom of the press. While Stalinism correctly points out that, under capitalism, freedom of the press is primarily designed to benefit those who have the money to invest in the heavily capitalized means of communication, when in power Stalinists generally establish media regimes that are even less democratic than those under capitalism. Instead of a capitalist media oligopoly, the rulers of the so-called socialist countries establish a media monopoly controlled by the Communist Party. This party, as the self-appointed, exclusive, and perpetual spokesperson for the working class, operates the mass media organs with a crude form of news management and society-wide censorship, basing itself on the elitist notion that the party knows best what the people are ready to see and hear. Stalinism does not believe in an open ideological combat against the bourgeoisie and other tendencies in the working class, and does not expect to prevail on the basis of greater truthfulness and persuasive appeal to the interests and the potential, if not actual rationality, of the masses. No, Stalinism, which even in opposition was pessimistic and elitist about the masses, additionally developed, when in power, distinctive class interests that led it to use police–administrative methods to silence rather than debate opponents.

Some of the key arguments used by Stalinists to defend their conceptions concerning freedom of the press often draw on several of Lenin's positions and policies, which I have previously described, particularly those adopted after the Civil War. However, as we have seen above, given a state-controlled press, Lenin's opposition to 'capitalist freedom of the press' was in fact an opposition to the dissemination of bourgeois *views*, real or putative. In the light of this, Lenin's determination to eliminate those views through administrative and police methods, rather than through strictly ideological and other means of persuasion, was in fact quite incompatible with working-class and/or popular rule, as was Lenin's defense of a so-called freedom of the press for workers and peasants alone. Instead, his post-Civil War views and actions on freedom of the press and other democratic questions *inevitably and necessarily* led to a thoroughly elitist form of government.

In the first place, there is no such thing as homogeneous classes and only one type of political consciousness and ideology per class. As Leon Trotsky himself succinctly put it at a very different stage of his political life (the 1930s):

> In reality classes are heterogeneous; they are torn by inner antagonisms, and arrive at the solution of common problems no otherwise than through an inner struggle of tendencies, groups and parties. It is possible, with certain qualifications, to concede that 'a party is part of a class.' But since a class has many 'parts' – some look forward and some back – one and the same class may create several parties. For the same reason one party may rest upon parts of different classes. An example of only one party corresponding to one class is not to be found in the whole course of political history – provided, of course, you do not take the police appearance for the reality.[78]

It is also important to point out that a heterogeneity of views will most likely exist within one stratum within a given class, owing to unavoidable group and individual differencs of opinion. These differences exist, in abundance, in even the most revolutionary of parties: In fact, they may involve grave strategic and tactical disagreements (e.g. Kamenev and Zinoviev vs. Lenin on the eve of the October Revolution). Or, there may even be conflicts within parties that, strictly speaking, are not political but may nonetheless have serious political consequences. This is the case, for instance, with conflicting ego needs (e.g. Trotsky's arrogance and abrasiveness alienating potential allies in his struggle against Stalin).

Second, real bourgeois ideological influences in the working class will persist for a long time after the revolutionary overthrow of the old society. The degree and extent to which these will survive will depend, in part, on actual and objective changes in the structure of society and, in part, on the course followed by ideological and political struggles. To attempt to shortcircuit such a process through the use of police and administrative methods would lead, again, to actions incompatible with popular rule. As a relatively recent critique of Stalinism has pointed out:

> If one says that only parties and organizations [or newspapers] that have no bourgeois (or petty bourgeois?) program or ideology, or are not 'engaged in anti-socialist or antisoviet propaganda and/or agitation' are to be legalized, how is one to determine the dividing line? Will parties with a majority of working-class members but with a bourgeois ideology be forbidden? How can such a position be reconciled with free elections for workers' councils? What is the dividing line between 'bourgeois program' and 'reformist ideology'? Must reformist parties then be forbidden as well? Will the Social Democracy be suppressed?[79]

In contrast to the liberal point of view, I submit that an authentically socialist and democratic revolution cannot allow the media to be monopolized by the rich or the few. All 'industrial' media that entail the investment and expenditure of significant material and human resources must be socialized. All 'cottage industry' media such as personal computers, duplicating and mimeograph machines, and other relatively, inexpensive equipment used to print leaflets and newsletters, make home videos, etc. can be left alone to be sold or traded as individuals and small groups may wish. But, contrary to the Stalinists, I also contend that the valuable socialized resources must immediately be placed at the disposal of political parties, workers' and community councils, and other organizations, in rough proportion to their relative numbers in the population. Special care would have to be taken to ensure that minorities got a full hearing and that social and political innovators are encouraged to present their views and proposals; otherwise, the media would be frozen in the mold of yesterday's issues and majorities.

Furthermore, in the aftermath of a successful revolution, workers' control of a society's means of communication cannot be established on the basis of control by only those who work in the media. It is rather obvious that the views expressed in the printed and electronic press should not be limited to the views held by such people as journalists and print workers. A post-revolutionary media should be very diverse, and communication workers would, to a considerable degree, have to act as facilitators, technical advisers, and implementers of the views and policies of a wide variety of groups. This would be especially necessary in the case of non-party media; for example, helping poorer communities, workplaces, etc. to use not only newspapers but more modern means of communication such as cable television and computer-based media.

The post-revolutionary media would likely be dominated by a variety of socialist views, but socialist hegemony should not be based on the use of police–administrative methods to prevent any ideological or political challenge to that hegemony. Once the media, and their firms and fortunes, have been taken away from the capitalists and socialized, why should socialists be afraid of former bourgeois cranking mimeo machines with the sweat of their own brows, or even getting access to the 5 percent of the mass media that they might be entitled to by virtue of the size of their own group in proportion to the total population? Moreover, the question of the rights of the defeated bourgeoisie would be, in all likelihood, a less serious matter than the strong temptation to use censorship as a 'corrective mechanism' for the *mass* of the population in the post-revolutionary society.

In sum, socialist points of view would have to prevail on their own merits. Needless to add, the content and presentation of these views would have to change in accordance with the rise in the cultural level of the population. Besides, highly conscious socialist journalism, even in the strictly party media, cannot be created by decrees externally imposed from above. As Engels wrote to August Bebel in 1892:

> it is a hard fate to be dependent – even on the workers' party. But aside from the financial aspect, to be the editor of a paper belonging to the party is a thankless job for anyone who possesses initiative. Marx and I were always in agreement that we would never occupy such a post, and that we would publish only a paper that was financially independent, even of the party. Your 'nationalization' of the party press can have great disadvantages if it is taken too far. It is absolutely necessary for you to have a party press that is quite independent of the party leadership and even of the party congress, i.e., one that is free *within the framework of the program* and the tactics agreed upon to come out against any particular steps taken by the party and also, as long as it does not overstep the bounds of party ethics, to criticize the program and tactics themselves. You, as the leadership, should encourage or even, if necessary, create such a press. Your moral influence will be much greater than if it were to arise independently against your will.[80]

Of course, a post-revolutionary society would have to acknowledge those minimal limitations on freedom of the press that are necessary to preserve other rights, such as the right to a fair trial and the individual's right to privacy. Furthermore, as I shall argue at greater length in chapter 4 on repression, a war situation may warrant the temporary suppression of those opposition materials the publication or transmission of which would create a 'clear and present danger' to the revolutionary regime. These may include, for example, the dissemination of information of military value to the counterrevolution, or inciting and helping to organize people to engage in violent actions against the government.

I take it for granted that it is impossible to anticipate every conceivable incident that may or may not justify media censorship, and that there will always be a 'gray area' of hard-to-decide cases, e.g. rumors spread by the opposition media causing panic buying or a run on the banks. Yet, it is still possible to establish a firm policy preventing the use of civil war conditions as an excuse for a general, permanent, and indiscriminate suppression of press freedom. More specifically, it should be possible to prevent the use of censorship as a tool to combat what the government may perceive or define as flagging enthusiasm and ideological and political 'confusion' among the masses in the face of material hardships. In all likelihood, these are real problems that will need to be confronted by the revolutionary leadership. But this leadership will need to do so through political means rather than police and administrative measures, if the democratic essence of the revolution is to be preserved.

In any case, as I will argue at greater length in chapter 5 on socialist legality, these limitations on press and media freedoms should be decided by courts directly responsible to the people who democratically elected them, and not by the party or parties in power. Furthermore, as soon as this civil war period is over, it should no longer be necessary to control or censor the opposition media, since whatever the opposition might say can and should be adequately dealt with in the political and ideological realm rather than through police–administrative action.

4

Repression

It is highly unlikely that violence and/or repression can be eliminated from the struggle for social change, let alone from revolution. We also know only too well that revolutions are necessarily dramatic and violent processes that elicit extreme emotions such as intense hatred, desperation, and desire for vengeance. Thus, it could be argued that it is fruitless, or even irrelevant, to analyze such events rationally in the hope of developing some general political criteria or guidelines for the benefit of democratic revolutionaries. I would argue, on the contrary, that the unavoidably bloody reality of revolutions does not at all diminish the need for rational policies on the part of the politically conscious revolutionaries. If anything, it only increases their responsibility for attempting, insofar as feasible, to direct the revolutionary rage against rationally and selectively chosen targets.

Thus, for example, given the virtual certainty of violent resistance to the revolutionary process, Lenin was undoubtedly right when he exclaimed, shortly after the seizure of power in November 1917: 'How can one make a revolution without firing squads?'[1] Yet, on further examination, one finds that this statement by Lenin can be interpreted in at least two different ways. It is one thing to acknowledge the fact that revolutions will usually require shootings, and that consequently revolutionaries should train and be ready for the worst, rather than count on the best, post-revolutionary situation. It is an altogether different matter for this statement to stand for the defense of 'toughness' or 'hardness' as such. In this latter instance, the desirability of these qualities is no longer limited to situationally justified actions, but is transformed instead into *prescribed* life-long political character traits *intrinsically* signifying revolutionary dedication and authenticity.

At a minimum, revolution, or the struggle for significant social change, will as a rule be accompanied by one degree or another of what Hal Draper has called 'coercion through intimidation,'[2] of which shooting is of course an extreme example. Beyond this, in any concrete revolutionary situation one must ask the following questions: are violence and repression being used *defensively*, i.e. only as limited last-resort actions, or are they being used *instead* of political and ideological struggle, and to demonstrate the merits of 'toughness' and 'hardness'? Furthermore, are measures being implemented that can be rationally justified in the light of the specific *situation* confronting the revolutionaries; and is there a conscious effort to maintain the greatest possible consistency between the stated and developing goals of the revolution and the methods it uses? The answers to questions such as these may indeed show that the specific ways in which 'coercion through intimidation' is practiced are far from constituting obvious and unproblematical responses to specific situations. Furthermore, these responses will likely reveal particular sets of political values and assumptions on the part of the revolutionary leaders. Concretely, we are dealing here with political belief systems that shape what are considered to be the appropriate actions against real or supposed dangers, and the manner in which those actions are justified.

Repression from the October Revolution to the Civil War

On 4 November of 1917, V. I. Lenin declared that 'we have not resorted, and I hope will not resort, to the terrorism of the French revolutionaries who guillotined unarmed men. I hope we shall not resort to it, *because we have strength on our side.*'[3] Indeed, the record of overall repression in this initial post-revolutionary period parallels the situation with regard to freedom of the press, i.e. a state of arbitrary, inconsistent, and yet comparatively mild repressive activities. Lenin once confronted Gorky's criticisms of governmental abuses and challenged him to present alternative criteria for determining which blows delivered by a revolutionary government were necessary and which blows were superfluous. While Lenin may have indeed spotted a weakness in Gorky's frequent use of absolutist arguments, it does seem that the Bolshevik leader did not develop consistent criteria of his own in these matters.[4]

In fact, Lenin had shown a very unproblematic attitude towards the application of capital punishment even before the onset of the Red Terror and the Civil War. Thus, in late December 1917, he suggested, as one of the possible ways of dealing with 'the rich, the rogues and the idlers,' that 'one out of every ten idlers will be shot on the spot.'[5] Moreover, the Cheka (the All-Russian Extraordinary Commission for Combatting Counterrevolution and Sabotage), founded in December 1917, had become a most disturbing institution, since it soon acquired *uncontrolled* repressive powers.[6] The Cheka's omnipotence was neither accidental, nor merely a situational response to objective difficulties confronting the revolutionary government. In general, Lenin, notwithstanding his statement quoted above, tended to be uncritical of the Jacobin political tradition and of the Jacobin terror in particular (see the discussion of this issue in chapter 6). Furthermore, in what may have been an overreaction to the extreme moral absolutism of other political tendencies (e.g. populism), mainstream Bolshevism seems to have taken an almost perverse pride in an equally extreme moral relativism. This extreme relativism was accompanied by an insensitivity to the question of whether particular means were consistent with, rather than subversive of, declared revolutionary ends. Mainstream Bolshevik thought was, if anything, even more resistant to the establishment of general criteria, rather than purely ad hoc decisions, concerning what were permissible and impermissible means of repression.

The Civil War Period: the Red Terror as Surplus Repression

The massacre of the whites was a tragedy: not for the whites. For these old slave-owners, those who burnt a little powder in the arse of a Negro, who buried him alive for insects to eat, who were well treated by Toussaint, and who, as soon as they got the chance, began their old cruelties again; for these there is no need to waste one tear or one drop of ink. The tragedy was for the blacks and the Mulattoes. It was not policy but revenge, and revenge has no place in politics. The whites were no longer to be feared, and such purposeless massacres degrade and brutalise a population, especially one which was just beginning as a nation and had had so bitter a past.

C. L. R. James[7]

Has not the moment come to declare that the day of the glorious year of 1918 when the Central Committee of the party decided to permit the Extraordinary Commission to apply the death penalty *on the basis of secret procedure, without hearing the accused who could not defend themselves, is a black day?* That day the Central Committee was in a position to restore or not restore an Inquisitorial procedure forgotten by European civilization. In any case, it committed a mistake. It did not necessarily behoove a victorious socialist party to commit that mistake. The revolution could have defended itself better without that.

Victor Serge[8]

As Hal Draper has indicated, Marx and Engels seemed to have thought of 'revolutionary terror' in at least two clearly different ways. First, they thought of it in the positive general sense equivalent to what I referred to above as 'coercion through intimidation' – a necessary feature of all truly revolutionary upheavals. But Marx and Engels also thought of 'revolutionary terror' in another sense. In this second negative sense, Robespierre, for example, is seen by Engels as having used terror as a 'means of self-preservation' in his struggle against Danton and the Commune, 'and thereby [the Terror] became absurd. . .'[9] Likewise, on another occasion, Engels viewed the 'Reign of Terror' in this same negative sense as

the reign of people who are themselves terrorstricken. *La terreur* is in large part useless cruelties committed by people who are in fear themselves, for their own self-assurance. I am convinced that the blame for the Reign of Terror in '93 lies almost exclusively on the shoulders of the terribly frightened bourgeois behaving like patriots, and on the little philistines who are shitting in their pants, and on the lumpen-mob making a profit out of the *terreur*.[10]

These negative views of the Jacobin terror can be fully understood only if we realize that Marx and Engels were critical of Robespierre for a variety of reasons, not the least being that, as Marx put it: '[For Robespierre] The principle of politics is the *will*. The more onesided . . . the *political* mind is, the more does it believe in the *omnipotence* of the will, the more is it blind to the *natural* and spiritual *limits* of the will, and the more incapable is it therefore of discovering the source of social ills.'[11]

But what about the Red Terror in the Russian Revolution? This began in the Summer of 1918, shortly after the onset of the Civil War. It has usually been claimed that the Red Terror was sparked by several assassination attempts on Bolshevik leaders, some of them successful, and particularly by the attempt on Lenin's life on 30 August. Nevertheless, at least one historian has argued that the Terror actually began on 9 August and was primarily a response to peasant risings against the revolutionary regime.[12] Be that as it may, what exactly did the Red Terror mean? To my knowledge neither Lenin nor anybody else has provided a textbook definition of the term. However, the historian William Henry Chamberlin is very misleading when he implied that the Red Terror was simply a matter of revolutionary survival in the midst of chaos, i.e. getting 'orders obeyed . . . by flourishing a revolver,' since 'the national morale was completely shattered by the World War. No one, except under extreme compulsion, was willing to perform any state obligation.'[13]

If this is all there had been to the Red Terror, it would have been purely instrumental and consequently rather limited in scope. Chamberlin's Red Terror would also have been understandable, if not necessarily justified, as a fundamentally desperate, non-ideological response to a very difficult objective situation. However, I would like to argue that there was a lot more to the Red Terror than this. The Red Terror was also an instrument to impose what had become, in the course of the Civil War, the government's dogmatic and *willful* (in the Robespierran sense) endorsement of the policies of War Communism. In particular, these policies were being forced on a peasantry among whom the Bolshevik Party had no historical roots or support. The party's estrangement from the peasantry rapidly grew as it lost a good deal of the sympathy it had recently gained with the land redistributions carried out after the October Revolution. The policies of War Communism, which as I discussed in chapter 1 were only partly dictated by necessity, had in the eyes of the rural majority converted the admired Bolsheviks of late 1917 into the hated Communists of late 1918. In other words, the opposition confronting the Bolshevik leadership was caused not only by the hardships resulting from the bitter armed *political* struggle against the Whites, but also by the specific *social* and *economic* policies pursued by the government. What Rosa Luxemburg said about why the Jacobins carried out the French Terror and how it differed from what she thought would be the behavior of the socialist proletariat in its revolution is to a considerable extent applicable to the Bolshevik government's Red Terror:

> [The socialist proletariat] enters the revolution not in order to follow utopian illusions *against* the course of history, but to complete the iron necessities of development, to make socialism *real* . . . It therefore does not require to destroy its own illusions with bloody acts of violence in order to create a contradiction between itself and bourgeois society.[14]

Last but not least, as I showed in chapter 1, the government had also lost a great deal of support among the urban working class, as demonstrated by the results of the soviet elections that took place in the Spring of 1918. In sum, the Red Terror was not only aimed against the counterrevolution but was in fact also an attempt to compensate for the regime's declining popularity, a good part of which can be attributed to the specific set of policies chosen and pursued by the government. Lenin had stated in November 1917, as noted above, that the Bolshevik leadership hoped not to engage in Terror 'because we have strength on our side.' As this strength diminished, the condition underlying Lenin's promise not to use terror ceased to prevail.

The Scope and Nature of the Red Terror

William Henry Chamberlin estimated that 50,000 persons were put to death by the government in the course of the Civil War. This figure does not include insurgents who were shot down with arms in their hands or people who were killed by mobs or by uncontrolled groups of soldiers and sailors.[15] Chamberlin also pointed out that Terror was not a tactic limited to the Soviet regime but was also widely practiced by its White opponents. However, he found it harder to estimate the number of victims of the White Terror since the Whites did not keep as good records as the centralized Cheka. Besides, as Chamberlin pointed out,

> by far the largest number of persons who met a violent end under the regime of the Whites seem to have come to their death not as a result of any regular trial, or even of a summarry verdict by a drumhead courtmartial, but were simply slaughtered by more or less irresponsible bands of soldiers whose leaders certainly kept no records of their actions.[16]

Nevertheless, my main concern here is not the total *number* of people killed by both sides, shocking as these figures are. Instead, my purpose is to analyze the types of actions carried out by the Bolshevik leaders of the Russian Revolution as a positive or negative model for a democratic and revolutionary socialist workers' movement. In addition, I shall attempt to provide an answer to Lenin's challenge to Gorky mentioned earlier in this chapter. Consequently, I will focus on the political control over the repressive agencies of the revolutionary regime and the criteria guiding the latter's work in such matters as choice of victims and types and severity of punishment. The atrocities carried out by the White Terror are assumed to be a given in this context, and are thus of interest only insofar as they may be said, in given instances, to justify or not justify the particular tactics carried out by the Red Terror. From this vantage point, several features of the Red Terror are extremely troublesome and indeed highly disturbing.

First of all, punishments were primarily carried out, in summary fashion and with fundamentally no external controls, by the Cheka – the government's political police. As Felix Dzerzhinsky, the first head of the Cheka, described its character in mid-1918:

> The Cheka is not a court. The Cheka is the *defence of the revolution* as the Red Army is: as in the civil war the Red Army cannot stop to ask where it may harm particular individuals, but must take into account only one thing, the victory of the revolution over the bourgeoisie, so the Cheka must defend the revolution and conquer the enemy even if its sword falls occasionally on the head of the innocent.[17]

E. H. Carr has also pointed out that 'the Cheka established at an early stage . . . the rule that shootings required the approval of a commission of three (troika). These troikas, though administrative bodies, inevitably acquired the aspect of summary courts.'[18] In other words, this was an administrative agency of the Bolshevik government with *de facto* judicial powers. Dzerzhinsky's justification of the Cheka is revealing in that it shares a common characteristic of the ideology of 'Leninism in power;' namely, the readiness to gloss over critical distinctions. In this case, a secret police that by definition acted primarily in the rearguard was not at all in the same situation as a Red Army facing armed combatants who were in a position to *immediately* kill or be killed.

In addition, the omnipotence and lack of external controls over the Cheka made it highly prone to corruption even though its top leader, Felix Dzerzhinsky, was personally a revolutionary puritan beyond the slightest suspicion and was ready to execute whoever attempted to use the Cheka for personal gain. Nonetheless, corruption did become widespread, particularly in the Ukrainian Cheka, which became notorious for such behavior as the appropriation for personal use of goods confiscated from arrested persons.[19] Cheka's deputy chief, Latsis, was well aware of the *structural* factors involved in such corrupt behavior. As Latsis described it, work in the Cheka,

> in an atmosphere of physical coercion, attracts corrupt and outright criminal elements who, profiting from their position as Cheka agents, blackmail and extort, filling their own pockets . . . however honest a man is, however pure his heart, work in the Cheka, which is carried on with almost unlimited rights and under conditions greatly affecting the nervous system, begins to tell. Few escape the effect of the conditions under which they work.[20]

The uncontrolled behavior of the Cheka not only opened the door to venality, but also encouraged another sort of *political* corruption; namely, an attitude of contempt for legality, including the very laws and regulations adopted by the Cheka's own government. Thus, for example, the Cheka conducted administrative convictions and deportations without any legal or constitutional authority, as evidenced by the fact that the decrees of amnesty issued during 1920 specifically included the category of those under administrative arrest. Since the Cheka had been, in early 1919, legally restricted to carrying out administrative detention only against those engaged in open armed rebellion, who were as a matter of course excluded from every amnesty, the 1920 amnesty for non-combatant administrative detainees was thus applied to a category of people that legally was not supposed to exist.[21] In fact, it has been estimated that more than half of those serving time in labor camps in 1919 and 1920 were there as a result of administrative, and not judicial, action. Furthermore, in this period, virtually all the formal trials held on the basis of a Cheka investigation took place without the presence of either the defendant or the prosecutor.[22]

Even more extreme and dramatic is Victor Serge's description of how, on 17 January 1920, the Bolshevik government abolished the death penalty except in districts where there were military operations still taking place. Nevertheless, as Serge was horrified to find out,

> while the newspapers were printing the decree, the Petrograd Chekas were liquidating their stock! Cartload after cartload of suspects had been driven outside the city during the night, and then shot, heap upon heap. How many? In Petrograd between 150 and 200; in Moscow, it was said, between 200 and 300. In the dawn of the days that followed, the families of the massacred victims came to search that ghastly, freshly dug ground, looking for any relics, such as buttons or scraps of stocking, that could be gathered there.[23]

Not only did the Cheka rush to beat the deadline, but it found a way to circumvent the decree. Having discovered the loophole, the Cheka leadership quickly took advantage of it in the following secret order: 'In view of the abolition of the death penalty, it is suggested that persons whose crimes would otherwise have rendered them liable to the supreme penalty now be dispatched to the zone of military operations where the decree concerning capital punishment does not apply.'[24]

The Cheka's powers were thus far in excess of anything that could possibly be justified by the strictly military needs of the Civil War. Victor Serge many years later pointed out how secret procedures that could have been reasonably invoked in cases of conspiracy were also invoked 'for the housewife who sells a pound of sugar that she has bought (speculation), ... the socialist or the anarchist who has passed some remark or other in the street ... cases of this sort literally swamped those of conspiracy.' Furthermore, Serge contended that 'during the civil war there was perfect order behind the front itself, in the interior of Soviet territory ... There was nothing to prevent the functioning of regular courts, which might in certain cases have sat *in camera*.'[25]

Moreover, there was also a qualitative broadening of punishments and reprisals with the intention of preventing as well as punishing counterrevolutionary deeds. Specifically, this meant not only drastic and summary sanctions against suspected perpetrators of specific counterrevolutionary acts and their accomplices (this was, of course, already in effect before the Red Terror), but it could also mean the punishment of random individuals for the sake of frightening others. Thus, for example, on 16 June 1919, commissar Nikolai Razin lined up the garrison of the Obruchev Fort in Kronstadt and had every fifth man, for a total of 55, shot in full view of their comrades.[26]

The broadening of punishments additionally meant the carrying out of massive retaliation against broad categories of people regardless of their actual or suspected involvement in specific political crimes. These categories included, for example, members of certain political parties. Many of these parties, such as the Socialist Revolutionaries (SRs) and the Anarchists, were non-disciplined associations where the behavior of any specific member could not be at all deduced from that of the leaders, let alone from the behavior of other members. Categorical punishments were also applied to people with particular class, and sometimes ethnic or national, backgrounds. It should be noted that the use of categorical punishments raises an even more serious question than whether or not an individual accused of committing a crime received a fair trial. This is because categorical punishments *by definition* establish the punishment of those who have committed no crime except belonging, sometimes by birth, to a certain group. As we shall use, the arguments that were occasionally given in support of these categorical measures indicated a logic going far beyond the military defense of the revolution. In fact, these arguments suggested the physical removal, if not the liquidation, of the actual or potential social base of support for dissidents and counterrevolutionaries.

Besides, the criterion of categorical or collective punishments is the very opposite of the criterion of selectivity that Leon Trotsky very cogently articulated in the 1930s in the context of defending the Bolshevik practice of taking hostages. As Trotsky put it:

> the moralist might perhaps try to argue that an 'open' and 'conscious' struggle between two camps is one thing, but the seizure of non-participants in the struggle is something else again. This argument, however, is only a wretched and stupid evasion ... modern warfare, with its long-range artillery, aviation, poison gases, and finally, with its train of devastation, famine, fires and epidemics, inevitably involves the loss of hundreds of thousands and millions, the aged and the children included, who do not participate directly in the struggle. People taken as hostages are at least bound by ties of class and family solidarity with one of the camps, or with the leaders of that camp. A conscious selection is possible in taking hostages.[27]

Indeed, Marx had approved of the Paris Commune's selective hostage taking, as for example in the proposed exchange of Archbishop Darboy and several priests for the revolutionary Blanqui.[28] Unfortunately, the factual claims made by Trotsky in the 1930s bear little relation to what actually happened in Russia in the period subsequent to 1918. Thus, by the middle of 1919, there were more than 13,000 hostages in Cheka prisons.[29] Throughout the Civil War hostages were taken in hundreds and thousands. In Nizhnii Novgorod, for example, the local Cheka bulletin published a list of 41 persons shot and reported the taking of 700 hostages in that city in one day alone.[30] Popular reaction to the massive seizure of hostages was so negative that, on 6 November 1918, the 'moderate' Bolshevik Kamenev moved a resolution at the Sixth All-Russian Congress of Soviets to release all hostages 'except those whose temporary detention is essential to ensure the safety of comrades fallen into enemy hands.'[31] In other words, it was the 'right-wing' Communist Kamenev who was in this instance reasserting the principle of selectivity that the Cheka had systematically ignored in practice, and that the 'left-wing' Trotsky was later to defend in the 1930s.

It should be pointed out that the practice of taking hostages was not completely abolished with the end of the Civil War. For example, in 1922, the difficult international situation created by the sentencing to death of 12 leading Socialist Revolutionaries was 'resolved' by the postponement of the death sentences provided that, and for as long as, the SR Party as a whole did not engage in any further sabotage or terror against Soviet Russia. This trial, discussed at greater length in chapter 5 on socialist legality, took place while Lenin was seriously ill. Nevertheless, he had earlier strongly rebuked Bukharin and Radek for having agreed not to invoke the death penalty against the SR defendants at a meeting of representatives of the three Internationals in Berlin in April 1922.[32]

The policy of taking very large number of hostages was by no means the only manifestation of a collective or categorical approach to punishment. Let us examine, for example, the following advice by Latsis, deputy chairman of the Cheka:

> Do not ask for incriminating evidence to prove that the prisoner opposed the Soviet power by arms or by word. Your first duty is to ask him what class he belongs to, what were his origin, education, and occupation. These questions should decide the fate of the prisoner. This is the meaning and essence of Red Terror.[33]

Latsis' comments provoked widespread criticism from a variety of Bolshevik leaders including Lenin. *Pravda* itself sarcastically noted that under Latsis' criteria Marx and Lenin themselves would have had to be put to the wall.[34] Now, while Latsis' pronouncement was of course crude to a ludicrous degree, the fact remains that the prevailing government policy shared more of Latsis' logic than Lenin and other Bolshevik leaders would have cared to admit. In fact, the government did punish or threatened to punish whole groups of people purely on the basis of their social origins. I. N. Steinberg, the Left SR party leader who was Commissar of Justice during the Left SR–Bolshevik coalition, mentions this issue as one of his major objections to Lenin's and the Cheka's policies during his ministry in late 1917 and early 1918, i.e. before the beginning of the Civil War and the Red Terror. Steinberg singled out one such incident when the Bolshevik Amvelt, chairman of the soviet in the city of Reval, capital of Estonia, issued the following order: 'Whereas the German Barons are open counter-revolutionaries, who will aid the German armies; and whereas a plot of these Barons has been uncovered, martial law is hereby proclaimed throughout Estonia. The entire class of the Barons, men from 17 and women from 20 years of age, are declared outside the law.'[35] As it turned out, nothing happened to the German Barons, not primarily out of any consideration of revolutionary or humanitarian principles, but because negotiations with German resumed and it was not advisable to arouse her anger.[36] Less fortunate were the Cossacks. Thus, during the Civil War the Central Committee of the Communist Party sent the Kamensky Executive Committee a secret circular, which included the following categorical instruction: 'Institute a wholesale terror against the wealthy Cossacks and peasants, and having destroyed them altogether, carry out a pitiless mass terror against the Cossacks in general who took any direct or *indirect* part in the fight against the Soviet government.'[37]

One cannot but conclude that, at a minimum, Lenin's and the Cheka's policies were not interested in clearly distinguishing between measures designed to deprive the former ruling classes of their social and economic power (e.g. confiscation) and the quite different matter of legally penalizing people on the basis of group membership and social origins, rather than of particular criminal or political offenses committed by specific individuals. Needless to say, the issue here is not one's love or hatred for the former ruling classes, but what all this reveals about the government's legal conceptions, and the future consequences of this for *all*. Likewise with the government's crude 'workerism' – this turned out to be far more consequential and damaging in the government's relationship with the peasantry than whatever wrongs may have been committed against groups such as the Baltic Barons.

The policies sometimes pursued by the Bolshevik government in its successful attempt to put down the so-called 'Green' peasant rebellions (which were socially and politically quite different from the 'White rebellions) in the Tambov region in 1920–1 dramatically illustrate these points. This rebellion, primarily directed against the policies of War Communism, was very bloody. Numerous atrocites were committed by both sides. As Oliver H. Radkey, the author of a scholarly study of the rebellion, put it when attempting to draw the balance sheet of cruelty: 'our impression is that there was an excess of torture on the side of the Greens, an excess of killing on the side of the Reds – battle deaths excluded.'[38] Again, my main interest here is not cruelty *per se* but the implications of the Bolshevik government's apparent affinity for the principle of collective or categorical guilt and punishments. This notion strongly pervades the seven articles of the Decree of 11 June 1921, subsequently identified as Order No. 171, designed for the struggle against the Tambov Greens:

1   'Bandits' refusing to give their names were to be shot on the spot without trial.

2   Hostages were to be taken from settlements where arms were hidden and were to be shot unless the weapons were given up.

3   From a household where a concealed weapon was found, the oldest worker would be taken and shot out of hand without trial.

4   A family giving shelter to a 'bandit' was to be arrested and exiled from the province, its property confiscated, and its eldest breadwinner shot on the spot without trial.

5   A family giving shelter to members of a 'bandit's' family or hiding the property of a 'bandit' was to be considered itself as 'bandit' and would have its eldest breadwinner shot forthwith without trial.

6   In case of the flight of a 'bandit's' family, its possessions were to be distributed among peasants loyal to Soviet authority and the dwelling was to be burned.

7   The decree was to be read before village assemblies and was 'mercilessly to be carried out.'[39]

One place where this decree was enforced was the village of Parevka, a Green stronghold, where many of its inhabitants were shot in batches as an object lesson to the others.[40] Radkey points out that the percentage of voluntary enlistments in the Green forces exceeded 80 per cent of the male population only in the case of a few villages, and that a 50 per cent enrollment was considered high in most instances, even according to Soviet estimates.[41] Therefore, given that only a minority of the peasants were involved in the insurgency, there cannot be any doubt that *collective* punishments of people not actively involved in the rebellion were indeed applied in the suppression of the Tambov peasant upheaval.

One of the key causes of these collective punishments was that, while the government at various points offered concessions to the peasants in Tambov and occasionally even made some moves to win them over,[42] its basic War Communist hostility to the peasants as a class remained fundamentally unchanged. This attitude considerably facilitated the development of the government's posture as an occupying army, and thus the attempt to terrorize the rebels' base into inactivity and refusal to cooperate with the rebellion. It is clear that the economic crisis facing Russia at the time was an important reason why Lenin and the Bolshevik government had little, if anything, to offer to the peasantry. But neither can there be any doubt that the regime's dogmatic embrace of War Communism, long after its lack of viability had become evident, powerfully contributed to the profound alienation of the rural population in places like the Ukraine and Tambov. In fact, the implementation of the New Economic Policy (NEP) did as much as anything else to bring about the end of peasant rebellions in Soviet Russia.[43]

Finally, I would like to emphasize that the issue of collective guilt and punishment in the Russian Revolution was not merely a utilitarian tactic raising only the question of what would or wouldn't have worked in the effort to obtain peasant support and defeat peasant resistance. This approach was also based in part on a monstrous distortion and schematic mockery of Marxist class analysis.

Of course, this issue became above all a political and moral matter powerfully affecting the very nature of the revolution itself and, eventually, its internal strength and ability to resist the logic of Stalinist politics.

Repression against the Opposition Parties: the Red Terror and after

As we just saw, the Red Terror brought about large-scale repression, which was often carried out in an indiscriminate fashion and against whole groups and categories of people. Yet, as in the case of the press, the repression of opposition parties was somewhat tentative during this period, particularly when applied against those political tendencies that coincided with the government in opposing the counterrevolutionary White armies. In fact, the opposition political parties actually fared worse under the more limited, but in some crucial respects more systematic, repression of the years after the Civil War when the New Economic Policy was put into effect. Let us now examine how this shift in government policy affected the most important opposition parties.

The Mensheviks

While the right wing of the Menshevik Party under the leadership of Potresov did ally itself with and support the White counterrevolution, at no point did the majority Mensheviks, led by Martov and Dan, do so. Quite to the contrary, Mensheviks who associated with the Whites were expelled from the party.[44] Nevertheless, the Mensheviks did act as an opposition party; among other things, they called for the reconvening of the Constituent Assembly and organized working-class protest in the cities.[45] Consequently, they were the targets of continual harassment by the Cheka. Excluded, like other opposition parties, from the national soviets in June 1918, they were briefly reinstated on 30 November 1918. This took place after the Central Committee of the Menshevik Party in October 1918 approved a series of theses that, among other things, recognized the October Revolution as 'historically necessary' and rescinded their demand for a Constituent Assembly. At this time, Lenin also directed some conciliatory remarks towards his one-time party comrades.[46] According to Simon Liberman, a member of the Menshevik Party, after the Communist revolts in Bavaria and Hungary were quelled in 1919, there were even unsuccessful negotiations involving Lenin that might have led to the appointment of some leading Mensheviks to important government positions.[47]

By the Autumn of 1919, while remaining in opposition, the Mensheviks were nonetheless greatly concerned with the possibility of a White victory and actively recruited for the Red Army.[48] This did not however protect them from government persecution, albeit a not fully consistent one as yet. Thus, as E. H. Carr noted, in 1920 the Mensheviks had party offices and a club in Moscow, although the Cheka raided the premises, sealed them up, confiscated papers, and arrested those assembled. Carr further recorded that in the same year the Mensheviks held party conferences in the open, which were reported in the Soviet press, and also held an open public meeting with the British Labour Party delegation at which SR leader Chernov showed up in disguise (according to Dan, 'the last such meeting in Bolshevik Moscow').[49]

The situation changed substantially at the end of the Civil War in 1921, when the Mensheviks still had significant, and probably growing, influence in the working class.[50] Zinoviev is reported to have estimated that at that time as many as 90 per cent of the union rank-and-file were opposed to the regime.[51] This may have been the main reason for the greatly increased repression directed against the Mensheviks. Approximately 2,000 members of that party were arrested in the first three months of that year,[52] and in May 1921 a new wave of repression descended on Mensheviks, SRs, and Anarchists. Some of these were allowed to emigrate, but many were arrested and banished to the far north, Siberia, and Central Asia.[53] Again, and in contrast to the Right SRs for example, the Mensheviks remained aloof from anti-Bolshevik subversion. Thus, for example, they made no move to materially aid the Kronstadt rebellion.[54]

The Right SRs

The Socialist Revolutionaries, whether of the Right or of the Left, were organizationally far less disciplined than the Bolshevik or Menshevik parties. Therefore, in speaking about them one cannot assume a homogeneous position and attitude towards the Bolshevik government. Nonetheless, it is fair to say that many Right SRs, unlike the Left SRs, tended to be sympathetic to the Civil War opponents of the Bolsheviks. In this they were not too far from the party immediately to their right – the Kadets or Constitutional Democrats – who openly came out in support of the counterrevolution after they were banned by the revolutionary government in late 1917.[55] Chernov, the Right SR leader associated with one of the relatively 'leftish' wings of that party, sent a circular letter on 24 October 1918 calling the Civil War 'a struggle between Soviet Russia and the Russia of the constituent assembly, between ochlocracy and democracy.' Furthermore, anti-Bolshevik governments in Samara, Omsk, and Archangel, born shortly after the beginning of the Civil War in the Summer of 1918, had Right SR leaderships. These governments proceeded to abolish soviet rule and reinstated the municipal *dumas* and *zemstvos*. Yet there was a section of the party that refused to fight the Bolsheviks and they too were able to benefit from the occasional concessions from the Bolshevik government. Thus, in February 1919 they were briefly able to publish the old SR newspaper *Delo Naroda*;[56] besides, the SRs not allied with the counterrevolution were reinstated in the soviets by a resolution of the Central Executive Committee on 25 February 1919.[57] Shortly after this, the Right SRs again split into several factions, one interested in cooperating with the Bolsheviks, one hostile to the government, and a third under the leadership of Chernov, who now wanted to establish 'a third force equally removed from Bolshevism and restoration.'[58]

The Left SRs

Although sharing the party name with the Right SRs, the Lefts were in fact the authentic inheritors of peasant-oriented revolutionary Russian populism – a significantly different political perspective from the often tepid liberalism acquired by their erstwhile party comrades. In my estimation, the Left SRs and the Anarchists were, among the major political groupings, the only truly revolutionary forces in Russia besides the Bolsheviks. On 19 March 1918, the Left SRs resigned from their coalition government with the Bolsheviks in protest against Russia's signing of the Treaty of Brest-Litovsk. However, in the meantime, the Left SRs remained in the CEC of the soviets and continued to hold government positions, including high positions in the Cheka. In fact, their criticisms of the government in connection with the peace treaty were remarkably similar to those of the Left Communists under the leadership of Bukharin. The Left SRs first attempted to obstruct the treaty by propaganda in the army and peasantry, but further differences with the Bolsheviks on the application of the death penalty and on the agrarian policies of the revolutionary regime only increased their hostility to the government. This eventually led the Left SRs to resume the time-honored tradition of direct armed action against the powers that be. On 6 July 1918, two Left SRs assassinated the German Ambassador in Moscow; and simultaneously, the Left SRs attempted an armed coup against the Bolsheviks, which was quickly put down.[59] Needless to add, this brought about the outlawing of the Left SRs, and also the beginning of the Red Terror, which ended up being directed mostly against people who did not have the remotest connection to the Left SR Party. The political gulf between the Left SRs and the government was then greatly widened by the policies of War Communism in the countryside. Even so, a group of Left SRs around former People's Commissar of Justice Steinberg was briefly allowed in 1920 to publish a periodical called *Znamia*, which advocated a 'genuine soviet democracy' that would be a 'dictatorship of the working classes.'[60] As we have seen, this was similar to the occasional concessions that the Bolshevik government had given to other groups and parties during the Civil War.

The Anarchists

The Anarchists had actually been an unnamed coalition partner of the Bolsheviks in the October Revolution. Furthermore, several Anarchists played important roles in the revolutionary government, and some of them, like Bill Shatov, actually sided with the Bolsheviks when the Anarchists split with them in the early years of the Russian Revolution.[61] At least in the period up to 1921, the government tried to encourage the development of more Bill Shatovs inside the Anarchist movement. In pursuit of this tactic, the Bolshevik leadership spoke kindly of what they called 'ideological' (*ideinye*) Anarchists. These were to be distinguished from oppositionists and from what the government described as plain criminal and irresponsible elements using the flag of Anarchism as a cover for their depredations. The 'ideological' Anarchists were in fact welcomed if they set aside action on behalf of their ideological differences with the Bolsheviks, and in the meantime cooperated with the government in a variety of practical tasks. It was also in this spirit that, in 1920, the Right Bolshevik Kamenev offered the Moscow Anarchists freedom to publish their newspapers and maintain open clubs and bookshops in exchange for their adopting party discipline and purging their ranks of criminal and uncontrollable elements. This offer was indignantly rejected by the Anarchists.[62]

It goes without saying that the government was not concerned with truth and justice when it accused the Anarchist oppositionists of banditry (whether or not banditry had occurred),[63] or when the government used the prosecution of real banditry as a cover for the pursuit for other political ends. Thus, for example, on 9 April 1918, when a band of Moscow Anarchists stole an automobile belonging to the friendly representative of the American Red Cross, the Cheka used this as an excuse to raid no fewer than 26 Anarchist centers in the capital. Most Anarchists surrendered without a fight, but some resisted and as a result a dozen Cheka agents were killed, 40 Anarchists were killed or wounded, and more than 500 were taken prisoner.[64] None of this is to deny that the Anarchists were quite capable of violently striking back at the government. For instance, on 25 September 1919, a group of Anarchists and Left SRs seeking to avenge the arrests of their comrades bombed the headquarters of the Moscow Committee of the Communist Party while a plenary meeting was in session. The explosion killed 12 members of the committee and injured 55 others, including such figures as Bukharin, Iaroslavskii, and Steklov.[65] Also, some oppositionists such as the Anarchist Makhno in the Ukraine led a 'Green' revolt against the government's policies of War Communism after having worked with the Bolsheviks in the struggle against the Whites.

During the Civil War, the Anarchists were able, like other opposition groups, to operate sometimes underground and sometimes openly, and intermittently to publish their newspapers. During this pre-1921 period, they were apparently better able to maintain their clubs open than to keep their newspapers from being shut down.[66] The last open and public Anarchist demonstration took place when Kropotkin died on 8 February 1921. His family declined the government's offer of a state burial, and a committee of Anarcho-Communists and Anarcho-Syndicalists arranged the funeral. Several imprisoned Anarchists were allowed a day's liberty to participate in the funeral procession. This turned out to be a 20,000 strong demonstration with placards and banners demanding, among other things, the release of all Anarchists from prison. As the procession passed the Butyrki prison, the inmates shook the bars on their windows and sang Anarchist hymns.[67] With the end of the Civil War and the beginning of the New Economic Policy the suppression of the Anarchists became thorough and complete.

Was Repression Practical?

Quite aside from all principled objections to the Red Terror and the subsequent repression after the end of the Civil War – whether from a socialist, democratic, or humanitarian point of view – it is also questionable whether repressive activities were necessarily practical. Take, for example, the persecution of opposition parties. Lenin seems to have been only episodically interested in distinguishing among them, not on the question of their relative degree of leftness or rightness – that is not our concern here – but on their degree of willingness to be a loyal opposition as opposed to a subversive force aiding the counterrevolution. Thus, we just saw how the Mensheviks, under the leadership of Dan and Martov, the majority faction since late 1917, actually moved somewhat to the Left under the impact of the October Revolution and became, in a variety of ways, the logical candidates for a loyal opposition.[68] Yet Lenin failed to take advantage, in a systematic fashion, of these important political differences. Instead, we find Lenin making pronouncements such as the following in 1919:

> Even supposing the Menshevik Central Committee is better than the Mensheviks in Tula who have been definitely exposed as fomentors of strikes – in fact I have no doubt some of the regular members of the Menshevik Committee are better – in a political struggle when the white-guards are trying to get us by the throat, is it possible to draw distinctions? Have we time for it? Facts are facts. Let us suppose that they were not aiding and abetting, but were weak and yielded to the Right Mensheviks; so what of it? The Right Mensheviks foment strikes, and Martov, or others, condemned these Rights in the newspapers. What does this teach us? We get a note saying 'I, to, condemn, but' . . . (A voice: 'What else can they do?') They can do what the Bolshevik Party does – take their stand, not in words, but in deeds.[69]

One can certainly sympathize with Lenin's impatience with what, in my view, he correctly perceived as Menshevik political bankruptcy, and with the sheer lack of time created by the urgencies of the Civil War. Yet the question nonetheless remains as to what was the appropriate policy to be followed vis-à-vis the Mensheviks. It is precisely in this context that I would argue that Martov's and Dan's consistency in rejecting revolutionary methods, both before and after the Bolsheviks came to power, made them potentially invaluable from the point of view of avoiding the creation of a one-party state in the new society. A permanent legalization[70] of Martov's party, as long as it continued to disassociate itself from the counterrevolution, would have deepened the Menshevik split. Besides, such a policy might have conceivably encouraged loyalist attitudes among other opposition forces such as the Left SRs, particularly after the Bolshevik government brought to an end its short-lived 'poor peasant' policy in the Russian countryside.

It is also worth wondering what would have happened if the Bolsheviks had adopted a policy of 'those who are not our active enemies, are our friends,' or, in other words, the opposite of what seemed to have been Lenin's War Communist policy of 'he who is not with us, is against us.'[71] Such a policy would have been especially welcome at the time of the growing isolation and loss of support for the Bolsheviks even before the Civil War broke out in mid-1918. In any case, it may well be that the Red Terror strengthend rather than weakened the determination and even obstinacy of many enemies. After all, if one is going to be punished whether or not one *does* something, many a person may conclude that one may as well do it. Adam Ulam, certainly no friend of the Left or of the October Revolution, has nonetheless persuasively made the point that,

> it is arguable that insurgency and bitterness against the Communist rule grew in fact in the wake of executions and other inhumanities perpetrated by the Cheka and other authorities, and that many elements, at first friendly or lukewarm in their opposition to the Bolshevik power, became its fanatical enemies because of terror. One does not have to consult White propaganda to reach that conclusin. The most famous novel of the Civil War written by a Communist eyewitness, Mikhail Sholokhov's *And Quiet Flows the Don*, presents an instructive tale of how it was mostly through Bolshevik atrocities that the rank-and-file apolitical Don Cossack, like the hero of the novel, Gregory Melenkov, was turned into an anti-Bolshevik fighter. Far from being a regrettable necessity, the extent of the Bolshevik terror was one of the factors that made their victory in the Civil War more difficult.[72]

The Red Terror and subsequent repression also created serious practical problems in the technical and economic fields. Simon Liberman, one of the many Menshevik experts who worked for the Bolshevik government, tells the ominous yet somehow amusing story of the Communist inventor who was sent over to him by Dzerzhinsky, the head of the Cheka. It turns out that the particular 'invention' being proposed was based on the long discredited notion of perpetual motion. When Dzerzhinsky was informed of the negative appraisal, he replied, as reported by Liberman: 'That's strange. Our technical committee has examined this proposal and has found it worthwhile.' Whereupon, Liberman fearfully called up Rykov and requested that the project be sent over to the Scientific Committee for its decision. Liberman then adds: 'I was passing the buck, to be sure, but somehow I had to take this awful responsibility off my shoulders.'[73] This incident is a textbook example of the bureaucratic irresponsibility and consequent inefficiency that would also systematically characterize Stalinist Russia.

The Revolutionary Opposition to the Cheka

As much as many current and subsequent supporters of 'Leninism in power' may have argued that the Cheka's abuses were necessary, inevitable, or 'objectively' unavoidable excesses incurred in the higher calling of preserving the revolution, this attitude was by no means universally shared at the time. Political disagreements concerning the nature and legitimacy and the revolutionary government's repression were both strong and widespread, and reached the highest levels of the revolutionary government itself. In this critical respect, the early Soviet experience was unique, since none of the subsequent self-styled socialist revolutions (e.g. the Chinese, Cuban, and Vietnamese revolutions) ever witnessed debates of this sort.

The first clashes concerning revolutionary repression began during the Left SR–Bolshevik coalition government, which lasted from the end of November 1917 until March 1918. The Left SRs, particularly through their party representatives in the Cheka and through Commissar of Justice I. N. Steinberg, a Left SR Party member, consistently and continuously exercised a restraining influence on the government's repressive apparatus through such actions as repeatedly vetoing the use of the death penalty, and by their refusal to prosecute categories of people rather than *individuals* suspected of counterrevolutionary activities.[74] It is also worth noting that Steinberg emphasized the prosecution of overt counterrevolutionary actions rather than of opinions.[75] Much more significant, however, was the widespread opposition to the Cheka that developed in soviet and Bolshevik circles, demonstrating, among other things, how their revolutionary worldview was still quite distant from the Stalinist monolithism of a few years later.

Shortly after the Cheka was established, a struggle for power developed between the Cheka and the local soviets in 1918. In many localities, the soviets were attempting to subordinate the secret police organs to themselves. As Dukhovsky, a high-ranking official of the Commissariat of Internal Affairs summarized the conflict: 'The question can be put quite bluntly: to whom does power in the provinces belong? To the soviets in the person of their executive committees, or to the Chekas?'[76] Dukhovsky went on to state that the soviet executive committees were elected locally and that the Cheka personnel were, of course, appointed and controlled from the center. At about the same time (20 October 1918), another functionary of the same Commissariat revealed the results of a poll in which 118 out of 147 (80 per cent) local soviets responding expressed the view that the Cheka should be subordinated to themselves.[77]

In some extreme cases, the party and government as a whole were forced to publicly criticize and even take measures against elements within the Cheka. Thus, in 1918 the *Cheka Weekly* published a letter from the chairman of the Nolinsk party committee and Cheka regretting that the arrested British spy Bruce Lockhart had not been subjected to the most 'refined tortures' and then sent 'to the other world.' The Nolinsk people further suggested that the Cheka's failure to torture and kill Lockhart was due to its still being influenced by petty bourgeois ideology. The government denounced the letter, banned its authors from holding any government office, and closed down the *Cheka Weekly*. In contrast to the strong response by the central government and party authorities, it is worth noting the quite different initial response by the Cheka's central organization. It read: 'Not at all objecting in substance to this letter, we only want to point out to the comrades who sent it and reproached us with mildness that the "sending to the other world" of "base intriguers" representing "foreign peoples" is not at all in our interest.'[78]

Much more numerous were the occasions when opposition to repression in general and the Cheka in particular was expressed by leading members and/or sections of the Bolshevik Party. Several leading Bolsheviks were also greatly concerned with the lack of judicial controls over the Cheka, leading Shklovsky, a member of the All-Russian Cheka to complain about 'the "legal limitations" which certain tender-minded Bolsheviks would impose upon the Cheka.'[79] Perhaps one of the most persistent of these 'tender-minded' Bolsheviks was Mikhail Stepanovich Olminsky (1863–1933), an Old Bolshevik, member of the editorial staff of *Pravda* from 1918 to 1920, and a long-time personal friend of Lenin and Krupskaya.[80] Although predictably the target of workerist 'intellectual baiting' by Cheka deputy chairman Peters, Olminsky was apparently not intimidated by this or other criticisms and subjected the Cheka to strong and substantive, and not merely formal or jurisdictional, criticism from the very pages of *Pravda*. Olminsky charged that nobody except perhaps the highest government officials enjoyed any guarantees of personal security from the secret police. To Olminsky, it was clear that establishing the proper scope of the Cheka was of great urgency.[81] On another occasion, in February 1919, Olminsky pointed out that in the provinces the Chekists were continuing to 'execute and execute for no apparent reason, as if they were competing in the invention of grounds for shooting people: this one for playing cards, that one for making "false denunciations" – what other grounds can be devised for executions?'[82] Again, in March 1919, *Pravda* accused the Cheka of Vladimir of keeping a special den for 'pricking prisoners' heels with needles.'[83] In late 1918, *Pravda*, then under the editorship of Bukharin, was publishing more articles by detractors than by supporters of the Cheka. This was not the case with *Izvestiya*, but even this newspaper at one or another time published articles such as one under the title 'Do medieval torture chambers still exist?,' which was published on 26 January 1919. This article, written by a Communist who had been erroneously arrested, denounced a Cheka prison attached to one of the quarters of the city of Moscow where people 'were flogged until their senses left them, and then, still unconscious, taken down to a cellar which had been the refrigerator chamber, and thenceforth beaten for eighteen hours out of the twenty-four. Things of the sort so impressed me that I nearly lost my reason.' Sometime earlier, on 4 December 1918, a writer by the name of Diakonov had written an article in *Izvestiya* under the title 'A Cemetery of Still Living Bodies,' where he described some of the cells attached to the inquisitorial department of the Taganka prison where he reported seriously ill patients living under extreme, inhuman conditions.[84]

In the light of all these denunciations, it is not surprising that Dzerzhinsky appeared before the Central Committee of the Communist Party on 12 December 1918 to complain about what he considered to be unfounded and malicious articles that had appeared in the Soviet press. The Central Committees upheld Dzerzhinsky's position, but even this did not stop the debates, which, as we have just seen, continued into early 1919.[85]

The 'Tribunalist' Opposition to the Cheka

Olminsky's primarily substantive criticism of the Cheka overlapped with strong criticism from another quarter, which was in all likelihood motivated primarily by jurisdictional considerations. I am referring to the Revolutionary Tribunals, which had been established on 17 May 1918 as the proper judicial bodies to try counterrevolutionary crimes. The Tribunals were under the supervision of N. Krylenko,[86] who was to become a defender of the worst kinds of abuses and a top Stalinist jurist. Given the Cheka's *de facto* judicial powers, it is hardly surprising that friction developed between the two bodies. Yet, this jurisdictional friction did have significant substantive implications. According to Lennard D. Gerson:

> despite Lenin's proddings, the death penalty was rarely applied by the tribunals during the first frenzied months of the Red Terror ... Of the fourteen persons executed during this formative period of the Tribunals twelve were convicted of counterrevolutionary activity, but this represented less than 2 per cent of those actually charged with this most serious political offense. Most counterrevolutionaries were either sentenced to prison or were fined; some received even lighter sentences.[87]

The clash between the 'Tribunalists' and the Cheka even reached the point of an open debate at a district meeting of the Moscow Communist Party in late January 1919. Krylenko's statements at this meeting combined jurisdictional and substantive considerations. According to him,

> The lack of control [over the Chekas] creates an atmosphere fully favorable to abuses and provocation. The Chekas consider themselves to be organs completely detached from the general system of Soviet institutions. That which is decided in the closed offices of a Cheka inspires a lack of trust. Only the publicity of a court and the possibility of controlling investigations can achieve the desired results. A complete reform, converting the Chekas into investigative departments of the revolutionary tribunals, will give order and unity to the judicial system. The reform of the Cheka is inevitable, for on this depends the future development of the revolution.[88]

At the end of this meeting, a vote was taken and the Cheka point of view prevailed by a margin of 214 to 57 over the Tribunalists. Krylenko claimed, however, that the meeting had been packed by employees of the Cheka.[89]

Shortly after this, as I mentioned earlier, Dzerzhinsky's prodding of the Central Committee eventually brought these types of open party and press debates to an end. Then, through a series of decrees in the years 1919 and

1920, the party formally established the Cheka as an investigative agency and the Tribunals as judicial organs, but with enough loopholes still to allow the Cheka considerable freedom of action, including the right to confine persons to forced labor camps, by administrative decision, for a maximum period of five years.[90] Furthermore, in exchange for being formally limited to an investigative role, the Chekas gained the right to be represented in the Revolutionary Tribunals, i.e. the Tribunals were instructed to include on their three-person panels a collegium member of the local provincial Cheka.[91] Besides, the Tribunals were now given discretion to dispense with calling witnesses, and their sentences were exempted from appeal. As George Leggett points out, 'indeed, session in public, in the presence of the accused, was one of the few safeguards which distinguished their trial procedure from that of the Chekas.'[92] In sum, the Cheka had clearly come out ahead. And yet it would still take some time before the Cheka and its successor organizations would be entirely immune from criticism. For example, the Second Congress of the Members of Revolutionary Tribunals, held on 26–28 April 1920, passed a resolution that, among other things, criticized the Cheka for unnecessary deprivation of liberty of accused persons, keeping these persons under arrest for too long a period of time, illegal actions such as beatings, and arrests of persons for doing things not forbidden by the laws of the country.[93] Besides, independent thought and some concern for personal freedoms must have been still alive within the Communist Party itself when, in the Spring of 1921, Communist deputies to the Moscow Soviet joined with the tiny Menshevik fraction in that body and, in defiance of the chairman Kamenev, approved a resolution that no deputy to the soviet could be arrested until the presidium of the soviet had been informed and a full meeting of the soviet had consented to the arrest.[94]

Lenin and Repression

On the whole, Lenin's position in the political spectrum inside the Bolshevik Party tended to be much closer to the Cheka than to its detractors and opponents. Lenin became a forceful and frequent defender of the Red Terror, and explicitly defended the Cheka in the face of its revolutionary, let alone other critics. Thus, he told a rally of Chekists on 7 November 1918:

> It is not at all surprising to hear the Cheka's activities frequently attacked by friends as well as enemies. We have taken a hard job. When we took over the government of the country, we naturally made many mistakes, and it is only natural that the mistakes of the Extraordinary Commissions strike the eye the most. The narrow-minded intellectual fastens on these mistakes without trying to get to the root of the matter. What does surprise me in all these outcries about the Cheka's mistakes is the manifest inability to put the question on a broad footing. People harp on individual mistakes the Chekas made, and raise a hue and cry about them.

We, however, say that we learn from our mistakes ... When I consider its activities and see how they are attacked, I say this is all narrow-minded and futile talk.[95]

It is true that Lenin did not stand for the stupidities of Cheka deputy chief Latsis or for the defense of torture by the Nolinsk Cheka. Furthermore, Lenin often went to considerable lengths to stop Cheka excesses in *individual* cases. Maxim Gorky was one of the those personalities who would desperately contact Lenin to stop one or another arrest or execution, often successfully.[96] On the other hand, Lenin was equally likely to criticize other Bolshevik leaders for not being sufficiently zealous in their pursuit of the Red Terror. Thus, on 26 June 1918, after the assassination of Volodarsky by members of the SR Party, Lenin wrote to Zinoviev in Petrograd:

> Only today we heard at the C.C. [Central Committee] that in Petrograd the *workers* wanted to reply to the murder of Volodarsky by mass terror and that you (not you personally, but the Petrograd Central Committee) restrained them. I protest most emphatically. We are discrediting ourselves: we threaten mass terror, even in resolutions of the Soviet of Deputies, yet when it comes to action we *obstruct* the revolutionary initiative of the masses, a *quite* correct one. This is im-poss-ible! The terrorists will consider us old women. This is wartime above all. We must encourage the energy and mass character of the terror against the counter-revolutionaries, and particularly in Petrograd, the example of which is *decisive*.[97]

It is worth emphasizing that, in this instance, Lenin was not limiting himself to the justifiable demand for retribution against the actual perpetrators of Volodarsky's assassination but was clearly advocating wholesale terror. However, even this exhortation to his comrades in Petrograd was still presumably directed against political opponents. But, in February 1920, Lenin instructed the Cheka to direct 'revolutionary coercion' against 'the wavering and unstable elements among the masses themselves.'[98] On this occasion, Lenin could not have had open political opponents in mind when he referred to 'wavering and unstable elements.'

Most important of all, Lenin did nothing substantive, from an *institutional* point of view, to significantly reverse the unlimited powers of the Cheka. Lenin's penchant for personnel changes as a solution to political and structural–bureaucratic problems led him in mid-1919 to respond to Kamenev's complaint about Cheka's depredations in the Ukraine by attributing this to the inferior quality of the people involved. He then ordered a purge of the Ukrainian Cheka.[99] Likewise, in 1918–19, Lenin appointed Bukharin, whose *Pravda* as we have seen had strongly criticized the secret police, as the Politburo's representative on the Cheka collegium with the right of veto. Characteristically, Lenin did this at the same time that he rejected a proposal, made from within the government itself, to abolish the Cheka altogether and transfer its functions to a reorganized Commissariat of Justice. Instead, he subordinated the Cheka directly to the Politburo, appointing Bukharin with the comment; 'Let him go there himself, and let him try to keep the terror within limits, if it is possible. We shall all be very glad if he succeeds.'[100]

Worst of all, the evidence indicates that terror remained for Lenin an instrument of political and social policy even after the end of the Civil War. Recently, with the liberalization of the Soviet press under Gorbachev, the magazine *Ogonyok* edited by Vitaly A. Korotich has campaigned to rehabilitate Nikolai Stepanovich Gumilev, a romantically 'monarchist' poet shot by the Petrograd Cheka on 23 or 24 August 1921 for 'participation in the conspiracy of Tagantsev.' This execution was carried out without Gumilev having the benefit of a trial, and without the public being provided any account of the supposed 'Tagantsev conspiracy.' Moreover, the execution was carried out in spite of Maxim Gorky's efforts to save Gumilev, and even though the Academy of Sciences, the Institute of World Literature, and Proletkult petitioned the Cheka to release the poet into their custody. In addition, the Academy of Sciences offered to guarantee his appearance in court.[101] A few months before this incident, Lenin had declared in a letter to Kamenev dated 3 March 1922 that 'it is a great mistake to think that the NEP put an end to terror; we shall again have recourse to terror and to economic terror.'[102] And, in a letter to D. I. Kursky on 17 May 1922, Lenin stated:

> The courts must not ban terror – to promise that would be deception or self-deception – but must formulate the motives underlying it, legalise it as a principle, plainly, without any make-believe or embellishment. It must be formulated in the broadest possibly manner, for only revolutionary law and revolutionary conscience can more or less widely determine the limits within which it should be applied.[103]

Two days later, Lenin showed how categorical, extra-judicial punishments were still in force more than a year after the end of the Civil War. On that day, Lenin wrote to Dzerzhinsky on how to go about deporting writers and professors helping the counterrevolution. In this context, Lenin mentioned the right-wing academic journal *Ekonomist* and pointed out that the journal carried 'a list of its members on the cover. These, I think, are *almost all* the most legitimate candidates for deportation.' Lenin then concluded by telling Dzerzhinsky to 'show this confidentially, without making any copies, to the *Politbureau* members, *returning it to you and to me*, and inform me of their opinion and your conclusion.'[104]

A Note on the Origins of Stalin's Concentration Camps

Solzhenitsyn's *Gulag Archipelago*[105] focused again the world's attention on the millions of people who were compelled to work and perished in Stalin's slave labor camps. This would not be strictly relevant to the topic and period covered by this book if it were not for the fact that Solzhenitsyn traced the origins of these camps to as early as 1918. He is therefore among those who stress the continuity between Lenin's and Stalin's camps and treat them as essentially the same phenomena. However, there have been scholars who have noted substantial differences between the camps under Lenin and under Stalin. This they have done without at all minimizing the significance and magnitude of Stalin's camps, or denying the ominous legal and political precedents established by the use of the camps under Lenin, never rescinded or abolished while he was alive.

First of all, it is important to distinguish between the Civil War camps strictly speaking (closed in 1922) and what were called the Northern Camps of Special Designation (SLON) established in 1921 and 1922. Civil War camps, as Peter H. Solomon Jr has noted, were located in the heartland of Russia, not in remote regions of Siberia or the north; and some of their prisoners were allowed to live in residences outside of the camps.[106] Living conditions in these camps were poor and inmates were often treated with cruelty. There were also executions without trial, often of innocent people. Yet the prisoners had contact with the outside world, from which they often received material aid. Political activity was permitted in these camps and many inmates actually survived and regained their freedom.[107] In fact, Civil War camps were to a significant degree established to punish labor offenses, and prisoners were paid 70–75 per cent of normal trade union wages, the remainder being deducted by the state to defray the costs of the camps. For peasant prisoners this was, in a cruel irony, more than they could have earned at home.[108] The payment of prisoners was, to be sure, a very bizarre illustration of some of the contraditions of early Soviet rule.

The Northern Camps of Special Designation (SLON), in contrast, were situated in remote locations in the northermost region of Russia, on the White Sea islands and adjacent regions on the mainland. The core of the camps was located in the Solvetsky Islands;[109] escape from these islands was virtually impossible. The first prisoners to be brought to the SLON camps were former White officers; shortly afterwards they were joined by participants in the Kronstadt revolt in early 1921, and then shortly after that by Socialists and Anarchists.[110] Brutality was also known in these camps, and a certain Bachulis became particularly notorious as the commandant of the concentration camp at Pertominsk. He was eventually replaced by Moscow in the Spring of 1923 after the Anarchists went on a hunger strike to protest his behavior.[111] However, political activity was permitted, as had been the case in the Civil War camps. In fact, the SLON administration recognized to the politicals of leftist parties, but not to right-wingers, the right to refuse to work entirely and to organize themselves and elect representatives to negotiate with the camp administration.[112] Finally, it should be noted that neither the SLON nor the Civil War camps were established for the purpose of increasing the productive capacity of the Russian economy – even as late as 1928, convict labor produced only 0.02 per cent of the national income in the Soviet Union.[113] As Stalin consolidated his rule, this changed quite radically. The number of prisoners increased by leaps and bounds. By the middle of 1930 there were 662,000 prisoners in the camps, and by 1932 the total number of inmates had reached the very high figure of nearly 2 million.[114] Prison labor was now becoming an important part of the Russian economy.

The immediate forebears of the Stalinist camps were indeed those of the OGPU (the Unified State Political Administration – the political police) in the Solovetsky Islands, but as Peter H. Solomon Jr has again pointed out: 'The historical significance of Solovki [as Solovetsky was known] lay not in maintaining a tradition of forced labor (which it did not do), but in keeping the Chekists in the prison business, thereby allowing them to develop a cadre of task-masters and a tradition of ruthlessness, which could be drawn upon later.'[115]

Implications and Conclusions

The argument can and has been made that the Red Terror worked: the Bolshevik government stayed in power and successfully confronted the counterrevolution. But this argument completely begs the question. One must still ask: *what* was won and at whose cost? For one key thing, the power of the working class and peasantry was only a shadow of its former reality by the time the Red Terror and War Communism came to an end in early 1921.

In the 1930s, Leon Trotsky indignantly rejected the attempt by Victor Serge and others to go beyond the necessary condemnation of and opposition to Stalin's barbarous political and social system and critically examine the earlier record of the Bolshevik regime. Trotsky treated these criticisms of Lenin's government with a contemptuous attitude. As he put it: 'Idealists and pacifists always accused the revolution of 'excesses.' But the main point is that 'excesses' flow from the very nature of revolution which in itself is but an 'excess' of history. Whoever so desires may on this basis reject (in little articles) revolution in general. I do not reject it...'[116] If we accept Trotsky's reasoning, then there is indeed no reason to write a chapter like this one, provided of course we know the presumed class nature of the revolution in question. However, Trotsky's polemical posture, as the man of action sharply responding to intellectual nit-pickers who don't know what war and revolution are all about, was in the last analysis nothing less than a request that we suspend our critical faculties and issue him and the rest of the mainstream Bolshevik leadership with a blank cheque of uncritical approval. At the very least, this attitude is a serious obstacle to the prevention of avoidable excesses in the future. More importantly, it prevents an examination of the systematics of such excesses and thus the development of a revolutionary politics that will minimize the driving of future 'Don Cossacks' into opposition, let alone the corrupting influence of uncontrolled power on revolutionary personnel and institutions.

Yet we can in fact speak of 'unavoidable excesses' in a truly revolutionary upheaval if by that we mean such things as the following:

1　Actions that run beyond or even contrary to the policies of the revolutionary organizations and leadership and for which of course they are not responsible e.g. indiscriminate looting, 'wine pogroms' during the Bolshevik Revolution.[117] Excess of this sort are in fact unavoidable in any truly popular upheaval.

2   Abuses carried out in the process of implementing orders that do not intrinsically require abuses for their successful implementation. For example, an arrest order carried out against an unresisting unarmed suspect certainly does not require physical or verbal abuse, let alone torture. Yet such abuses are very likely to occur in the course of the inevitable hatreds created by a civil war situation. These are also unavoidable excesses that, if appropriately condemned and punished by the responsible revolutionary authorities, would most likely greatly reduce the frequency and scope of the abuses, and thus earn these leaders praise rather than criticism.

However, there is a huge difference between these cases, occurring in the course of more or less spontaneous behavior among the masses, or even among rank-and-file government functionaries, and 'excesses' that occur as the result of conscious policy choices by the revolutionary leaders. Thus, we cannot meaningfully talk about 'excesses' if the policies of the revolutionary authorities themselves call for objectionable and unjustifiable behavior, e.g. the Cheka's policy of 'assembly-line' arrests and executions without any external controls whatsoever. I would also place under this heading the cynical policy on the part of the Cheka's leadership of transferring suspects from pacified to military zones where the death penalty still applied. Neither can we meaningfully talk about 'unavoidable excesses' if the policies of the revolutionary leaders are such that they cannot possibly be carried out successfully without excesses.[118] This was the case, for example, with Lenin's and the Bolshevik government's infatuation with the anti-market policies of War Communism – policies that Marxists, more than anybody else, should have known were totally incompatible with the objective realities of the Russian economy and society.

Furthermore, and in light of the above discussion, can we reach any conclusion as to how all of this affected the eventual development of Stalinism? I submit that the victory of those Bolshevik currents represented by the leadership of the Cheka (Dzerzhinsky, Latsis, Peters) in close alliance with Lenin's 'pragmatic' institutional adaptation to their politics and overall practices and the politics of such other Bolshevik leaders as Stalin and Trotsky (until 1923) helped to consolidate a specific political practice and ideology. This type of politics, especially in its perceptions of danger, the appropriate means to deal with it, and the justifications of those means, at the very least did not contribute to the creation of significant defenses, resistances, let alone immunity to the later Stalinist virus. Needless to say, unfavorable objective conditions (e.g. war, economic scarcities, etc.) played a crucial role in strengthening these tendencies over others, but such an 'objective' analysis cannot ignore that political beliefs, inclinations, and tendencies had a dynamic of their own and were not merely a reflex response to objective conditions. This is not to say that Stalinism was inevitable given the prevailing climate of 'Leninism-in-power.' Subsequent objective developments or timely changes of political course, particularly at the end of the Civil War in 1921, might have turned the tide in at least a somewhat different direction.

Revolution and Civil Liberties

Even the most democratic of working-class socialist revolutions will in all likelihood, as I suggested at the beginning of the chapter, be confronted with strong and forceful resistance by the defeated ruling classes. Moreover, this resistance will be aided by some members of the exploited and oppressed groups that have been politically and ideologically influenced by the old ruling classes. In the light of this, the new revolutionary government will need to suppress, in order to defend itself, violent and subversive acts against the new socialist state. Moreover, the revolutionary government cannot wait until these violent acts take place, but must try to prevent their occurrence whenever possible. In order to do this successfully, the government will also be forced, in specific instances, to curtail the civil liberties of those actively supporting the violent opponents of the revolution, e.g. the detention of individuals who are providing or helping to provide supplies to a counterrevolutionary guerrilla army.

Nevertheless, the repression that the revolutionary government will be forced to carry out, particularly right after the overthrow of the old ruling classes, can be justified and controlled by democratic aims and purposes. Certain general rules can be established. First of all, repression can be limited and controlled in its effects if it is guided by the general criteria that repressive acts be proportional, relevant, and specific to the nature of the counterrevolutionary acts committed. Moreover, punishmment should generally be applied selectively to the actual individuals involved in preparing and/or committing those acts, and not against broad categories of people. In other words, collective punishments should be avoided.

It is interesting in this context to study the evolution of US jurisprudence during the twentieth century. This, from a strictly analytical point of view, and not of course because we are entitled to make totally ahistorical analogies between revolutionary Russia and the USA. I must also emphasize that I am referring only to the legal theory involved here, since there has always been a gap between the theory and practice of free speech in the US and other societies. Wholesale violations of the most elementary rights have taken place in the United States during such critical periods as the Cold War, World War II and World War I, the Civil War, and the War of Independence and its aftermath. Let me also note that the legal tradition I will be discussing was primarily established in a society at peace and one that, for many decades, had not waged warfare in its own territory even when it was at war.

Nonetheless, in the North American legal tradition, a body of thought has been developed dealing with what are considered to be legitimate and illegitimate curtailments of the right of free speech. Because of the strong elements of *analytical reasoning* invoked in this body of thought, I believe it is useful and that it can be adapted to the very different situations confronted by post-revolutionary societies. Specifically, I found it helpful to study the evolution of US jurisprudence during this century in regard to three 'degree-of-danger tests' that the US courts have utilized at various times in the past in order to determine when speech is and is not protected by the Constitution.[119]

First, there is the 'bad tendency' test. This has been the most restrictive test, and one that the courts have tended to move away from in recent decades. Judges applying this test have stopped or punished speech that, if allowed to continue, they believed had a tendency to create a serious danger at some indefinite time in the future. This test has also been described as 'killing the serpent in its egg' and as 'putting out the spark before the conflagration.'[120] As it turns out, this was an issue addressed by Karl Marx in his very first political article written in 1842 and published in 1843. In criticizing his government's decree on censorship, Marx declared: 'The writer is thus subjected to the *most frightful terrorism*, the *jurisdiction of suspicion*. Laws about *tendency*, laws that do not provide objective norms, are laws of terrorism, such as were conceived by the state's exigencies under Robespierre and the state's rottenness under the Roman emperors.'[121]

Second, there exists the 'clear and present danger' test, which tended to replace the 'bad tendency' criterion. Originally articulated by Justice Holmes in the case of Schenk [General Secretary of the Socialist Party] vs. the United States in 1919, the test initially constituted a narrow and restrictive interpretation of free speech and was applied against Schenk in the spirit of the 'bad tendency' test.[122] In later years, while the label remained unchanged, the test was given a clear libertarian logic. In this latter version, the test permits speech to continue until it creates a danger to society that is both clear, obvious, and present, i.e. immediate. Justice Brandeis articulated this new view of the test in the 1927 case of Whitney vs. California as follows:

> To justify suppression of free speech there must be reasonable ground to fear that serious evil will result if free speech is practiced. There must be reasonable ground to believe that the danger apprehended is imminent. There must be reasonable ground to believe that the evil to be prevented is a serious one . . . no danger flowing from speech can be deemed clear and present, unless the incidence of the evil apprehended is so imminent that it may befall before there is opportunity for full discussion. If there be time to expose through discussion the falsehood and fallacies, to avert the evil by the processes of education, the remedy to be applied is more speech, not enforced silence. Only an emergency can justify repression . . . It is therefore, always open to Americans to challenge a law abridging free speech and assembly by showing that there was no emergency justifying it . . . The fact that speech is likely to result in some violence or

in destruction of property is not enough to justify its suppression. There must be the probability of serious injury to the state. Among freemen, the deterrents ordinarily to be applied to prevent crime are education and punishment for violations of the law, not abridgment of the rights of free speech and assembly.[123]

Third, there is the 'incitement' test. This is the least restrictive of the three tests. It allows speech to continue 'past clear and present danger to a point just short of actual incitement to illegal conduct.'[124] Analytically akin to the 'clear and present danger' doctrine, this test seems to be more liberal in that it places even greater stress on the 'imminence' of the lawless action advocated by the speech in question.[125]

The application of the 'bad tendency' test in a post-revolutionary situation would leave the society wide open to the worst kinds of arbitrariness. Without a doubt, this test would make it easier to argue that every open expression of discontent was potentially, if not actually, supportive of the counterrevolution. On the other hand, the 'incitement' test seems to be more appropriate for a later period, i.e. that of a fully consolidated revolutionary society, which could then formally adopt that criterion. Such a regime could well afford to take risks that would be inadvisable for a still violently challenged post-revolutionary government. I submit, then, that the 'clear and present danger' doctrine would serve as the best general guideline for a revolutionary government that must take drastic measures to defend itself, without at the same time negating its overall democratic character. Obviously, this doctrine would be invoked with far greater frequency in a post-revolutionary society confronting violent resistance than in either a consolidated socialist society or a stable capitalist democracy such as the United States is today.

However, the 'clear and present danger' doctrine, which assumes a fair trial and other guarantees of due process, does not apply to some very specific situations often produced by war. Again, let us take the principles of due process and of open and public trials. An open and public trial with the observance of due process may take place even in a situation of civil war, but only in an area or city where revolutionary rule has been consolidated and is not being violently challenged. Such rights could not be observed, for obvious practical reasons, in a combat zone or in an area or city that finds itself in the midst of a 'moving front.' Likewise with the principles of punishment being proportionate to the gravity of the offense and the right to full and relatively lengthy appeal procedures. These rights may not be fully applicable when, for example, it is not clear whether the new rulers have a serious chance of staying in power. In such a situation, a long prison sentence is a practically meaningless punishment, at least insofar as its deterrent effects are concerned. This may justify the death penalty for offenses that in a peaceful situation would deserve only long prison terms. The same reasoning applies to appeal procedures, which may keep a person free for a long enough period of time to avoid punishment altogether. Last but not least, a moving front may create an even more obvious obstacle; namely, the lack of correctional facilities where a proportionate sentence may be carried out.

One can also think of highly stressful war situations where extreme measures may be justified. There are not many penalties available, besides execution, for desertion in the midst of battle. The same goes for indiscriminate looting and rape carried out against the populations inhabiting the areas where the military action is taking place.[126] Much less clearcut, but in my view still justifiable from a 'situational' point of view, is the execution of a handful of highly visible political leaders who: (a) may serve as a rallying point for the armed opposition to the revolution, and (b) represent an element of continuity with the past that is, or can easily become, an important source of restorationist legitimacy.

There is an underlying analytical distinction at the heart of the revolutionary democratic socialist case for the temporary restriction of some civil liberties in the period immediately after the revolutionary seizure of power. I am referring to the difference between two forms of struggle available to a socialist government. First, there is the ideological, political struggle appealing to an attempting to change popular consciousness, that is, to persuade people. Not that this persuasion and appeal to reason can convince people to act against their own interests. Nevertheless, it is possible to persuade the waverers and the doubtful. It is even possible to persuade opponents within one's own broad class camp, if their ideas are treated with respect and their sincerity is not questioned or attacked through the use of character assassination. Successful persuasion can even win over a small minority from the opposite class camp and neutralize a group larger than those won over.

Second, there is the kind of struggle primarily carried out through police, military, and administrative methods. During relatively peaceful periods, the first type of method is the appropriate one to combat the opponents of the revolution. However, this is not as likely to be the case in a situation of civil war or armed combat. The crucial difference lies, as indicated in the quotation from Brandeis noted above, in the element of time. The effects of an inflammatory article in the opposition press, e.g. calling on people to take arms against the government, can be mediated through a process of counterargument and debate during a relatively peaceful time. This is all shortcircuited in a civil war situation. That inflammatory article immediately and directly becomes an organizing tool for the armed opposition. Naturally, in a civil war, the revolutionary government not only engages the armed opposition, but tries to prevent it from recruiting new combatants, and attempts to destroy the organization(s) that make their combat materially possible.

Moreover, even as significant restrictions on civil liberties are being implemented for the duration of the civil war, there is no reason why the democratic organizations of the working class and its allies should stop functioning. It is virtually inevitable that there will be people within the revolutionary camp, in economically developed as well as in less developed countries, who will argue that the revolutionaries cannot 'afford' to debate or disagree with each other, or at least reveal these disagreements to the public at large because this will 'play into the hands of the enemy.' Of course, what is often involved here is not a fear of the enemy, but a fear of the revolution's own supporters. It is assumed that the undoctored and unvarnished truth will disorient, confuse, and make the masses less resolute in their revolutionary convictions and actions. Furthermore, this is also a major reason why it is often argued that the ruling party must be monolithic; otherwise, the enemies of the revolution will use the revolution's own internal disagreements to undermine the 'immature' supporters who are not ready to understand differences of opinion among the revolutionary leaders. In other words, according to this view, the very real political problems that any revolution is likely to encounter will not be resolved through political education, open discussion, and debate. Instead, secrecy and manipulation, if not police and administrative measures, are seen as the answers to these problems.

Also at issue here is the assumption that enforced political agreement is more effective than disagreement, a monolith more practical and desirable than the unity of action arrived at through debate and a democratic vote. The advocates of monolithism always point to the presumed delays and inefficiencies of democracy but ignore the far greater inefficiencies of the lack of democracy – e.g. systematically misinformed decision making, lack of initiative and responsibility, widespread resentment resulting in withdrawal of efficiency and self-mobilization, to say nothing of the withdrawal of organized dissident political tendencies from the struggle against the counterrevolution.

Furthermore, the position outlined here is also different from the fashionable unspoken assumption, if not the explicit view, that holds that the socio-economic underdevelopment of a country merits the restriction or elimination of democratic rights. In practice, this amounts to arguing for permanent restrictions since the conditions justifying them are not likely to be removed within a short time, even if civil warfare promptly comes to an end. Again, this argument is based not on a specific situation of armed conflict, but rather on long-term assumptions about people. This frequently involves the colonialist argument, often reformulated in 'leftist' terms today, that the poverty-stricken natives, like children, are not ready for self-government.

Finally, nothing can provide an *iron-clad guarantee* for the preservation of democracy in a society that has undergone a social revolution. The actions and institutions resulting from the politics and value commitments hegemonic in the revolutionary movement are, in the last analysis, the only safeguards subject to human control that may promise a humane and liberating outcome to the revolutionary process. In any case, authentic revolutions happen not because their outcomes are guaranteed, but because no other options remain.

5

Socialist Legality

I am told that, just beyond the horizon, new forms of working-class power are about to arise which, being found upon egalitarian productive relations, will require no inhibition and can dispense with the negative restrictions of bourgeois legalism. A historian is unqualified to pronounce on such utopian projections. All that he knows is that he can bring in support of them no historical evidence whatsoever. His advice might be: watch this new power for a century or two before you cut your hedges down.

E. P. Thompson[1]

The Nature of Post-Revolutionary Legality

Soon after the Bolsheviks came to power, the new government tried to implement a legal philosophy that emphasized simplicity, flexibility, and mass participation in the administration of justice. However, what prevailed in practice in the chaotic conditions of the early years of the revolution was a much more mixed legal system. One scholar has described it as a

> jerry-built legal order comprised of miscellaneous proletarian principles of jurisprudence, former tsarist laws, an essentially local court system staffed by a lay and often illiterate bench guided mainly by its revolutionary consciousness, blurred and generally indistinguishable legal and social roles, and the vaguely defined rights and duties of both citizen and state.[2]

Yet it is possible to discern important and consequential legal tendencies in these early years of the revolution. These developed in response to the situation facing the government, or were rooted in the politics of mainstream Bolshevism, or both.

Egalitarian and Humanitarian Aspects of Early Bolshevik Legality

The great upheaval that brought the Bolsheviks to power touched all areas of social and political life in Russia. The legal system was no exception. The

Bolsheviks instituted civil marriage and no-fault divorce. They also declared full legal and civil equality, and promised equal educational and occupational opportunities, for women. The revolutionary government also committed itself to the establishment of publicly funded maternity and day care.[3] Moreover, the classification of children as legitimate or illegitimate was abolished.[4] The courts and correctional systems were similarly affected by an egalitarian spirit some-times verging on chaos. As John N. Hazard describes it,

> no one respected the dignity of the new court. Parties to suits sat on the benches wearing their hats, replying to questions without rising from their places, while a hum of conversation among those waiting to be heard drowned out the hearing ... The policemen on duty made no effort to stop conversations between spectators and those brought in under arrest.[5]

Yet, aside from these chaotic tendencies, contemporary accounts very often show the prevalence of a strong spirit of compassion and equity among the popular elements involved in these trials.[6] Moreover, the establishment of lay judges to sit together in the courts with professional judges was part of a process that eventually brought about a radical change in the class composition of the judiciary. For example, in 1923 it was estimated that 76 per cent of people's judges were workers and peasants. Of course, one short-term byproduct of this transformation was a low educational level among the new judiciary.[7] Neverthe-less, as early as June of 1920 the system of lay judges began to be challenged, although still unsuccessfully, with the argument that 'it is time once and for all to finish with this institution, which was born of liberalism and which is at the present time unnecessary under the dictatorship of the proletariat.'[8] In this context, 'liberalism' was an ideologically revealing term of abuse against the notion that the people might still need protection against the full-time repre-sentatives of the state: i.e. the professional judges.

Furthermore, early Soviet policies in the field of correction and punishment made some considerable advances in the treatment of common crime. In this area, Soviet policies before Stalin tended to be guided by the most humanita-rian and progressive notions then available in Western Europe and America. A decree issued on 14 January 1918 by the Council of People's Commissars proclaimed that 'there shall be no courts or prisons for children,' and raised the lowest age for criminal liability from the Tsarist 10 years to 17. Criminal suspects below that age were to be referred to the educational- and welfare-oriented Commissions on Juvenile Affairs. However, subsequent legislation adopted in 1919, 1920, and 1922 marked a retreat from the 1918 decree, although without quite returning to Tsarist age limits and other practices in this field.[9] During the early years of the Soviet regime most criminals did not serve prison terms, and the average length of terms served by the minority who did go to prison decreased markedly.[10] In one of the more ideologically overstated innovations, the term 'guilt' was deleted from the official vocabulary – society alone was guilty when its members perpetrated crimes. In 1922, the maximum sentence for a criminal sentence was raised from the previous revolutionary maximum of five years to ten, but this still compared favorably with the Tsarist maximum of 20 years. Parole was introduced and used on a large scale.[11] Common prisoners were, at least in theory, human beings who needed to be educated in self-discipline, and it was argued that it was desirable to have them serve as their own guards and sometimes even to carry weapons. Besides, these prisoners were to be provided with full educational opportunities and have their own publications. Last but not least, a new 'half-way house' form of criminal punishment was introduced: obligatory work without confinement, at a some-what reduced rate of pay, and without being able to change jobs without permission of the local agents of the Commissariat of Justice.[12] By the mid-1920s, however, this particular innovation had virtually ceased to exist.[13] Moreover, by the Stalinist late twenties, the situation described above had radically changed and the number of people in Soviet prisons was significantly higher than even during the worst years of the Tsarist period.[14]

The Repressive Aspects of Early Bolshevik Legality

Any significant, let alone revolutionary, legal innovation will likely be accompa-nied by an unavoidable cost in procedural and substantive legal safeguards and predictability. Thus, for example, flexibility and discretion on the part of judges is incompatible with the full standardization and fixity of punishment for particular crimes – a dilemma that continues to plague legal reformers in many countries to this very day. Likewise, the simplification and popularization of any revolutionary legal system would very likely have at least a temporary negative effect on procedural safeguards, particularly in a situation such as that of early Soviet Russia where the country confronted a civil war situation for approxi-mately two and a half years (1918–20). However, I would argue that these real dilemmas can be seen as having decisive weight only when they act to thwart or impede an already existing general commitment to the *basic and elementary* rules of due process on the part of the legal innovators. It thus follows that this would not be the case when the political and philosophical assumptions and predis-positions of the new judiciary authorities already show a clear bias against the very *principles* of due process. Furthermore, this bias against the rules of due process would be all the more consequential if it was adhered to whether or not there was a contradiction between due process and a specific substantive legal reform, or regardless of the objective circumstances prevailing in the country, such as war or peace. Since I have already discussed in previous chapters the unfavorable objective situation prevailing after the Bolsheviks came to power, my most important task here will be the exploration of the revolutionaries' most fundamental legal principles, rather than the outlining of a solution to the likely contradictions of a fully functioning socialist legal system, e.g. the conflicting demands of formal law and substantive justice.

Indeed, as I showed in the previous chapter, the Civil War witnessed a dramatic rise in governmental arbitrariness, particularly in the case of the Extraordinary Commission for Combating Counterrevolution and Sabotage (the Cheka). Therefore, it is not surprising that during this period there was also a general and wholesale deterioration of the legal procedural rights and guarantees that had remained in force in the period following the October Revolution. Nevertheless, one must very seriously question whether and which of these changes can be justified or even explained strictly on the basis of the *objective* needs and problems posed by Civil War conditions. Thus, for example, as I pointed out in the previous chapter, a moving military front may often require the administration of summary forms of justice for common criminal acts, let alone for sabotage, treason, and desertion.

However, let us examine, for instance, the changes in the very important area of trial procedure. In the first few months after the October Revolution, many liberal reforms in criminal procedure introduced under the Provisional Government in 1917 had remained in force. Lawyers had retained at least the formal right to participate in pretrial investigations and were sometimes even permitted to attend the investigator's interrogation of witnesses. While minor criminal trials were held in local people's courts consisting of a professional judge, two lay assessors, and no jury, more serious criminal cases such as murder were tried before a jury in higher courts. After the beginning of the Civil War, the Cheka and the Revolutionary Tribunals took over primary responsibility for the investigation and trial of criminal cases from the ordinary courts and investigative agencies. Moreover, the bar associations and union of advocates were closed and private practitioners were banned from the courts. We can clearly detect, particularly in these last changes concerning the individual practice of law, the state socialist *politics* of War Communism rather than any situationally justified response to the Civil War emergency. Besides, at the very time the war was coming to an end, in October of 1920, the jury system was abolished and the defender was prohibited by law from participating in the criminal process before the indictment had been issued.[15]

Another very important instance of the deterioration of procedural rights and guarantees during the Civil War took place in the labor field. On 14 November 1919 'comradely courts' were established attached to trade union organizations on every level of the enterprise in order to deal with violations of labor regulations and wage agreements. The possible penalties that could be ordered by these informal courts included censure, reprimand, the denial of the right to run for office, and, much more seriously, demotions, reductions in pay for one month, dismissal, and the sending of serious offenders to labor camps. In spite of the fact that these courts could impose very serious penalties, no provision was made for the establishment of legal procedures or measures of due process to protect the accused or help the court.[16]

By the time the New Economic Policy established in 1921 had taken root, further significant changes had taken place in the Soviet legal system with the restoration of the procuracy (a system of centralized political supervision of all the courts originally established by Peter the Great and abolished by the liberal reforms of the judiciary carried out in the nineteenth century),[17] the reestablishment of the bar abolished under War Communism, and the introduction of

a new hierarchical judiciary and professional legal education.[18] The introduction of the NEP required a certain degree of stability and predictability at least
in the field of civil law;[19] and it was in this context that codification was carried
out for civil and criminal law and procedure, and for land law and labor law, and
new statutes were created for such topics as patents and copyright.[20]

It should be noted that, while at this time the Cheka was reorganized and its
name changed to GPU, its arbitrary mode of operation remained fundamentally
unchanged. Although the end of armed conflict and the Bolshevik victory in the
Civil War naturally brought about a reduction in the sheer numbers of people
directly experiencing the government's legal arbitrariness, this began to express
itself in altogether new areas. By the beginning of 1921, the ruling Communist
Party had been left with very little popular support and a very small social base.
The party had also acquired a bureaucratic apparatus and had virtually eliminated the participation of other parties in the political life of the country. This
was followed shortly after by the banning of factions inside the ruling party
itself. All of this established the political basis for Lenin's apparently unproblematic legal assumption in November 1921 (i.e. a year after the end of the Civil
War) that the central party authorities – although not the local ones – had the
right to force judicial authorities to discontinue proceedings against members of
the Communist Party and have them released from custody.[21]

A no less serious abuse of the judicial process for strictly political ends was
the government's staging of the so-called SR trial held in June 1922. This was a
trial of 32 leaders and members of the Right SR party charged with having
carried out counterrevolutionary and terrorist activities at the beginning of the
Civil War. However, it is virtually certain that the real reason for this carefully
prepared trial was not at all a governmental interest in settling Civil War scores,
but rather an attempt on the part of the Communist Party leadership to
intimidate and squelch the anti-Bolshevik socialist parties that had experienced
a certain resurgence after the end of the Civil War. Be that as it may, the trial
was full of violations of due process. In the first place, the accused were judged
under provisions of a brand new Penal Code which had come into force on 1
June 1922, i.e. a week before the start of the trial and several years after the
charged offenses had presumably been committed. Beyond that, other violations of due process included, but were not limited to, the following: the
defense had insufficient time to prepare its case; supporters of the prosecution
were allowed to pack the trial and to demonstrate right inside the courtroom,
while the defense were not provided any tickets for people sympathetic to their
views to be able to attend; documents were taken away from the defense by the
GPU, and defense lawyers were arrested after they had protested various
irregularities and had withdrawn from the case. Eventually, in January 1924,
after pressure was exerted by Western socialists, the sentences of those
condemned to death were commuted to five years' imprisonment and the
sentences of those condemned to prison terms were halved.[22]

The Politics of Early Soviet Legal Arbitrariness

It does not seem that the dire *objective* necessities posed by the Civil War and its aftermath, as I earlier suggested, were the only or perhaps even the principal reasons for the existence of a large degree of legal arbitrariness during early Bolshevik rule, let alone after Stalin came to power. In fact, the central Bolshevik leadership shared certain notions and preconceptions about legality that greaty influenced if not determined *how* they responded to the Civil War emergency. Furthermore, after the Civil War was over, the dreadful economic situation and very thin popular base of support for the regime further consolidated the regime's negative attitude to legal curbs on its unlimited powers. In other words, the difficulties of the Civil War and post-Civil War situations interacted with previously existing legal notions, or lack thereof, among the revolutionary leaders. Thus, one cannot but conclude that, even if the revolution had consolidated its power under highly favorable and peaceful circumstances, that would not have solved the major problems posed by the legal politics of the mainstream Bolshevik leadership.

As the Marxist scholar Hal Draper has noted, Lenin argued as early as April 1906, in the pamphlet *The Victory of the Cadets and the Tasks of the Workers' Party*, that the soviets that had arisen in 1905 'represented a dictatorship in embryo, for they recognized *no* other authority, *no* law and *no* standards, no matter by whom established. Authority – unlimited, outside the law, and based on force in the most direct sense of the word – is dictatorship.'[23] Reviewing another similar formulation utilized by Lenin in this pamphlet, Draper wondered whether a lynch mob could not also be considered an example of what Lenin had termed 'dictatorship of the people.'[24] More than 12 years later, Lenin, now the head of the revolutionary government, was still defining the revolutionary dictatorship of the proletariat as a rule 'won and maintained by the use of violence by the proletariat against the bourgeoisie, rule that is unrestricted by any laws.'[25] I would like to stress that Lenin was writing here about something much more consequential than the unavoidable *time lag* that any authentic social revolution would encounter as it went about solving emergencies and implementing radical changes before it had the time formally to legislate on these matters. For a revolutionary Marxist like Lenin, the term 'dictatorship of the proletariat' referred to a whole transitional epoch lasting many years, which is of course a qualitatively lengthier period than that of the civil war and social upheaval that immediately follows the violent overthrow of the old ruling classes.

In practice, however, Lenin on more than one occasion insisted on the strict observance of revolutionary legality. Thus, for example, in November 1918, he drafted a number of theses for a decree on the precise observance of revolutionary laws.[26] Ironically, it was the introduction of NEP and the need to provide a degree of security to *capitalists* that later brought about Lenin's greatest degree of emphasis on legality. In sum, it seems that his attitude to legality was that of expediency at best and of contempt at worst. It should be noted that Lenin's chronic distaste for codified rules, legal or otherwise, had sometimes played an important role in his political practice concerning internal party organization. Lenin's party rules, shortly after the Bolshevik–Menshevik split, were limited to 12, and this 'informality' greater facilitated his ability to make changes contrary to the democratic decisions of the party. When, after the Second Congress of the Bolshevik Party, he could no longer count on the support of his own Central Committee, he reorganized his own followers around a newly convened conference that elected a Russian Bureau. When in 1909 he split with Bogdanov, he removed him at a meeting of a enlarged editorial board of the journal *Proletary*, even though Bogdanov had been properly elected to the Bolshevik Center by the 1907 Congress.[27] Of course, there can be extraordinary circumstances that a revolutionary leadership committed as a *matter of principle* to internal democracy may invoke to justify the violation or bypassing of any set of rules. But for 'pragmatists' such as Lenin, who did not seem to place much value on the notion that there are or should be matters of principle in questions related to internal party organization, there was no need to invoke the existence of extraordinary circumstances. And indeed he infrequently invoked them for Soviet Russia as a whole, even when, as head of the state, he would have been fully justified in doing so, e.g. during the Civil War period.

On the other hand, there were other occasions when Lenin defended strict formality in matters concerning party organization. It was Lenin himself who in 1904, in a different organizational context, provided a devastating argument in favor of formal rules as an antidote to capriciousness and arbitrariness. As he argued against his Menshevik opponents in *One Step Forward, Two Steps Back*:

> To people accustomed to the loose dressing-gown and slippers of the . . . circle domesticity, formal Rules seem narrow, restrictive, irksome, mean, and bureaucratic, a bond of serfdom . . . Aristocratic anarchism cannot understand that formal Rules are needed precisely in order to replace the narrow circle tie by the broad Party tie. The Party tie . . . must be founded on *formal*, 'bureaucratically' worded rules (bureaucratic from the standpoint of the undisciplined intellectual), strict adherence to which can alone safeguard us from the wilfulness and caprices characteristic of the circles.[28]

I would add that Lenin's argument against the Mensheviks can be easily extended to mean that a revolutionary party, if democratic, is not the property of its leaders to do with it as they see fit. Besides this, Lenin's case for formality is, if anything, even more relevant for safeguarding democracy and preventing the 'wilfulness and caprices' of rulers in society at large.

In light of Lenin's view of the role of the law under the dictatorship of the proletariat, it is hardly surprising that he advocated 'revolutionary law consciousness,' and not the writing and codifying of *new* laws, as the *primary* guideline for lay and professional judges alike. Lenin's followers in legal circles such as A. Traynin interpreted 'revolutionary law consciousness' as meaning 'instinct'[29] – indeed a most subjective and arbitrary concept. Along the same lines, Commissar of Justice Kursky found some examples of court decisions taken in the early years of Soviet power 'just in a high degree,' but acknowledged that 'these decisions are shot through with the spirit of unhindered imagination. They are as far from the opinion of a legally trained judge as they are from the heartless form of the old written law.'[30]

Mainstream Leninist, as well as radical Left Bolsheviks, not only tended to downplay the importance of socialist legality, but also were inclined to downplay, if not ignore, the need for individual and minority rights against unlimited state power even under normal peacetime conditions, let alone in a civil war situation. Thus, the first Soviet Constitution adopted on 10 July 1918 had no section broadly equivalent to the first ten amendments, i.e. the Bill of Rights, added to the US Constitution in 1791. No mention was made of a number of fundamental freedoms such as the right of habeas corpus, the right to a public trial, and the prohibition of unreasonable searches of persons and their dwellings. This Constitution did commit itself to the provision of facilities to workers and poor peasants for the publication of newspapers and other printed materials (Article Two, Chapter Five, section 14), and for the holding of free meetings (Article Two, Chapter Five, section 15). Finally, the Constitution also established freedom of conscience and the separation of church from the school and the state and added, perhaps inconsistently, that 'the *right* of religious and anti-religious propaganda is accorded to every citizen' (Article Two, Chapter Five, section 13).[31]

Similarly, since the very beginning, both mainstream Leninists and radical Left Bolsheviks tended to oppose not just those inequities, abuses, and class biases in courtroom procedure and the administration of justice that could be *specifically* traced to the pernicious influence of capitalist society. These revolutionaries were also inclined to see a legal process where the job of the defense was to be independent from and oppose the prosecution as incompatible with socialism. This, notwithstanding that the independence of the defense attorneys from judges and prosecutors was a victory and progress achieved in the course of centuries of worldwide struggles against unlimited, arbitrary authority. In their highly schematic view, which undoubtedly was also an important ideological background factor influencing the Bolshevik leadership's reaction to adverse objective conditions, socialism was conceived as eliminating the fundamental antagonism between the individual and the state. This antagoinism was in turn seen as constituting the logical basis for a legal process based on the notion of independent, conflicting parties.

In the light of this, it is not surprising that another Civil War measure, the Law on the People's Court of 30 November 1918, stipulated that citizens could no longer turn to a specific lawyer for help. Requests for legal assistance were made to a college of salaried state functionaries or to the court, which then appointed the lawyer. Furthermore, in civil cases, representatives were assigned to argue a case only when the college felt the complaint was justified. As Eugene Huskey has suggested, this meant that the state was thereby ruling on the validity of a case before it had been put before the court.[32] This was all of a

piece with the early Soviet legal assumption that defense lawyers were supposed
to work as members of a team in court rather than as the representatives of
individuals. The lawyer had to come to think of himself as an 'assistant' to the
judge, and to subordinate individual rights to the public policy of the state.
Moreover, it was also argued that the old efforts at maintaining the independence of lawyers had been progressive when the state was a representative of the
bourgeoisie, but that was no longer the case when the state had become a
defender of the masses.[33] In fact, it took some time before these new norms
were effectively observed in courtroom practice. Ironically, because most
members of the colleges of accusers and defenders had been educated and
socialized professionally under the Tsarist legal system, they still regarded the
criminal process as a conflict between the prosecution and the defense.[34]

'Instinct,' 'unhindered imagination;' these notions soon found their counter-
part at a higher and more systematic level of abstraction in the writings of the
radical Left Bolshevik legal philosopher E. B. Pashukanis. In his *General Theory
of Law and Marxism* published in 1924, Pashukanis put forward his 'commodity
exchange' theory of law, which saw the source of law as the market where
commodities were exchanged, and consequently argued that it was only
bourgeois–capitalist society that could create all the conditions essential to the
attainment of complete definiteness of the juridical element in social relationships. That is, the law was a form of equivalence among individualized and
egoistic subjects. Or, as Pashukanis explained elsewhere:

> The *categories* most characteristic of bourgeois law – the subject of a right,
> ownership, contract, etc., primarily and most clearly reveal their material
> basis in the phenomenon of exchange. The category of the legal subject
> corresponds to the category of the value of labour. The impersonal and
> general quality of commodities is enhanced by the formal qualities of
> equality and freedom which owners of commodities confer upon one
> another.[35]

Pashukanis also contended that the role of the dictatorship of the proletariat as
a transition period was not to create a system of proletarian law but to pave the
way for the dying out of the juridical form in general. This form would
completely disappear with the coming of communism.[36]

Undoubtedly, the work of Pashukanis constituted a serious theoretical
contribution to a Marxist sociology of law *under capitalism*. In my view, the most
valuable and significant insights in Pashukanis' theory related to the development of civil law (e.g. contracts) in bourgeois society. Indeed, it was reasonable
to expect that civil law as the law of the market place would begin to lose
importance in the Soviet social system. Furthermore, as I shall argue in greater
detail later in this chapter, to the extent that the political, economic, and
cultural level of the masses rose, it was not altogether utopian to assume that the
element of legal coercion would *gradually* become less important in the management of daily life.

However, far from helping to bring about communism, Pashukanis and his legal school did help to establish an ideology that eroded the legitimacy of law in Soviet society.[37] The efforts by Pashukanis and his followers to abolish law while workers' and peasants' democracy, let alone the abolition of classes and the hierarchical division of labor, was retrogressing rather than advancing could only have the practical effect of increasing arbitrariness and power disparities. In the late 1920s and early 1930s the punishment for acts not explicitly forbidden by the law greatly increased under the principle of 'analogy' that had been originally elaborated by Pashukanis' legal school.[38] In fact, this innovation entailed nothing less than a rejection of the elementary principle of *nulla poena sine lege* (no penalty without law). It should be noted that we can find an early expression of this principle in 1919, when the Guiding Principles on Criminal Law of the RSFSR introduced the 'material determination of the crime' into criminal legislation. What this meant in essence was that every 'socially dangerous' act (action or omission) directed against the Soviet state or against its economic, social, or political system was a criminal offense whether or not it was expressly forbidden by the criminal law. While this principle was originally established under Civil War conditions, it remained in force in the post-Civil War Russian Criminal Code of 1922 (article 6).[39] Moreover, this same 1922 Code 'created no procedure equivalent to the writ of habeas corpus to assure that the matter of arrest and detention would be brought to the attention of a judge.'[40]

The Pashukanis school also developed the principle of 'expediency,' which left to the complete discretion of the judge whether to apply a greater or lesser 'measure of social defense.'[41] Article 6 of the draft criminal code of 1930 was also a truly Orwellian product of this legal philosophy:

> Measures of class oppression and of enforced educational influence may be applied to persons who have committed a certain delinquency as well as to persons who, in spite of not having committed a definite crime, justify the serious apprehension that they eventually may commit delinquencies, in consequence of their relations to criminal surroundings or of their own criminal past.[42]

Given this record of legal 'accomplishments' it is hardly surprising that Pashukanis had also maintained that the state could not recognize absolute and inalienable private rights, for such inalienability was for him 'the inalienability of capitalist exploitation.'[43]

Nevertheless, viewed in its entirety, Pashukanis' record was much more mixed than the above discussion suggests. On the one hand, Pashukanis' *philosophy* was very useful to Stalin as a convenient legal front during the time when Stalin was in the process of consolidating his power through the first Five Year Plan and the forced collectivization of the peasantry. This was also the period when Stalin carried out a pseudo-egalitarian policy, against his actual or potential opponents in the intelligentsia, similar to Mao's Cultural Revolution of the 1960s.[44] On the other hand, it seems that in the meantime Pashukanis had genuinely changed or modified his views, aside from the fact that he was forced to recant many of his legal theories in the early 1930s. Thus, in the late twenties, the legal section of the Communist Academy headed by Pashukanis, while accepting the further politicization of legal processes, still favored a fuller statement of procedural guarantees and opposed the elimination of some of the more traditional elements of criminal procedure. This was one of the many repressive changes proposed by N. V. Krylenko, at the time Stalin's principal jurist and an early supporter of Pashukanis' legal philosophy. Apparently, Pashukanis had by then adopted the view that at this time Soviet society was not yet ready for the elimination of the legal form.[45] Also, in 1936, as head of the Institute of Law of the new Academy of Sciences, Pashukanis was the leader of a group of lawyers working on the reform of Soviet criminal law in a more humane and less repressive direction.[46]

In any case, after the period of the late 1920s and early 1930s – i.e. the first Five Year Plan and forced collectivization at home and the ultra-left and highly sectarian 'Third Period' Communism abroad – Stalin shifted gears again. He had won his 'revolution from above;' he had vanquished the Russian peasantry and fully consolidated his power at home by defeating the various inner-party oppositions. Internationally, the period of the Popular Front had now begun. Stalin, no longer needing to make 'revolution' at home, at the same time became increasingly concerned with his image among Western 'progressives' and quickly moved towards legal formalism and democratic appearances as exemplified by the Constitution of 1936. By this time, the 'revolutionary' theories of the original Pashukanis school had become superfluous if not counterproductive, and were duly denounced by the likes of the former Menshevik A. Vyshinsky. This man, who was to acquire great notoriety as the main prosecutor of the Moscow Trials in the mid and late thirties, was a true master of the new Stalinist legal order, i.e. the combination of terror with legal formality.[47] As I indicated above, although Pashukanis had been forced to repudiate his earlier views, he had continued to engage in legal work. Finally, on 20 January 1937, *Pravda* denounced him as an 'enemy of the people.' There was no public trial of Pashukanis – he simply disappeared.[48]

'Moderate' and Other Legal Views in the Early Soviet Period

Pashukanis' legal philosophy did not go unchallenged. Within the Communist Academy, a so-called 'moderate' wing led by Peter Stuchka opposed Pashukanis' 'radical' wing. While supporting the overall legal orientation established by mainstream Bolshevism, Stuchka nevertheless criticized, among other things, Pashukanis' overextension of the commodity exchange concept of law from civil law to other branches of law and his failure to distinguish public law (e.g. laws regulating relations among governmental institutions) from private law. Stuchka also insisted, against Pashukanis, on the necessity for Soviet law in the transaition period after the revolution.[49]

I find a striking parallel between the Communist legal 'moderates,' who were more likely than the mainstream and Left Bolsheviks to defend the traditional notions of individual rights in the state's judicial system, and those Right Bolsheviks such as Riazanov and Lozovsky who expressed similar concerns in the political and trade union arenas. In this context, it is interesting to note that, while in the late twenties Aron Solts, a prominent Communist discussing the future of the legal profession, maintained that socialism in Russia had eliminated the opposition between the state and the individual and thus the need for the adversary process, Stuchka defended the adversary process as a 'cultural achievement' that should not be discarded.[50] In fact, in 1918, Stuchka's influence had made itself felt along similar lines in the Moscow courts. There, unlike in Petrograd, clients were then allowed to choose their attorneys. However, this did not mean that wealthier people were thereby supposed to acquire an advantage, since no money changed hands between client and lawyer. Instead, clients paid their fees into a central fund on the basis of a schedule of set fees. These earnings were in turn disbursed to the working attorneys on the basis of a formula that took into account the number and complexity of cases handled. Also, the local soviet in Moscow permitted legal representatives, when they were occasionally called upon to prosecute cases, to excuse themselves if they disagreed with the bases of the prosecution.[51] It should not then be surprising that Stuchka on one occasion even questioned Lenin's views on the role of law under the dictatorship of the proletariat, although he did this subtly and indirectly, given that he said what follows as late as the year 1931:

> We know Lenin's definition of dictatorship as 'a power basing itself on coercion and not connected with any kind of laws,' . . . [but] what should be the relationship of the dictatorship of the proletariat *to its law* and to law in general as the means of administration?[52]

We also find less important Soviet jurists who, while still defending Lenin's concept of 'revolutionary legal consciousness,' quite openly expressed the view that the suppression or limitation of individual rights was justified only by the existence of the extraordinary conditions of civil war. As I. Slavin discussed the Civil War period in 1922:

> The court quite properly became an instrument of the proletarian class struggle. This is completely logical, and can not be otherwise, because its purpose is to protect the interests of the ruling class in Russia – the proletariat . . . However, the past activities of the judicial organs have revealed a very vulnerable Achilles' heel – the insufficient defense of the interests of the individual vis-à-vis the state. But one should not forget the objective conditions that existed, namely, the impact of the extremely intensive and ceaseless struggle on both sides . . . Consequently, when the present objective conditions evoked by the Civil War change, the courts of Soviet Russia will be free to defend the rights of the individual in the near future.

Moreover, in an article published in 1922, Stuchka reported how, in November 1917, Lunacharsky and other unnamed leading Bolsheviks had expressed significant opposition to the initial decree abolishing the old courts on the grounds that the newly established courts would be functioning without laws. In any case, as Stuchka tells it, Lunacharsky did change his mind and became a strong supporter of the decree.[53]

However, it is fair to say that, in general, Soviet jurists tended to minimize the role to be played by law in the post-revolutionary period, although, as I have just shown, not all of them arrived at the Pashukanis school's extreme conclusions on this matter. One who seemed to have taken law very seriously was the early Soviet jurist and 'Old Bolshevik' M. A. Reisner, a member of the Bolshevik Party since 1905, who had been greatly influenced by L. I. Petrazhitskii, the well-known Russian–Polish legal philosopher of pre-revolutionary times. While Reisner was a proponent of the notion of legal intuition, he did maintain that law would be 'killed' only in the highest stages of Communism with the establishment of the formula 'to each according to his need.'[54] Contrary to the predominant tendencies in Marxism then or now, Reisner strongly argued for 'the necessity of utilizing legal motivation' as a mass revolutionary tool and added:

> Legal emotions are distinguished as being of a character which demands as of right, which realizes its rights by force, which defends its rights by battle, and which takes pitiless vengeance if its rights are violated. The legal psyche is a psyche of struggle and of dangerous and destructive collisions; failure by the obligor to fulfill an obligation is conceived of by the other side as a positive injury, as an encroachment, as a cruel insult, as a wrong caused to a human being. And a similar consciousness operates with extraordinary force and sharpness upon the legal feeling; for this reason those thereabout are extensively infected with anger and impatience when a right is trampled under foot and we see the picture of a collective explosion of vengeance and hatred directed against the criminals – against the persons who have broken the law.[55]

Here we can see an interesting and striking contrast between, on the one hand, Pashukanis' mastery of abstraction flawed by a dangerous schematism and, on the other hand, Reisner's socio-psychological subtlety that nonetheless seemed to ignore the double-edged nature of his insights. After all, legal emotions can and have been directed against both the oppressors as well as the oppressed, e.g. the slogan of 'law and order' in the contemporary USA. Besides, legal approaches to social change can and have been a serious obstacle to the development of social and political movements – e.g. the frequently conservatizing impact of the legal strategies of the National Association for the Advancement of Colored People on the Black movement, and of many labor lawyers on trade union insurgents in the USA today.

Towards a Democratic Revolutionary Legal Theory

Capitalist Legality and Socialist Legality

As liberalism has increasingly lost whatever combativeness it may have had in the past, it has at the same time developed a strong inclination to legal strategies as its preferred solution to fundamental political and social problems. In the present context of studying the origins of the Soviet system, there is no better representative of this approach than the legally trained and well-known Sovietologist Leonard Schapiro. A very telling and succinct formulation of Schapiro's views on law and social change appeared in a posthumous collection of his writings:

> What the common law taught me is what I believed for years – that a society can only progress by evolution, and not by convulsions, by growth and not by surgery dictated by belief in some system. And further, that the only safeguard against convulsion, and the only condition for ensuring organic growth, is a well-rooted legal system and a strong and independent judiciary to safeguard it. Never must these primary requirements of a civilized society be sacrificed to the demands of the uncultured masses which will readily yield to the blandishments of demagogues in the hope of achieving their material aims.[56]

Aside from its crude and extreme elitism, this formulation, and Schapiro's work as a whole, ignores enormous class and power disparities that cannot be radically changed through legal methods. Hence his inability to understand, let alone explain, the need for revolution. Schapiro was even incapable of developing a clear notion of the *social structural* impediments to the development of a 'well-rooted legal system and a strong and independent judiciary' in societies such as pre-revolutionary Russia. In contrast to views such as his, the Marxist tradition has been in my view quite correct and justified in seeing legal systems as less important than the existing relation of forces as these are expressed in social, economic, and political power structures. But this basically sound perspective has also carried over, far more often than not, into something else; namely, a dismissal of the law as if it were inconsequential, particularly in the context of the transition to socialism. In this latter context, I would like to suggest that, just as the socialist revolution signifies, among other things, the emergence of the political 'superstructure' as a dominant 'structure' over the blind and chaotic social and economic processes inherited from capitalist society, so it will be necessary for a new dominant legal 'structure' to arise to help establish the 'rules of the game' for the newly developing socio-economic and political system.

My reasoning is based on the notion that the legal system is not only a set of devices designed to help the ruling class preserve its power against the rest of society. It is that, but it is other things as well. The legal system also registers changes and developments in the relations and struggles among classes, and is itself an arena of class struggle. Thus, in 1864, Marx praised the Ten Hours' Bill and declared that it 'was not only a great practical success; it was the victory of a principle; it was the first time that in broad daylight the political economy of the middle class succumbed to the political economy of the working class.'[57] Moreover, the legal system is also an indispensable means to help settle disputes within the ruling classes themselves. Incidentally, this is one major reson why the legal systems in democratic capitalist societies are autonomous spheres with their own rules and dynamic not at the immediate beck and call of the government of the day. The proletariat as the ruling class would not be immune from similar internal disputes. For example, the administration of a democratically planned economy under workers' management would necessarily have to be conducted under rules with the force of law. As Tom Campbell commented in his critique of Pashukanis:

> There is, in fact, little reason to accept Pashukanis's arbitrary refusal to regard as law the non-bourgeois system of societal rules. His conclusions follow only if we accept contract and power theories of rights and give them a very special locus in certain economic relations of capitalism. He himself allows, following Engels, that where there are no clashes of commercial interests there will still have to be administration, that is, the organisation of joint activities on the basis of agreed objectives, as in an army, a religious order, or the running of a railway system ... such organisational activities generate rules and ... some of these rules will include provisions for entering into agreements and having some legal power over others. The fact that these institutions are not used for the purpose of bourgeois commerce is an insufficient reason to decline to call them legal.[58]

More important than what I call the 'horizontal' conflicts discussed by Campbell above, are the potential 'vertical' disputes in a revolutionary society; namely, those conflicts arising out of the relationship between the revolutionary state on one hand, and local forms of government, groups, and individuals on the other hand. These become especially important if we keep in mind that even the most democratic and egalitarian workers' state would still retain, for an indefinite period of time, a *hierarchical division of labor*. This is the implication I draw from Christian Rakovsky's observation, cited in the Introduction to this volume, that 'when a class takes power, one of its parts becomes the agent of that power.' Moreover, even the most democratic, but complex, society would need legally codified rules and precedents to adjudicate such 'vertical' disputes. Otherwise, the representative bodies of the society would become completely jammed and therefore unviable in the effort to take up and resolve every single question and dispute *anew*.

Along the same lines, post-revolutionary legality could not do without at least a minimum of procedural rigor. Yet procedural rigor need not necessarily be a matter of the extreme degree of empty formalism and elitist pomposity that revolutionaries rightly condemn in the old bourgeois courts. In the last analysis, procedural matters often have great substantive implications. For example, whether or not a warrant for search and arrest is properly executed is a grave matter since it involves the very serious question of who, and under what clearly defined circumstances, is entitled to carry out such an important action.

Last but not least, law can be an important tool in helping to *institutionalize* democratic practices and the social and political conquests achieved by the mass of the population. If we make the reasonable assumption that the initial revolutionary enthusiasm and intense political involvement may decline with the passage of time, then a post-revolutionary legal system may help to 'freeze' the gains made by the revolution, although of course such legal 'freezing' could not possibly overcome by itself a counterrevolutionary reversal of the previous wide distribution of political and social power among the people. I am of course suggesting that the revolution must create a new legal system – the very notion rejected by Pashukanis and other early Soviet legal scholars – as soon as it is practicable after the violent overthrow of the old ruling classes. In sum, this new legal system would sanction the end of the old inequalities while helping to avoid the creation of new ones; in other words, its key function would be to strengthen the newly acquired power of the working class and its allies against both would-be restorationists and would-be usurpers.

Inalienable Rights under Socialism?

The historical experience of twentieth-century 'really existing socialism' conclusively proves that a revolutionary democratic socialist society would need to recognize the existence of certain inalienable rights. By this I mean a series of civil rights and liberties that, under normal conditions, should not be abolished by a routine majority vote of a representative political body or of the electorate in a duly organized referendum. In other words, the majority would not be entitled to do away with what are the very presuppositions of a socialist society based on democratic popular power; e.g. freedom of speech, press, assembly, and workplace and political organization. In the field of penal codes and justice this would include such rights as the following: the necessity of written law, avoidance of retroactive delinquency, burden of proof to be on the accuser, assumption of innocence until proven guilty, full right of individuals to determine the nature of their defense, full immunity for legal defenders from prosecution for lines of defense used in such trials, rejection of the notion of collective responsibility, prohibition of torture, suppression of the death penalty outside of civil war and war situations, universal system of public trials by juries of peers, and, last but by no means least, the democratic election of all judges, and the right for the mass of the working population to recall elected judges.[59] This concept of inalienable rights would be established by the majority of society itself and it is only that majority, or its duly elected representatives, that would make the determination about whether or not truly extraordinary circumstances existed that justified the curtailment of one or more of these rights.

In any case, as I have argued elsewhere in this volume, these restrictions should be strictly temporary and relevant, specific and proportionate to the social dangers involved. I, for one, would also be open to the idea that such drastic measures should require the approval of a higher percentage of the representative bodies than just 50 per cent plus one of those voting.

As far as the concept of judicial review is concerned, it would most likely be desirable to retain an institution fulfilling this function and making the ultimate determination of whether or not day-to-day violations of fundamental and basic rights had taken place and/or were justified. This, with the provision that all judges from the highest to the lowest should be subject to popular election and recall and their tenure limited to a finite number of years, thereby avoiding the creation of some kind of non-elected and thus elitist Socialist Supreme Court. Here again we can draw on the experiences of 'really existing socialism.' Thus, on the one hand, I would contend that nothing in the history of those societies has invalidated the Paris Commune ideal of abolishing the separation between the executive and legislative powers. However, given the very short duration of forms of democratic and libertarian socialism in some of these societies, it could also be argued that neither is there anything in the history of these countries that has validated the ideal. On the other hand, I would draw different conclusions regarding the separation of the judiciary from the executive and the legislature, given the necessity to preserve fundamental human freedoms as a *prerequisite* for a democratic workers' state.

Thus, in the same spirit I would support the efforts of the 2,000 lawyers who gathered in Moscow on 25 February 1989 to form an independent Soviet Advocates' Association in spite of the opposition from the Ministry of Justice. It is very revealing, and reminiscent of the debates of the 1920s, that among the topics discussed at the Moscow meeting were the right of defense lawyers to see their clients as soon as they are arrested, guarantees for the independence of judges, and equal rights for the defense and the prosecution. Similarly, I would also endorse the changes proposed by the Chinese Marxist dissident Li Zhengtian in the speech entitled 'Lawless Laws and Crimeless Crimes' delivered on 5 April 1979. There he proposed a division of powers in the Chinese legal system among the security organs, i.e. police, the procuracy, and the courts. He also proposed the creation of an institution solely dedicated to the protection of the interests of the defendant. Furthermore, Li Zhengtian maintained that defense lawyers should have the right to argue in court against the public prosecutor sent by the procuracy, and with the plaintiffs. These lawyers should also have the right to hold talks with the defendants, to accept copies of their appeals, and to support the appeals they lodge. Lastly, he strongly argued that police agencies shoud have no right to engage in prosecutorial work, let alone have any right to conduct a trial.[60]

It is not at all necessary to defend a notion of inalienable rights on the basis of some metasocial, let alone metaphysical, theory about their ultimate source. In this context, it is worth noting that Rosa Luxemburg postulated that 'every right of suffrage, like any political right in general, is not to be measured by some sort of abstract scheme of 'justice,' or in terms of any other bourgeois–democratic phrases, but by the social and economic relationships for which it is designed.'[61] While Rosa Luxemburg did not in that context systematically discuss the concept of rights, more recently the philosopher Mary Gibson has done so along similar lines. Mary Gibson defended the idea of rights even though she rejected the notion of 'natural' and 'human' rights, by which she meant rights that individuals are believed to have independently of social institutions, solely in virtue of being human. Instead she proposed that rights are social relations, which is reflected in the fact that the full specification of a right requires identification of the right holder as well as the person(s) or agency against whom the right is held. Moreover, Mary Gibson insisted that these social relations are as real as the entities that engage in them.[62] But, one may ask, if rights are not 'natural' or 'human,' why bother with the notion of rights at all? In that case, one very major reason to stick to the notion of rights would be that, as Mary Gibson herself put it,

> once the courts or the legislature declare that persons have certain rights, then political and legal arguments have to proceed according to different rules. The burden or proof, so to speak, shifts, and the opposition has to show that the consequences of respecting such rights in specific circumstances will be, not just worse than not respecting them, but so terrible as to justify the suppression or restriction of rights.[63]

Thus, although we do not need to defend the notion of rights as absolute, we can still defend many rights and principles as being of such profound and long-run importance that we have to ensure them; this gives them the status of rights or principles, even though not absolute. Moreover, beyond any consequentialist arguments in support of rights, I would further argue that the right to think and act independently is a good thing in and of itself, provided, of course, that it doesn't interfere with the rights of others. In other words, we should have rights not just because they will help produce a better society but because they are a constituent element of a good society.[64] Finally, rather than basing my arguments in defense of individual self-determination on some notion of pre-social individuals confronting society, I would contend the very opposite; namely, that individuals are no less social entities than groups and society (in this I would go farther than Mary Gibson). Moreover, different social functions are primarily lodged in one or more, but not all, of these various and different social entities. Thus, for example, the power of rational thought is lodged in individuals, i.e. strictly speaking groups and societies do not think. However, it goes without saying that the individual ability to think was not developed in isolation à la Robinson Crusoe and that the potential that such rational thought can reach is enormously dependent on social arrangements. Nonetheless, the point I am trying to make is that there are no valid arguments against individual or group self-determination on the basis that these are pre- or non-social entities.

It is obvious, however, that sometimes there are problems in the practical application of rights. As Tom Campbell has pointed out:

> It can also be allowed that where human rights conflict with each other (as when A's right to privacy thwarts B's right to free speech), or with themselves (as when A's right to choose the kind of education that is given to his children cannot be reconciled with other people's choices regarding the education that their children receive), such rights cannot all be upheld in every circumstance ... this sort of difficulty arises even in the case of old-style civil liberties, for not everyone can exercise their rights of free speech and assembly at the same place and at the same time...[65]

Of course, these real difficulties do not invalidate a rights approach any more than relatively scarce resources and conflicting preferences and priorities would invalidate the need for democratic ecnomic planning in a socialist society.

Aside from these philosophical considerations, there also exist powerful *historical* arguments in support of the concept of rights. Working-class and oppressed peoples throughout the world can draw on their own long and rich experiences to realize that rights are needed in order to make it possible for current minorities peacefully to become new majorities, and to provide room for innovation and therefore progress. Rights constitute a sort of 'safety net' that encourages the necessary free discussion to arrive at the closest possible approximation of the truth.

Rights and the Higher Phase of Communism

Would the adoption of the rights approach by a post-revolutionary socialist society force it to give up on the central goal of Communist society as proclaimed by Marx and Engels, i.e. the disappearance of the state and the establishment of the formula 'to each according to his or her need'? Not necessarily. Rights may gradually disappear for lack of use; for example, free speech would be taken for granted and would no longer have to be claimed as a *right* against the state or against other individuals and groups. Indeed, Mary Gibson has argued that 'it is conceivable that a genuine community in which the promotion of the good of each were actually the goal of all might have no needs for rights as we know them, yet might be equally or more conducive to self-respect than our society is.'[66]

Yet, it seems to me that the real controversy, at least among Marxists, arises not in connection with whether such a future situation is possible, but rather in assessing or analyzing the process of how it will come about, or, stated in plainer terms, of how we will get there. I would contend that rights cannot be abolished in a democratic socialist society. Rights may gradually disappear, to be replaced by something better such as was suggested by Marx, Engels, and Gibson above, only in a democratic socialist society of increasing abundance that has carefully and scrupulously respected rights for an indefinite, although probably quite prolonged, period of time. Anything else would constitute a possibly dangerous shortcut. Thus, for example, the feminist author Alison Jaggar may be right in concluding that to achieve the legal right to decide about abortion is the first step on the way to women's liberation, but the last step may be the achievement of a society in which the whole notion of individual rights against the community is senseless. Nevertheless, I find her gravely misleading when she *counterposes* the defense of rights to other worthy goals, as when she states that 'the abortion issue shows clearly why, in our search for justice, freedom and equality, it may well be more fruitful to change our emphasis from the establishment of individual rights to the fulfillment of human needs.'[67] A far more serious shortcut than this of course was the attempt by the followers of the legal school of Pashukanis to eliminate anything resembling the notion of rights while there was still a strong and powerful need for them in the early years of the Russian revolution.

Again, it is possible to conceive of a society that, as it has achieved increasing material abundance and cultural enlightenment, would become increasingly non-coercive, which of course is not necessarily the same as conflict-free. Furthermore, to take an extreme case, even if disputes were to be as frequent as in the USA, the most litigious of capitalist societies, it does not follow that these disputes would necessarily be resolved through the legal intervention of the state, i.e. the institution ultimately distinguished by its monopoly of the means of violence. An increasingly egalitarian and democratic society could, for example, utilize truly voluntary third-party arbitration of many complaints and disputes, except perhaps for major offenses such as murder, to replace the role of state legal coercion. This would be a democratic and egalitarian socialist version of what has for a long time existed in many ethnic minority and religious communities, although, since these communities usually reproduce the inequalities of the outside society, arbitration is far more often than not handled in those cases in an authoritarian, hierarchical, and paternalistic fashion. In this context, it seems to me that the only meaningful *materialist* interpretation of Marx's prediction of the disappearance of the law and the state in communist society is the following: as social classes and the hierarchical division of labor gradually tend to diminish or disappear in a post-revolutionary society of increasing abundance, then the need for a specialized juridical sphere will also gradually tend to diminish or disappear.

What is 'Class Justice'?

The early history of the Russian Revolution also poses for use the question of the proper relation between, on the one hand, the universalistic political and legal requirements of socialist democracy and, on the other hand, the class character and commitment that should be distinctive features of authentically revolutionary societies. In this context, I would argue that the class character of a socialist revolution consists, first of all, in the fact that the working class and its allies, in addition to having taken over and established their management of the means of production, are also the creators of and have control over the new form of state. However, unlike the bourgeoisie, which can be a ruling class with or without political democracy, these new ruling classes can collectively control their state only through a democratic political system. One would also expect such a state to carry out policies that radically redistribute the economic surplus. Moreover, a society-wide system of 'affirmative action' for the working-class, low-income groups and, of course, racially and sexually oppressed groups, would also be indispensable in order to bring about a quick end to the educational, occupational, and other related monopolies of the old society.

However, this society-wide 'affirmative action' would have to avoid some pitfalls. First of all, political discrimination must be avoided at all costs. What I mean is that the state's 'affirmative action' policy should not be taken to mean rewards for *political* merits. The only thing that should count here is disadvantaged social background of one kind or another; not 'the correct' views and activities. Thus, even civil war veterans would be given compensation because of the disadvantages they suffered as a result of their being, for a period of time, displaced from their occupations, having their family life disrupted, injured, etc., but not as a reward for their having chosen the right politics in the conflict.

To provide a concrete and positive historical example of what I am proposing, I will cite the layoff policies adopted by some factory committees in Petrograd at the end of 1917, as the production of war industries began to decline after the October Revolution. According to S. A. Smith:

> at the Okhta explosive works the factory committee agreed that workers should be made redundant in the following order: first to go would be volunteers; second, merchants, traders, yardkeepers, caretakers and others who had entered the factory in order to avoid conscription; third, those who had refused to join a trade union; fourth, members of families in which more than one member worked at the factory; fifth, youth under the age of eighteen, unless they had dependants or were without families; sixth, those with some property or element of fixed income; seventh, those from families in which other members were still employed, though not at the factory; eighth, single people with no dependents; ninth, and last to go, would be workers with dependants, according to the number of dependants they had. Similar redundancy plans were drawn up at the Old Parviainen works and at Putilov.[68]

Noticeably absent from these instructions was any attempt to benefit workers who were members of the political parties and groups supporting the revolution at this time, e.g. Bolsheviks, Left SRs, Anarchists, or, even more noticeably, any attempt to discriminate against workers supporting parties opposed to the revolution, e.g. Mensheviks and Right SRs. Nor did these layoff policies make any reference to the varying degrees of revolutionary dedication and merit that many individual workers could have easily claimed as a justification for keeping their jobs. Yet, while these redundancy plans were carried out at a time when party and revolutionary activities were at a fever pitch in Petrograd, the cradle of the revolution, we should not really be surprised by them. After all, these policies were developed under the still-prevailing multi-party political climate in Petrograd factories and elsewhere.

It is also clear that practically all of these instructions were inspired by strong class sentiments of equity and protection of the institutional gains of the working class, e.g. emphasis on union membership and rejection of bourgeois draft evaders, who in any case were far more able to draw on family resources to support themselves while remaining unemployed. Moreover, it is also worth noticing that these guidelines had advanced beyond what, to the North American or British reader, would be the more familiar unionist emphasis on seniority, and were instead using material need as the principal criterion of judgment.

Of course, political parties, as voluntary associations distinct from the state, are a different matter. Provided that these parties have no access to the resources of the state, they may want and are entitled to reward political merit in whichever legal way they see fit. Furthermore, certain policy-making positions will be rightly given to those people who represent the prevalent or majority political point of view. These are obvious commonsensical exceptions to a general rule of impartiality.[69] Formulating this in the terminology of the Chinese Cultural Revolution, I would then say that being a Red is no reason, in an egalitarian society, to be given the more desirable jobs. A policy of political discrimination would only be a systematic source of non-bourgeois, but no less serious, bureaucratic corruption. It would also lead to the most pernicious kinds of dissimulation, since having the 'correct' politics would then be the necessary accompaniment to successful bureaucratic and professional careers. In fact, this has often been a major source of oppression for independent scientists, skilled workers, technicians, and artists in the countries of 'really existing socialism.' These people often experience the humiliation of being displaced by, or having to submit to, colleagues who are far less competent in their specialized fields of endeavor, but 'compensate' for their incompetence through having learned only too well how to mouth the appropriate slogans and how to 'work' the party and bureaucratic systems. Of course, it is also no less true that being an expert is no reason to occupy policy-making positions that are primarily political rather than technical in nature.

Affirmative action should be *for* some groups rather than *against* other groups. People of disadvantaged backgrounds should be given preference, but that is not all the same thing as establishing a blanket and absolute prohibition *against* people of advantaged backgrounds. Such a prohibition would constitute a serious step in the creation of a society of hereditary estates and of categorical forms of 'justice.' 'Affirmative action' is or should be a policy directed to the redress of an inequitable situation, not an instrument of permanent social vengeance or resentment against the descendants of the former exploiters or of the pre-revolutionary middle classes.

At the level of the administration of criminal justice and the correctional system, an 'affirmative action' policy requires, of course, the elimination of the myriad class biases and the humanization of the previous bourgeois system of justice. In the case of early Soviet Russia, this was not only true of policies with a clear differential class impact such as decarceration, reduction of sentences, and popularization of justice, but also in regard to the adoption of the model of rehabilitation to replace the notions of punishment and deterrence.[70] At the same time, however, as we saw in chapter 4 on repression, early Soviet criminal penal policy was also animated by a rather primitive workerism. Thus, membership in the bourgeois class was, in itself, sufficient reason to obtain a heavier criminal penalty than would otherwise have been prescribed by the laws and the judge.[71] Yet, if we examine the evolution of this principle a little closer, we will find that originally, according to the Guiding Principles on Criminal Law established by the revolutionary government in 1919, the class situation of the offender did not constitute in itself an aggravating or extenuating circumstance, but had the status of a sort of background factor to place the offense committed in its proper perspective. It was only later, in 1924, that the shift took place to class situation becoming an explicitly aggravating or extenuating circumstance.[72] Most ironically, at the very same time a tendency was developing moving away from class position being used as an extenuating case *in favor* of the workers. Thus, while in January 1921 Dzerzhinsky was still supporting greater leniency for workers and peasants, by February 1924 he was already referring to that very same attitude as 'liberal nonsense.'[73]

PART II

Before Stalinism

Political Alternatives

6

Revolutionary Alternatives to Lenin

Mainstream and Dissident Bolshevism

In chapter 2, I described how the Right and Left Bolshevik opponents of the mainstream party leadership raised a variety of different and, although not realized at the time, sometimes *complementary* democratic-type objections to the government's conduct of industry. Similarly, in chapter 5 I noted how the 'moderate' or 'Right' Bolshevik legal thinkers were relatively more sensitive to the need to preserve individual freedoms. Writing about the early 1920s, the historian Vladimir Brovkin has suggested the existence of a body of opinion inside the ruling party holding consistently liberal or moderate views in a variety of areas. As Brovkin put it, 'those forces in the CP which advocated normalization of criminal justice procedures, curtailment of the powers of the Cheka, accountability and responsibility of local administration were, more often than not, in favor of a tolerant attitude toward the legal, and in many ways positive, activity of the Mensheviks.'[1] Unfortunately, Brovkin did not provide us sufficiently detailed information to help us determine the extent to which the specific individuals involved in raising the general political criticisms may have been the same or different people from those active in legal, or industrial, controversies, and, to the extent that they were different people, whether and how they communicated with each other.

While neither the Left Bolsheviks nor the Right Bolshevik opposition of people like Riazanov and Lozovsky could match Lenin in political and leadership skills, both of these currents nonetheless raised penetrating democratic objections in the broader political realm. In fact, I would argue that these different types of dissidents demonstrated a much better understanding of the importance of democratic institutions for the development of socialism than did the principal Bolshevik leader. During the early post-revolutionary period, the Left oppositions emphasized what we would today call institutions of participatory democracy, while the Right raised objections relevant to the more traditional democratic rights and civil liberties.

On the other hand, as we saw in previous chapters, Lenin's post-revolutionary understanding of democratic practices at best consisted of his insistence on worker staffing and inspection. Again, Lenin's insistence on worker staffing contained an important democratic element to the extent that it removed the stranglehold that the old ruling classes and their immediate, and formally well-educated, descendants had over the important positions in state and society. Nevertheless, changes in the social composition of those occupying leadership positions did not and could not do anything to help institutionalize the *democratic control* from below of social and state institutions. Likewise, inspection, in the absence of a free press and democratic controls truly independent of the party, was not and could not be of much use.

For Lenin, bureaucracy was indeed an evil; but as he saw it the problem was in great part due to cultural backwardness and to the social background of the administrative personnel, e.g. Tsarist and bourgeois functionaries. Lenin had little, if any, insight into how the hierarchical division of labor established by the revolutionaries themselves, particularly in the absence of democratic controls, could also create a horrendous bureaucracy. Likewise with the party: insure the working-class social background of the party ranks and their ability to inspect what the leaders do. This was essentially Lenin's prescription for cure in what was in fact a remarkably unproblematic view of the problems presented by one-party rule in a society moving towards the abolition of the separation between the economic and political spheres. Needless to add, Lenin's inadequate post-revolutionary views on democracy and socialism still proved to be a lesser evil to what came later; namely, Stalin's unlimited rule by naked force, the conversion of the Communist Party from what waas during Lenin's lifetime at least partly a body of independent-minded revolutionaries into a cult of total sycophants, and the development of 'Marxism–Leninism' as a ritualistic ideology or state religion.

The critical question is whether these Right and Left oppositions, singly or in combination, constituted programmatic and leadership alternatives to Lenin's mainstream Bolshevik leadership, particularly after the end of the Civil War. The political possibilities for change at this early time were in some ways greater than when Leon Trotsky and others attempted to organize a political opposition to Stalin in the less fluid period of the mid and late twenties. Moreover, the whole point of political action is to organize while there is still a 'fighting chance' to win, or at least obtain significant concessions within a reasonable span of time. We can now see, perhaps with the benefit of hindsight, the special dangers of delay in the cases of revolutions that attempt to reorganize the whole society. In those situations, it is sheer political suicide to wait for the organization of an opposition until after political closure has occurred, let alone after the consolidation of the new ruling class as a *social class* – a necessarily protracted process. Instead, a political opposition – if it is not going to be a futile heroic gesture – must be organized by the time there is a *threat* of *political* closure but the more or less open organization of political opposition groups might still be possible. In any case, we need to take a closer look at the nature of these oppositions in order to see whether they could have constituted a meaningful alternative to the central Bolshevik leadership.

The Right and Left Bolsheviks

First of all, it is necessary to be cautious when generalizing about the political inclinations and positions adopted by the various currents within the Bolshevik Party in the early post-revolutionary period. For one thing, leading Bolsheviks were not always consistent, and they changed their political attitudes a great deal, a most dramatic example of this being Bukharin's shift from the extreme Left to the extreme Right within the party. It also happened that a tendency would formally disappear as such while remaining as a latent current or mood within the party, e.g. the evolution of what was called the Bolshevik 'Right' at the time of the October Revolution. To a certain extent, these types of political behavior may all have been understandable responses to the often desperate objective situation facing the country. However, as I suggested in an earlier chapter, it is also the case that, perhaps as a result of a Marxist overreaction to utopianism, the Bolsheviks had been politically and theoretically unprepared for the actual practical tasks of the transition to socialism even under the best of possible circumstances. Similarly, Bolshevik theory and strategy up to Lenin's 'April Theses' in 1917 had not contemplated socialism being on the immediate agenda after the overthrow of the autocracy. Thus, it is also reasonable to assume that this lack of preparation further contributed to the apparent political instability of many of the party's leading tendencies and figures.

The Right Bolsheviks

In an interesting monograph on the October Revolution, Marc Ferro uses the term 'Bolshevik democrats' to refer to people such as Kamenev and Rykov, 'who hoped for a chance to define some new form of state, in which legitimate power could lie both with the soviets and a constituent assembly.'[2] In fact, Kamenev, and his then ally Zinoviev, had opposed the launching of the October Revolution on the grounds that the Bolsheviks had excellent prospects in the elections to the Constituent Assembly. They expected their party to win as much as one-third of the votes, and thought that the party's opponents would then have to yield or otherwise the Bolsheviks would form a 'governing bloc' with the Left Socialist Revolutionaries (SRs) and non-party peasants to carry out the party's program.[3] Ferro also claimed that Kamenev was at bottom opposed to the dictatorship of a single party, and on this issue was actually closer to the Left Menshevik leader Martov than to Lenin. Neither did Kamenev think that the preconditions for socialism had been fulfilled in Russia, and this he saw as posing a serious threat to the Bolshevik Party, since it could be discredited by not being able to build true socialism.[4] I do not propose to discuss here my criticisms of the Right Bolshevik position vis-à-vis the October Revolution, except to recall that my discussion of these issues in chapter 1 suggests profound disagreements with their strategy and tactics. Likewise, many of my criticisms of Rosa Luxemburg's assessment of the Russian

Revolution, especially her advocacy of a Constituent Assembly, are also applicable to the Right Bolsheviks.

However, in the end, most of the Right Bolsheviks and the Left Socialist Revolutionaries acquiesced in the dissolution of the Constituent Assembly. Riazanov and Lozovsky were the only Bolshevik leaders to vote against the dispersal of that body when the question was taken up in January 1918 at a meeting of the Central Executive Committee of the soviets.[5] Kamenev and the 'softer' Right of the Party then proceeded to more or less adapt themselves to Lenin's mainstream leadership. Still, there is no doubt that the spirit of this Bolshevik Right continued to exist, especially in Moscow where a relatively more coalitionist and moderate political atmosphere prevailed for some years; this, in contrast with the relatively more hard-line spirit then predominant in Petrograd. Moreover, Kamenev, as chairman of the Moscow Soviet since August 1918, attempted to implement measures restricting the arbitrary powers of the Cheka. For a brief period of time, he even came close to the positions of the Democratic Centralists (discussed below). Thus, at the Moscow Guberniia (province) Conference of Soviets, which met from 15 to 17 December 1920, Kamenev acknowledged that the soviets had been emptied of their democratic functions. He then proposed a series of reforms such as the soviets reviving the plenary sessions and opening their sessions to the public, an increase in their political and economic powers, and better links between the soviet deputies and the factories.[6] There is also evidence indicating that several years later, in 1921, at a time when Lenin was considerably tightening the restrictions on the opposition parties, Kamenev and Bukharin were among some Communist leaders who felt 'that it was time to bring other socialist parties into the picture.'[7] Lozovsky, with Riazanov a leading member of the harder Right within the Bolshevik Party, was expelled from the party in early 1918 and readmitted, much chastened, in 1919. He later became a Stalinist, only to be purged for being a Jew in 1952.[8] For his part, Riazanov, a perennial pro-democratic gadfly inside the leadership of the Communist Party, eventually disappeared in the 1930s after serving as the director of the Marx–Engels Institute for several years.[9]

It is worth indicating, as another example of the vagaries and instability of internal Bolshevik Party politics, that even as generally consistent a democratic critic as Riazanov would on the occasion of the 1921 Tenth Party Congress be rebuffed by Lenin when he proposed that the ban on party factions (relatively permanent and internally disciplined sub-groups within the larger party) be extended to party electoral platforms (a relatively temporary programmatic coalition organized for a party congress).[10] Since the 1921 ban on factions was primarily aimed at the Left, and Riazanov was a Right critic of the mainstream leadership, this may be further evidence of the Right and Left oppositions failing to even perceive a degree of commonality of views and interests.

The Left Bolsheviks

There exists a contemporary infatuation with Bukharin, in his right-wing phase, as a critic of Stalinism. Yet the majority of the democratic objections to the degeneration of the Russian Revolution, since the very beginning, came from the Left rather than the Right oppositions in the party. Of course, not all of the Left oppositions were directly concerned with the question of democracy. To cite an important example, the formation of the original Left Communist opposition in 1918 was primarily due to the sharp debates around the Brest-Litovsk Treaty, although many of its leaders (V. Osinsky and V. Smirnov, but not Bukharin) were a short time later involved in the formation of pro-democratic factions such as the Democratic Centralists.

The 'Military Opposition' and the Democratic Centralists The first two pro-democratic Left opposition groups were created in 1919. At the time of the Eighth Party Congress in March of that year, the short-lived 'Military Opposition' was formed. V. Smirnov, acting as one of its main spokesmen, conceded the need for the use of specialists of alien class and political backgrounds, but strongly opposed the introduction of traditional forms of military discipline – e.g. special forms of address and salutation, and special living quarters and other privileges for officers. The party leadership, speaking primarily through Trotsky and his supporter G. Y. Sokolnikov, raised a red-herring by falsely counterposing irregular guerrilla warfare as the only alternative to traditional army discipline. In the end, Smirnov's resolution received 95 votes against 174 in support of Trotsky's policies. However, not all of the 95 votes were principled votes in support of a more democratic army, since some were cast by those animated by the petty jealousies and rivalries that Trotsky's arrogant brilliance was already beginning to foster inside the revolutionary government.[11]

The Democratic Centralists, also established in 1919 and whose leadership overlapped with that of the Military Opposition, were a longer-lasting pro-democratic opposition group with a much broader range of concerns, perhaps because they were not really a single, homogeneous tendency. As Richard Sakwa has pointed out, one group around Osinsky emphasized the inadequacies of the party center, while another group, which was later to support the Workers' Opposition, was formed by supporters of Moscow leader Ignatov and criticized the usurpation of the rights of the soviet fractions by the party committees; and still others reflected Ukrainian 'localism,' or merely a generalized political dissatisfaction. Nevertheless, it can generally be said that this tendency, most characterized by the leadership of Communist intellectuals such as V. Smirnov, V. V. Osinsky, and by the 'Old Guard' Bolshevik worker T. V. Sapronov, adopted as its main focus the restoration of the democratic features of the soviet and party constitutions. As we have seen in chapter 2, Osinsky had already in 1918 been quite concerned with the issues of balancing local and central control and extending democracy in the factory. However, the

Democratic Centralists placed even greater stress on arguing for reforms that would make the Central Committee of the party more representative and that would restore power to the executive committees of the local soviets. Specifically, they also proposed to limit the powers of the party's Central Committee and open most of its deliberations to the party membership. This, after the Democratic Centralists had initially advocated a stronger party center as an antidote to bureaucratization at the local level. Finally, this opposition group also insisted that minorities should be assured representation in party elections and that they be given facilities to publish their views.[12]

At the Ninth Party Congress held in March 1920, A. G. Shliapnikov, a leader of the Workers' Opposition (see below), called for a three-way separation of powers among the party, the soviets, and the trade unions, each to be responsible for work in its respective area. Osinsky, speaking on behalf of the Democratic Centralists, endorsed Shliapnikov's idea and noted that there was a 'clash of several cultures' among the 'military–soviet culture,' the 'civil–soviet culture' (with which the Democratic Centralists identified themselves), and the trade union movement, which had 'created its own sphere of culture.' Osinsky maintained that it was incorrect to impose the authority or methods of one type of culture on the others. It is clear that by this time the Democratic Centralists had become more critical of the trends that had developed during the Civil War. Earlier, as I noted above, the Democratic Centralists had tried to combat bureaucracy by bureaucratic means, maintaining that an improved mechanism would facilitate the practice of a more democratic centralism. Now, Sapronov declared that a dictatorship of the party bureaucracy was being established as elections were being replaced by appointments and transfers. He also argued that the apparatus could not rescue the revolution since there was no self-activity by the masses of workers.[13] In sum, the Democratic Centralists maintained that the worst problem affecting the party was the decline of collective decision making and election of officers. The right balance between democratic accountability on one hand and discipline and hierarchy on the other hand had been lost. Every possible measure (e.g. holding party conferences every three months) had to be taken to restore that lost balance.[14]

The Workers' Opposition   A bigger and more broadly based pro-democratic opposition group than the Democratic Centralists was established in 1920, under the name of the Workers' Opposition. Geographically, this group was concentrated in the southeastern parts of European Russia – the Donets Basin, and the Don and Kuban regions. They also had strength in Moscow province, and for brief periods of time they controlled or had a majority of the party's membership in the Ukrainian republic and in the region of Samara province on the Volga. The Workers' Opposition was, in addition, far more proletarian in its leadership and membership than the Democratic Centralists. It was particularly strong in the Union of Metalworkers, an industry whose workers had been in the vanguard of the movement towards worker self-management.[15]

Similarly to the Democratic Centralists, the Workers' Opposition demanded freedom of discussion within the party, complete abolition of the system of appointments, to be replaced by election to all posts, and the freeing of the highest soviet and trade union organs from too much interference by the party's Central Committee.[16] As I mentioned above, one of its main leaders, Shliapnikov, demanded a separation of powers among the party, soviets, and trade unions. The Workers' Opposition was also especially concerned to maintain the proletarian nature of the Communist Party and proposed, among other things, a thorough purge of alien class elements from that organization. At the same time every party member was to be required to live and work as a peasant or worker for three months of every year.[17]

However, the most distinctive proposal of the Workers' Opposition was the one they made at the fateful Tenth Party Congress in March 1921. In the Theses that the Workers' Opposition prepared for the Congress it was advocated that 'the organization of the administration of the economy belongs to the All-Russian Congress of Producers, united in trade production unions, who elect the central organs which administer the whole economy of the Republic.'[18] In a separate pamphlet entitled *The Workers' Opposition*, also published shortly before the Congress, Aleksandra Kollontai, another key leader of the group, explained that the transfer of the economy to this new body would not take place until the All-Russian Central Executive Committee of the Trade Unions 'has found the said unions to be able and sufficiently prepared for the task.' However, Kollontai's arguments for the proposal that the 'existing dualism' between the Supreme Council of National Economy and the All-Russian Executive Committee of the Trade Unions be abolished in order to create a 'singleness of will' of the newly proposed Congress of Producers must have made it difficult for the Workers' Opposition to refute the accusations of syndicalism made by the mainstream party leadership. However, Kollontai certainly had a point when she rejected this charge by claiming that she was just being faithful to the party program adopted in 1919[19] (see my earlier discussion of this issue in chapter 2).

As we have just seen, the Democratic Centralists and the Workers' Oppositionists shared many of the criticisms of the government and agreed on a variety of reform proposals designed to cure the ills affecting the Communist Party in particular and Russian society in general. Yet, while they occasionally joined forces in struggles against the party's leadership, these two groups were far from being united. Partially as a result of this disunity, they were never serious contenders for power or, unlike the earlier 1918 Left Communist opposition to the Treaty of Brest-Litovsk, real threats to the Bolshevik mainstream led by Lenin. In addition to their clear political disagreements and different social class compositions, the history of the two factions showed substantially different orientations towards the central party leadership. At one point, Democratic Centralist leader A. S. Bubnov accused the Workers' Opposition of being demagogic, and his associate T. V. Sapronov depicted their own tendency as consisting exclusively of supporters of the Central Committee's political program who differed on what were the best methods to implement that program. The Workers' Opposition had in turn accused the Democratic Centralists of being no better than the run-of-the-mill party officials in the localities where the Democratic Centralists were in charge.[20] In the end, the Democratic Centralists strongly fought the proposed ban on factions at the Tenth Party Congress, and particularly criticized the leadership's threat to expel oppositionist groups from the party. Yet, they did not protest, and actually voted in favor of, the motion condemning the Workers' Opposition as an anarcho-syndicalist deviation.[21]

It is also very true, as Robert V. Daniels has reminded us, that neither the Right nor the Left Communist Party oppositions objected to or resisted the outlawing of other political parties, although there were some very honorable exceptions such as Miasnikov on the Left and Riazonov on the Right. Besides, it cannot be denied that the analysis of bureaucracy developed by the Workers' Opposition tended to overemphasize the issue of social orgins, e.g. the entry into the party of careerist elements, and how this could be effectively counteracted by bringing in more workers.[22] Yet, it is clear that the solutions proposed by the Workers' Opposition were not limited to this and actually went far beyond the sociological-type remedies usually recommended by Lenin. Furthermore, even though the democratic Centralists and Workers' Oppositionists did not, at least openly, raise objections to the existence of a one-party state in Russia, the nature and dynamic of their proposals for inner party and soviet democracy were so profound and far-reaching that even a limited degree of success would have significantly changed the future development of Russian society.[23] This is especially true in light of the fact that at that time the Communist Party itself was politically still fairly diverse. Furthermore, the party rank-and-file had not yet been fully educated to the support of the one-party state as a good in itself.

It is also important to clarify that, for the first couple of years after the Bolsheviks came to power, both the Left and Right Communist Party opponents of the central party leadership held highly responsible positions in the government; and that it was only later, in the early twenties, when this ceased to be the case. Consequently, these critics or opponents were 'losers' only in the sense that their policies were not being accepted by the top party leadership – in other words, this was not, at this time, a situation of the 'ins' versus the 'outs' insofar as administering the revolutionary state was concerned. Consequently, the differences between Lenin and his party opponents on questions concerning democracy cannot be attributed to the lack of governmental responsibility on the part of the critics.

Why Wasn't There an Alternative?

It is unlikely that the stark objective realities of post-revolutionary Russia would have permitted the implementation of all the democratic changes proposed by the early Right and Left oppositionists. In any case, none of these changes were ever put to the test because these various dissident tendencies were at no point in the *political* position to be contenders for power, either singly or in combination. Yet, they could have conceivably played a still limited, but more important role. They could have, in spite of very serious policy differences and even class orientations, worked together as a *tactical bloc* (not to be confused with a merger or a permanent alliance) to extract more democratic-type concessions from the mainstream leadership of the Communist Party. Or perhaps more important, even if these tendencies had been numerically unimportant, they could have performed a role of political educators in their common democratic criticisms of the leadership, thus facilitating a more effective future resistance to what had not of course been foreseen at the time; i.e. the rise of Stalinism. From this educational political point of view, a tactical bloc for 'democratic survival' among Democratic Centralists, Workers' Oppositionists, and those who were rooted in what had recently been the right-wing of the Bolshevik Party would have been indeed extremely helpful and illuminating. Of course, this did not and probably could not have taken place – in fact, as far as I know, it was never even considered. However, it is of some interest to note in this context that both Shliapnikov and Kollontai had initially, i.e. in late 1917, agreed with the Right opposition in supporting a coalition government with the other socialist parties.[24]

Moreover, as I just showed, not even the two main left-wing opposition groups, the Democratic Centralists and the Workers' Oppositionists, were able to unite against the Bolshevik center in spite of their many common principles. Clearly, there were many real political differences standing in the way of such a bloc. There were also significant differences among these tendencies in terms of institutional origins and affiliations (e.g. unions vs. factory committees), and class orientation and background. The class factor can of course be exaggerated, as exemplified by the vice, peculiarly widespread among schematic Marxists, of attributing every conceivable political disagreement to differences in class background and/or orientation. Last but by no means least, the enormous power and prestige of Lenin's central leadership was doubtlessly a major obstacle to the formation of a serious opposition bloc. Thus, as we saw above, the Democratic Centralists wanted to maintain at least a political allegiance to the mainstream leadership of the party and consequently failed to fully support the Workers' Oppositionists in 1921.

Yet, I believe that the single most important obstacle preventing these tendencies from even perceiving the need for such a tactical bloc was ideological in nature. In the first place, the different concerns of the early Right and Left oppositions can be seen as in part reflecting different aspects of democratic politics. In a seminal article,[25] George H. Sabine has noted two different democratic traditions: one tradition, Anglo-American in origin, stressed the defense of liberty against arbitrary state power; the other tradition, French and Continental in origin, stressed social and political equality. Indeed, the early Left Communist oppositions strongly advocated the earliest possible establishment of economic equality as well as what I earlier referred to as participatory democracy. Moreover, the Right opposition stressed the need to limit state power in various social realms, and particularly defended the independence of the unions from the state. Missing here was precisely the kind of synthesis that Sabine recommends as indispensable to a truly democratic society:

> Equality does depend on liberty and liberty on equality, because each expresses a phase of the kind of human relationship that democracy hopes measurably to realize. If, as continually happens in the democratic experiment, an attempt to advance one puts an obstacle in the way of the other, the simple device of rejecting one is not a live option.[26]

Second, most Bolsheviks, as well as members of other parties, tended to perceive the dynamics of the revolutionary process through the prism of what they knew about the one major and familiar historical model, i.e. the French Revolution. This may have prevented most Bolsheviks from even perceiving the qualitatively smaller bureaucratic dangers involved in the French case. The French Revoution had been, after all, a political revolution (i.e. a radical transformation of the form of government) and a social revolution (i.e. a transfer of class power from the Church, nobility, and royalty to the peasantry and bourgeoisie). In comparison to this, the Russian case was radically diffe-rent: a qualitatively more comprehensive social revolution resulting, *inter alia*, in a tremendous growth in the powers of the central state. But there was something else that made the analogy between the two revolutions particularly misleading if not altogether dangerous; I am referring to the vast differences between the scope and possibilities of modern political organization and the modern state in late eighteenth-century France as compared with twentieth-century Russia. Thus, while Lenin and Robespierre used such similar terms as 'terror' and 'dictatorship,' their *social* and *political* nature and consequences could not have possibly been the same. In fact, Robespierre and his associates had no intention or desire to interfere with the predominant form of private property in the France of his times, i.e. small private property. But even if their intentions had been different, the scope of their power was greatly limited by the technical and organizational possibilities of a nation still on the threshold of modernity. While post-revolutionary Russia was still primitive in many funda-mental respects, it had made tremendous strides towards the modern world, at least when compared with France in the 1790s. Moreover, the reach of the Russian state had been quite considerably extended during the period of War Communism. In retrospect, we can see how even some of Lenin's earlier political innovations (e.g. the establishment of a centralized nationwide news-paper and political organization) would have been inconceivable under the material and political conditions prevailing at the time of the French Revolu-tion. In sum, I am suggesting that what they knew of the dynamics of the French Revolution may have misled the Russian revolutionaries, thus helping to prevent a proper understanding of the dangers of state power and bureaucracy, and consequently of the imperative need for an anti-bureaucratic tactial bloc among the various dissident factions in the Bolshevik Party.

What is 'Right' and What is 'Left'?

Another ideological or intellectual obstacle to the formation of a bloc between Left and Right Bolshevik dissidents was the lack of full clarity regarding the very notions of 'Right' and 'Left' within the context of the broad revolutionary camp. It is true that the categories of 'Left' and 'Right' are based on historically rooted distinctions that have always been by their very nature at least somewhat loose and vague. However, the fact remains that at the time of the Russian Revolution some meanings of 'Rightness' and 'Leftness' had become relatively clear while other meanings had perhaps not even been detected, let alone clarified. Thus, the debates within international socialism on reform vs. revolution had fairly clearly established that revolutionaries were considered to be to the left of reformists of revisionists. This latter word, which should merely suggest the permanent rational need for the 'revision' of all theories, turned into a synonym for reformists. Ironically, this synonym was used as such by people like Rosa Luxemburg who would otherwise have had good reasons to think of themselves as 'revolutionary revisionists.'

This particular Right–Left debate concerned questions of tempo as well as of the actual goals to be attained. Reformists were gradualists, revolutionaries were not. But there was also the implication that this was not just a difference concerning the speed of attaining a given goal shared by reformists and revolutionaries alike. As it turns out, many reformists were not really too concerned about actually attaining the goal. This attitude was exemplified by Edward Bernstein's belief that the social democratic movement was everything, while the goal did not mean much at all.

However, this does not mean that there could not be strategic and tactical differences among people presumably sharing the same goal, not for some remote time, but for a reasonably immediate and actionable future. A good example of this were the differences over the Treaty of Brest-Litovsk. Incidentally, Lenin did not differ from the Left Communists insofar as the assessment of the treaty was concerned – all Bolsheviks in fact agreed that it was a terrible treaty and a setback for the Russian Revolution. The real difference was over whether or not the Russian revolutionaries were in any position to engage in a campaign of revolutionary guerrilla warfare against the imperialist powers. This strategy in turn required that the working classes of those countries respond *immediately* to the revolutionary appeal, attempt to overthrow their own governments, and join in the struggle for world revolution with the Russian revolutionary guerrilla armies. Lenin's answers to all of these questions was 'no' while the Left Communists' answered a resounding 'yes' in all instances. We can then choose to speak in this instance of a Left and an 'Ultra-Left.' In this case, as in others, the Left advocated a more cautious strategy, presumably to avoid a worse defeat, while the 'Ultra-Left' was willing to take its chances, or perhaps even denied that there was any risk of a worse defeat at all. In any case, as it should be clear from this example, relative 'rightness' and 'leftness' was not just a matter of political ethics and courage, but also a question requiring a thorough understanding of the political juncture at hand, and thus of the correct use of political judgment and skill, an activity at which Lenin, for one, greatly excelled.

On the basis of this discussion of the types of issues and positions that determined the *explicit and perceived* degrees of Rightness and Leftness within the broad revolutionary camp by the time of the Russian Revolution, it should hardly be surprising that the tactical bloc for 'democratic survival' about which I speculated above did not take place and was probably not even considered. Such a bloc would only have been possible on the basis of what were then, and to a great extent are still today, undetected or dormant dimensions of Left and Right. Today, we are in a position to learn from the lessons of how the two major wings of the Left evolved in the course of the twentieth century. One degenerated into a totalitarian Stalinism, which was even capable of engaging in mass murder. The other major wing degenerated into social democracy: hopelessly pro-capitalist and pro-imperialist, heavily bureaucratized, and increasingly more concerned with stabilizing capitalism than with the introduction of even mild reforms. For many years the Left has been correctly associated with a critique of, or opposition to, capitalism. However, this conception retains a sometimes fatal ambiguity. Anti-capitalism is not necessarily pro-socialism, if we define socialism as a movement 'from below' attempting to establish the democratic rule of the working class and its allies among the oppressed sections of the population. Anti-capitalism can also be elitist, paternalistic, undemocratic, and bureaucratic; that is, 'from above' as opposed to 'from below.'[27]

Furthermore, and as I have discussed elsewhere in this volume, there are also questions of individual freedom, their relationship to socialist democracy, and the grounds and degree to which one or more of these freedoms may legitimately be curtailed. In this context, it should be pointed out that there are those who conceive of the pursuit of equality in a post-revolutionary society in terms of the elimination of individual diversity and freedom, in the manner of a beehive. This 'Communionist' tendency, identified by Hal Draper as one of several strains of 'socialism from above,' has been particularly strong in recent years among many Maoists and among many religious and so-called ethical socialists.[28] On the other hand, it is particularly appropriate to cite here Jan Josef Lipski, one of the founders of the Polish Workers' Defense Committee (KDR) group and more recently one of those involved in reviving the Polish Socialist Party (PPS), who described 'being on the left' as 'an attitude that emphasizes the possibility and the necessity of reconciling human liberty with human equality, while being on the right is understood as an attitude that may mean scarificing the postulate of human freedom in favor of various kinds of social collectives and structures, or foregoing the possibility of equality in the name of laissez-faire.'[29]

Last but by no means least, there was another relatively undetected dimension of Leftness and Rightness, particularly relevant to my earlier critique of the Democratic Centralists and Workers' Oppositionists. I am referring to the notion of popular sovereignty or self-government, which bears heavily on the question of the second-class citizenship of the Russian peasantry discussed elsewhere in this volume. In fact, David Caute sees popular sovereignty as *the* overarching concept that defines the Left:

> Popular sovereignty signifies at least the *liberty* to a voice in public affairs, to a share in the control of one's own destiny; the *equality* of men [sic] in so far as they all enjoy this liberty and are likely to use it to achieve a wider measure of social and economic equality; a certain *optimism* about men's ability to govern themselves; *rationalism* in the sense that it denies metaphysically derived sources of authority such as Divine Right; *anti-militarism* by analogy, for if the people of one nation can attain sufficient harmony to distribute sovereignty among themselves, then surely the different nations can also learn to regulate their differences peacefully; *sympathy for the oppressed* in so far as it puts them within reach of changing their own condition; *social reform* because a sovereign people could hardly avoid reforming the society over which they had previously not been sovereign and because the long-term effect of the totality of social reforms is, whatever their intention, to increase popular sovereignty; and finally *movement* because this insistent demand has proved to be the most dynamic force of change in modern European history.[30]

In reality, it is only in the light of all of the above dimensions of Rightness and Leftness that one can today, in retrospect, see the need for an intra-Bolshevik tactical bloc for 'democratic survival.' Not only that, but the traditional and conventional meanings of Right and Left in the Russian Revolution also become retrospectively transformed. Thus, for instance, a figure like Dzerzhinsky, while being close to the extreme Left of the Communist Party on the question of the Treaty of Brest-Litovsk, could be seen at the same time as being on the extreme Right of the party insofar as the questions of freedom and repression were concerned. While D. K. Riazanov was on the extreme Right of the party, and G. T. Miasnikov on the extreme Left, in relation to the degree of radicalism of socio-economic transformations that each advocated; yet they would both be on the extreme Left, as opposed to Dzerzhinsky's extreme Right position, on the issues of freedom and repression mentioned above.

It is also interesting to speculate whether, if Trotsky had been able to consider all of the possible dimensions of Left and Right discussed above, and had also freed himself from the straitjacket of the French Revolution, he would have continued to see, in the mid-1920s, Stalin's 'Center' position as the lesser threat and even potential ally against Bukharin's 'Right.' However, in all fairness to Trotsky, it should be mentioned that he did initially come to see the need for at least a 'United Opposition' with Zinoviev against Stalin and Bukharin in the years 1926–7.[31] However, it was only much later – in mid-1938, after Stalin's Great Purges – that Trotsky finally made it clear that his differences with the Bukharinist Right were of a qualitatively different nature than his differences with Stalin. As Trotsky then put it, 'the Right group of the old Bolshevik Party, seen from the viewpoint of the bureaucracy's interests and tendencies, represented a *left* danger.'[32]

Trotsky's 1938 pronouncement had been preceded some years earlier by a very gradual shift in the perspectives of his followers inside Russia. Thus, Christian Rakovsky, the most important Trotskyist leader not yet exiled, felt, as late as the Summer of 1929, still at least as distant from the Bukharinist Right as he was from Stalin.[33] But by 1930, i.e. at the high point of the collectivization campaign, a certain *de facto* convergence had taken place between Rakovsky and the right-wing Bukharinists. As R. W. Davies has observed, 'there [was] no doubt that Left and Right shared common assumptions about the limits which should be voluntarily imposed on state policy, assumptions which Stalin and his supporters had rejected.'[34] However, Rakovsky minimized the significance of this convergence. While it is true that his 'Declaration of April 1930' is already more critical of Stalin than of the Right, he still speaks of the Right as opponents and most definitely does not call for any alliance or even for a tactical bloc with them against Stalinism. Instead, Rakovsky at this point restated the Trotskyist position of October 1929 when it affirmed

> the need to regroup all the revolutionary communist forces around the five-year plan in industry and around the struggle against agrarian capitalism and the rightists. Such a regroupment – including the democratic centralists – on the basis of the recognition of the unity of the party is needed even more today, when it is necessary to confront the emerging Thermidor with the firm proletarian ranks. However, in so far as the introduction of the slogan of regroupment of all communist forces means the end of the monopoly of centrism, the centrist bureaucracy will stand against it with the same violence as in the past. *The slogan of regroupment of all the revolutionary communists can only be introduced through the struggle of the mass of the party against the centrist bureaucracy.*[35]

One cannot but reach the sad conclusion that, once again, in failing to see the need for a tactical bloc with the Right opposition, this was indeed too little and too late.

That the approach I suggested above to defining Right and Left is far from being widely accepted even today is demonstrated by, for example, the terminological inversion that seems to have prevailed in China at least since the Cultural Revolution. Thus, in May 1987, a *New York Times* reporter writing about Mao's home province of Hunan quoted a young college-educated Chinese describing it as a very conservative province because many officials were still Leftists. The reporter explained that 'Leftism' referred to party control over all facets of life, and also cited Mr Weng Hui, a high official of the provincial government, as acknowledging that 'Leftism' was still a problem there.[36] Later, in November 1987, the same reporter interviewed an innovative movie studio director in Xian who complained about interference by the head of the propaganda department of the party in Shaanxi province, calling him 'a typical bureaucrat . . . He doesn't understand films but he wants to control film making. He's a bureaucrat who is influenced by leftist thinking. He is a conservative and ossified thinker.'[37] However, can we really say that Mao and the 'Gang of Four' were Leftists? Or that Deng is a Rightist? Isn't the problem here at least in part that the notions of Leftness and Rightness are not being applied along the variety of criteria that I spelled out above?

Or take, for example, the notion particularly widespread in the 1960s and 1970s that Maoism and Guevaraism were to the Left of the traditional pro-Moscow Communist parties. This was certainly true along the dimensions of tactical militancy and socio-economic radicalism. Nevertheless, at least a few of these Maoist and Guevaraist tendencies even resurrected the cult of Stalin and thus tended to be way to the Right of the so-called Eurocommunist parties insofar as the issues of freedom and democracy were concerned. Today, the lessons of twentieth-century politics, and particularly those of the degeneration of the Russian Revolution, should help us understand the need for a left revolutionary politics that puts forward policies attempting, as much as possible, to maximise the degree of Leftness on *all* of the above-mentioned political dimensions. It stands to reason that this may often require a conscious attempt to *reconcile* all these dimensions of Leftism over a period of time, since it may not be possible to do so at any particular moment – owing, for example, to the adoption by a revolutionary regime of temporary and situationally justified repressive measures. The purpose of these temporary measures, as I earlier suggested in this volume, would be strictly limited to the defense of a workers' and popular revolution against violent restorationist attempts by the former ruling classes and their domestic and foreign allies.

The Question of the Peasantry

Even if the Right and Left Bolshevik dissidents had seen the need for, and agreed on, the formation of a pro-democratic bloc, they would have still had to deal with a very difficult issue, i.e. what attitude to take to the peasantry. This would have been as much of a problem for the early Bolshevik Left and Right as it became for Bukharin and Trotsky in the mid and late twenties. The early Left oppositions in particular were far more pro-worker and anti-peasant than the Leninist mainstream and tended, at best, to leave the mass of the peasantry out of their proposals for democratic reform and, at worst, to see the peasantry as a necessary class enemy of the working class and the revolution.[38] Thus, for example, Osinsky had been an advocate of many of the harshest War Communism measures against the peasantry while opposing such concessions as the introduction of the tax in kind.[39] Nevertheless, it is interesting to note that the Old Bolshevik and Left oppositionist Miasnikov, leader of the smaller but more proletarian Workers' Group, while strongly opposed to the NEP was nonetheless favorably disposed towards the peasantry, especially its poorer elements, and advocated the formation of peasant unions. This earned him the government's accusation of being a sympathizer of the Socialist Revolutionaries, perhaps a symptom of the Bolshevik mainstream's alienation from the peasantry.[40] A probably even smaller opposition group, led by the sailor Bolshevik Panyushkin, echoed the rebels of Kronstadt and raised the slogan of 'All power to the Soviets, and not to parties' in the Summer of 1921. Again, like the Kronstadt rebels, Panyushkin showed a great deal of sympathy for the peasantry, as was indeed suggested by the name adopted by his group: 'Workers' and Peasants' Socialist Party.'[41]

Of course, as I will discuss in greater detail in the next chapter, the rebellion of Kronstadt, in March 1921, had taken place outside and against Communist Party rule, although many individual Communists participated in it. The Kronstadt program also called for a fully democratic worker and peasant *soviet* democracy, not for an all-class democracy or for a Constituent Assembly. Furthermore, two of the points in the rebel program at Kronstadt anticipated the New Economic Policy that was very shortly after inaugurated by the government. These were the demands for the removal of all roadblock detachments and that the peasants be given 'full freedom of action in regard to the land, and also the right to keep cattle, on condition that the peasants manage with their own means, that is, without employing hired labor.'[42] However, it is possible to identify with and justify the Kronstadt rebellion and even admire its political program, let alone criticize the tactics used by the government in suppressing the rebellion, without at the same time having any illusions as to whether the Kronstadt rebels offered or presented any credible *governmental alternative* to the Communist Party. It is highly doubtful that they had the political and organizational coherence to articulate, let alone administer, a detailed governmental program going beyond doctrinal generalities. The record of at least one of the dominant groups in the Kronstadt rebellion was not exactly encouraging. In the Spring of 1918, the SR Maximalist-dominated Red Guard units in the city of Izhevsk rebelled. As the historian Stephen M. Berk describes it, 'the result was near anarchy. The Maximalists set off on a rampage, killing and arresting Bolsheviks, Mensheviks, Socialist Revolutionaries, and even ordinary workers.'[43]

The fact remains that, social democratic (i.e. Bolshevik *and* Menshevik) suspicion of the peasants' class nature aside, there was always a strong reservoir of populist, pro-peasant sentiment in the Russian working class. Thus, for example, S. A. Smith has noted how in 1917, in the months before the seizure of power and before the dispersal of the working class that began in 1918, workers' resolutions on control of the economy tended to be couched in terms of control by the 'toiling people' rather than in the more precise Bolshevik formula of 'workers' control of production and distribution.' Smith's 'impressionistic survey' of these resolutions on control of the economy found that Menshevik, Anarchist, and syndicalist formulations were rare and that the populist-type resolutions were second in frequency only to the Bolshevik ones.[44]

The Other pro-October Left

While the formation of an early Left–Right Bolshevik pro-democracy bloc would have increased the chances for a more effective resistance to the bureaucratic degeneration of the Russian Revolution, this would not have been sufficient to ensure a healthier and less despotic future for the Russian peoples. As I will argue in the next chapter, all parties willing to renounce the use of violence against the Soviet system should have been legalized. In particular, such a conciliatory measure might have very possibly convinced these groups to give up arms and/or the use of terror and play the role of a revolutionary loyal opposition. Such a process would have of course facilitated the reorganization and growth of groups and parties that had supported the October Revolution and yet were more sympathetic and responsive to the peasantry than all of the wings of the Bolshevik party. These groups and parties, due to their undeniable weaknesses, could not have possibly offered an alternative to the Bolsheviks as a party of government. Yet they could have played a major role in *peacefully integrating* the bulk of the peasantry into the post-October revolutionary process.

The Left Social Revolutionaries

The Left SRs could, more than any of the other important parties, claim to be the ideological and political descendents of revolutionary Russian populism. As such, this party would have gradually gone out of step with an increasingly proletarian and capitalist Russia. Although a youthful party,[45] it was nonetheless very weak both politically and organizationally. Oliver Henry Radkey, the historian of the Socialist Revolutionary Party, a source not hostile to the Left SRs, noted the ineffectiveness of the Left SRs even in one of their major strongholds – Ufa province in the Southern Urals. In this area, although the Left SRs had complete control of the peasants' soviets and were equal in strength to the Bolsheviks in the army and in the workers' and soldiers' soviets, it was the Bolsheviks and not the Left SRs who took the initiative in forming a soviet militia.[46] This should perhaps not surprise us considering the SRs' vacillation and attempts at playing a mediating role at the critical time of the October Revolution. The leadership of the Left SR Party was also usually inclined to the strong expression of rather vague revolutionary sentiments, although far more often than not these revolutionary sentiments were phrased in libertarian rather than authoritarian language. Yet their fondness for terrorism played an extremely negative role in helping to provide the justification for the unleashing of the Red Terror in the Summer of 1918. Like the mass of the peasantry that the Left SRs oriented to, this party could function at its best as allies and as an important channel of peasant political support and legitimacy for other social and political forces. Individual members of the Left SR Party for a while occupied important positions in the Bolshevik-led government, including the security forces, although for a shorter time than the anarchists.

This continued to be the case even after the Left SRs left the coalition government protesting the Treaty of Brest-Litovsk in March 1918, but not of course after the Left SRs began to use terroristic methods against the Bolshevik government in July 1918.

A note on the Anarchists

The Anarchists had similar weaknesses to those of the Left SRs in the realms of political leadership and organization. However, the term 'anarchism' – like the term 'socialism' – covered a rather wide spectrum of political shadings and organizations. This spectrum included a significant peasant presence in the form of Makhno's peasant anarchism in the Ukraine. Viewed from a Marxist and shopfloor-oriented working-class revolutionary point of view, one of the more interesting currents in Russian Anarchism were the Anarcho-Syndicalists, in contrast for example to the more community-oriented Anarchist–Communist followers of Kropotkin.[47] At the end of August 1918, the Anarcho-Syndicalists held their First All-Russian Conference in Moscow with the intention of organizing themselves and adopting a common program. This Conference strongly criticized the government for abolishing workers' control in favor of one-man management and labor discipline. The Anarcho-Syndicalists also criticized the Bolsheviks for abandoning the factory committees in favor of the trade unions; and, while strongly supporting the military struggle against the Whites, the Conference called for the arming of the workers and peasants to replace the standing army. In agriculture, the Anarcho-Syndicalists supported the equalization of land allotments and the gradual formation of autonomous peasant communes, and proposed that the state should turn over the tasks of grain requisitions to worker–peasant organizations.[48]

Some of the above demands were definitely positive and others were at least debatable. But the Conference also proposed a variety of measures that were totally out of touch with the reality of revolutionary Russia. Among these were the Anarcho-Syndicalists' opposition to the employment of bourgeois engineers and technicians and their call for the abolition of the Sovnarkom (Council of People's Commissars), to be replaced by a 'federation of free soviets.' How this 'federation of free soviets' could have done without an executive body to organize its deliberations and implement its decisions, which is precisely what the CEC of the soviets and the Council of People's Commissars were at least originally *supposed* to do, was not specified. Last, but by no means least, the Anarcho-Syndicalists certainly had a point in accusing the Bolsheviks of creating, particularly with their policies of War Communism, a 'state capitalist' monster rather than socialism. Nevertheless, their call for an 'immediate and radical revolution' against the government carried out by the workers themselves – right in the middle of the Civil War[49] – was an empty and idle threat that could only have played into the hands of the worst and most repressive elements in the Bolshevik Party and in the Cheka.

The 'liberatarianism' of the Anarcho-Syndicalists as well as of most other Anarchists in Russia consisted in their being, similar to the Left Communists, strongly in favor of participatory democratic forms at the local level. Furthermore, the Anarchists were of course typically opposed to the central state and professed to be in favor of group and individual autonomy. Yet, as we have seen above, they tended to be quite naive about, if not hostile to, the need for institutional arrangements to ensure effective majority rule at the national level. Neither were they particularly sensitive to the need for the design of institutions to address the practically inevitable conflicts between majority rule and minority rights. Similarly, Anarchist opposition to the central state also translated itself into suspicion of, if not opposition to, *legally* sanctioned majority and minority *rights*. Besides, a certain cult of spontaneity prevented most Anarchists from seeing that, as I suggested in chapter 3 on freedom of the press, there was a lot more to establishing a true freedom of communication then seizing newspapers from the bourgeoisie. Beyond this, the Anarchists had not made any systematic proposals as to who should be entitled to press facilities, how, where, and when.

Conclusion

This overview of the SR and Anarchists political tendencies again leads me to emphasize that any potentially viable revolutionary alternatives to mainstream Bolshevism in this period would have had to be primarily, although not exclusively, centered around tendencies within the Bolshevik Party itself. There is little doubt that, at least within the pro-October camp, the Bolsheviks were the best organized and politically the most self-conscious party. Besides, since the Summer of 1917, with the entry into the party of the Inter-District Committee (Trotsky's group) and a variety of former Left Mensheviks and independent revolutionaries, the Bolsheviks had lost at least some of their earlier and narrower distinctiveness. At that point, Lenin and his older and newer associates became the leaders of an authentic mass party practically encompassing the great majority of revolutionaries in the country. This is one major reason why the following observation from Victor Serge, besides being an accurate description of reality, constitutes one of the principal assumptions or points of departure for this book:

> It is often said that 'the germ of all Stalinism was in Bolshevism at its beginning'. Well, I have no objection. Only, Bolshevism also contained many other germs – a mass of other germs – and those who lived through the enthusiasm of the first years of the first victorious revolution ought not to forget it. To judge the living man by the death germs which the autopsy reveals in a corpse – and which he may have carried in him since his birth – is this very sensible?[50]

7

Lenin's NEP as an Alternative (1921–1923)

Working-class and Peasant Unrest

A red victory finally concluded the Civil War against the Whites in November of 1920. While the Bolsheviks had indeed won an impressive military victory against the right-wing opposition, this by no means brought to an end the series of devastating defeats that the government had suffered on other fronts. The economy was in a shambles. The great majority of the peasantry had also turned against the regime in reaction to the confiscatory and anti-market policies of War Communism; indeed, the Red Army was still fighting the so-called 'Green' peasant revolt in the area of Tambov, and was in the process of liquidating a similar rebellion under Nestor Makhno's anarchist leadership in the Ukraine. Moreover, as I showed in chapter 2 on workers' control and trade union independence, the industrial working class, the principal social base for the ruling Communist Party, had been reduced to a little less than half its 1913 size. More important was the fact that the government did not have much support among this smaller and in many ways different working class. In the early part of 1921, Zinoviev even declared that the government's support among the working class had been reduced to 1 per cent! While Trotsky attacked Zinoviev's claim as a 'monstrous exaggeration', he conceded that there were still a 'substantial number' of dissatisfied people. Trotsky added that 'information arriving from the provinces shows that the local communists are helpless in resisting the pressure of anarchic elements.'[1] In fact, in the early part of 1921, a spontaneous strike movement accompanied by a Menshevik resurgence took place in the industrial centers of European Russia. In Petrograd, this movement developed in late February and was centered at the Trubochny, Baltic, and Patronny metal plants, the Laferme tobacco and Skorokhod shoe factories, the Admiralty shipyards, and the Galernaya drydocks. Initially, the strikes put forward primarily economic demands, particularly the demand for food, warm clothing, freedom to trade with the villages, and the elimination of privileged rations for special categories of workers. Later, the workers began to raise demands that were primarily political in content. Among these were the

removal of special squads of armed Bolsheviks from the factories, the disband-
ment of labor armies, and the restoration of political and civil rights. At the
beginning of the strike movement, a worker demonstration at Vasilevskii Island,
on the northern side of the Neva, was dispersed without bloodshed. Later, the
government took stronger measures such as carrying out widespread arrests
and attempting to starve the strikers by depriving them of their rations and
shutting down the principal factories involved in the walkouts. However, the
workers also obtained some concessions such as being allowed to trade with the
villages, thus anticipating the about to be inaugurated New Economic Policy.[2]

The working-class unrest in Petrograd had been preceded by similar developments in Moscow where a strike wave engulfed a number of Moscow's
major factories in the metal, chemical, printing, and garment industries. There,
as in Petrograd, the Mensheviks played a significant role in the strike movement. In the case of Moscow, Menshevik influence was at this time particularly
significant in the printing and chemical industries, while the Communist Party's
Workers' Opposition was developing a major influence in the metal industry.[3]
One of the fateful consequences of these events was that the Petrograd strike
movement in particular helped to set the stage for the rebellion that broke out
shortly afterward, in early March, in nearby Kronstadt. However, the Mensheviks, consistent with their strategy of non-violent opposition to the regime,
played no role whatsoever in that armed rebellion.[4] In sum, the 'Green' peasant
revolts in the Tambov and the Ukraine, large-scale strikes in Petrograd and
Moscow, armed rebellion in Kronstadt – all of these events cumulatively
demonstrated the isolation of the regime, despite its major victory against the
Whites in the Civil War.

The Kronstadt Rebellion

The armed clashes in Kronstadt were, in my view, historically no more
important than the widespread working-class strike movement in early 1921.
However, subsequent debates, particularly within the Left, have made Kronstadt a symbol. Moreover, these debates have often been a surrogate for a
thorough discussion of the complete record of 'Leninism in power.' Be that as it
may, these debates and sybolism warrant a closer look at those events.

In 1921, approximately 50,000 people – half civilian, half military – lived in
Kronstadt, a fortified city and naval base located on an island in the Gulf of
Finland some 20 miles west of Petrograd.[5] On 26 February, in response to the
events in the nearby city, the crews of the warships *Petropavlovsk* and *Sevastopol*
held an emergency meeting and agreed to send a delegation to the former
capital to report on the ongoing strike movement. On their return from
Petrograd two days later, the emissaries told Kronstadters of their full sympathy
for the strikers and about the governmental repression to which the strikers
were being subjected. Those present at the meeting, which took place on the
Petropavlovsk, then approved a long resolution that was to become a sort of

Kronstadt Manifesto, which included the following demands:

1. In view of the fact that the present soviets do not express the will of the workers and peasants, immediately to hold new elections by secret ballot, with freedom to carry on agitation beforehand for all workers and peasants;

2. To give freedom of speech and press to workers and peasants, to anarchists and left socialist parties;

3. To secure freedom of assembly for trade unions and peasant organizations;

4. To call a nonparty conference of the workers, Red Army soldiers, and sailors of Petrograd, Kronstadt, and Petrograd province, no later than March 10, 1921;

5. To liberate all political prisoners of socialist parties, as well as all workers, peasants, soldiers, and sailors imprisoned in connection with the labor and peasant movements;

6. To elect a commission to review the cases of those being held in prisons and concentration camps;

7. To abolish all political departments because no party should be given special privileges in the propagation of its ideas or receive the financial support of the state for such purposes. Instead, there should be established cultural and educational commissions, locally elected and financed by the state;

8. To remove immediately all roadblock detachments;

9. To equalize the rations of all working people, with the exception of those employed in trades detrimental to health;

10. To abolish the Communist fighting detachments in all branches of the army, as well as the Communist guards kept on duty in factories and mills. Should such guards or detachments be found necessary, they are to be appointed in the army from the ranks and in the factories and mills at the discretion of the workers;

11. To give the peasants full freedom of action in regard to the land, and also the right to keep cattle, on condition that the peasants manage with their own means, that is, without employing hired labor;

12. To request all branches of the army, as well as our comrades the military cadets (*kursanty*), to endorse our resolution;

13. To demand that the press give all our resolutions wide publicity;

14. To appoint an itinerant bureau of control;

15. To permit freed handicrafts production by one's own labor.[6]

In light of the main themes discussed in this volume, it is worth noting that the Kronstadt program called for a fully democratic worker and peasant *soviet* democracy, not for an all-class democracy or for a Constitutent Assembly. Furthermore, two of the points in the rebel program at Kronstadt anticipated the New Economic Policy that was about to be inaugurated by the government. I am referring specifically to the demands for the removal of all roadblock detachments, and for economic freedom for peasants who did not hire labor. In this connection, the point is not whether 'it would have been *sufficient* to inform the Kronstadt sailors of the N.E.P. decrees to pacify them,' as Trotsky disingenuously asked in 1938,[7] but rather whether the government was willing to grant concessions, as it had just done in Petrograd, thereby *helping* to avoid the bloodletting. Moreover, the specific demands of the Kronstadt program were in some ways consistent with the political basis of what I described in the previous chapter as a conceivable tactical bloc of Right and Left Communist dissidents. But in other ways, the garrison's program went beyond what could have probably been expected at this time from any Communist Party faction(s), particularly in regard to the peasantry and the demand for a multi-party system. As it happened, Communists belonging to all tendencies at the Tenth Party Congress then meeting in Petrograd joined in the attack on the garrison.

Initially, the Communist Party leadership appealed to the insurgents to desist from their rebellious activities, but, again, without offering any concessions. Instead, the government soon delivered what was in effect an ultimatum: either give up or suffer the consequences. The regime's impatience might be explained in terms of its justified fear that the rebellion would spread outside of Kronstadt. Also, there were short-term tactical considerations that moved Lenin and his associates to act more quickly – as Trotsky explained shortly after the suppression of the rebellion. In a short time the ice in the Gulf of Finland would have melted, making an infantry assault on the fortress impossible.[8] Thus, the government forces began the attack on 7 March; after a few days of bloody fighting, the rebellion was crushed.

After the suppression of the Kronstadt rebellion, the Communist Party leadership fostered a variety of myths to discredit the defeated movement. It is important to point out that Kronstadters expressed widespread support for the notion that 'all power should go to the soviets but not to the parties.' Nevertheless, there is no evidence, in the text of the *Petropavlovsk* resolution or elsewhere, to support the emigre claim, later echoed by the government and by Leon Trotsky in particular as late as 1938,[9] that the Kronstadt rebels agitated for the quite different demand of 'soviets without Communists.' Besides, it seems that, contrary to the propaganda of the higher party leadership, the majority of Communists in the garrison actually voted for the Kronstadt program, and even the remaining minority of Communist Party members did not oppose it, but merely abstained. Moreover, while it is true that Communists were not part of the leadership of the rebellion, in the new Kronstadt soviet elections held under rebel sponsorship at the beginning of March, close to one-third of those elected were Communists, with the majority of the delegates elected belonging to no party.[10] It is also true that subsequently, as the hostilities between the rebels and the government escalated into armed combat, some 300 Communists were arrested. These prisoners were generally well treated except that they were deprived of 280 pairs of boots and shoes, which were then given to the rebel fighters.[11]

Beyond this, Paul Avrich has shown that the contact established between leaders of the rebellion such as Petrichenko and the emigre group in Paris known as the National Center occurred *only after* the rebel leaders fled Kronstadt in the period subsequent to the suppression of the movement. In addition, Avrich has also demonstrated that there was no advanced preparation for the Kronstadt rebellion and that, at least during the early stages of the revolt, the Kronstadters 'saw themselves not as revolutionary conspirators but as a pressure group for social and political reform.'[12] As far as the navy officers in the ships and naval base are concerned, they played, as a group, no leadership or political role in the rebellion. They did provide technical advice to the rebels, just as they had previously provided it to the Bolsheviks during the Civil War.[13]

Nevertheless, there exists a more sophisticated line of criticism of the Kronstadt rebellion, which places more emphasis on Marxist sociology than on the typical police approach looking for the cause of political movements in plots, conspiracies, and evil elements misleading the masses. This sociological critique, strongly established in the Trotskyist tradition, claims that 'Kronstadt in 1920 was not Kronstadt of 1917. The class composition of its sailors had changed. The best socialist elements had long ago gone off to fight in the army in the front line. They were replaced in the main by peasants whose devotion to the revolution was that of their class.'[14]

However, this interpretation has failed to meet the historical test of the growing and relatively recent scholarship on the Russian Revolution. This literature has shown this type of analysis to be mistaken on a variety of grounds. In the first place, even if the claim concerning the degree to which the Kronstadt sailors in 1921 were of recent peasant background was factually correct, it would still be a fundamentally misleading point. In fact, in 1921, a smaller proportion of Kronstadt sailors were of peasant social origin than was the case with the Red Army troops supporting the government.[15] Second, it is true that the total number of active sailors had significantly diminished due to Civil War casualties, and that, understandably, a greater proportion of these casualties took place among those navy men most committed to the revolutionary regime. Nevertheless, while this obviously had an effect on the *political* composition of the Kronstadt garrison, there is no evidence suggesting that this had any effect on the *class* background or origins of the Kronstadt sailors. On the other hand, recently published data strongly suggest that the class composition of the ships and naval base had probably remained unchanged since before the Civil War. We now know that, given the war-time difficulties of training new people in the technical skills required in Russia's ultra-modern battleships, very few replacements had been sent to Kronstadt to take the place of the dead and injured sailors. Thus, at the end of the Civil War in late 1920, no less than 93.9 per cent of the members of the crews of the *Petropavlovsk* and the *Sevastopol*, ships renowned for revolutionary zeal and Bolshevik allegiance, were recruited into the navy before and during the 1917 revolutions. In fact, 59 per cent of these crews joined the navy in the years 1914–16, while only 6.8 per cent had been recruited in the years 1918–21.[16] The historian Evan Mawdsley has also found that, of the approximately 10,000 recruits who were supposed to be trained to replenish the Kronstadt garrison, only a few more than 1,000 had arrived by the end of 1920, and those had been stationed not in Kronstadt, but in Petrograd, where they were supposed to be trained.[17]

Indeed, what had changed dramatically in Kronstadt was not the sailors' class origins, but the navy's Communist Party membership. Without a doubt, some of this was due to the selective impact of heavy Civil War casualties during the period 1918–20. However, we also know that while toward the end of the Civil War, in March 1920, there had been 5,630 party members, the number had dropped to 2,228 by the end of the year. Many members had been purged (for whatever good or bad reasons), and many others had simply dropped out. Moreover, 88.1 per cent of these Communists had been recruited since October 1919, with 64 per cent having joined between October 1919 and January 1920.[18]

Of course, there still remains a somewhat remote possibility that more sailors of working-class than of peasant background had been injured or killed during the Civil War. In other words, it could still be argued, although without any supporting evidence, that deaths among the sailors were unduly concentrated among Communists, and that in turn Communists were more likely to come from working-class backgrounds than sailors supporting other parties. However, I would suggest that the principal causes of the Kronstadt rebellion are not to be found in some far-fetched sociological analysis of the supposedly changing class composition of the Kronstadt garrison, but at a more immediate level? i.e. the sailors' and civilians' profound *political and economic* discontent. The news of the February strike wave in Petrograd only exacerbated political tensions already existing in Kronstadt. This discontent had been created by the highly voluntaristic and often arbitrary policies of War Communism, the economic crisis confronting the country, and a number of specific political events that helped to discredit the government among these people. First of all, the radical naval democracy that seemed to have been consolidated at the time of the October Revolution began to be eroded in mid-1918, and was finally destroyed on 18 January 1919 when Trotsky abolished all ships' committees, appointed commissars to all ships, and replaced the elected 'comradely courts' with Revolutionary Tribunals.[19] Likewise, with the beginning of the Civil War in mid-1918, Kronstadt's multi-party radical soviet democracy was abolished by the central government (the Kronstadt Soviet will be discussed in more detail below). Moreover, the prestige of the party was also undermined as a consequence of the struggle between Trotsky and Zinoviev for political control of the fleet, with a resultant loss of control over the rank-and-file.[20] Last but not least, there was also growing resentment among the sailors, including the party membership, concerning the special rations, allocations, and housing enjoyed by commissars, senior party functionaries, and trade union officials. In particular, Kronstadters seemed to have been shocked by the high lifestyle displayed by the chief commander of the Baltic Fleet, Fiodor Raskolnikov, and his flamboyant wife Larissa Reissner.[21]

In the light of the above considerations, it should hardly be surprising that the political prestige of the government and ruling party declined, and that sailors and civilians would be attracted to other political programs and views that had strong roots in the city of Kronstadt. The underlying ideology of the Kronstadt rebellion has been described as a not fully coherent anarcho-populism, 'whose deepest urge was to realize the old *Narodnik* program of 'land and liberty', and 'the will of the people,' the ancient dream of a loose-knit federation of autonomous communes in which peasants and workers would live in harmonious cooperation, with full economic and political liberty organized from below.'[22] On the negative side, this ideology could, as populist movements sometimes do, turn to antisemitism and deeply conspiratorial views of power relations.[23] As one might expect, other elements of traditional Russian ideology also found an echo among the rebels, as exemplified by the return to the use of religious ceremonies and by the notion prevailing among many Kronstadters that Lenin himself was a well-intentioned ruler who had unfortunately become the prisoner of his associates.[24]

Specifically, the overall ideological climate in Kronstadt was very close to the politics of the Socialist Revolutionary Maximalists, a left-wing splitoff from the SR Party, politically located somewhere between the Left SRs and the Anarchists. The SR Maximalists had supported the overthrow of the Provisional Government and its replacement by a government of soviets. They had also advocated worker seizure of the factories, the expropriation of state and church land by the peasants, the 8 hour workday, and the immediate cessation of the war. Moreover, this grouping also had approved of the use of assassination and terror as legitimate weapons in the revolutionary struggle.[25] Indeed, one could speak of this and other political tendencies close to it as forming a loose 'anarcho-populist coalition' (my term), which had been at least as numerous as the Kronstadt Bolsheviks in the period between the October Revolution and the beginning of the Civil War. At any rate, this was certainly a time when the class composition of Kronstadt would not have yet undergone the changes cited by the above-mentioned Trotskyist sociology.

Thus, in late 1917, at a time when the people of Kronstadt were overwhelmingly supporting the national revolutionary government, the Bolsheviks did not prevail in the Kronstadt Soviet; instead, the main part of the 'anarcho-populist coalition,' constituted by SR Maximalists and Left SRs, maintained a majority in that body.[26] Then, in the Soviet elections held in late January 1918, the Bolsheviks improved their position by electing 139 deputies as compared to their previous 96. But even in this election, when the Bolsheviks had obtained their highest vote ever during the era of multi-party soviets, they still fell short of an absolute majority (46 per cent). Also elected at this time were 64 SRs (21 per cent), 56 Maximalists (19 per cent), 21 non-party delegates (7 per cent), 15 Anarchists (5 per cent), and 6 Mensheviks (2 per cent). These delegates then elected a Left SR as the chairman of the soviet, but two out of the three deputy chairmen also elected were Bolsheviks.[27] Elections were held again on 1 April 1918 and at this time, consistent with what was then taking place throughout the country, the position of the Bolsheviks significantly deteriorated. On this occasion, only 53 Bolshevik deputies were elected (29 per cent) as compared to 41 SR Maximalists (22 per cent), 39 Left SRs (21 per cent), 14 Menshevik Internationalists (8 per cent), 10 Anarchists (5 per cent), and 24 non-party delegates (13 per cent). While a Bolshevik was nonetheless elected chairman of the soviet, he had to share power with a chairman and deputy chairman of the executive committee who belonged respectively to the Left SR and SR Maximalist parties. Likewise, the chairmanships of 17 departments that came to replace the vast network of commissions were carefully distributed among the various competing tendencies. Moreover, the relative weakness of the Bolsheviks in this city was demonstrated on 18 April 1918 when, by a vote of 81 to 57, with 15 abstentions, the Kronstadt Soviet denounced the Moscow Soviet's repressive measures against the Anarchists.[28] By July 1918, the Kronstadt Soviet had finally come under complete Bolshevik domination, but only after the other parties had been suppressed. Under these kinds of conditions, when soviet elections were again held in January 1919, the outcome was pretty such predetermined: 73 Communists, 91 Communist sympathizers, 22 non-partisans, 1 Menshevik (whose party had temporarily been allowed to run in soviet elections in November of 1918), and 1 delegate described as a sympathizer of the Maximalists had been elected.[29]

The New Economic Policy (NEP) and Democracy

the social–political order of NEP, with its officially tolerated social pluralism in economic, cultural–intellectual, and even (in local soviets and high state agencies) political life, represents a historical model of Soviet Communist rule radically unlike Stalinism.

Stephen F. Cohen[30]

the maximum political control and *political* police repression was to be accompanied by economic flexibility and free trade.

Alec Nove discussing Lenin's views of the NEP[31]

The New Economic Policy – i.e. a variety of measures relaxing government economic controls and permitting private enterprise, particularly among the peasantry – was the Bolshevik government's immediate response to the massive working-class and peasant unrest that I have just described. The NEP was of course also a recognition of the many failures and indeed absurdities of War Communism. This was indeed a very delayed recognition since the masses of workers and peasants had long before rejected this highly voluntaristic policy. As Lenin clearly stated it, the NEP was a policy of 'retreat,' of concessions to the peasantry (e.g. restoration of private trade and the establishment of a tax in kind to replace the forcible confiscation of grains and other staples), and to domestic and foreign capitalists.

Supporters of Gorbachev in the USSR and Western historians such as

Stephen Cohen, in their partly well-founded efforts to distinguish Leninism from Stalinism, have nevertheless greatly exaggerated the degree of political freedom existing during NEP. It is true that there was a significant degree of cultural freedom during this period. Indeed, the prevailing situation in the arts was not only a far cry from Stalin's later 'socialist realism,' but there was also a flourishing of artistic expression and experimentation.[32] However, as a I discussed it in chapter 3, while the intelligentsia benefited from this situation, at the same time Krupskaya had presided over the establishment of a system of book censorship primarily affecting the popular classes.

In fact, the end of the Civil War in some critical respects brought about a deterioration rather than an improvement in the degree and extent of political freedom in Russia. While Lenin inaugurated the NEP and thus relaxed state economic controls, in the political realm he moved from the very widespread but still somewhat tentative repression of the Civil War years towards the complete and systematic repression of opposition parties and groups. At about the same time he also successfully pressed for the abolition of party factions at the Tenth Party Congress (Mrach 1921). I have also shown in chapter 2 how by 1922 the application of party fraction discipline and other organizational measures had considerably accelerated the process of converting the trade unions into transmission belts for Communist Party policies. It was also in 1921, as I showed in chapter 4 on repression, that a qualitative change for the worse took place in the location and administration of labor camps. In addition, by 1922 the last opposition newspapers and journals had been shut down, never to be reopened. Finally, in August 1921, as the reader may recall from chapter 3, Lenin wrote to Miasnikov putting forward a most undemocratic view of freedom of the press. This significant reduction in political freedom was causally connected to the granting of economic concessions. As Lenin explicitly linked the political and economic questions at the Eleventh Party Congress in 1922 (his last party congress):

> It is terribly difficult to retreat after a great victorious advance, for the relations are entirely different. During a victorious advance, even if discipline is relaxed, everybody presses forward on his own accord. During a retreat, however, discipline must be more conscious and is a hundred times more necessary, because, when the entire army is in retreat, it does not know or see where it should halt. It sees only retreat; under such circumstances a few panic-stricken voices are, at times, enough to cause a stampede. The danger here is enormous. When a real army is in retreat, machine-guns are kept ready, and when an orderly retreat degenerates into a disorderly one the command to fire is given, and quite rightly so.[33]

This citation is quite revealing because Lenin is essentially saying that an economic retreat required a political closing of the ranks. The military imagery helped to disguise a crisis that had just ceased to be primarily military and had become mainly political and economic. It is clear that Lenin was greatly afraid of a split in the party and had no great trust in the party leadership. The Menshevik resurgence in the Spring of 1921 and that party's partly justified claim that NEP had vindicated their political–economic program could have only exacerbated Lenin's fears. It is very likely that Lenin felt, consciously or otherwise, that in the absence of a military threat, the internal solidarity of the regime could not be maintained merely through political means and therefore had to be accomplished through administrative and police measures.

This appears to be a conclusion consistent with the overall thrust of Lenin's actions in the 1921–3 period. In this context, it should also be noted that repression was assuming a new character. During the Civil War, a certain degree and type of state repression was justified by the very physical needs of civil war. After 1921, repression increasingly became an *alternative* to persuasion and the open struggle for mass political hegemony. Thus, on 17 April 1921, Lenin criticized a Cheka report written by the Chekist I. Vardin (Mgeladze) recommending that certain groups within the Menshevik, SR, and Anarchist parties should be legalized, and that individual Mensheviks and SRs should be released to take part in elections to the Moscow Soviet.[34] Again, it was obvious that Lenin did not want to allow political competition precisely because his NEP was similar to the policies that had long been advocated by at least some of his opponents.[35] As he stated at the 1922 Eleventh Party Congress: 'when a Menshevik says, "You are now retreating; I have been advocating retreat all the time, I agree with you, I am your man, let us retreat together," we say in reply, "For the public manifestations of Menshevism our revolutionary courts must pass the death sentence, otherwise they are not our courts, but God knows what." '[36]

Yet one can easily underestimate the complexity of the NEP period. On one hand, there is no doubt, as we have seen above, that these years witnessed a qualitative deterioration of many important aspects of political freedom. Most of all, the repression that had previously been in many ways more brutal but at least somewhat tentative, became, with the end of the Civil War and the Red Terror, less brutal but also more politically hardened and crystallized. On the other hand, if one carefully analyzes Lenin's actions and speeches from 1921 until his withdrawal from political activity due to severe illness in 1923, one can appreciate the difference between what from a democratic point of view was indeed Lenin's very undesirable regime, and the truly monstrous alternative that was beginning to take shape around the person of Stalin. Thus, in this period we can also find a Lenin attempting to develop an economically very moderate perspective, moving *toward* a *de facto* socialism in one country, and intensely preoccupied by the growing national chauvinism and bureaucraticization of Russian society. The latter concerns increasingly distanced and eventually made the Bolshevik leader quite hostile to Stalin's developing power and political orientation. Nevertheless, at the same time, Lenin remained no less distant from conceiving or recommending *democratic* solutions to the problems of bureaucracy.

One can detect in this particular combination of economic and political policies an at least implicit governmental strategy aimed at staying in power even in the absence of any real social base of support. The best that can be said about this strategy is that Lenin's government was trying to buy time. Indeed, even if the NEP had been unlikely to make enthusiastic supporters out of the peasantry, or of the working class, it did have a fighting chance of at least winning the grudging acquiescence of significant sections of these social forces. However, it goes without saying that acquiescence, as compared to participatory control or even mere support, encourages cynicism and increases the alienation between leaders and led, thus altogether transforming their mutual relationship.

Many well-meaning Western liberals and socialists and some recent Russian reformers have praised the NEP as their preferred Leninist period. And indeed, there are many good things to be said for Lenin's NEP (1921–3) when compared with the horrors structurally built into the policies of War Communism (1918–20). Yet there is also something very disturbing about the *politics* of what has often been an unproblematic support for the NEP frequently coupled with an admiration for Bukharin in his 'right-wing' phase in the 1920s. I would call this the 'politics of the possible,' by which I mean the notion that it would have been utopian to expect democratic institutions from below in a country like the Soviet Russia of the twenties. Consequently, according to this view, one must get the best one can, i.e. a benevolent, Western-influenced, and culturally enlightened dictator such as the late Lenin or, after his death, Bukharin. In my view, this position expresses a view of the world that confuses, through an intellectual sleight of hand, two quite different things: (1) a realistic understanding of the objective obstacles that indeed would have faced any attempt to establish workers' democratic institutions in the Russia of the twenties; (2) *determinism*, a very different approach to social reality, already discussed in the Introduction to this volume. In the present context, I want to underline determinism's characteristic and systematic failure to understand that what the masses of people *do* and *think* politically is as much part of the process determining the outcome of history as are the objective obstacles that most definitely limit peoples' choices. The determinist outlook can produce some surprising agreements, as when the 'revisionist' historian Stephen Cohen coincided with his opponent Leonard Schapiro, the most accomplished of the historians representing the orthodox 'totalitarian' school, in their joint praise for Bukharin.[37]

Moreover, I would propose a non-deterministic view of NEP, stressing that the fortunes of political democracy in Russia would have been helped the most not by a passive acceptance of whatever the late Lenin or Bukharin had to offer, but with whatever independent initiatives or pressures, no matter how modest, could have been continued to be organized and carried out from below. In other words, the terms of 'the best one could have gotten' were not a historically predetermined and fixed category. The eventual political outcome would itself have been affected by the respective strengths of conflicting political pressures and ideas from above and from below, *both* of which would have been vectors or components of objective political reality. While the *overall* objective reality may have indeed completely precluded the development of a Russian socialist democracy in the 1920s, there could have also been a stronger vector or component of resistance from below. For example, this could have happened if Trotsky had not failed to appeal for mass self-organization, both inside and outside party ranks, in support of the relatively democratic opening outlined in his proposed 'New Course' policy of December 1923.[38] This might have also in turn helped to preclude the eventual rise of Stalinist totalitarianism. Again, as I suggested in the Introduction, it was not a matter of indifference which one of the various possible kinds of non-democratic society might have come to prevail in Soviet Russia.

Toward 'Socialism in One Country'

The NEP could also be seen as a return to a version of what Lenin had referred to earlier, before the establishment of War Communism in mid-1918, as 'state capitalism.' And yet Lenin, in the last year of his life, at least implied that he and the Communist Party were building socialism. This was a move in the direction of what I would call a moderate, *de facto* socialism in one country, to differentiate it from Stalin's later *de jure* and venomously immoderate version of that notion. Lenin's version did not, on the whole, include the Great Russian chauvinist subordination of the fate of other revolutionary movements to Russia's national interest. I say 'on the whole' because, evidence provided by Fernando Claudin has shown how occasionally, i.e. not systematically, the protection of the Russian state had already, under Lenin's leadership, placed great strains on Communist internationalism. This expressed itself in Russia's relations with Germany and Britain, but most dramatically in the case of Turkey. Thus, in March 1921 a treaty of friendship and aid was signed with Mustafa Kemal. In spite of the dire economic situation at home, Moscow provided the Turkish leader with 10 million gold roubles and substantial quantities of arms. This aid helped Kemal repeal the armed intervention of the Entente powers, carried out through the surrogate Greek army. However, this assistance was provided *after* Kemal had pitilessly repressed the peasant movement fighting for agrarian reform and the Turkish Communist Party. A month and a half before the treaty with Turkey was signed, the Kemalists had arrested 42 leading Turkish Communists. Fifteen of these were immediately strangled and their bodies thrown into the sea. The rest were put on trial on charges of 'high treason.' Subsequently, when the Third Congress of the Communist International met, it protested the suppression of the Communists in Germany. However, rather than openly confront the dilemma presented by the Turkish situation, it remained completely silent about the murder of the Turkish Communists.[39]

Furthermore, while it is true that the Comintern in Lenin's time was already dominated by the Russian party, this was still as much due to the Russian party's political prestige as to the application of sheer organizational muscle and resources. However, it is not surprising that, by the time of NEP, Lenin's view of the development of socialism in Russia was no longer premised, at least in the short run, on a successful German or other West European revolution coming to the economic and political aid of his country. Instead, we find again a marked voluntarism. Thus, for example, on 16 and 17 January 1923, in his reflections on Sukhanov's history of the Russian Revolution, Lenin described what had been after all the old Marxist notion shared by both Mensheviks *and* Bolsheviks that the 'economic premises for socialism do not exist in our country' as an 'infinitely stereotyped' argument 'learned by rote during the development of West-European Social Democracy.' Lenin then asked, 'what if the complete hopelessness of the situation, by stimulating the efforts of the workers and peasants tenfold, offered us the opportunity to create the fundamental requisites of civilisation in a different way from that of the West-European Countries?' and finally, 'why cannot we begin by first achieving the prerequisites for that definite [higher] level of culture in a revolutionary way, and *then*, with the aid of the workers' and peasants' government and the Soviet system, proceed to overtake the other nations?'[40] Stalin, Mao, and Fidel Castro would have gladly put their signatures under this pronouncement.

In this period Lenin also began to develop an incipient form of what in contemporary language one might call 'Third Worldism.' In this context it is worth quoting at some length from his very revealing article 'Better Fewer, But Better' published in *Pravda* on 4 March 1923. There, Lenin the Marxist pointedly asked himself whether his government would 'be able to hold on with our small and very small peasant production, and in our present state of ruin, until the West-European capitalist countries consummate their development towards socialism?' and then answered that these countries were 'consummating it not as we formerly expected. They are not consummating it through the gradual 'maturing' of socialism, but through the exploitation of some countries by others, through the exploitation of the first of the countries vanquished in the imperialist war combined with the exploitation of the whole of the East.' Thus, in this article Lenin clearly *implied* that he was no longer counting on or expecting help from revolution in the West, at least in the near future. Therefore, the reader could not help but conclude that Russia had little practical choice left but to go it alone. Again, Lenin the Marxist asked himself whether Soviet Russia would not then have to endure 'a reign of peasant limitations?' and answers, 'No. If we see to it that the working class retains its leadership over the peasantry, we shall be able, by exercising the greatest possible thrift in the economic life of our state, to use every saving we make to develop our large-scale machine industry, to develop electrification, the hydraulic extraction of peat, to complete the Volkov Power Project, etc. In this, *and in this alone*, lies our hope.' While revolution was not about to take place in the West, Lenin nevertheless concluded that, in the last analysis, the outcome of the struggle will be determined by the fact that Russia, India, China, etc., account for the overwhelming majority of the population of the globe. And during the past few years it is this majority that has been drawn into the struggle for emancipation with extraordinary rapidity, so that in this respect there cannot be the slightest doubt what the final outcome of the world struggle will be. In this sense, the complete victory of socialism is fully and absolutely assured.

Apparently lost in this ideologico-political card shuffle was the notion held up to then by *all* Bolsheviks that the economic backwardness of Russia could only be overcome with the material help provided by one or more successful revolutions in *economically developed* Western Europe. Yet, again, Lenin's 'Third Worldism' was not yet fully crystallized. The old ideas of the long-time opponent of Russian populism had not completely disappeared from this article, as when he indicated, as a kind of reservation or afterthought, that the majority of the 'Orientally backward countries ... must become civilised. We, too, lack enough civilisation to enable us to pass straight on to socialism, although we do have the political prerequisites for it.'[41]

Still and all, Lenin's proposed internal economic measures were very moderate. It was in this context of economic moderation that Lenin expressed a very sanguine view of the future role of the cooperatives in becoming collectivist schools for the peasantry. Actually, according to the economic historian Alec Nove, what Lenin had in mind were primarily consumer retail rather than producer cooperatives.[42] Nevertheless, the Bolshevik leader's very positive views of the coops are still remarkable if we keep in mind the Bolshevik Party's problematic relationship, and sometimes hostile attitude, to those institutions. Thus, it is not surprising that historically the producers' and credit cooperatives, which were almost all rural, had been linked to the SR Party, and the consumer cooperatives, which were predominantly urban, to the Menshevik Party.[43]

In sum, Lenin's attitude at the time, although at one level highly voluntarist, was still very far removed from Stalin's later forcible collectivization of agriculture or of its rough equivalent in Mao's China: The Great Leap Forward of the 1950s. As Lenin put it towards the end of his political life on 4 January 1923:

> it will take a whole historical epoch to get the entire population into the work of the co-operatives through NEP. At best we can achieve this in one or two decades. Nevertheless, it will be a distinct historical epoch, and without this historical epoch, without universal literacy, without a proper degree of efficiency, without training the population sufficiently to acquire the habit of book-reading, and without the material basis for this, without a certain sufficiency to safeguard against, say, bad harvests, famine, etc. – without this we shall not achieve our object.[44]

The Political 'Last Struggles'

It was precisely in this period that Lenin searched for an alliance with Leon Trotsky to defend the Georgians against the national chauvinist abuses of Stalin and his associates. Lenin's speeches and writings also dealt with the essential need to raise the cultural level of the Russian people.[45] Most significant for my present task, however, were the governmental reforms that Lenin advocated as a means to struggle against the bureaucratization of the Soviet state. It has been suggested[46] that Lenin, from the point of view of his governmental reforms, saw the Soviet state as being composed of three sectors: policy formation, administration, and control. He saw the Communist Party as being in charge of policy formation. However, as a way of establishing control over bureaucratic degeneration, Lenin proposed that the party's Central Committee be considerably enlarged from the then current 27 members to 50 or even 100 people. In Lenin's view, the new members of the Central Committee would be rank-and-file workers and peasants unconnected with the old leaders and factions. In effect, these new CC members would be watching the old members. Furthermore, Lenin also proposed that a presidium of members of the also enlarged Party Central Control Commission (CCC) would take part in all Politburo meetings, have the right to examine all documents and materials, and 'watch over' the Politburo and Central Committee. Besides, Lenin was proposing a kind of Super Central Committee (my term) formed by as many as 150–200 members comprising the rank-and-file-enlarged Central Committee and Central Control Commissions. This 'super' Central Committee would meet at party conferences held six times a year.[47] Finally, insofar as the actual day-to-day administration of the government was concerned, Lenin proposed the merger of the Central Control Commission with the RKI (the Commissariat of Workers' and Peasants' Inspection) – an agency that, while originally designed to control bureaucracy, had itself become hopelessly bureaucratized under the direction of Stalin. Lenin hoped that this newly merged organization would become a sort of institute devoting part of its time to study, under the direction of experts, management, control, and the rationalization of work. In other words, this 'institute' would become the center around which a sort of technically proficient Communist 'civil service' would be constructed. This 'civil service' would draw on the most advanced administrative techniques then in use in the capitalist West, and disseminate them throughout the whole administrative apparatus.[48]

Lenin's emphasis on raising the level of culture of the masses was very much on target, although 'civilization' would perhaps be a more accurate term in our present-day language to describe what the Communist Party leadership in the early 1920s had in mind. As Peter Kenez has pointed out, 'where Lenin and his comrades spoke and wrote about 'culture', they rarely had in mind mankind's highest creative and artistic achievements. For them culture was the opposite of backwardness, a combination of a certain economic well-being, industrial and technical accomplishments, modern attitudes to the problems of existence, and certain very basic intellectual accomplishments.'[49] In this context, I find quite superfluous and lacking in perspective those evaluations of the Bolshevik cultural program that are based on philosophical discussions, currently fashionable among many Left intellectuals and academics, concerning the true nature and ideological presuppositions of science. Likewise, I am not impressed by the recent Maoist criticism that Lenin unquestioningly accepted the legacy of bourgeois culture, science, and technology, and that 'we never find appearing in Lenin the central idea of the Chinese cultural revolution, . . . namely, the need for a specific struggle to be waged in the actual terrain of culture-as-ideology.'[50] To be sure, there was no reason for the state to interfere with the intellectual, educational, and artistic freedom that would have allowed a variety of currents of opinion and schools of thought to challenge the Western intellectual heritage if they so desired. And, in fact, this is what did happen in Soviet Russia for a number of years with the proliferation of vanguard art, Proletcult, etc.

Yet, 'modern attitudes to the problem of existence' were indispensable in order to reduce the brutality so pervasive in Russian life. Moreover, a greater degree of mass literacy and understanding of the workings of society could have only enhanced the potential for socialist democracy in Soviet Russia. Lenin was quite correct in emphasizing *basic* educational priorities, for example literacy and the acquisition of a rational scientific outlook, in what was still an overwhelmingly peasant and unschooled country. Of course, none of these welcome cultural changes would have by themselves democratized Russia given the clear absence of specifically *political* democratic institutions.

Lenin's withdrawal of support for, and attempt to organize against, Stalin and his associates on the Georgian question was also positive. However, it is legitimate to wonder whether some of Lenin's former policies had not helped to create the propitious climate for the sort of national chauvinism he was now lamenting. For example, in 1920, after retaliating against Pilsudski's earlier incursions into Russian territory, Lenin was defeated in his attempt at a full invasion of Poland. This succeeded in making a hero of Pilsudski to this very day. It is important to note that at the time the leader of the Russian revolutionary government was warned against such a move by Trotsky. Likewise, a number of leaders with much greater experience in Polish affairs, and certainly not suspect of 'softness' towards Polish nationalism, such as Dzerzhinsky and Radek, argued against the invasion and pointed out that a march on Warsaw could succeed only in the event of a workers' uprising in Poland itself. Even Stalin is reported to have had misgivings about Lenin's Polish plans.[51] Furthermore, the overthrow of the reformist Menshevik government in Georgia early in 1921 was itself highly questionable – Moscow had sent in the Red Army to 'assist' an alleged Georgian Communist uprising. Also questionable was of course Lenin's immediately subsequent support for Stalin's policies in that region.[52] Ironically, the abolition of Georgian independence had not taken place earlier, during the Civil War, at a time when it could have been justified, on a *temporary* basis, as a military self-defense measure. During the Civil War period, the Georgian government had been 'neutral in favor of the Whites.' Indeed, this conduct had even earned them the repudiation of the Russian Mensheviks, who then severed all organizational links with their Georgian comrades in December 1918.[53]

But what about applying to Georgia the Leninist principle of the self-determination of nations, particularly after the Civil War had been over? After all, in spite of their collaboration with the Whites and Western imperialism during the Civil War, this was no reactionary government. The Menshevik government, with a strong base in the Georgian working class, while the much smaller Georgian Bolsheviks had primarily recruited from the local peasantry, had carried out an authentic program of domestic reforms. This government had confiscated all private landholdings in excess of 40 acres, as well as the land belonging to the Tsarist family, the Imperial government, and the Church, and later, after 1919, sold these lands to the peasants at a nominal price. Moreover, this same Menshevik government had nationalized the main industries and means of communication, with the result that, by 1920, 90 per cent of all non-farm laborers worked in state or cooperative enterprises. However, it should also be pointed out that the Georgian government's own nationalism prevented it from recognizing the legitimate demands for political and cultural autonomy raised by minority groups within their region.[54] In fact, in May 1920, Lenin's government had actually signed an agreement with the Georgian Mensheviks that recognized without reservations the independence and sovereignty of the Georgian state. As a result of this agreement, the Georgian Communist Party was legalized by the Menshevik government, and almost 1,000 Communist were released from prison where they had been detained since the coup they had unsuccessfully attempted to carry out in November 1919.[55]

Insofar as his governmental reforms are concerned, it is clear that Lenin's disgust with bureaucracy was authentic and he did not mince words in expressing it. However, what is shocking and surprising in Lenin's program is its apparent naivety. Politics, let alone political struggle, is completely absent from this governmental reform program. Lenin apparently ignored such key issues as how the new 'rank-and-file' members of the Central Committee and Central Control Commission were to be recruited, not to mention their structural position and thus how they would be controlled (or not) by various groupings. Apparently, not by elections with the open competition of electoral platforms if not factions. If so, it was inevitable that this new personnel would be recruited by the very people that had to be watched. Neither did Lenin propose that these new leaders have bases of support (e.g. unions, political associations of various kinds) that could have made it possible for them to be in a more equal standing with the previous members of the Central Committee and the Central Control Commission. Characteristically, Lenin's 'reforms' emphasized the rank-and-file worker and peasant *background* of the proposed new leadership as if this was sufficient for the new Central Committee and Central Control Commission to represent worker and peasant interests independently of the bureaucracy. In the absence of politics and political struggle, Lenin's reforms would at best have meant a degree of circulation of elites and, through its new approach to staffing, would have perhaps constituted a very limited check on the worst vices of the state bureaucracy. But one hesitates to call it a true institutional reform because, in the last analysis, what Lenin proposed was a set of apolitical bureaucratic changes to fight bureaucracy, which were therefore of not much use.

A Possible Alternative Scenario

The Bolsheviks had, shortly after the fall of Tsarism, insisted against the Mensheviks that favorable political conditions existed for a workers' and peasants' revolution in the Russia of 1917. They also indicated that, in fact, the eventual alternative to this revolution would not have been a bourgeois democracy, but a ruthless landlord–bourgeois dictatorship. Moreover, while Russia was not economically ready for socialism, there existed realistic prospects for a revolution in at least one economically advanced country in Western Europe, which would then come to the political and economic assistance of the Russian workers' and peasants' republic. Thus, the revolutionary 'gamble' of October 1917 was both necessary and justified.

Now, in the period immediately after the end of the Civil War, Lenin and the mainstream Bolshevik leadership were trying to square the circle. Lenin's actions and writings in 1921–3, and the shift of the Comintern towards the tactics of the United Front, indicated that the Communist leadership no longer saw revolution in Western Europe as an immediate or short-term possibility. At the same time, as a result of the Civil War, a good part of the working class, including some of its most revolutionary elements, had been killed or dispersed. Within the newly reconstituted and much smaller working class, support for the Bolsheviks was at best precarious. The situation among the peasantry was, if anything, worse. In sum, the Communist Party had been left ruling a country without a social base of support. To make matters even worse, serious divisions over fundamental matters existed within the ruling party itself. Besides, the uprising in Kronstadt and the peasant 'Green' rebellions in Tambov and the Ukraine were the latest warning signals that the government could not indefinitely continue to rely on primarily military and repressive means to remain in power, as it had done at least since the beginning of the Civil War. In any case, the Communist Party leadership could not continue to engage in such behavior and honestly regard itself as socialist. If it did attempt to maintain a monopoly of power, the result could not possibly have been a workers' and peasants' state, let alone socialism, but what Bukharin once called an 'imperialist pirate state' with a monstrous state machine controlling the minutest aspects of life in society. In other words, the Bolsheviks had lost, in the most fundamental respects, the necessary gamble they had taken in October 1917.

Of course, it can and has been argued that Lenin and the Communist Party acted the only way they could have, given the situation in which they found themselves by the end of the Civil War. It is indeed difficult to respond to such an argument without sounding arrogant and/or ahistorical. Yet, it is impossible to analyze that political conjuncture without asking oneself precisely that question: what else could have been done?

First of all, at the level of general political principles, I would like to suggest that while there were plenty of organizationally conservative and Realpolitik reasons justifying the Communist Party's attempt to maintain a monopoly of political power, such efforts could no longer be justified in Marxist or socialist terms. This, given the political, social, and economic conditions prevailing in Russia and abroad between 1921 and Lenin's withdrawal from political activity in 1923. However, looking further at these issues from this Marxist and socialist perspective, the Communist Party did have a legitimate and indeed vital interest in assuring, as a minimum, the physical integrity of its members and supporters, the party's freedom to organize politically, especially in relation to the support of revolutionary movements abroad, and the prevention of chaos in the country at large. I should clarify that I am using the term chaos here to refer to the real thing, i.e. massive societal breakdown. I am certainly not defining as chaotic the dissolution of the boundary lines of the old Russian empire through the exercise of the right to self-determination by the oppressed nations.

Starting from this point of departure, and with the preservation of these legitimate interest in mind, I would like to suggest an alternative political scenario, at least as a heuristic construct. A still politically active Lenin could have had sufficient political strength and prestige to propose, by no later than say the 1922 Eleventh Party Congress, a New Political Policy (NPP) to accompany the NEP. Lenin could have argued that, just as the party took a gamble for revolution in 1917, he was now proposed to take a gamble against the total degeneration of the revolution in 1921–2. This NPP could have consisted of at least the following features: the Communist Party would have accepted the Cheka report that I. Vardin (Mgeladze) had written in early 1921 advocating the legalization of certain opposition groups, and, going beyond that report, would have legalized all parties and political groups willing to accept, and pledge loyalty to, the Soviet system of government. Any parties – e.g. the Mensheviks – doing this would have then been allowed to run slates in open soviet elections, as it had been normal practice from October 1917 until at least April 1918. Moreover, in accordance with the spirit of Lenin's press proposals of September 1917, these parties would have also been provided press facilities roughly proportionate to their size. In addition, the government would have immediately closed all labor camps, placed the secret police under strict judicial control, and declared an immediate amnesty for all political prisoners, with the possible exception of those who had directly engaged in violent acts or economic sabotage in support of the White armies during the Civil War.

This NPP, like the NEP, would have also been an attempt to buy time in the hope of an improvement in the Russian economy and of the longer-term prospects of a revolution breaking out in one or more economically advanced countries in Western Europe. But this sort of attempt to buy time, unlike the policy of combining economic concessions with political repression, would have been consistent with the at least partial preservation, rather than the total extinction, of the strong democratic elements of the October Revolution. It is also reasonable to assume that the very announcement of such a political turn, let alone the implementation of the NPP, would have allowed the Communist Party to recover a good deal of its lost prestige and popularity.

However, it is certainly possible that the NPP would have *first* resulted in a temendous growth of soviet electoral strength for the reconstituted social democratic and populist parties. In that case, the Communist Party should have been ready to enter into negotiations with these parties to explore all avenues of possible compromise. After all, in September 1917, although naturally under different circumstances, Lenin had been ready to compromise. At that time, Lenin had expressed a willingness to support a government of SR and Mensheviks exclusively responsible to the soviets, with the Bolsheviks remaining outside of the government. Lenin's party would have then retained full freedom of propaganda.[56] In 1921 and 1922, such negotiations might have led to a power-sharing arrangement with these other Soviet parties, or even, in the most extreme outcome, to the Bolsheviks leaving the government altogether. In the event of such an extreme and unprecedented situation developing, certain minimum conditions could have been agreed through the above-mentioned negotiations. First, a programmatic iron-clad guarantee preserving the major gains of the October Revolution, e.g. that there would be no attempt to return the major industries to private capitalists, and that the growth of private capitalism in the countryside would remain subject to strict controls. The Communist Party could have insisted on these conditions on the high moral and political grounds that, just as bourgeois democratic countries could not allow the 'democratic' restoration of slavery, neither could a popular soviet democracy allow the wholesale restoration of wage slavery. Second, the Communist Party would have retained full freedom of agitation and propaganda, including the right to support revolutionary movements abroad, although obviously it could only have done so as an independent party, and not in its capacity as a partner in a coalition government. Lastly, the Communist Party would have *publicly* announced that it possessed the determination *and* material ability to resort to armed struggle if the stipulated agreements or the physical integrity of the Communist Party membership were violated by the new government.

This would have indeed been a bold policy and a gamble. Indeed, one cannot underestimate the difficulties involved in a policy that may not have worked after all. However, there was *no* policy that could have confidently promised positive results if we consider the desperate situation facing the country and the complete isolation of the Communist Party. In fact, Lenin's NEP approach combining economic concessions with a political crackdown was in many ways riskier than his earlier policies relying on a relatively short-term world revolution. For one thing, it made it extremely difficult for the working class and the peasantry to *organize* and defend themselves against *NEP* abuses, e.g. widespread corruption and the exploitative and oppressive activities of both bureaucrats and born-again capitalists. Ironically, the new working class that was reconstituting itself out of the remnants of the old working class that won the Civil War against the Whites badly needed a Bolshevik Party unencumbered by state bureaucratic responsibilities and liabilities in order to struggle against the inequities of NEP. Such a party might have been able to help these new workers reorganize and repoliticize themselves from the grassroots, i.e. from below rather than from above. In any case, Lenin's policies *did not work* at least on the grounds that they deprived Russian society of the political and organizational ability to resist the later totalitarian Stalinism.

In late 1917, the Right Bolsheviks had proposed an all-socialist coalition government as a way of insuring that the government would represent a majority of the population. However, it would not have been possible or desirable to establish a coalition government with parties such as the SR and the Mensheviks. At the time, these parties rejected the very legitimacy of the October Revolution, as exemplified by their boycott of the soviets immediately after the insurrection. Later, in the Spring of 1918, a case *could* still have been made justifying the Bolshevik overthrow of the results of the unfavorable soviet provincial elections. The short-term prospects for international revolution were then very much alive, and the Bolsheviks still enjoyed a considerable social base and popular support. However, by 1921, none of these compensating factors were valid any longer. To be sure, it had never been anticipated that the first workers' and peasants' state would have been confronted with such a paradoxical situation. Nonetheless, the alternatives to this NPP policy were, as again Kronstadt, Tambov, and the Ukraine amply demonstrated, increased repression, a slow but steady bureacratic strangulation of the revolution, and a devasting defeat for the very idea of revolutionary socialism.

The Evolution of Lenin's Mainstream Bolshevik Politics

However, by 1921 neither Lenin nor his close associates in the leadership of the Communist Party would have even considered such a political opening and the specific proposals associated with it. But not because of the obvious difficulties involved in the course of action proposed above, or because the radically different choice they made was inevitable, or the only course compatible with objective reality. Rather, the political turn and proposals I spelled out above only make sense or are meaningful from a socialist perspective that sees political democracy as an essential and indeed defining element of socialism. By 1921, the political views and practices of Lenin and mainstream Bolshevism had ceased to be significantly affected by democratic considerations and priorities. As Leon Trotsky put it in 1921 with a characteristic bluntness and clarity that Lenin partly shunned in theory but not in practice:

The Workers' Opposition has come out with dangerous slogans, making a fetish of democratic principles. They place the workers' right to elect their representatives – above the party, as it were, as if the party were not entitled to assert its dictatorship even if that dictatorship temporarily clashed with the passing moods of the workers' democracy. It is necessary to create among us the awareness of the revolutionary birthright of the party, which is obliged to maintain its dictatorship, regardless of temporary wavering even in the working classes. This awareness is for us the indispensable unifying element. The dictatorship does not base itself at every given moment on the formal principle of a workers' democracy, although the workers' democracy is, of course, the only method by which the masses can be drawn more and more into political life.

When I argued that workers' democracy should be subordinated to the criterion of the economic interest of the working class … Comrade Kamenev stated that in Trotsky's eyes workers' democracy is a conditional proposition. Of course it is, although it is not a conditional but a conditioned proposition. If we were to assume that workers' democracy is unconditional, that is above everything else, then Comrade Shlyapnikov would have been right when, in his first draft, he stated that every factory should elect its own management, that every district conference of producers should elect its leading bodies, and so forth up to the All-Russian Producers' Congress.[57]

It should be emphasized that Trotsky was not justifying undemocratic party rule in situational terms here. To the contrary, Trotsky's quasi-Hegelian talk about the 'revolutionary birthright' of the party, his rejection of what democracy is all about, i.e. the right and duty of representative bodies to carry out their 'passing moods' – otherwise, who is to judge what is a 'passing' and a 'lasting' mood? – clearly expressed a non-conjuntural point of view. That is what Trotsky thought at the time concerning the nature of the dictatorship of the proletariat; it was not simply a necessary tactical response to an admittedly most difficult conjuncture. Neither had Lenin, in any of his voluminous speeches and writings, offered a conjunctural or situational justification for the lack of demcoracy, at least since the Civil War. This suggested, at the very least, an indifference to democracy as a central element of socialism.

This had not always been Lenin's attitude. Originally, Lenin's thoughts and actions contained important democratic elements, not only in the context of the demands to be raised in the political struggle against Tsarism, but also in his vision of the post-revolutionary society. Let us take us an example Lenin's arguments against 'Parabellum' in the latter part of 1915:

We must *combine* the revolutionary struggle against caplitalism with a revolutionary programme and tactics on *all* democratic demands: a republic, a militia, the popular election of officials, equal rights for women, the self-determination of nations, etc. While capitalism exists, these demands – all of them – can only be accomplished as an exception, and even then in an incomplete and distorted form. Basing ourselves on the democracy already achieved, and exposing its incompleteness under capitalism, we demand the overthrow of capitalism, the expropriation of the bourgeoisie, as a necessary basis both for the abolition of the poverty of the masses and for the *complete* and *all-round* institution of *all* democratic reforms. Some of these reforms will be started before the overthrow of the bourgeoisie, others *in the course* of that overthrow, and still others after it ... It is quite conceivable that the workers of some particular country will overthrow the bourgeoisie *before* even a single fundamental democratic reform has been fully achieved. It is, however, quite inconceivable that the proletariat, as a historical class, will be able to defeat the bourgeoisie, unless it is prepared for that by being educated in the spirit of the most consistent and resolutely revolutionary democracy.[58]

An examination of other elements of Lenin's political trajectory does show that he was perfectly capable of conceiving, and in fact did outline, institutionalized political mechanisms that would establish at least a minimum of authentic democracy in the post-revolutionary society. As I have already indicated in chapter 3, Lenin proposed, shortly before coming to power, some specific measures that would have created a diverse and pluralist press in the aftermath of a triumphant soviet power. Actually, Lenin was, compared to other socialist leaders of his time, uniquely aware of the nature and importance of democratic struggles and demands for revolutionary strategy. Even at one of his most elitist points, Lenin's *What is to be Done?* contains a strong plea for the struggle for political democracy against the indifference and hostility of the 'Economists.'[59] Lenin also sharply polemicized against those such as Rosa Luxemburg who dismissed what he considered to be a key democratic demand: the right of nations to self-determination.[60] In sum, there are sufficient politically democratic elements in Lenin's writings to have provided the basis for a society that would have been, on the whole, democratic and socialist. In fact, several democratic socialists in the Soviet Union such as Roy Medvedev have based their political philosophy precisely on those elements of Lenin's political ideas.[61] Other sympathetic writers such as Marcel Liebman have also expounded on the libertarian side of Lenin.[62]

This does not mean, of course, that there were no serious flaws and gaps in Lenin's conception of democracy. Socialist scholars such as Ralph Miliband[63] and Carmen Sirianni,[64] while not hostile to Lenin, have nonetheless made some perceptive criticisms of his political thought. They note, in particular, how in *State and Revolution* Lenin wrote extensively about workers *administering* society but not about political processes to settle the inevitable differences of opinion within the working class (i.e. a key element of socialist democracy), and the absence of any discussion of the party. In other words, they claim that Lenin looked towards a kind of apolitical administration not specially conducive to a democratic perspective on the nature of socialism. This present volume is full of criticisms pointing to Lenin's democratically deficient conceptions, even before the revolution. These criticisms concern Lenin's thoughts and practices vis-à-vis soviet rule, workers' control, socialist legality, and particularly his failure to see democracy as the institutionalization of a *participatory and democratic* new way of life for the working class and its class allies. This may, for example, help to explain the tendency displayed by Lenin as head of the Russian government to conceive of democratization as appointing people with a working-class or peasant background to governmental and economic administrative positions. This, as distinct from the establishment of institutionalized mechanisms that would allow workers and peasants to control and hold responsible those in positions of power, quite independently of the latter's social origins or background.

Yet an elementary sense of proportion and perspective demands that we distinguish between Lenin's flawed conception of democracy, which he by and large upheld until at least the Spring of 1918, and the clearly anti-democratic perspective that, with his associates, he began to adopt shortly before and especially during the course of the Civil War. As we have seen, these anti-democratic views and practices fully crystallized in the period 1921–3, even as Lenin reacted in genuine horror against the practical outcomes of those very views and actions. It was particularly during and after the Civil War that many undemocratic practices that may have indeed been justified as necessary came to be seen and defended by Lenin and the other mainstream party leaders as intrinsically virtuous. The existence of this attitude is also demonstrated, as I mentioned earlier, by the virtual absence of statements by Lenin attesting to the temporary or conjunctural nature of his repressive and anti-democratic measures, except in a few isolated instances, e.g. when the 1921 ban on party factions was originally declared to be temporary. This is one reason I think Sirianni, Miliband, and other intelligent criticis of Lenin's political theory[65] are in a sense missing the key issue. That is, in the last analysis the main problem was not the theoretical inadequacies of *State and Revolution*. Rather, the problem was Lenin's willingness to forget about it as a guideline for government policy, even if that meant merely to go on record indicating why he had to depart from it given the circumstances facing Soviet Russia. Consequently, the political vision of *State and Revolution* became in fact social poetry rather than an actual guideline for social policy.

Such a political evolution on the part of the mainstream Bolshevik leadership was neither automatic nor obvious, and must be explained. From a strictly *logical* point of view, this anti-democratic evolution of the Bolshevik leadership in the face of the Civil War and its aftermath is actually much less understandable than, say, the standpoint adopted at the time (1920) by Martov, the leader of the Left Mensheviks. As he put it:

> In a class struggle which has entered the phase of civil war, there are bound to be times when the advance guard of the revolutionary class, representing the interests of the broad masses but ahead of them in

political consciousness, is obliged to exercise state power by means of a dictatorship of the revolutionary minority. Only a short-sighted and doctrinaire viewpoint would reject this approach as such. The real question at stake is whether this dictatorship, which is unavoidable at a certain stage of any revolution, is exercised in such a way as to consolidate itself and create a system of institutions enabling it to become a permanent feature, or whether, on the contrary, it is replaced as soon as possible by the organized initiative and autonomy of the revolutionary class or classes as a whole. The second of these methods is that of the revolutionary Marxists who, for this reason, style themselves Social Democrats; the first method is that of the Communists.[66]

The point, however, is that the Bolshevik mainstream leaderhsip did not approach the situation confronting them at the time of the Civil War strictly or even primarily as a problem of Marxist political theory or logic. In my estimation they were reacting, more than anything else, to the fact that the ever-growing popular support that their party had enjoyed in the period of September 1917 to the early part of 1918 had begun to shrink by the Spring of 1918, as shown by the sharp decline of Bolshevik strength in the soviet elections held at the time. The peasantry, always a real or potential problem, turned sharply against the government as a consequence of the general policies of War Communism, and even more so as a result of the short-lived 'poor peasant' policy. By the end of the Civil War, as we have seen above, the Communist leadership could not count on the support of the any social class.

It was in the context of the Bolsheviks' general tendency to have a relatively narrow social base, combined with the serious economic difficulties and sharply declining support confronting them in early 1918, that certain democratically flawed *predispositions* of mainstream Bolshevism degenerated into an outright indifference if not hostility to democracy. In particular, one specific 'flaw' of the Leninist view of democracy became quite decisive, and considerably facilitated the subsequent evolution to a clear anti-democratic position. I am referring to the ambiguous status of majority rule in the political theory of the Bolshevik mainstream, as compared for example with the views of Rosa Luxemburg on this matter. We have already seen, in chapter 1 on the soviets, that, while it is true that Lenin recognized the different functions and democratic raison d'être for both the soviets and his party, in the last analysis it was the party that was more important than the soviets. In other words, the party was the final repository of working-class sovereignty.[67] Thus, Lenin did not seem to have reflected on or have been particularly perturbed by the decline of the soviets after 1918, or by the implications for workers' democracy of the abandonment of the slogan 'All Power to the Soviets' in the Summer of 1917 – although, as I suggested in chapter 1, he was justified in setting the slogan aside at that time. This is why one must take seriously Oskar Anweiler's claim that 'with all the idealized glorification of the soviets as a new, higher, and more democratic type of state, Lenin's principal aim was revolutionary–strategic rather than social–structural.'[68]

Likewise, I believe that a greater sensitivity to majority wishes might have led the Bolsheviks to modify or avoid altogether many of the disastrous policies of War Communism, which were in part inspired by ideology and doctrine (e.g. on the role of the market), rather than solely by what were strictly speaking the imperatives of the Civil War and the need to feed the population. It is also important to emphasize that the effects of viewing the party as more important than the working class are very different when the revolutionaries are in opposition than when they are ruling the country. When in opposition, the worst that can happen if the party is unresponsive to the working classes is that the workers and allied strata will not follow the party, and that therefore the revolutionaries will end up in sectarian isolation. However, the stakes are far higher and more dangerous when the party is in power. Here the cost of isolation is not merely sectarian irrelevance, but the extremely high price to be paid by a ruling party attempting to stay in power through an increasing reliance on repression and undemocratic practices.

Nevertheless, as I already discussed it in chapter 1, Lenin was neither the creator nor the inventor of this conception of the party. He simply shared a notion established early in the development of Russian social democracy by G. G. Plekhanov.[69] Similarly, it is critical that we do not project back into Lenin's original political ideology either his own post-Civil War notions, or even less Stalin's later views on the party. Lenin at no point glorified the party as some supra-historical, omniscient institution. In Lenin's original scheme of things, the party was no more and no less than the organized revolutionary activists. In this context, it is very important to note that Lenin was on more than one occasion willing and ready to denounce and even organize against the party itself when he felt that it was not truly acting in this revolutionary capacity. Nor was Lenin particularly concerned, unlike Stalin's later views, with preserving the party as the repository of the true science of Marxism and knowledge. Thus, it was quite characteristic for Lenin to have been seriously bothered by the existence of a body of party opinion sympathetic to Bogdanov's philosophical views *only* when they advocated a significantly different *political* course of action from that of Lenin.

Therefore, in a very real sense, Lenin's original views on the party and society were closer to Jacobinson than to Stalinism. His sometimes uncritical endorsement of the Jacobins is very suggestive in this regard.[70] One of the principal features of what I would call Lenin's 'quasi-Jacobinism' was his frequent emphasis on what the revolutionary dedication and consciousness of a few individuals and groups such as parties could accomplish. This emphasis was usually accompanied by an insistence that these groups have organizational roots in the working class and that individual leaders have an appropriate working-class (or peasant) background. This, as distinct from an approach that, while recognizing the indispensability of political leadership, still places the central emphasis on the development of class democratic *institutions* such as factory committees, unions, and soviets. Here I may recall Rosa Luxemburg's criticism that, when the Bolshevik leadership was speaking about their revolutionary dictatorship, it was 'a dictatorship, to be sure, not the dictatorship of the proletariat, however, but only the dictatorship of a handful of politicians, that is a dictatorship in the bourgeois sense, in the sense of the rule of the Jacobins.'[71] Moreover, Lenin's 'quasi-Jacobinism' was also characterized by an insufferable arrogance that is, unfortunately, too often found among revolutionaries in general. This arrogance seems to be based on the attitude or belief that the truth of the revolutionary activists' vision is sufficient guarantee of their authority to act.[72]

besides this fundamental evolution to an anti-democratic perspective, there were also additional reasons why Lenin was not inclined to make a democratic turn in the last years of his life. Perhaps the most important of these was Lenin's evident lack of confidence in the leadership of the Communist Party. As shown in his Testament,[73] Lenin was, to a greater or lesser degree, critical of all the prominent Bolshevik leaders. He was thus not very likely to trust that the Communist Party could or would win a major open political battle. Moreover, Lenin's 'political perception of danger' did not allow him to perceive of the possibility of a new and durable type of repressive society originating from *within* the revolutionary camp. One must beware of practicing '20–20 hindsight' and not forget that the worst monstrosities of Stalinism took place after Lenin had long been dead. Furthermore, in Lenin's Marxism – in spite of all, still influenced by the Second International's evolutionism – only socialism could, by definition, replace capitalism as a mode of production. It followed from this schematic view of history that capitalist restoration was, by definition, the only major qualitative danger confronting the revolution.

Another part of the problem may have been, as I already suggested in the previous chapter, Lenin's adherence to the model of the French Revolution and his consequent underestimation of the differences between the bourgeois and socialist revolutions. The French revolutionary model, very popular among the Bolsheviks, was very misleading for at least two reasons. First, the bourgeoisie, through the system of individual private property, can at least *economically* rule under a dictatorship as much as under a democracy. The working class can rule only through political means; i.e. through its collective and democratic control of the state. This is why the sharp differentiation that many 'Marxists' have made between the question of *who* rules in a post-capitalist society and that of *how* they rule is a fundamentally false distinction, at least insofar as the class rule of the working class is concerned. Second, a socialist revolution is, by definition, far greater in its social scope than a bourgeois revolution. One necessary result of this is the development of a state apparatus the strength of which would not have been imaginable to even the most hard-line Jacobin. Obviously, the popular control of such a powerful state requires at least equally strong democratic institutions and safeguards.

Finally, there was an additional sense in which the model of the French Revolution may have greatly influenced the Communist leadership's perception of the scope of the dangers facing them. Yes, there had been a dictatorship and a bloodbath during the Jacobin terror. But wasn't there also an even more serious bloodbath of revolutionaries after the 1871 Paris Commune was defeated? Lenin would have obviously preferred the former. Besides, and more to the point, the Jacobin terror, if for no other reason than because it had been overthrown, was relatively short-lived and without long-lasting institutional consequences. The Jacobins had not, after all, established an enduring terrorist political, let alone social, system. Therefore, Lenin could have perceived the Jacobin dictatorial atrocites, and by analogy the dictatorial atrocites of his own government, as relatively inconsequential in the longer historical run.

Conclusion

We know now, and some Bolsheviks had at least an inkling of it at the time, that a socialist revolution, even more than a bourgeois revolution, can be lost in more than one manner or fashion. Not only can the revolution be lost to the counterrevolutionary restorationists wanting to reestablish the Old Order. It can also be lost to a perhaps less obvious but no less devastating counterrevolution – namely, those supporting a New Order devoid of democratic control from below unavoidably opening the road for the formation of a new type of ruling class.

None of this is to suggest that the new revolutionary society can be totally free from the vices of the old society, or that it can be a complete 'prefiguration' of the future utopia. But, precisely because of this, it is therefore indispensable that there exist abundant political freedom to organize against the old as well as against the new vices. Sometimes, the well-founded skepticism concerning the new society's ability to cure *all* ills can be used as an ideological cover for the quite different claim that nothing can be done from within the revolutionary camp to prevent *most* ills. Along the same lines, there is also often a great eagerness to seize on Marx's anti-utopianism while distorting its essence and the political context in which it developed. Marx rejected utopianism precisely because of its ahistoricism and arrogant attempt to preempt the creativity of the working-class subject. For many 'Leninists' and other revolutionaries in power, anti-utopianism can become not merely the healthy refusal to elaborate detailed blueprints for the socialist future, but also the refusal to consider what strategy and tactics are or are not compatible with the road towards the socialist goal. These arguments can be particularly pernicious when, under the guise of the 'pragmatic' maxim 'hold on to power no matter what,'[74] institutional arrangements completely opposed to the original revolutionary goals are being established.

Epilogue

Democracy, as a goal of political struggle and as a subject of enquiry, has become a central question in Eastern Europe, China, and many other parts of the world. Indeed, this is the other side of the coin of the major crises that one-party-state political systems have experienced from Mexico to Poland, and from Algeria to China. I certainly did not expect such dramatic developments when I began to research and write this book in 1984, i.e. before *glasnost*, *perestroika*, not to speak of such recent phenomena as the massive collapse of Stalinism throughout Eastern Europe and the 'people power' democratic movements in the Philippines and especially China. In particular, Gorbachev's limited reforms from above have, at the time of this writing (December 1989), already placed on the political agenda many of the issues discussed in this volume. Moreover, there are clear signs that the opening initiated by the top leadership in the USSR has found a response from below in what may become a great movement for democracy unwilling to respect the limits of Gorbachev's program. If so, it is likely that more of the issues discussed here will be added to the political agenda. Thus, for example, it seems that sooner or later, Gorbachev and his associates will no longer be able to avoid or postpone confronting the question of the monopoly of power by the CPSU (the Communist Party of the Soviet Union), an important obstacle to a full democratization of the country. This, at a time when this central feature of Stalinism is in the process of being eliminated from many of the Soviet bloc countries in Eastern Europe.

So far, the democratizing changes in the USSR have taken place more along the lines of what George H. Sabine, as I noted in chapter 6, identified as the Anglo-American democratic tradition stressing the defense of liberty against arbitrary state power. Here, I would include current Soviet changes and/or debates concerning such matters as greater freedom of the press, the ban on political parties other than the Communist Party, artistic and educational freedom, and enhanced legal protection for individuals and groups. Until now, relatively less emphasis has been placed on what Sabine described as the French and Continental tradition emphasizing greater social and political equality, and on demands concerning what I have referred to in this volume as participatory democracy. A major exception to this trend, of course, has been the demands for greater political equality and control formulated by the democratic mass movements of the non-Russian nationalities, especially those in Transcaucasia and in the Baltic.

While various non-Russian nationalities have already spoken for themselves, the Russian working class has only recently begun to do so, as in the huge miners' strikes that swept the country in the Summer of 1989. Many workers have been for some time *individually* sympathetic to Gorbachev, Yeltsin, and other reform politicians. But the workers have only just begun to move in a direction that may lead them to speak *as a class* through their own organizations and spokespeople. At the same time, relatively little has been said or done so far concerning topics discussed in this book, such as workers' management or control or union independence, while a law establishing a very limited right to strike has been approved. However, there has been some discussion concerning the relative merits of political representation based on the shopfloor as compared to geographically defined electoral districts, and on whether the legislative and executive powers should be separated.[1] Moreover, whatever can be said for or against the enterprise autonomy legislated by the Law on State Enterprises that came into effect on 1 January 1988, it has been to a great extent subverted by compulsory state procurement. As of this writing, the majority of enterprises continue to find themselves obliged to deliver almost all of their production to state bodies. In any case, while this law was supposed to grant workers the right to elect their enterprise leaders, this right was considerably limited by a new clause entered in Article 6 stating that: 'If the candidate elected by the work collective is not approved by the superior organ, new elections are held.' According to an earlier version of the law, such an action was supposed to have been possible only 'following a decision by the general meeting of the work collective.'[2]

The working class, as it endures the effects of *perestroika*, may be increasingly compelled to speak and act strongly in its own name, since the workers will likely end up experiencing the worst of all worlds. That is, a situation where there is no significant increase in the quality and availability of consumer goods while at the same time the workers suffer the negative effects of economic rationalization and restructuration such as growing unemployment and production speedups. When this happens, the workers may act for themselves, in the manner of the Polish *Solidarność* of the early 1980s. If they do, they will have resisted the temptation to ally with the most backward sectors of the bureaucracy opposed to Gorbachev's reforms. After all, these backward-looking bureaucrats are also likely, in their capacity as directors of bankrupt firms and obsolete industrial sectors, to be hurt by *perestroika*. At the same time, the comparatively greater elitism of the Russian intelligentsia may or may not turn out to be a decisive impediment to the kind of worker–intellectual alliance that greatly facilitated the rise of *Solidarność*. I am referring in particular to the critical role played by the Polish KOR (Workers' Defense Committee).[3] However, an aroused Soviet working class would have an advantage not enjoyed by the Polish workers in the early 1980s; namely, there will be no imperial power to the East threatening to intervene, thus frustrating the development of the radical aspirations of the Soviet peoples.

Still, the most important democratic issue of all, which is very relevant to both of the above-mentioned democratic traditions, has just begun to emerge in the USSR. I am referring again to the monopoly of power by the Communist Party. Of course, the Soviet leadership did hold partly open parliamentary elections, which, while assuring the continued monopoly of the Communist Party, allowed for the defeat of individual and particularly unpopular party bureaucrats. Nevertheless, it is by no means established that all or most of these rejected candidates will necessarily lose all of their power, at least insofar as their positions inside the ruling Communist Party are concerned. Still, it does appear that the newly elected Supreme Soviet has acquired some influence in the appointment of government ministers, at least through its power to reject undesirable nominees.

In the last analysis, the one-party political regime existing in the USSR has been the protector of the interests of the Soviet class system. The ruling class consists of a central bureaucracy that has maintained a monopoly of political and economic power and has used the *nomenklatura* as the device through which it appoints and controls those to whom it delegates parts of its power throughout the society. At any rate, the key point to understand in this context is that an overthrow or even a serious breakdown of this one-party political regime *in a democratic and pluralistic direction* – as distinct, for example, from an army takeover as took place in Poland in 1981 – could gravely endanger the existing class system. Given this, it remains to be seen whether the current tendency in Eastern Europe to develop political pluralism and to diminish, if not eliminate, the role of the Communist Party, while keeping key structures of the existing *state* (i.e. the Interior and Defense Ministries, armed forces and security services) essentially unaltered, is a viable option for the governance of these societies.

In this context, it is worth discussing what I believe to be the shallowness of the self-styled 'new evolutionism' in Poland and Hungary associated with the names of very important democratic oppositionists such as Adam Michnik and Jacek Kuron in Poland and Miklos Haraszti in Hungary. One of the ideas that has recently gained currency in these circles is the parallel that they have drawn between some of the Eastern European regimes and Franco's Spain, thus postulating the possibility and desirability of a 'Juan Carlist' peaceful transition to democracy.[4] Given the Marxist background of many of these 'new evolutionists,' it is surprising how they have ignored a crucial difference between Francoism and East European Communism; namely, in Franco's Spain there existed a separation between the political institutions and the economic system, while in Poland and Eastern Europe no such separation exists. That is, Francoism was a dictatorial *political regime* governing over a capitalist *social system* fundamentally distinct in its composition and interests from the political regime. Moreover, Franco's political tools, such as the Falange, were organizations different from, and not organically connected to, the bulk of the capitalist class owning and controlling the Spanish economy. On the other hand, East European Communism has represented both a political regime and a particular form of non-capitalist social system to which the political regime has been inextricably linked.

Of course, it is theoretically possible to conceive of a transition, as some have in Eastern Europe, where the former Communist bosses became capitalist bosses, i.e. compensating members of the *nomenklatura* for their loss of political power with economic power acquired and maintained on an individual proprietary basis.[5] While this phenomenon has already occurred in some instances in Poland, it is unlikely to be converted into a wholesale, system-wide process, without this being accompanied by major social and political upheavals. It is true that many educated and highly skilled bureaucrats and technicians well placed at the top of the political and economic pyramids, or located in the most modern and dynamic sectors of the economy, may welcome privatization. However, neither many middle and lower full-time functionaries of the Communist parties, nor many heads of central ministries and plant directors, are likely to look kindly on giving up the current system of nationalized property which insures their bureaucratic existence, and instead allow themselves to be thrown into the 'sink or swim' processes of the marketplace. In any case, even if such a change was possible, there is no guarantee that the new society would be much more democratic than the current system in those countries.

One of the possible outcomes of the current massive upheavals in Eastern Europe is that the rulers, instead of adopting a Spanish-type model, will be attracted to something closer to the Mexican political model. Mexico has been governed by a political system that has allowed the legal existence of – and, since 1978, legally subsidized – opposition parties. This, while the ruling party for 60 years insured that the opposition *never won a single state or national executive office even if this necessitated the use of force and/or electoral fraud.* The opposition has been allowed to function and speaks, sometimes loudly, inside the weak parliament, and has some access to the print media. Most of this print media is controlled by the government through a complex system of co-optation and corruption – and intimidation, whenever peaceful means prove to be insufficient. Moreover, this access by the opposition to the media is minimal when it comes to the far more important radio and television. In addition, there is ample freedom to publish all sorts of magazines and books and the courts are supposed to be independent, although in reality they are not, at least whenever vital government interests are affected. Violations of human rights by the government or elements linked to it are common – including killings and disappearances – and as a rule go unpunished.

In other words, Mexico has a formally democratic but fundamentally authoritarian system where there is not, unlike 'Juan Carlist' Spain, an opportunity to replace the party in office. In addition, and this is specially relevant to a comparison with Eastern Europe, in Mexico there is no real separation between the party in power and the state, and consequently the ruling party is free to use and dispose of state resources as if they were its own. However, I should also point out that the Mexican political system has in recent years entered a serious crisis owing to a variety of reasons, of which the principal ones are the decline of the strongly statist and corporatist economic model in the direction of a modernizing, capitalist free-market economy, and the growth of a powerful and leftist-inspired democratic opposition movement. One result of this crisis has been that the ruling party, for the first time in its history, recently conceded one state governor's election to the right-wing opposition party. This, while at the same time it continued its refusal to acknowledge the victory of the Left opposition party in the legislative elections in another state.

In sum, the effort to maintain the monopoly of political power has underlined the limits of Gorbachev's reform program. This, plus Gorbachev's attempt to stimulate the economy through the encouragement of a certain degree of private enterprise, suggests a similarity with the Leninism of the post-1921 period. Consequently, it should not be surprising to find that Gorbachev and his followers have often identified his program with Lenin's NEP, or even with its subsequent embodiment in Bukharin's program and policies. By the same token, while Leon Trotsky is likely to be retrospectively decriminalized and his works published, the regime will continue to attack and distort his views. Most distasteful to Gorbachev and his followers would be the Trotsky of his more strongly democratic 1933–40 period. This was a Trotsky who, while still retaining his faith in the progressiveness of Soviet nationalized property, at the same time had abandoned his previous hope of reforming the heavily bureaucratized Communist parties, and had also by then clearly repudiated the identification of socialism with the one-party state. In this period, Trotsky did all of this while also maintaining his long-standing revolutionary internationalism. The current Soviet leadership would correctly perceive revolutionary internationalism as an obstacle to its foreign policy strategy, i.e. what could be called 'detente from above:' a sort of late twentieth-century version of the Holy Alliance 'peacefully' dividing geopolitical spheres of influence between the USSR and its heretofore rival imperialisms. Similarly, Gorbachev is not going to embrace either the early Right or Left oppositions to Lenin, precisely because these tendencies stood as significant obstacles to the political monopoly of the post-1921 Leninist system that is so much in Gorbachev's interest to symbolically embrace.

However, the developing movement from below will probably go much farther and beyond Bukharin's program and Lenin's NEP in its search for models and political programs that can be useful in the development of the Soviet society of the future. In the process it is likely to discover that the Bolshevik Party, at least until 1921, was a monolith only in the mythologies fostered by Stalinists and Western Cold Warriors alike. The ideas and practices of the early Right and Left Bolshevik oppositions will be reexamined, as no doubt will also be the case with the ideas and practices of Mensheviks,

Anarchists, and Right and Left SRs. If this volume turns out to make even a tiny contribution to this rebirth of political activity and discussion in the USSR, and to the creation of a new Soviet Left, this project will have been truly worth while.

Notes

INTRODUCTION

1 Abraham Brumberg, 'Moscow: The Struggle for Reform', *New York Review of Books*, vol. 36, no. 5 (30 March, 1989), p. 39, and 'Gorbachev's Progress', letter to the Editor, *New York Review of Books*, vol. 36, no. 9 (1 June, 1989), p. 41; Zbigniew Brzezinski, *The Grand Failure. The Birth and Death of Communism in the Twentieth Century*, New York: Charles Scribner's Sons, 1989, p. 49; Bill Keller, 'Lenin Faulted on State Terror, and a Soviet Taboo is Broken,' *New York Times*, 8 June, 1988, pp. 1–12; Bill Keller, 'In USSR, a Painful Prying At Roots of Stalin's Tyranny', *New York Times*, 11 June, 1988, pp. 1–6; and Bill Keller, 'Soviet Party Conference to Try to Relax Authoritarian Grip', *New York Times*, 27 June, 1988, pp. 1–8. See also R. W. Davies, 'Soviet History in the Gorbachev Revolution: The First Phase', in Ralph Miliband, Leo Panitch, and John Saville (eds), *Socialist Register 1988*, London, England: The Merlin Press, 1988, pp. 37–78.

2 See the Democratic Union's 'Declaration' approved at the Democratic Union's Founding Congress, 9 May, 1988 in 'The Democratic Union (DS)', *Labour Focus in Eastern Europe* (London, England), vol. 10, no. 3, 1989, p. 25, and Ronald Tiersky, *Ordinary Stalinism. Democratic Centralism and the Question of Communist Political Development*, Boston: Allen & Unwin, 1985. The Italian Communist Party may have been a partial exception. At one time, factions more critical of the lack of democracy in the Soviet bloc were also more militant on domestic matters than the mainstream party leadership (see Tiersky, pp. 125–35).

3 Of course, the original development of the Cuban Revolution towards Communism differs in some important respects from the Chinese and Vietnamese cases. However, these differences do not affect the commonality relevant to my point; namely, the Fidelista leadership chose Communism as a good thing in itself and not simply as a lesser evil imposed by objective reality. See my works *Revolution and Reaction in Cuba. 1933–1960*, Middletown, Conn. Wesleyan University Press, 1976, and 'The Cuban Communists in the Early Stages of the Cuban Revolution: Revolu-

tionaries or Reformists?' *Latin American Research Review*, vol. 18, no. 1, 1983, pp. 59–83.

4   I am indebted to David Finkel for helping me to articulate this approach. Personal communication of 29 May 1986.

5   For example, Frederick Kaplan, *Bolshevik Ideology and the Ethics of Soviet Labor 1917–1920. The Formative Years*, New York: Philosophical Library, 1968, and Maurice Brinton, *The Bolsheviks and Workers' Control*, Montreal, Black Rose Books, 1975.

6   Carmen Sirianni, *Workers' Control and Socialist Democracy. The Soviet Experience*, London, England: Verso Editions and New Left Books, 1982.

7   ibid., pp. 302, 325, and relevant notes on pp. 409–10.

8   Sheldon S. Wolin, *Politics and Vision. Continuity and Innovation in Western Political Thought*, Boston: Little, Brown and Company, 1960, p. 431.

9   ibid., p. 434.

10 Christian Rakovsky, 'The "Professional Dangers" of Power', in Tariq Ali (ed.), *The Stalinist Legacy*, Middlesex, England: Penguin Books, 1984, pp. 49, 53.

11 Charles Bettelheim, *Class Struggles in the USSR. First Period: 1917–1923*, New York: Monthly Review Press, 1976, translated by Brian Pearce.

12 S. A. Smith, *Red Petrograd. Revolution in the Factories 1917–1918*, Cambridge, England: Cambridge University Press, 1983, pp. 264–5. Smith's emphasis.

13 Daniel Bell, 'Ten Theories in Search of Reality: The Prediction of Soviet Behavior', in *The End of Ideology. On the Exhaustion of Political Ideas in the Fifties*, New York: The Free Press, 1960, pp. 325–6; Fang Lizhi, 'China's Despair and China's Hope', *New York Review of Books*, vol. 36, no. 1, 2 February 1989, p. 3.

14 Marvin Harris, *Cultural Materialism. The Struggle for a Science of Culture*, New York: Vintage Books, 1980, p. 260.

15 ibid., p. 261.

16 Stephen F. Cohen, *Rethinking the Soviet Experience. Politics and History Since 1917*, New York: Oxford University Press, 1985, pp. 5–6.

17 See, for example, the many works by Alexander Rabinowitch, particularly *The Bolsheviks Come to Power. The Revolution of 1917 in Petrograd*, New York: W. W. Norton, 1978, and the essays by a variety of scholars such as S. A. Smith, Ronald Grigor Suny, and William G. Rosenberg in Daniel H. Kaiser (ed.), *The Workers' Revolution in Russia, 1917. The View From Below*, Cambridge, England: Cambridge University Press, 1987. For the deep divisions in the Bolshevik Party in 1917 and ealry 1918, see *The Bolsheviks and the October Revolution*, Central Committee Minutes of the Russian Social-Democratic Labour Party (Bolsheviks), August 1917–February 1918, London, England: Pluto Press, 1974, translated from the Russian by Ann Bone. It is also important to note and emphasize that there exist, and I draw upon in this book, many other approaches to the Russian Revolution and the early Soviet state besides the orthodox and revisionist schools

discussed above. Among these I will presently mention the work of British 'empiricists' such as E. H. Carr and R. W. Davies, and that of the 'post-revisionist' scholarship of a younger generation of historians such as Vladimir Brovkin, Jane Burbank, and John B. Hatch.

18 Cohen, *Rethinking the Soviet Experience*; Stephen F. Cohen, *Bukharin and the Bolshevik Revolution. A Political Biography 1888–1938*, New York: Oxford University Press, 1980. This is also true, to a somewhat lesser extent, of some of the works by Robert C. Tucker such as *Political Culture and Leadership in Soviet Russia. From Lenin to Gorbachev*, New York: W. W. Norton and Company, 1987.

19 Victor Serge, *Memoirs of a Revolutionary*, London, England: Oxford University Press, 1963, translated by Peter Sedgwick; Ante Ciliga, *The Russian Enigma*, London, England: Ink Links, 1979, translated by Fernand G. Fernier and Anne Cliff (part I) and by Margaret and Hugo Dewar (part II).

20 Arthur O. Lovejoy, *The Great Chain of Being*, Cambridge, Mass.: Harvard University Press, 1948, p. 11; Alvin W. Gouldner, 'Metaphysical Pathos and the Theory of Bureaucracy', *American Political Science Review*, vol. 49, 1955, p. 378.

21 See for example, the article by *New York Times* reporter John Tagliabue on Leszek Moczulski, leader of the Confederation for an Independent Poland. 'Leader of Choice for Polish Radicals', *New York Times*, Friday, 24 March, 1989, p. A10.

22 Adam Michnik, *Letters from Prison and Other Essays*, Berkeley, Calif.: University of California Press, 1985, pp. 89–90, 294, translated by Maya Latynski.

23 Karl Kautsky, *Terrorism and Communism. A Contribution to the Natural History of Revolution*, Westport, Conn.: Hyperion Press (Reprint), 1973, p. 107, translated by W. H. Kerridge.

24 George Orwell, *The Lion and the Unicorn. Socialism and the British Genius*, London: Secker & Warburg, 1962, p. 85.

25 Gouldner, 'Metaphysical Pathos', p. 507.

26 Cohen, *Rethinking the Soviet Experience*, p. 29.

27 E. J. Hobsbawm, *The Age of Revolution. 1789–1848*, New York: Mentor Book, New American Library, 1964, p. xv.

CHAPTER 1   THE RISE AND DECLINE OF DEMOCRATIC SOVIETS

1 Oskar Anweiler, *The Soviets: The Russian Workers, Peasants, and Soldiers' Councils, 1905–1921*, New York: Pantheon Books, 1974, translated from the German by Ruth Hein, pp. 45–7.

2 ibid., p. 113.

3 Boris Souvarine, *Stalin. A Critical Survey of Bolshevism*, New York: Octagon Books, 1972, p. 209.

4 Anweiler, *The Soviets*, p. 113.

5 ibid., pp. 205–6.

6 John L. H. Keep (translator and editor), *The Debate on Soviet Power, Minutes of the All-Russian Central Executive Committee of Soviets, Second Convocation, October 1917–January 1918*, Oxford, England: Clarendon Press, 1979.

7 Malvin Magnus Helgesen, 'The Origins of the Party-State Monolith in Soviet Russia: Relations between the Soviets and Party Committees in the Central Provinces, October 1917 – March 1921,' PhD dissertation, State University of New York at Stony Brook, 1980, pp. 63, 78–91; Ronald W. Clark, *Lenin. A Biography*, New York: Harper & Row, 1988, p. 336.

8 T. H. Rigby, *Lenin's Government: Sovnarkom 1917–1922*, Cambridge, England: Cambridge University Press, 1979, p. 165; Richard Sakwa, *Soviet Communists in Power. A Study of Moscow during the Civil War, 1918–1921*, New York: St Martin's Press, 1988, pp. 186–7.

9 Rigby, *Lenin's Government* pp. 168–9. See also Robert Abrams, 'The Local Soviets of the RSFSR, 1918–1921', unpublished PhD dissertation, Columbia Universtiy, New York, 1966, p. 377.

10 Alexander Rabinowitch, 'The Evolution of Local Soviets in Petrograd, November 1917–June 1918: The Case of the First City District Soviet', *Slavic Review*, vol. 46, no. 1, Spring 1987, p. 27.

11 ibid., pp. 28–9.

12 Helgesen, 'Origins of the Party-State Monolith', pp. 163–4.

13 John L. H. Keep, *The Russian Revolution. A Study in Mass Mobilization*, New York: W. W. Norton, 1976, pp. 265–342.

14 Vladimir Brovkin, 'Politics, Not Economics Was the Key', *Slavic Review*, vol. 44, no. 2, Summer 1985, p. 246.

15 David Mandel, *The Petrograd Workers and the Soviet Seizure of Power. From The July Days 1917 to July 1918*, New York: St Martin's Press, 1984, p. 356.

16 ibid., p. 406.

17 ibid., pp. 407–8.

18 ibid., p. 356.

19 S. A. Smith, *Red Petrograd. Revolution in the Factories 1917–1918*, Cambridge, England: Cambridge University Press, 1983, p. 166; Mandel, *The Petrograd Workers*, p. 356.

20 Israel Getzler, *Kronstadt 1917–1921. The Fate of a Soviet Democracy*, Cambridge, England: Cambridge University Press, 1983, pp. 183, 186.

21 A. M. Spirin, *Klassy i partii v grazhdankou'voine v Rossii (1917–1920 gg)*, Moscow: 'Mysl'', 1968, pp. 173–4.

22 Vladimir Brovkin, 'The Mensheviks' Political Comeback: The Elections to the Provincial City Soviets in Spring 1918,' *The Russian Review*, vol. 42, no. 1, 1983, p. 47.

23 I am indebted to Professor Gerald Surh for his invaluable assistance in

translating excerpts from Spirin's book and in interpreting the relevant findings.

24   Silvana Malle, *The Economic Organization of War Communism, 1918–1921*, Cambridge, England: Cambridge University Press, 1985, p. 367.

25   Brovkin, 'The Mensheviks' Political Comeback', pp. 7, 23, 31, 43; Abrams, 'The Local Soviets of the RSFSR', p. 376.

26   Brovkin, 'The Mensheviks' Political Comeback', pp. 47–8. For a more extensive discussion of this regionalism and fragmentation, see John L. H. Keep, 'October in the Provinces', in Richard Pipes (ed.), *Revolutionary Russia*, Cambridge, Mass.: Harvard University Press, 1968, pp. 180–223.

27   Stephen M. Berk, 'The "Class Tragedy" of Izhevsk: Working-Class Opposition to Bolshevism in 1918', *Russian History*, vol. 2, no. 2, 1975, p. 181.

28   Marcel Liebman, *Leninism under Lenin*, London, England: Jonathan Cape, 1975, translated by Brian Pearce, pp. 225–6.

29   ibid., pp. 226–7.

30   Mandel, *The Petrograd Workers*, p. 391.

31   William G. Rosenberg, 'Russian Labor and Bolshevik Power after October', *Slavic Review*, vol. 44, no. 2, Summer 1985, p. 223. For a Menshevik view of these issues and for a discussion of labor protests at the time, see Raphael R. Abramovitch, *The Soviet Revolution 1917–1939*, New York: International Universities Press, 1962, pp. 151–67.

32   Rosenberg, 'Russian Labor and Bolshevik Power', pp. 229, 233. For further details on the Petrograd Conference of Factory Representatives, see Abramovitch, *The Soviet Revolution*, and also Vera Broido, *Lenin and the Mensheviks. The Persecution of Socialists Under Bolshevism*, Aldershot, England: Gower/Maurice Temple Smith, 1987, pp. 76–9, and Vladimir N. Brovkin, *The Mensheviks after October. Socialist Opposition and the Rise of the Bolshevik Dictatorship*, Ithaca and London: Cornell University Press, 1987, pp. 161–96.

33   Richard Sakwa, 'The Commune State in Moscow in 1918', *Slavic Review*, vol. 46, nos 3/4, Fall/Winter 1987, pp. 442, 441.

34   Rosenberg, 'Russian Labor and Bolshevik Power', p. 237.

35   Vladimir Brovkin, 'Politics, Not Economics Was the Key', pp. 244–5.

36   Mandel, *The Petrograd Workers*, p. 376.

37   Rosenberg, 'Russian Labor and Bolshevik Power', p. 227.

38   Smith, *Red Petrograd*, p. 234.

39   Brovkin, 'Politics, Not Economics Was the Key', p. 247.

40   Anweiler, *The Soviets*, p. 230.

41   Leonard Schapiro, *The Origin of the Communist Autocracy, Political Opposition in the Soviet State: First Phase, 1917–1922*, Cambridge, Mass.: Harvard University Press, 1956, pp. 178–9.

42   Rigby, *Lenin's Government*, pp. 161–2.

43   E. H. Carr, *The Bolshevik Revolution, 1917–1923*, vol. 1, London, England: Pelican Books, 1966, p. 183.

44 Schapiro, *The Origin of the Communist Autocracy*, p. 178.

45 For details on the working-class unrest and Menshevik resurgence in 1921, see Vladimir Brovkin, 'The Mensheviks and NEP Society in Russia', *Russian History*, vol. 9, parts 2–3, 1982, pp. 352–5. For discussions of similar developments in Moscow, see John B. Hatch, 'Working-Class Politics in Moscow during the Early NEP: Mensheviks and Workers' Organizations, 1921–1922', *Soviet Studies*, vol. 39, no. 4, October 1987, esp. pp. 558–60, 561, and William J. Chase, *Workers, Society, and the Soviet State. Labor and Life in Moscow, 1918–1929*, Urbana, Ill.: University of Illinois Press, 1987, pp. 50–1.

46 Cited in Roy Medvedev, *Leninism and Western Socialism*, London, England: Verso, 1981, translated by A. D. P. Briggs, p. 128.

47 Carr, *The Bolshevik Revolution*, p. 236.

48 ibid., p. 236.

49 Schapiro, *The Origin of the Communist Autocracy*, pp. 170, 206.

50 Cited in Medvedev, *Leninism and Western Socialism*, pp. 233–4.

51 Sakwa, 'The Commune State in Moscow in 1918', p. 436.

52 Rigby, *Lenin's Government*, p. 161.

53 ibid., p. 169.

54 ibid., pp. 171, 174.

55 ibid., pp. 165, 175–6; Jonathan R. Adelman, 'The Development of the Soviet Party Apparat in the Civil War: Center, Localities and Nationality Areas', *Russian History*, vol. 9, part I, 1982, pp. 87–9; Leonard Schapiro, *The Communist Party of the Soviet Union*, New York: Random House, 1960, p. 253; Abrams, 'The Local Soviets of the RSFSR', p. 376. For a detailed description and analysis of these processes in the central provinces, see Helgesen, 'The Origins of the Party-State Monolith'; and, for Moscow, see chapter 4 of Richard Sakwa's *Soviet Communists in Power*.

56 T. H. Rigby, 'Staffing USSR Incorporated: The Origins of the Nomenklatura System', *Soviet Studies*, vol. 40, no. 4, October 1988, p. 530.

57 Robert Service, *The Bolshevik Party in Revolution. A Study in Organizational Change*, London, England: Macmillan, 1979, pp. 126–8; Charles Duval, 'Iakov Mikhailovich Sverdlov: Founder of the Bolshevik Party Machine', in Ralph Carter Elwood (ed.), *Reconsiderations on the Russian Revolution*, Cambridge, Mass.: Slavica Publishers, 1976, pp. 230–1.

58 Cited in Tony Cliff, 'Trotsky on Substitutionism', in *Party and Class. Essays by Cliff, Hallas, Harman and Trotsky*, London, England: Pluto Press, n.d., p. 35.

59 Service, *The Bolshevik Party in Revolution*, pp. 167–8; Abdurakhman Avtorkhanov, *The Communist Party Apparatus*, Chicago, Ill.: Henry Regnery Company, 1966, p. 101.

60 Anweiler, *The Soviets*, pp. 115–6.

61 Keep, *The Russian Revolution*, p. 122.

62 Carmen Sirianni, *Workers' Control and Socialist Democracy. The Soviet Experience*, London, England: Verso Editions and New Left Books, 1982,

p. 71; Marc Ferro, 'The Birth of the Soviet Bureaucratic System', in Ralph Carter Elwood (ed.), *Reconsiderations on the Russian Revolution*, pp. 114, 116.

63   Anweiler, *The Soviets*, p. 115.

64   Ferro, 'The Birth of the Soviet Bureaucratic System', pp. 102–3, 126.

65   Keep, *The Russian Revolution*, p. 120.

66   Ferro, 'The Birth of the Soviet Bureaucratic System', pp. 102–3, 110–13; S.A. Smith, review of Marc Ferro's *October 1917: A Social History of the Russian Revolution*, (London: Routledge & Kegan Paul, 1980) in *Soviet Studies*, vol. 33, no. 3, July 1981, pp. 454–9; Rex A. Wade, 'The Rajonnye Sovety of Petrograd: The Role of Local Political Bodies in the Russian Revolution', *Jahrbücher für Geschichte Osteuropas*, vol. 20, no. 2, June 1972, pp. 226–40.

67   Wade, 'The Rajonnye Sovety of Petrograd', p. 231.

68   Article Four, Chapter 13, section a, *The Russian Constitution. Adopted July 10, 1918*, reprinted by *The Nation*, 4 January 1919, p. 16; my emphasis.

69   Keep, *The Russian Revolution*, p. 122.

70   Rabinowitch, 'The Evolution of Local Soviets in Petrograd', p. 36, 48.

71   Graeme J. Gill, *Peasants and Government in the Russian Revolution*, London and Basingstoke, England: Macmillan 1979, pp. 117–20, 130. See also Anweiler, *The Soviets*, p. 236.

72   Orlando Figes, 'The Village and *Volost* Soviet Elections of 1919', *Soviet Studies*, vol. 40, no. 1, January 1988, pp. 26–8, 31.

73   Anweiler, *The Soviets*, p. 225; Abrams, 'The Local Soviets of the RSFSR', ch. 5, pp. 180–204.

74   Orlando Figes, 'The Village and *Volost* Soviet Elections of 1919', p. 42.

75   Cited by Robert Service, *Lenin: A Political Life. Vol. 1. The Strengths of Contradiction*, Bloomington, Ind.: Indiana University Press, 1985, p. 147.

76   See Tony Cliff, *Lenin. Vol. 1: Building the Party*, London: Pluto Press, 1975, pp. 159–68; Solomon K. Schwarz, *The Russian Revolution of 1905: The Workers' Movement and the Formation of Bolshevism and Menshevism*, Chicago: University of Chicago Press, 1976, p. 57.

77   Hal Draper, *The 'Dictatorship of the Proletariat' from Marx to Lenin*, New York: Monthly Review Press, 1987, See, in particular, pp. 39–41, 46, 92–3.

78   Allan K. Wildman, *The Making of a Workers' Revolution. Russian Social Democracy, 1891–1903*, Chicago: University of Chicago Press, 1967, pp. 252–3; V. I. Lenin, 'Our Tasks and the Soviet of Workers' Deputies. A Letter to the Editor', written 2–4 November 1905, first published 5 November 1940 in *Pravda*, no. 308; in *Collected Works*, vol. 10, November 1905–June 1906, Moscow: Foreign Languages Publishing House, 1962, pp. 19, 23.

79   V. I. Lenin, 'Socialism and Anarchism', written 24 November (7 December), 1905, published in *Novaya Zhizn*, no. 21, 25 November 1905; in *Collected Works*, vol. 10, p. 72.

80 V. I. Lenin, 'The Socialist Party and Non-Party Revolutionism', published in *Novaya Zhizn*, nos 22 and 27, 26 November and 2 December 1905; in *Collected Works*, vol. 10, p. 81; my emphasis. For a Menshevik interpretation of Lenin's inconsistent attitude towards the soviets at this time, see Solomon K. Schwarz, *The Russian Revolution of 1905. The Workers' Movement and the Formation of Bolshevism and Menshevism*, Chicago: University of Chicago Press, 1967, pp. 189–95.

81 Cited in Anweiler, *The Soviets*, p. 145.

82 Rosa Luxemburg, 'The Russian Revolution', in *The Russian Revolution and Leninism or Marxism?*, Ann Arbor, Mich.: University of Michigan Press, 1961, p. 39.

83 V. I. Lenin, 'On Slogans', written mid-July 1917, published in pamphlet form in 1917 by the Kronstadt Committee of the RSDLP (B); in *Collected Works*, vol. 25, June–September 1917, Moscow: Progress Publishers, 1964, pp. 184, 189.

84 Alexander Rabinowitch, *The Bolsheviks Come to Power. The Revolution of 1917 in Petrograd*, New York: W. W. Norton, 1978, p. 59.

85 Mandel, *The Soviets*, p. 233.

86 Rabinowitch, *The Bolsheviks Come to Power*, pp. 60–1; Mandel, *The Soviets*, p. 234.

87 Schapiro, *The Communist Party of the Soviet Union*, p. 167.

88 Rabinowitch, *The Bolsheviks Come to Power*, pp. 83–90.

89 Anweiler, *The Soviets*, pp. 172–3.

90 Mandel, *The Petrograd Workers*, pp. 235, 240–1.

91 Rabinowtich, *The Bolsheviks Come to Power*, p. 90.

92 ibid., pp. 219–23, 247, 250–4.

93 Jerry F. Hough and Merle Fainsod, *How the Soviet Union is Governed*, Cambridge, Mass.: Harvard University Press, 1979, pp. 38–9. See also Rabinowitch, *The Bolsheviks Come to Power*, p. 59; *The Bolsheviks and the October Revolution*, Central Committee Minutes of the Russian Social-Democratic Labour Party (Bolsheviks) August 1917–February 1918, London: Pluto Press, 1974, translated from the Russian by Ann Bone, and the essays by a variety of scholars such as S. A. Smith, Ronald Grigor Suny, and William G. Rosenberg in Daniel H. Kaiser (ed.), *The Workers' Revolution in Russia, 1917. The View From Below*, Cambridge, England: Cambridge University Press, 1987.

94 Robert C. Tucker, *Political Culture and Leadership in Soviet Russia. From Lenin to Gorbachev*, New York: W. W. Norton, 1987, p. 84.

95 Schapiro, *The Communist Party of the Soviet Union*, pp. 188–9.

96 E. H. Carr, *The Bolshevik Revolution. 1917–1923*, vol. 2, London, England: Pelican Books, 1966, pp. 55–6; Lars T. Lih, 'Bread and Authority in Russia: Food Supply and Revolutionary Politics, 1914–1921', PhD dissertation, Princeton University, 1984.

97 Malle, *The Economic Organization of War Communism*, p. 336.

98 Ferro, *October 1917*, p. 138; Teodor Shanin, *The Awkward Class. Political*

Sociology of Peasantry in a Developing Society. Russia 1910–1925, Oxford, England: Clarendon Press, 1972, p. 2. For an informative and interesting discussion of how various Left parties classified the peasantry, see Lars T. Lih, 'Bread and Authority in Russia', pp. 190, 287–300, 315.

99   Malle, *The Economic Organization of War Communism*, p. 406; Shanin, *The Awkward Class*, p. 174; Lazar Volin, *A Century of Russian Agriculture. From Alexander II to Khrushchev*, Cambridge, Mass.: Harvard University Press, 1970, pp. 136–7.

100   Mandel, *The Petrograd Workers*, p. 234.

101   ibid., p. 240.

102   Gill, *Peasants and Government in the Russian Revolution*, p. 124.

103   William Henry Chamberlin, *The Russian Revolution. 1917–1921*, vol. 2, New York: Macmillan, 1935, pp. 43–5.

104   For a detailed discussion on the evolution of the committees of the rural poor, see Malle, *The Economic Organization of War Communism*, pp. 367–72.

105   From an article by Vasili Seliunin entitled 'Istoki' ('Sources') published in *Novyi Mir* (no. 5, 1988) and cited by Abraham Brumberg in 'Moscow: The Struggle for Reform', *New York Review of Books*, vol. 36, no. 5, (30 March 1989), p. 39. The data on the degree of collectivization during the period of War Communism are available in Volin, *A Century of Russian Agriculture*, p. 154.

106   Chamberlin, *The Russian Revolution*, pp. 97–8.

107   ibid., p. 102.

108   Maurice Dobb, *Soviet Economic Development since 1917*, London, England: Routledge & Kegan Paul, 1978.

109   Paul Craig Roberts, 'War Communism: A Re-Examination', *Slavic Review*, vol. 29, no. 2, June 1970, pp. 238–61.

110   Simon Liberman, *Building Lenin's Russia*, Chicago: University of Chicago Press, 1945, p. 24.

111   Stephen F. Cohen, *Bukharin and the Bolshevik Revolution. A Political Biography 1888–1938*, Oxford, England: Oxford University Press, 1980, p. 87.

112   ibid., p. 87. For a discussion of Bukharin's *The Economics of the Transition Period*, see pp. 87–96, and for a description of War Communism, see pp. 78–87.

113   Alec Nove, 'Lenin and the New Economic Policy', in Bernard W. Eissenstat (ed.), *Lenin and Leninism. State, Law and Society*, Lexington, Mass.: Lexington Books, D. C. Heath, 1971, p. 155.

114   Roy A. Medvedev, *The October Revolution*, New York: Columbia University Press, 1979, translated by George Saunders, p. 183.

115   Jan M. Meijer, 'Town and Country in the Civil War', in Richard Pipes (ed.), *Revolutionary Russia*, Cambridge, Mass.: Harvard University Press, 1968, p. 269.

116   Medvedev, *The October Revolution*, p. 180.

117 ibid., pp. 183–4.
118 Thomas F. Remington, *Building Socialism in Bolshevik Russia. Ideology and Industrial Organization 1917–1921*, Pittsburgh, Pa.: University of Pittsburgh Press, 1984, p. 171. See also a highly detailed critique of the food requisition policies of War Communism in Malle, *The Economic Organization of War Communism*, pp. 372–80.
119 Paul Avrich, *Kronstadt 1921*, New York: W. W. Norton, 1974, p. 23.
120 Schapiro, *The Communist Party of the Soviet Union*, p. 192.
121 Lih, 'Bread and Authority in Russia', pp. 403–4; Lih's emphasis.
122 ibid., p. 440.
123 Schapiro, *The Communist Party of the Soviet Union*, p. 192.
124 ibid., p. 189.
125 Isaac Deutscher, *The Prophet Armed. Trotsky: 1879–1921*, vol. 1, New York: Vintage Books, 1965, p. 496.
126 Avrich, *Kronstadt 1921*, p. 20.
127 Esther Kingston-Mann, *Lenin and the Problem of Marxist Peasant Revolution*, New York: Oxford University Press, 1983, p. 100.
128 For an interesting exchange concerning the Bolshevik Party's attitudes to the peasantry, see the 'Discussion' of Meijer's 'Town and Country in the Civil War', pp. 278–81.
129 David Lane, *The Roots of Russian Communism. A Social and Historical Study of Russian Social-Democracy 1898–1907*, Assen, Holland: Van Gorcum, 1969, pp. 25–6; Avtorkhanov, *The Communist Party Apparatus*, p. 101; Adelman, 'The Development of the Soviet Party Apparat', pp. 94, 100, 101; Gill, *Peasants and Government in the Russian Revolution*, p. 225; Abrams, 'The Local Soviets of the RSFSR', pp. 207–15.
130 Ferro, *October 1917*, p. 112; Adelman, 'The Development of the Soviet Party Apparat', p. 91.
131 Adelman, 'The Development of the Soviet Party Apparat', pp. 94, 102, 103.
132 Neil Harding, *Lenin's Political Thought. Vol. 2. Theory and Practice in the Socialist Revolution*, London and Basingstoke, England: Macmillan, 1981, p. 230.
133 V. I. Lenin, 'The Constituent Assembly Elections and the Dictatorship of the Proletariat', in *Collected Works*, vol. 30, September 1919–April 1920, Moscow: Progress Publishers, 1965, p. 257; Lenin's emphasis.
134 Harding, *Lenin's Political Thought*, p. 230.
135 V. I. Lenin, 'Deception of the People with Slogans of Freedom and Equality', second speech to the First All-Russia Congress on Adult Education (6–19 May 1919); in *Collected Works*, vol. 29, March–August 1919, Moscow: Progress Publishers, 1965, p. 359.
136 ibid., p. 365.
137 Cited in Avrich, *Kronstadt 1921*, p. 9.
138 Lenin, 'Deception of the People with Slogans of Freedom and Equality', pp. 360–1; Lenin's emphasis.

139 Friedrich Engels, *Socialism: Utopian and Scientific*, in Robert C. Tucker (ed.), *The Marx–Engels Reader. Second Edition*, New York: W. W. Norton, 1978, pp. 716–17.

140 Lars T. Lih, 'Bolshevik *Razverstka* and War Communism', *Slavic Review*, vol. 45, no. 4, Winter 1986.

141 For a critical analysis of the Leninist point of view on economic development and its impact on the peasantry, see Shanin, *The Awkward Class*.

142 Tony Cliff, *Lenin, Vol. 3: Revolution Besieged*, London, England: Pluto Press, 1978, p. 31.

143 Oliver Henry Radkey, *The Election to the Russian Constituent Assembly of 1917*, Cambridge, Mass.: Harvard University Press, 1950, pp. 2–3, 14, 38.

144 Oliver Henry Radkey, *The Sickle under the Hammer. The Russian Socialist Revolutionaries in the Early Months of Soviet Rule*, New York and London: Columbia University Press, 1963, p. 284.

145 ibid., p. 305.

146 ibid., pp. 305–6.

147 *The Bolsheviks and the October Revolution*, pp. 154–5.

148 Luxemburg, 'The Russian Revolution', p. 60.

149 ibid., pp. 60–1.

150 ibid., p. 59.

151 V. I. Lenin, 'The Tasks of the Revolution', in *Collected Works*, vol. 26, September 1917–February 1918, Moscow: Progress Publishers, 1964, pp. 67–8.

152 Cited in Peter Nettl, *Rosa Luxemburg*, abridged edn, London, England: Oxford University Press, 1969, p. 307.

153 ibid., p. 452.

154 Rosa Luxemburg, 'The Question of Suffrage', in *The Russian Revolution*, pp. 63–7.

155 Carr, *The Bolshevik Revolution*, vol. 1, pp. 135–6.

156 V. I. Lenin, *The Proletarian Revolution and Kautsky the Renegrade*, in *Collected Works*, vol. 28, July 1918–March 1919, Moscow: Progress Publishers, 1965, p. 255.

157 Luxemburg, 'The Question of Suffrage', pp. 64–5.

158 ibid., p. 66.

CHAPTER 2   WORKERS' CONTROL AND TRADE UNION INDEPENDENCE

1 S. A. Smith, *Red Petrograd. Revolution in the Factories 1917–1918*, Cambridge, England: Cambridge University Press, 1983, pp. 139–40.

2 Marc Ferro, *October 1917. A Social History of the Russian Revolution*, London, England: Routledge & Kegan Paul, 1980, translated by Norman Stone, pp. 144–5.

3 ibid., pp. 146–8, 159.
4 Smith, *Red Petrograd*, p. 162; Marc Ferro, 'The Birth of the Soviet Bureaucratic System', in Ralph Carter Elwood (ed.), *Reconsiderations on the Russian Revolution*, Cambridge, Mass.: Slavica Publishers, 1976, pp. 108–10.
5 Ferro, 'The Birth of the Soviet Bureaucratic System', op. cit., pp. 108, 110. For a full discussion of the Red Guards, see Rex Wade, *Red Guards and Workers' Militia in the Russian Revolution*, Stanford, Calif.: Stanford University Press, 1984.
6 Thomas F. Remington, *Building Socialism in Bolshevik Russia. Ideology and Industrial Organization. 1917–1921*, Pittsburgh, Pa.: Univeristy of Pittsburgh Press, 1984, pp. 27–8.
7 Smith, *Red Petrograd*, p. 159.
8 Remington, *Building Socialism in Bolshevik Russia*, pp. 27–9.
9 ibid., p. 37.
10 Smith, *Red Petrograd*, pp. 209–10.
11 ibid., pp. 211–12; Remington, *Building Socialism*, p. 32.
12 Remington, *Building Socialism*, p. 32.
13 Smith, *Red Petrograd*, pp. 213, 216; Richard Sakwa, 'The Commune State in Moscow in 1918', *Slavic Review*, vol. 46, nos 3/4, Fall/Winter 1987, pp. 439–40.
14 David Mandel, *The Petrograd Workers and the Soviet Seizure of Power. From the July Days 1917 to July 1918*, New York: St. Martin's Press, 1984, p. 366.
15 Smith, *Red Petrograd*, p. 227.
16 Mandel, *The Petrograd Workers*, p. 368.
17 Cited in Maurice Brinton, *The Bolsheviks and Workers' Control. 1917 to 1921. The State and Counter-Revolution*, Montreal, Canada: Black Rose Books, 1975, p. 21.
18 Carmen Sirianni, *Workers' Control and Socialist Democracy. The Soviet Experience*, London, England: Verso Editions and New Left Books, 1982, pp. 131–2.
19 Paul H. Avrich, 'The Bolshevik Revolution and Workers' Control in Russian Industry', *Slavic Review*, vol. 22, no. 1, March 1963, pp. 60–1.
20 Smith, *Red Petrograd*, p. 223.
21 Ferro, *October 1917*, pp. 176–7; Remington, *Building Socialism*, pp. 39, 57.
22 Remington, *Building Socialism*, pp. 56–61.
23 ibid., pp. 60, 58.
24 ibid., p. 59.
25 Mandel, *The Petrograd Workers*, p. 378.
26 For examples of localism ('*mestnichestvo*') in Petrograd, see Mandel, *The Petrograd Workers*, pp. 372–3. For other examples illustrating not only localism but also problems of labor inefficiency and low productivity, see James Bunyan, *The Origin of Forced Labor in the Soviet State. 1917–1921*.

Documents and Materials, Baltimore, Md: Johns Hopkins Press, 1967, pp. 20–5.

27 Smith, *Red Petrograd*, p. 209.

28 Brinton, *The Bolsheviks and Workers' Control*, p. 19.

29 Remington, *Building Socialism*, pp. 37–8.

30 Mandel, *The Petrograd Workers*, p. 374.

31 Smith, *Red Petrograd*, p. 241.

32 ibid., p. 242.

33 Isaac Deutscher, *Soviet Trade Unions. Their Place in Soviet Labour Policy*, London, England: Royal Institute of International Affairs, 1950, pp. 33–4; Remington, *Building Socialism*, pp. 87–8.

34 Smith, *Red Petrograd*, p. 242; Remington, *Building Socialism*, p. 87.

35 Smith, *Red Petrograd*, p. 251.

36 Mandel, *The Petrograd Workers*, p. 379.

37 Remington, *Building Socialism*, p. 54.

38 Cited in Mandel, *The Petrograd Workers*, p. 373; Lenin's emphasis.

39 William J. Chase, *Workers, Society and the Soviet State. Labor and Life in Moscow, 1918–1929*, Urbana and Chicago: University of Illinois Press, 1987, pp. 33–4.

40 Robert C. Williams, *The Other Bosheviks. Lenin and His Critics, 1904–1914*, Bloomington, Ind.: Indiana University Press, 1986, pp. 38–9.

41 Smith, *Red Petrograd*, p. 153.

42 ibid., pp. 151, 154; Jane Burbank, *Intelligentsia and Revolution. Russian Views of Bolshevism, 1917–1922*, New York: Oxford University Press, 1986, p. 26.

43 Smith, *Red Petrograd*, p. 228.

44 V. I. Lenin, *State and Revolution*, in *Collected Works*, vol. 25, June–September 1917, Moscow: Progress Publishers, 1964, pp. 426–7; Lenin's emphasis.

45 Remington, *Building Socialism*, pp. 50–3.

46 ibid., p.70.

47 ibid., p. 146.

48 Sirianni, *Workers' Control and Socialist Democracy*, p. 216; Smith, *Red Petrograd*, p. 228. Emphases in citation are Lenin's.

49 Some Bolshevik leaders such as Trotsky even saw the militarization of labor as compatible with a workers' state. See Deutscher, *Soviet Trade Unions*, pp. 36–9.

50 Remington, *Building Socialism*, p. 89; William Chase, 'Voluntarism, Mobilisation and Coercion: *Subbotniki* 1919–1921', *Soviet Studies*, vol. 41, no. 1, January 1989, p. 119.

51 Remington, *Building Socialism*, pp. 110–11.

52 Silvana Malle, *The Economic Organization of War Communism, 1918–1921*, Cambridge, England: Cambridge University Press, 1985, p. 502.

53 For a very informative account of these and other oppositionists, see

Robert Vincent Daniels, *The Conscience of the Revolution. Communist Opposition in Soviet Russia*, New York: Clarion Books, 1960.

54 Remington, *Building Socialism*, p. 71.
55 Cited in Smith, *Red Petrograd*, p. 229.
56 Sirianni, *Workers' Control and Socialist Democracy*, pp. 143–4.
57 ibid., pp. 144–5; James Bunyan, *The Origin of Forced Labor in the Soviet State*, pp. 121–3.
58 Sirianni, *Workers' Control and Socialist Democracy*, pp. 146–7.
59 ibid., pp. 148–9.
60 Cited in ibid., p. 149; Lenin's emphasis.
61 ibid., p. 150.
62 Smith, *Red Petrograd*, p. 214.
63 Cited in ibid., p. 215.
64 ibid., pp. 215–16.
65 Cited in Brinton, *The Bolsheviks and Workers' Control*, p. 28.
66 Smith, *Red Petrograd*, p. 249.
67 Remington, *Building Socialism*, p. 138.
68 Sakwa, 'The Commune State in Moscow in 1918', p. 441.
69 Brinton, *The Bolsheviks and Workers' Control*, p. 59.
70 Mandel, *The Petrograd Workers*, pp. 280–1.
71 Jay B. Sorenson, *The Life and Death of Soviet Trade Unionism. 1917–1928*, New York: Atherton Press, 1969, p. 9. See also Malle, *The Economic Organization of War Communism*, p. 90.
72 Smith, *Red Petrograd*, p. 217.
73 Sorenson, *The Life and Death of Soviet Trade Unionism*, p. 25.
74 Cited by Deutscher, *Soviet Trade Unions*, p. 18.
75 Thus, for example, the resolution adopted by the Congress strongly attacked union 'neutrality' without even considering the possible merits of union organizational independence from the state. James Bunyan and H. H. Fisher (eds), *The Bolshevik Revolution 1917–1918. Documents and Materials*, Stanford, Calif: Stanford University Press, 1934, pp. 639–41.
76 Deutscher, *Soviet Trade Unions*, p. 21; Smith, *Red Petrograd*, p. 218.
77 Deutscher, *Soviet Trade Unions*, p. 24.
78 ibid., p. 19.
79 ibid., p. 20; Smith, *Red Petrograd*, p. 218.
80 Deutscher, *Soviet Trade Unions*, p. 22; Smith, *Red Petrograd*, p. 218.
81 Cited in Deutscher, *Soviet Trade Unions*, p. 23.
82 Bunyan and Fisher, *The Bolshevik Revolution*, p. 641.
83 Sorenson, *The Life and Death of Soviet Trade Unionism*, p. 34.
84 Deutscher, *Soviet Trade Unions*, pp. 25–6; Sorenson, *The Life and Death of Soviet Trade Unionism*, pp. 33–5.
85 Sorenson, *The Life and Death of Soviet Trade Unionism*, p. 35.
86 Cited in Deutscher, *Soviet Trade Unions*, p. 29.
87 ibid., p. 29.

88 Sorenson, *The Life and Death of Soviet Trade Unionism*, p. 83.
89 Deutscher, *Soviet Trade Unions*, p. 31.
90 ibid., pp. 31–2.
91 Cited in Brinton, *The Bolsheviks and Workers' Control*, p. 83.
92 ibid., p. 83; Daniels, *The Conscience of the Revolution*, pp. 157–8.
93 Brinton, *The Bolsheviks and Workers' Control*, pp. 82–3; Daniels, *The Conscience of the Revolution*, p. 157.
94 Sorenson, *The Life and Death of Soviet Trade Unionism*, pp. 173–4.
95 Barbara Evans Clements, 'Working-Class and Peasant Women in the Russian Revolution, 1917–1923', *Signs*, vol. 8, no. 2, Winter 1982, pp. 231–2.
96 Deutscher, *Soviet Trade Unions*, p. 43.
97 ibid., pp. 48, 56.
98 ibid., pp. 49–51.
99 Sorenson, *The Life and Death of Soviet Trade Unionism*, p. 84.
100 'The Role and Functions of the Trade Unions Under the New Economic Policy. Decision of the C.C., R.C.P.(B), January 12, 1922', in V. I. Lenin, *Collected Works*, vol. 33, August 1921–March 1923, Moscow: Progress Publishers, 1966, p. 192.
101 ibid., p. 193.
102 ibid., p. 193.
103 Duetscher, *Soviet Trade Unions*, p. 65; Sorenson, *The Life and Death of Soviet Trade Unionism*, pp. 170–1.
104 Sorenson, *The Life and Death of Soviet Trade Unionism*, pp. 175–6; Chase, *Workers, Society and the Soviet State*, p. 215.
105 Sorenson, *The Life and Death of Soviet Trade Unionism*, p. 219; Daniels, *The Conscience of the Revolution*, p. 158; Chase, *Workers, Society and the Soviet State*, pp. 258–9.
106 Mandel, *The Petrograd Workers*, pp. 397, 395–6.
107 Robert Service, *The Bolshevik Party in Revolution. A Study in Organisational Change*, London, England: Macmillan, 1979, p. 204.

CHAPTER 3 FREEDOM OF THE PRESS

1 S. A. Smith, *Red Petrograd. Revolution in the Factories 1917–1918*, Cambridge, England: Cambridge University Press, 1983, p. 34.
2 Albert Resis, 'Lenin on Freedom of the Press', *The Russian Review*, vol. 36, no. 3, July 1977, p. 275.
3 V. I. Lenin, 'Party Organisation and Party Literature', in *Collected Works*, vol. 10, November 1905–June 1906, Moscow: Foreign Languages Publishing House, 1962, p. 47.
4 Resis, 'Lenin on Freedom of the Press', pp. 280–1.
5 V. I. Lenin, 'The Tasks of the Revolution', in *Collected Works*, vol. 26,

September 1917–February 1918, Moscow: Progress Publishers, 1964, p. 68.

6 V. I. Lenin, 'How to Guarantee the Success of the Constituent Assembly', in *Collected Works*, vol. 25, June–September 1917, Moscow: Progress Publishers, 1964, p. 382; Lenin's emphasis.

7 V. I. Lenin, 'Draft Resolution on Freedom of the Press', written 4 November 1917; in *Collected Works*, vol. 26, September 1917–February 1918, p. 283.

8 Resis, 'Lenin on Freedom of the Press', p. 285; Vladimir N. Brovkin, *The Mensheviks after October. Socialist Opposition and the Rise of the Bolshevik Dictatorship*, Ithaca and London: Cornell University Press, 1987, p. 106.

9 James Bunyan and H. H. Fisher, *The Bolshevik Revolution 1917–1918. Documents and Materials*, Stanford, Calif.: Stanford University Press, 1934, p. 220.

10 Resis, 'Lenin on Freedom of the Press', p. 287.

11 John L. H. Keep (translator and editor), *The Debate on Soviet Power, Minutes of the All-Russian Central Executive Committee of Soviets, Second Convocation, October 1917–January 1918*, Oxford, England: Clarendon Press, 1979, p. 68.

12 ibid., pp. 68–9.

13 ibid., p. 70.

14 ibid., p. 71.

15 ibid., pp. 71–2.

16 ibid., pp. 72–3.

17 ibid., pp. 75–6.

18 ibid., pp. 73–5.

19 Peter Kenez, 'Lenin and the Freedom of the Press', in Abbott Gleason, Peter Kenez, and Richard Stites (eds), *Bolshevik Culture. Experiment and Order in the Russian Revolution*, Bloomington, Ind.: Indiana University Press, 1985, p. 136.

20 Keep, *The Debate on Soviet Power*, p. 76. Lozovsky was another Bolshevik siding with Larin and Riazanov. See Robert V. Daniels, *The Conscience of the Revolution. Communist Opposition in Soviet Russia*, New York: Clarion, 1960, p. 66.

21 Kenez, 'Lenin and the Freedom of the Press', p. 77.

22 *The Bolsheviks and the October Revolution. Central Committee Minutes of the Russian Social-Democratic Labour Party (Bolsheviks) August 1917–February 1918*, London, England: Pluto Press, 1974, translated by Ann Bone, pp. 140–1.

23 Bunyan and Fisher, *The Bolshevik Revolution*, pp. 22–3.

24 Peter Kenez, *The Birth of the Propaganda State. Soviet Methods of Mass Mobilization, 1917–1929*, Cambridge, England: Cambridge University Press, 1985, p. 44.

25 Resis, 'Lenin on Freedom of the Press', pp. 287–8.

26 Oliver Henry Radkey, *The Sickle under the Hammer. The Russian Socialist*

Revolutionaries in the Early Months of Soviet Rule, New York: Columbia University Press, 1963, p. 145.

27 Resis, 'Lenin on Freedom of the Press', p. 294, footnote 70; Brovkin, *The Mensheviks after October*, pp. 107–8, 123.

28 Keep, *The Debate on Soviet Power*, pp. 92–3; Brovkin, *The Mensheviks after October*, p. 108.

29 E. H. Carr, *Socialism in One Country. 1924–1926 Volume One*, Baltimore, Md: Penguin Books, 1970, p. 177.

30 Leonard Schapiro, *The Origin of the Communist Autocracy. Political Opposition in the Soviet State: First Phase, 1917–1922*, Cambridge, Mass.: Harvard University Press, 1956, p. 192.

31 See V. I. Lenin's reflections on the nationalization of commercial advertising in his 'Report on the New Economic Policy', to the Seventh Moscow Gubernia conference of the Russian Communist Party on 29 October 1921; in *Collected Works*, vol. 33, August 1921–March 1923, Moscow: Progress Publishers, 1966, pp. 89–91. See also Brovkin, *The Mensheviks after October*, pp. 106–8.

32 Kenez, 'Lenin and the Freedom of the Press', p. 141.

33 It should be pointed out that the Left SRs were not always defenders of freedom of the press since they took an active part in the suppression of the Right SR press in Helsingfors. See Radkey, *The Sickle under the Hammer*, pp. 108–9.

34 Resis, 'Lenin on Freedom of the Press', pp. 292–3.

35 Kenez, 'Lenin and the Freedom of the Press', p. 142.

36 Bunyan and Fisher, *The Bolshevik Revolution*, pp. 579–80.

37 Brovkin, *The Mensheviks after October*, pp. 110–17.

38 Keep, *The Debate on Soviet Power*, p. 109.

39 ibid., p. 128.

40 Marc Ferro, *October 1917. A Social History of the Russian Revolution*, London, England: Routledge & Kegan Paul, 1980, translated by Norman Stone, p. 264.

41 David Mandel, *The Petrograd Workers and the Soviet Seizure of Power. From the July Days 1917 to July 1918*, New York: St Martin's Press, 1984, pp. 361, 362–3.

42 Vera Broido, *Lenin and the Mensheviks. The Persecution of Socialists under Bolshevism*, Aldershot, England: Gower/Maurice Temple Smith, 1987, pp. 114–15; Brovkin, *The Mensheviks after October*, p. 273.

43 Schapiro, *The Origin of the Communist Autocracy*, pp. 163, 126, 186–7; Marc Jansen, *A Show Trial Under Lenin. The Trial of the Socialist Revolutionaries, Moscow 1922*, The Hague: Martinus Nijhoff 1982, translated by Jean Sanders, pp. 8, 10; Anthony D'Agostino, *Marxism and the Russian Anarchists*, San Francisco, Calif.: Germinal Press, 1977, p. 167.

44 Carr, *Socialism in One Country*, p. 77.

45 According to William Henry Chamberlin, Miasnikov 'seems by general

testimony to have been an uncommonly bloodthirsty individual.' William Henry Chamberlin, *The Russian Revolution. 1917–1921*, vol. 2, New York: Macmillan, 1935, p. 94.

46 Paul Avrich, 'Bolshevik Opposition to Lenin: G. I. Miasnikov and the Workers' Group', *The Russian Review*, vol. 43, no. 1, January 1984.

47 ibid., p. 9.

48 ibid., p. 10.

49 ibid., pp. 4–5, 10.

50 V. I. Lenin, 'A Letter to G. Myasnikov', 5 August 1921; in *Collected Works*, vol. 32, December 1920–August 1921, pp. 504–9.

51 ibid., p. 504; Lenin's emphasis.

52 ibid., p. 505.

53 ibid., p. 505.

54 ibid., p. 505.

55 ibid., pp. 505, 507.

56 ibid., p. 508.

57 ibid., p. 508.

58 Leon Trotsky, *Terrorism and Communism. A Reply to Karl Kautsky*, Ann Arbor, Mich.: Ann Arbor paperback, 1961, p. 61.

59 ibid., p. 59.

60 Avrich, 'Bolshevik Opposition to Lenin', p. 11.

61 ibid., p. 17.

62 Roy Medvedev, *On Socialist Democracy*, New York: Alfred A. Knopf, 1975, translated and edited by Ellen de Kadt, pp. 188–9.

63 R. W. Pethybridge, 'Railways and Press Communications in Soviet Russia in the Early NEP Period', *Soviet Studies*, vol. 38, no. 2, April 1986, p. 201.

64 Kenez, *The Birth of the Propaganda State*, pp. 225–6.

65 Medvedev, *On Socialist Democracy*, p. 189.

66 Carr, *Socialism in One Country*, pp. 63–77.

67 Jeffrey Brooks, 'The Breakdown in Production and Distribution of Printed Material, 1917–1927', in Gleason, Kenez, and Stites (eds), *Bolshevik Culture*, pp. 162–3; Jeffrey Brooks, 'Public and Private Values in the Soviet Press, 1921–1928', *Slavic Review*, vol. 48, no. 1, Spring 1989, p. 22.

68 Kenez, *The Birth of the Propaganda State*, pp. 96–7.

69 ibid., pp. 246–7.

70 Cited in Richard Sakwa, *Soviet Communists in Power. A Study of Moscow during the Civil War, 1918–21*, New York: St Martin's Press, 1988, p. 156.

71 'The "Index" of the Soviet Inquisition', *Slavonic Review*, vol. 4, 1926, pp. 725–32; Boris Korsch, *The Permanent Purge of Soviet Libraries*, Research Paper No. 50, Jerusalem: The Soviet and East European Research Centre, The Hebrew University of Jerusalem, April 1983, pp. 1–21; Robert H. McNeal, *Bride of the Revolution. Krupskaya and Lenin*, Ann Arbor, Mich.: University of Michigan Press, 1972, pp. 200–3; Boris Raymond, *Krupskaia and Soviet Russian Librarianship, 1917–1939*, Metuchen, NJ: The Scare-

crow Press, 1979, pp. 90–4; Bertram D. Wolfe, 'Krupskaya Purges the People's Libraries', *Survey*, no. 72, Summer 1969, pp. 141–55. See also Carr, *Socialism in One Country*, pp. 76–7.

72 Borris Kagarlitsky, *The Thinking Reed. Intellectuals and the Soviet State. 1917 to the Present*, London, New York: Verso, 1988, translated by Brian Pearce, p. 51.

73 Thomas I. Emerson, *The System of Freedom of Expression*, New York: Random House, 1970, p. 661.

74 ibid., p. 670.

75 Jerome A. Barron, *Freedom of the Press for Whom? The Right of Access to the Mass Media*, Bloomington, Ind.: Indiana University Press, 1973, p. 309.

76 A. M. Rosenthal, 'Save the TV giraffe', *New York Times*, Op-Ed Section, 21 May 1987, p. A31. See also the news report, 'Reagan Vetoes Measure to Affirm Fairness Policy for Broadcasters', *New York Times*, 21 June 1987, p. 1.

77 Pierre Frank, Livio Maitan, and Ernest Mandel, 'In Defense of the Portuguese Revolution', *Intercontinental Press*, 8 September 1975, pp. 1168–70.

78 Leon Trotsky, *The Revolution Betrayed*, New York: Merit Publishers, 1965, p. 267.

79 'Dictatorship of the proletariat and socialist democracy', in *Resolutions of the Twelfth World Congress of the Fourth International* (January 1985), in *International Viewpoint*, Special Issue, n.d., p. 77.

80 Cited by Medvedev, *On Socialist Democracy*, p. 183; emphasis in the original.

CHAPTER 4 REPRESSION

1 Cited by George Leggett, *The Cheka: Lenin's Political Police*, Oxford, England: Clarendon Press, 1981, p. 62.

2 Hal Draper, Special Note C, 'The Meaning of "Terror" and "Terrorism"', in *Karl Marx's Theory of Revolution. Volume III: The 'Dictatorship of the Proletariat'*, New York: Monthly Review Press, 1986, p. 363.

3 V. I. Lenin, 'Speech at a Joint Meeting of the Petrograd Soviet of Workers' and Soldiers' Deputies and Delegates from the Fronts', 4 (17) November 1917; in *Collected Works*, vol. 26, September 1917–February 1918, Moscow: Progress Publishers, 1964, p. 294.

4 Maxim Gorky, *Days With Lenin*, New York: International Publishers, 1932, pp. 44–5.

5 V. I. Lenin, 'How to Organise Competition?'; in *Collected Works*, vol. 26, p. 414.

6 E. H. Carr, *The Bolshevik Revolution. 1917–1923*, vol. 1, Middlesex, England: Pelican Books, 1966, pp. 166–72.

7 C. L. R. James, *The Black Jacobins*, New York: Vintage Books, 1963, p. 373.

8   Victor Serge, 'Once More: Kronstadt', *The New International*, vol. 4, no. 7, July 1938, pp. 211–14; Serge's emphasis.
9   Draper, 'The meaning of "Terror" and "Terrorism"', p. 365.
10 ibid., p. 364.
11 ibid., p. 362; emphasis in original.
12 John L. H. Keep, 'Lenin's Letters as an Historical Source', in Bernard W. Eissenstat (ed.), *Lenin and Leninism. State, Law, and Society*, Lexington, Mass.: Lexington Books, 1971, p. 259.
13 William Henry Chamberlin, *The Russian Revolution 1917–1921*, vol. Two, New York: Macmillan, 1935, p. 81.
14 Quoted in Peter Nettl, *Rosa Luxemburg*, abridged edn, London, England: Oxford University Press, 1969, pp. 454–5; Luxemburg's emphasis.
15 Chamberlin, *The Russian Revolution*, p. 75.
16 ibid., p. 80.
17 Cited in Carr, *The Bolshevik Revolution*, p. 175; Dzerzhinsky's emphasis.
18 E. H. Carr, 'The Origin and Status of the Cheka', *Soviet Studies*, vol. 10, no. 1, July 1958, p. 6.
19 Lennard D. Gerson, *The Secret Police in Lenin's Russia*, Philadelphia, Pa.: Temple University Press, 1976, p. 64.
20 ibid., p. 65.
21 Leonard Schapiro, *The Origin of the Communist Autocracy. Political Opposition in the Soviet State. First Phase 1917–1922*, Cambridge, Mass.: Harvard University Press, 1956, p. 175.
22 Eugene Huskey, *Russian Lawyers and the Soviet State. The Origins and Development of the Soviet Bar, 1917–1939*, Princeton, NJ: Princeton University Press, 1986, p. 67.
23 Victor Serge, *Memoirs of a Revolutionary 1901–1941*, London: Oxford University Press, 1963, translated by Peter Sedgwick, p. 99.
24 Cited by Gerson, *The Secret Police in Lenin's Russia*, p. 161.
25 Victor Serge, 'Secrecy and Revolution – a reply to Trotsky', unknown whether or when it was originally published – probably dating from 1939. Published in translation by Peter Sedgwick in *Peace News* (London, England), 27 December 1963, cited in Steven Lukes, *Marxism and Morality*, Oxford, England: Clarendon Press, 1985, pp. 110–11.
26 Israel Getzler, *Kronstadt 1917–1921. The Fate of a Soviet Democracy*, Cambridge, England: Cambridge University Press, 1983, p. 199.
27 *Their Morals and Ours. Marxist Versus Liberal Views on Morality. Four Essays by Leon Trotsky, John Dewey, George Novack*, New York: Merit Publishers, 1966, p. 47.
28 Karl Marx, *The Civil War in France*, New York: International Publishers, 1940, pp. 78–79.
29 Gerson, *The Secret Police in Lenin's Russia*, p. 152.
30 Leggett, *The Cheka*, p. 148.
31 Cited in ibid., p. 148.
32 Adam Ulam, *The Bolsheviks*, New York: Collier Macmillan, 1965, pp.

550–2. For an account of Lenin's anger at Radek and Bukharin see Carr, *The Bolshevik Revolution*, p. 189.

33 *Krasnyi Terror*, no. 1, November 1918, p. 1, quoted from *Pravda*, no. 281, 25 December 1918, p. 1; James Bunyan, *Intervention, Civil War, and Communism in Russia. April–December 1918. Documents and Materials*, Baltimore, Md.: Johns Hopkins Press, 1936, p. 261.

34 Gerson, *The Secret Police in Lenin's Russia*, p. 199.

35 I. N. Steinberg, *In the Workshop of the Revolution*, New York: Rinehart & Co., 1953, p. 97.

36 ibid., p. 105.

37 Martin McCauley (ed.), *The Russian Revolution and the Soviet State 1917–1921. Documents*, New York: Barnes & Noble, 1975, pp. 188–9; emphasis mine.

38 Oliver H. Radkey, *The Unknown Civil War in Soviet Russia. A Study of the Green Movement in the Tambov Region 1920–1921*, Stanford, Calif.: Hoover Institution Press, 1976, p. 336.

39 ibid., p. 324.

40 ibid., p. 325.

41 ibid., p. 330.

42 See a discussion of this issue in several places in Seth Singleton, 'The Tambov Revolt (1920–1921)', *Slavic Review*, vol. 25, no. 3, September 1966.

43 Radkey, *The Unknown Civil War in Russia*, p. 330.

44 Vera Broido, *Lenin and the Mensheviks. The Persecution of Socialists under Bolshevism*, Aldershot, England: Gower/Maurice Temple Smith, 1987, ch. 5, pp. 39–50.

45 For this and other relevant matters concerning the Mensheviks after the Bolsheviks came to power, see Leopold H. Haimson, 'The Mensheviks after the October Revolution', Parts I and II, *Russian Review*, vol. 38, no. 4, October 1979, and vol. 39, no. 2, April 1980. See also Leopold H. Haimson (ed.), *The Mensheviks. From the Revolution of 1917 to the Second World War*, Chicago, Ill.: University of Chicago Press, translated by Getrude Vakar, 1974; Israel Getzler, *Martov, A Political Biography of a Russian Social Democrat*, Melbourne, Australia: Melbourne University Press, 1967; Broido, *Lenin and the Mensheviks*; Vladimir Brovkin, 'The Mensheviks and NEP Society in Russia', *Russian History*, vol. 9, parts 2–3, 1982, and *The Mensheviks after October. Socialist Opposition and the Rise of the Bolshevik Dictatorship*, Ithaca and London: Cornell University Press, 1987; Abraham Ascher (ed.), *The Mensheviks in the Russian Revolution*, Ithaca, New York: Cornell University Press, 1976; and chapter 1 of Jane Burbank's *Intelligentsia and Revolution. Russian Views of Bolshevism, 1917–1922*, New York: Oxford University Press, 1986.

46 Carr, *The Bolshevik Revolution*, pp. 179–80; Oskar Anweiler, *The Soviets: The Russian Workers', Peasants', and Soldiers' Councils, 1905–1921*, New York: Pantheon Books, 1974, translated by Ruth Hein, p. 233.

47 Simon Liberman, *Building Lenin's Russia*, Chicago, Ill.: University of Chicago Press, 1945, pp. 60–70.

48 Schapiro, *The Origin of the Communist Autocracy*, p. 199.

49 Carr, *The Bolshevik Revolution*, pp. 182–3.

50 Schapiro, *The Origin of the Communist Autocracy*, pp. 202–3.

51 Leonard Schapiro, *The Russian Revolutions of 1917. The Origins of Modern Communism*, New York: Basic Books, 1984, p. 190.

52 ibid., p. 205.

53 Paul Avrich, *Kronstadt 1921*, New York: W. W. Norton, 1974, p. 226.

54 ibid., p. 125.

55 Carr, *The Bolshevik Revolution*, p. 122; William G. Rosenberg, *Liberals in the Russian Revolution. The Constitutional Democratic Party, 1917–1921*, Princeton, NJ: Princeton University Press, 1974, especially pp. 277–89.

56 Anweiler, *The Soviets:* p. 233. For further information on Right SR collaboration with the Whites, see Oliver Henry Radkey, *The Sickle under the Hammer. The Russian Socialist Revolutionaries in the Early Months of Soviet Rule*, New York and London: Columbia University Press, 1963, pp. 452–5.

57 Carr, *The Bolshevik Revolution*, p. 180.

58 ibid., p. 181. For a very detailed discussion of the diverse views and currents among the Right SRs, see Marc Jansen, *A Show Trial under Lenin. The Trial of the Socialist Revolutionaries, Moscow 1922*, The Hague, Holland: Martinus Nijhoff 1982, translated by Jean Sauders, pp. 2–22.

59 Anweiler, *The Soviets*, p. 230.

60 ibid., p. 232.

61 Paul Avrich, *The Russian Anarchists*, Princeton, NJ: Princeton University Press, 1967, pp. 197–8.

62 Schapiro, *The Origin of the Communist Autocracy*, p. 185.

63 Avrich, *The Russian Anarchists*, p. 189.

64 ibid., p. 184.

65 ibid., p. 188.

66 Schapiro, *The Origin of the Communist Autocracy*, p. 183.

67 Avrich, *The Russian Anarchists*, p. 227.

68 Martov considered the Bolsheviks a mistaken wing of the workers' movement and, as we saw above, strongly opposed any Menshevik collaboration with the White armies.

69 V. I. Lenin, in *Collected Works*, vol. 29, Moscow: Progress Publishers, 1965, pp. 296–7.

70 For a dramatic example of the sometimes ruthless suppression of the Mensheviks, see Serge, *Memoirs of a Revolutionary*, pp. 129–30.

71 See Gorky, *Days With Lenin*, pp. 39–41.

72 Ulam, *The Bolsheviks*, p. 426.

73 Liberman, *Building Lenin's Russia*, pp. 28–29.

74 See Steinberg, *In the Workshop of the Revolution*.

75 See, for example, the decree of 1 January 1918 establishing the scope and

functions of the Revolutionary Tribunals in McCauley, *The Russian Revolution and the Soviet State*, pp. 182–3.

76 Cited by Gerson, *The Secret Police in Lenin's Russia*, p. 192.

77 Cited by Gerson ibid., p. 305, n. 8.

78 Chamberlin, *The Russian Revolution*, pp. 70–1.

79 Cited in Bunyan, *Intervention, Civil War, and Communism in Russia*, pp. 259–60.

80 According to the *Great Soviet Encylopedia*, Mikhail Stepanovich Ol'minsky was born on 3 (15) October 1863 and died on 8 May 1933. At the time of his death he was said to have been a member of the board of the V. I. Lenin Institute since 1928. It is difficult to tell the degree of Olminsky's adaptation to Stalinism, but it is interesting to note that many years earlier he had strongly criticized Bukharin's defense of War Communism, associating it with 'penal servitude and shooting.' See Stephen Cohen, *Bukharin and the Bolshevik Revolution*, Oxford, England: Oxford University Press, 1980, p. 96. Moreover, he was reported as having complained in 1932 that ideological changes in official party historiography were leading to a 'castrated Leninism.' Stephen F. Cohen, *Rethinking the Soviet Experience. Politics and History since 1917*, New York: Oxford University Press, 1985, p. 179, n. 46.

81 Gerson, *The Secret Police in Lenin's Russia*, p. 194.

82 Cited by Gerson, ibid., p. 195.

83 Sergey Petrovich Melgounov, *The Red Terror in Russia*, Westport, Connecticut: Hyperion Press, 1975, p. 182.

84 Cited by Melgounov, ibid., pp. 181–2, 230.

85 Gerson, *The Secret Police in Lenin's Russia*, p. 200.

86 Carr, 'The Origin and Status of the Cheka', pp. 5–6.

87 Gerson, *The Secret Police in Lenin's Russia*, pp. 202–3.

88 ibid., pp. 214–15.

89 ibid., p. 215.

90 Leggett, *The Cheka*, pp. 145–7.

91 ibid., p. 146.

92 ibid., p. 146.

93 Samuel Kucherov, *The Organs of Soviet Administration of Justice: Their History and Operation*, Leiden, Holland: E. J. Brill, 1970, p. 70.

94 Schapiro, *The Origins of the Communist Autocracy*, p. 204.

95 V. I. Lenin, Speech at a Rally and Concert for the All-Russian Extraordinary Commission Staff, 7 November 1918; in *Collected Works*, vol. 28, July 1918–March 1919, Moscow: Progress Publishers, 1965.

96 See, for example, Serge, *Memoirs of a Revolutionary*, p. 130. For a very detailed and useful account, in spite of its Cold War tone, of the relationship between Gorky and Lenin, see Bertram D. Wolfe, *The Bridge and the Abyss. The Troubled Friendship of Maxim Gorky and V. I. Lenin*, New York: Praeger, 1967.

97 V. I. Lenin, Letter to G. Y. Zinoviev, 26 June 1918, also to Lashevich and other members of Central Committee; in *Collected Works*, vol. 35, February 1912–December 1922, Moscow: Progress Publishers, 1966, p. 336; Lenin's emphasis.

98 Cited by Marcel Liebman, *Leninism under Lenin*, London, England: Jonathan Cape, 1975, translated by Brian Pearce, p. 226.

99 Keep, 'Lenin's Letters as an Historical Source', p. 260.

100 Cited by Leggett, *The Cheka*, p. 162.

101 For this and other details on the Gumilev case, see Wolfe, *The Bridge and the Abyss*, pp. 121–131.

102 Cited by Moshe Lewin, *Lenin's Last Struggle*, New York: Vintage Books, 1970, p. 133.

103 V. I. Lenin, 'Letter to D. I. Kursky', 17 May 1922; in *Collected Works*, vol. 33, August 1921–March 1923, Moscow: Progress Publishers, 1966, pp. 358–9.

104 V. I. Lenin, 'To F. E. Dzerzhinsky', in *Collected Works*, vol. 45, November 1920–March 1923, Moscow: Progress Publishers, 1970, p. 555.

105 Aleksandr I. Solzhenitsyn, *The Gulag Archipelago 1918–1956. An Experiment in Literary Investigation. Vols. III–IV*, New York: Harper & Row, 1975, pp. 9–24.

106 Peter H. Solomon, Jr, 'Soviet Penal Policy: 1917–1934: A Reinterpretation', *Slavic Review*, vol 39, no. 2, June 1980, p. 200.

107 David J. Dallin and Boris I. Nicolaevsky, *Forced Labor in Soviet Russia*, New Haven, Conn.: Yale University Press, 1947, pp. 157–8.

108 ibid., p. 165.

109 ibid., p. 168.

110 ibid., p. 170.

111 ibid., p. 172.

112 ibid., p. 178; Solomon, 'Soviet Penal Policy', p. 203.

113 Dallin and Nicolaevsky, *Forced Labor in Soviet Russia*, p. 165.

114 Solomon, 'Soviet Penal Policy', p. 210.

115 ibid., p. 203.

116 Leon Trotsky, 'More on the Suppression of Kronstadt', *The New International*, vol. 4, no. 8, August 1938, pp. 249–50.

117 John Reed, *Ten Days That Shook the World*, New York: The Modern Library, 1935, p. 360.

118 I owe this point and insight to Professor Gerald Surh (personal communication of 30 December 1984.)

119 Thomas L. Tedford, *Freedom of Speech in the United States*, New York: Random House, 1985, pp. 448–55.

120 ibid., p. 450.

121 Cited by Hal Draper in Special Note C, 'The Meaning of "Terror" and "Terrorism",' p. 362; Marx's emphasis.

122 Tedford, *Freedom of Speech in the United States*, pp. 69–73. See also the

very critical discussion of Holmes' original 1919 test in Alexander Meiklejohn, *Political Freedom. The Constitutional Powers of the People*, New York: Harper & Brothers, 1960 pp. 29–50.
123 Tedford, *Freedom of Speech in the United States*, pp. 81–2.
124 ibid., p. 451.
125 ibid., p. 451. See his discussion of several cases where this test was invoked on pp. 92–5.
126 Some relevant examples from the guerrilla war against the Batista regime in Cuba are to be found in C. Fred Judson, *Cuba and the Revolutionary Myth. The Political Education of the Cuban Rebel Army, 1953–1963*, Boulder, Col.: Westview Press, 1984, p. 131.

CHAPTER 5 SOCIALIST LEGALITY

1 Edward P. Thompson, *Whigs and Hunters. The Origin of the Black Act*, New York: Pantheon Books, 1975, p. 266.
2 Robert Sharlet, 'Stalinism and Soviet Legal Culture', in Robert C. Tucker (ed.), *Stalinism. Essays in Historical Interpretation*, New York: W. W. Norton, 1977, p. 159.
3 Barbara Evans Clements, 'Working-Class and Peasant Women in the Russian Revolution, 1917–1923', *Signs*, vol. 8, no. 2, Winter 1982, p. 218.
4 Barbara Evans Clements, *Bolshevik Feminist. The Life of Aleksandra Kollontai*, Bloomington, Indiana: Indiana University Press, 1979, p. 128.
5 John N. Hazard, *Settling Disputes in Soviet Society. The Formative Years of Legal Institutions*, New York: Columbia University Press, 1960, p. 2.
6 Martin McCauley (ed.), *The Russian Revolution and the Soviet State 1917–1921. Documents*, New York: Barnes & Noble, 1975, pp. 178–9.
7 Ia. Brandenburgskii, 'On The Social Composition of the Soviet Judiciary', in Zigurds L. Zile (ed.), *Ideas and Forces in Soviet Legal History: Statutes, Decisions and Other Materials in the Development and Processes of Soviet Law*, 2nd edn, Madison, Wis.: College Printing and Publishing, 1970, p. 78.
8 A certain Kozlovskii at the Third Congress of persons engaged in the administration of justice on 15 June 1920 as quoted in Hazard, *Settling Disputes in Soviet Society*, pp. 103–4.
9 Peter H. Juviler, *Revolutionary Law and Order. Politics and Social Change in the USSR*, New York: The Free Press, 1976, pp. 263, 269–70.
10 Peter H. Solomon, Jr, 'Soviet Penal Policy, 1917–1934: A Reinterpretation', *Slavic Review*, vol. 39, no. 2, June 1980, p. 198.
11 David Dallin and Boris Nicolaevsky, *Forced Labor in Soviet Russia*, New Haven, Conn.: Yale Univeristy Press, 1947, p. 151.
12 ibid., pp. 153–4.
13 ibid., p. 162.
14 Juviler, *Revolutionary Law and Order*. p. 35.
15 Eugene Huskey, *Russian Lawyers and the Soviet State. The Origins and*

Development of the Soviet Bar, 1917–1939, Princeton, NJ: Princeton University Press, 1986, pp. 54–7, 74–5.

16 Jay B. Sorenson, *The Life and Death of Soviet Trade Unionism 1917–1928*, New York: Atherton Press, 1969, p. 147.

17 Leonard Schapiro, *The Communist Party of the Soviet Union*, New York: Random House, 1960, pp. 264–5.

18 Sharlet, 'Stalinism and Soviet Legal Culture', p. 160.

19 Ivo Lapenna, 'Lenin, Law and Legality,' in Leonard Schapiro and Peter Reddaway (eds.), *Lenin. The Man, the Theorist, the Leader. A Reappraisal*, New York: Frederick A. Praeger, Publishers, 1967, p. 258.

20 Sharlet, 'Stalinism and Soviet Legal Culture', p. 160.

21 Lapenna, 'Lenin, Law and Legality', p. 260.

22 Marc Jansen, *A Show Trial under Lenin. The Trial of the Socialist Revolutionaries, Moscow 1922*, The Hague: Martinus Nijhoff, 1982, translated from the Dutch by Jean Sanders, pp. 22–9, 54–5, 58–60, 62–3, 69–71, 74–5, 80–3, 170. Jansen also summarizes the procedural violations at the trial on pp. 186–95. For another brief, but critical, account of this trial, see Roy Medvedev, *Let History Judge. The Origins and Consequences of Stalinism*, New York: Alfred A. Knopf, 1971, translated by Colleen Taylor, edited by David Joravsky and Georges Haupt, p. 382. See also E. H. Carr, *The Bolshevik Revolution 1917–1923*, vol. 1, Middlesex, England: Penguin Books, 1966, pp. 189–90. For a comparison of the similarities and differences between the 1922 SR trial and the Stalinist show trials of the 1930s, see Michael Reiman, 'Political Trials of the Stalinist Era', *Telos*, no. 54, Winter 1982–3.

23 V. I. Lenin, 'The Victory of the Cadets and the Tasks of the Workers' Party', *Collected Works*, vol. 10, November 1905–June 1906, Moscow: Foreign Languages Publishing House, 1962, p. 244; Hal Draper, *The 'Dictatorship of the Proletariat' from Marx to Lenin*, New York: Monthly Review Press, 1987, p. 90.

24 Draper, *The 'Dictatorship of the Proletariat' from Marx to Lenin*, p. 92.

25 V. I. Lenin, *The Proletarian Revolution and Kautsky the Renegade;* in *Collected Works*, vol. 28, July 1918–March 1919, Moscow: Progress Publishers, 1965, p. 236.

26 V. I. Lenin, 'Rough Theses of a Decision on the Strict Observance of the Laws'; in *Collected Works*, vol. 42, October 1917–March 1923, Moscow: Progress Publishers, 1969, pp. 110–11.

27 Tony Cliff, *Lenin. Vol. 1, Building the Party*, London, England: Pluto Press, 1975, pp. 92–3.

28 V. I. Lenin, *One Step Forward, Two Steps Back;* in *Collected Works*, vol. 7, September 1903–December 1904, Moscow: Progress Publishers, 1961, pp. 390–1; Lenin's emphasis.

29 Samuel Kucherov, *The Organs of Soviet Administration of Justice: Their History and Operation*, Leiden, Holland: E. J. Brill, 1970, p. 593.

30 Cited in ibid., p. 594.

31 *The Russian Constitution. Adopted July 10, 1918*, Reprinted by *The Nation*, 4 January 1919, p. 7; my emphasis.

32 Huskey, *Russian Lawyers and the Soviet State*, p. 63.

33 Hazard, *Settling Disputes in Soviet Society*, pp. 46, 44. For a discussion of the mixed record and problematic status of the right to counsel and of the limits of adversarial procedures in early Soviet Russia, see pp. 267–76 and 281–97.

34 Huskey, *Russian Lawyers and the Soviet State*, p. 69.

35 E. B. Pashukanis, *The Marxist Theory of Law and the Construction of Socialism*, reprinted in Piers Beirne and Robert Sharlet (eds), *Pashukanis. Selected Writings on Marxism and Law*, London: Academic Press, 1980, translated by Peter B. Maggs, p. 193; Pashukanis' emphasis.

36 E. B. Pashukanis, *The General Theory of Law and Marxism*, reprinted in Beirne and Sharlet, *Pashukanis*, pp. 37–131.

37 Sharlet, 'Stalinism and Soviet Legal Culture', p. 163.

38 Robert Sharlet, 'Pashukanis and the Withering away of the Law in the USSR', in Sheila Fitzpatrick (ed.), *Cultural Revolution in Russia, 1928–1931*, Bloomington, Ind.: Indiana University Press, 1978, pp. 176, 181.

39 Lapenna, 'Lenin, Law and Legality', p. 261.

40 Hazard, *Settling Disputes in Soviet Society*, p. 314.

41 Sharlet, 'Pashukanis and the Withering away of the Law in the USSR', p. 177.

42 ibid., p. 177.

43 Pashukanis, *The Marxist Theory of Law and the Construction of Socialism*, p. 190.

44 See Sheila Fitzpatrick, 'Cultural Revolution as Class War', in Fitzpatrick, *Cultural Revolution in Russia*, pp. 8–40.

45 Huskey, *Russian Lawyers and the Soviet State*, pp. 171–3.

46 Leonard Schapiro, 'Bukharin's Way', in Leonard Schapiro, *Russian Studies*, edited by Ellen Dahrendorf with an Introduction by Harry Willetts, New York: Elisabeth Sifton Books, Viking Press, 1987, p. 298.

47 For further details of the legal methodology of Vyshinsky and his followers, see Huskey, *Russian Lawyers and the Soviet State*, pp. 186–9, 211–12. See also the article by the same author entitled 'Vyshinskii, Krylenko and the Shaping of the Soviet Legal Order', *Slavic Review*, vol. 46, nos 3/4, Fall/Winter 1987, pp. 414–28.

48 John N. Hazard, Introduction to John N. Hazard (ed.), *Soviet Legal Philosophy*, Cambridge, Mass.: Harvard University Press, 1951, pp. xxix, xxxii.

49 Piers Beirne and Robert Sharlet, Introduction to Beirne and Sharlet, *Pashukanis*, pp. 20–3.

50 Huskey, *Russian Lawyers and the Soviet State*, pp. 146–7.

51 ibid., pp. 59–61.

52 Cited in Beirne and Sharlet, *Paskukanis*, p. 23; Stuchka's emphasis.

53 I. Slavin, 'The Judiciary and the New Economic Policy', in Zile, *Ideas and Forces in Soviet Legal History*, p. 76; P. Stuchka, 'Five Years of Revolution in Law', in William G. Rosenberg (ed.), *Bolshevik Visions: First Phase of the Cultural Revolution in Soviet Russia*, Ann Arbor, Mich.: Ardis, 1984, pp. 257–8.

54 M. A. Reisner, *Law, Our Law, Foreign Law, General Law* (published in Leningrad and Moscow, 1925), in Hazard, *Soviet Legal Philosophy*, pp. 108–9.

55 Reisner, p. 88.

56 Leonard Schapiro, 'My Fifty Years of Social Science', in Schapiro, *Russian Studies*, p. 24.

57 Karl Marx, 'Inaugural Address of the Working Men's International Association', in Robert C. Tucker (ed.), *The Marx–Engels Reader*, 2nd edn, New New York: W. W. Norton, 1978, p. 517.

58 Tom Campbell, *The Left and Rights. A Conceptual Analysis of the Ideas of Socialist Rights*, London, England: Routledge & Kegan Paul, 1983, p. 91.

59 'Dictatorship of the Proletariat and Socialist Democracy', in *Resolutions of the Twelfth World Congress of the Fourth International* (January 1985), *International Viewpoint. Special Issue*, n.d., p. 83.

60 Li Zhengtian, 'Lawless Laws and Crimeless Crimes', in Anita Chan, Stanley Rosen, and Jonathan Unger (eds), *On Socialist Democracy and the Chinese Legal System. The Li Yizhe Debates*, Armonk, New York: M. E. Sharpe, 1985, pp. 171–2; Abraham Brumberg, 'Moscow: The Struggle for Reform', *New York Review of Books*, vol. 36, no. 5, 30 March 1989, p. 40.

61 Rosa Luxemburg, 'The Russian Revolution', in Rosa Luxemburg, *The Russian Revolution and Leninism or Marxism?* Ann Arbor, Mich.: University of Michigan Press, 1961, p. 63.

62 Mary Gibson, *Workers' Rights*, Totowa, NJ: Rowman & Allanheld, 1983, pp. 124–5.

63 ibid., p. 135.

64 I am indebted to Nancy Holmstrom for helping me to think through and formulate these issues (personal communication of 12 July 1988). For a discussion of the distinction between absolute and less than absolute rights, see Ronald Dworkin, *Taking Rights Seriously*, Cambridge, Mass.: Harvard University Press, 1977, p. 92.

65 Campbell, *The Left and Rights*, p. 115.

66 Gibson, *Workers' Rights*, p. 132.

67 Alison Jaggar, 'Abortion and a Woman's Right to Decide', in Carol C. Gould and Marx W. Wartofsky (eds), *Women and Philosophy. Toward A Theory of Liberation*, New York: Capricorn Books, G. P. Putnam Sons, 1976, pp. 358–9. For two analyses of abortion rights that avoid Jaggar's pitfalls, see Nancy Holmstrom, 'The Morality of Abortion', *Against the Current* (New York), vol. 2, no. 2, Spring 1983, pp. 18–22, and Rosalind

Pollack Petchesky, 'Reproductive Freedom: Beyond "A Woman's Right to Choose"', *Signs*, vol. 5, no. 4, Summer 1980, pp. 661–85.

68 S. A. Smith, *Red Petrograd. Revolution in the Factories 1917–1918*, Cambridge, England: Cambridge University Press, 1983, pp. 242–3.

69 A rule that has not, for example, existed in Cuba where there has been widespread discrimination in employment and education against those not active in the 'mass organizations,' homosexuals, political oppositionists, and people who have been actively involved in some types of religious activities. See Samuel Farber, 'Cuba: Still Stuck in the ABC's. . .', *Against the Current*, (New York), Fall 1983.

70 Solomon, 'Soviet Penal Policy, 1917–1934', p. 197.

71 Marcel Liebman, *Leninism under Lenin*, London, England: Jonathan Cape, 1975, translated by Brian Pearce, p. 326. For examples of the application of discriminatory class punishments to members of the bourgeoisie in the field of labor, see James Bunyan, *The Origin of Forced Labor in the Soviet State. 1917–1921. Documents and Materials*, Baltimore, Md: Johns Hopkins Press, 1967, pp. 54–7.

72 Rudolf Schlesinger, *Soviet Legal Theory. Its Social Background and Development*, London, England: Routledge & Kegan Paul, 1951, p. 75, 113.

73 Schapiro, *The Communist Party of the Soviet Union*, p. 263.

CHAPTER 6 REVOLUTIONARY ALTERNATIVES TO LENIN

1 Vladimir Brovkin, 'The Mensheviks and NEP Society in Russia', *Russian History*, vol. 9, parts 2–3, 1982, p. 357.

2 Marc Ferro, *October 1917. A Social History of the Russian Revolution*, London, England: Routledge & Kegan Paul, 1980, translated by Norman Stone, p. 211.

3 Leonard Schapiro, *The Origin of the Communist Autocracy. Political Opposition in the Soviet State. First Phase 1917–1922*, Cambridge, Mass.: Harvard University Press, 1956, p. 60.

4 Ferro, *October 1917*, p. 270.

5 John L. H. Keep, *The Debate on Soviet Power. Minutes of the All-Russian Central Executive Committee of Soviets. Second Convocation, October 1917 – January 1918*, Oxford, England: Clarendon Press, 1979, pp. 265–6.

6 See the works by Richard Sakwa, 'The Commune State in Moscow in 1918', *Slavic Review*, vol. 46, nos 3/4, Fall/Winter 1987, pp. 433–5, and *Soviet Communists in Power. A Study of Moscow during the Civil War, 1918–1921*, New York: St Martin's Press, 1988, pp. 173, 236–9.

7 Schapiro, *The Origin of the Communist Autocracy*, p. 208.

8 V. I. Lenin, *Collected Works*, vol. 42, October 1917 – March 1923, Moscow: Progress Publishers, 1969, pp. 49–51; Robert Vincent Daniels,

The Conscience of the Revolution. Communist Opposition in Soviet Russia, New York: Clarion Book, 1960, p. 69.

9   Daniels, *The Conscience of the Revolution*, pp. 379, 389.

10 V. I. Lenin, 'Remarks on Ryazanov's Amendment to the Resolution on Party Unity. March 16. Tenth Congress of the R. C. P. (B)'; in *Collected Works*, vol. 32, December 1920 – August 1921, Moscow: Progress Publishers, 1965, p. 261.

11 Daniels, *The Conscience of the Revolution*, pp. 104–7.

12 Schapiro, *The Origin of the Communist Autocracy*, pp. 223–4; Sakwa, *Soviet Communists in Power*, pp. 186, 256; Malvin Magnus Helgesen, 'The Origins of the Party-State Monolith in Soviet Russia: Relations between the Soviets and Party Committees in the Central Provinces, October 1917 – March 1921', PhD diss., State University of New York at Stony Brook, 1980, pp. 538–40.

13 Daniels, *The Conscience of the Revolution*, p. 125; Sakwa, *Soviet Communists in Power*, pp. 188–9.

14 Robert Service, *The Bolshevik Party in Revolution. A Study in Organisational Change*, London, England: Macmillan, 1979, p. 108.

15 Daniels, *The Conscience of the Revolution*, p. 127.

16 Schapiro, *The Origin of the Communist Autocracy*, p. 267.

17 ibid., p. 267; Daniels, *The Conscience of the Revolution*, p. 129.

18 Cited by Daniels, *The Conscience of the Revolution*, p. 128. For long excerpts of the Platform of the Workers' Opposition at the Tenth Party Congress, see also James Bunyan, *The Origin of Forced Labor in the Soviet State. 1917– 1921. Documents and Materials*, Baltimore, Md: Johns Hopkins Press, 1967, pp. 230–7.

19 Aleksandra Kollontai, *The Workers' Opposition*, Reading, England: Solidarity Pamphlet No. 7, n.d. (originally published in translation in *Workers' Dreadnought*, 22 April – August 19, 1921), pp. 31–2. See also the informative article by Barbara Evans Clements, 'Kollontai's Contribution to the Workers' Opposition', *Russian History*, vol. 2, no. 2, 1975, pp. 191– 206.

20 Service, *The Bolshevik Party in Revolution*, p. 144.

21 ibid., pp. 156–7.

22 Daniels, *The Conscience of the Revolution*, p. 401. I want to thank the historian S. A. Smith for calling my attention to the weaknesses of the Workers' Opposition analysis of bureaucracy.

23 For a powerful account of the views on the one-party state and many other matters of Democratic Centralists imprisoned in Stalin's labor camps in the late twenties and early thirties, see Ante Ciliga, *The Russian Enigma*, London, England: Ink Links, 1979, pp. 274–80.

24 Barbara Evans Clements, *Bolshevik Feminist. The Life of Aleksandra Kollontai*, Bloomington, Ind.: Indiana University Press, 1979, pp. 122–3.

25 George H. Sabine, 'The Two Democratic Traditions', *The Philosophical Review*, vol. 61, October 1952, pp. 451–74.

26 ibid., p. 474.

27 Hal Draper, 'The Two Souls of Socialism', *New Politics* (New York), vol. 5, no. 1, Winter 1966. Unfortunately, Draper's interpretation of socialism has not been very much discussed or even known. 'Socialism from above' interpretations are much better known and have been offered and widely accepted as the sole meaning of socialism, as, for example, those contained in Joseph A. Schumpeter, *Capitalism, Socialism and Democracy*, New York: Harper Torchbooks, 1962 and in Emile Durkheim, *Socialism*, New York: Collier Books, 1962.

28 Draper, 'The Two Souls of Socialism', p. 78.

29 Jan Josef Lipski, *KOR. Workers' Defense Committee in Poland. 1976–1981*, Berkeley, Calif.: University of California Press, 1985, p. 121.

30 David Caute, *The Left in Europe since 1789*, New York: World University Library, 1966, p. 44; Caute's emphases.

31 Chapter 12, 'The United Opposition', in Daniels, *The Conscience of the Revolution*, pp. 273–321.

32 Leon Trotsky, *The Transitional Program. The Death Agony of Capitalism and the Tasks of the Fourth International*; in the collection of writings by Leon Trotsky entitled, *The Transitional Program for Socialist Revolution*, New York: Pathfinder Press, 1973, p. 103; Trotsky's emphasis.

33 Christian Rakovsky, 'Declaration of August 1929', in Gus Fagan (ed.), *Christian Rakovsky. Selected Writings on Opposition in the USSR 1923–1930*, London, England: Allison & Busby, 1980, pp. 137–44.

34 R. W. Davies, 'The Syrtsov–Lominadze Affair', *Soviet Studies*, vol. 33, no. 1, January 1981, p. 37. See also Ante Ciliga's account of how this convergence found an echo among the inmates in Stalin's labor camps. Ciliga, *The Russian Enigma*, pp. 227–8, 262.

35 Christian Rakovsky, 'Declaration of April 1930', in Fagan, *Christian Rakovsky*, p. 176; Rakovsky's emphasis.

36 Edward A. Gargan, 'Mao's Home Province Proves Stubborn', *New York Times*, 26 May 1987, p. A12.

37 Edward A. Gargan, 'Movie Maker in China Rails at the Leftists', *New York Times*, 27 November 1987, p. A9.

38 This was also true of Bolshevik leaders who came out from socialist parties abroad. Thus, for example, Feliks Dzerzhinsky, in his many years as a principal leader of the Polish and Lithuanian socialists (the SDKPiL), is said to have shown a complete lack of interest in the Polish peasants. See Robert Blobaum, *Feliks dzierżyński and the SDKPiL: A Study of the Origins of Polish Communism*, Boulder, Col. and New York: East European Monographs, distributed by Columbia University Press, 1984, pp. 159–60.

39 Silvana Malle, *The Economic Organization of War Communism, 1918–1921*, Cambridge, England: Cambridge University Press, 1985, pp. 446–7. See also the discussion of Kollontai's great hostility to the NEP in Barbara Evans Clements, *Bolshevik Feminist*, pp. 202–7.

40 Paul Avrich, 'Bolshevik Opposition to Lenin: G. T. Miasnikov and the

Workers' Group', *The Russian Review*, vol. 43, no. 1, January 1984, pp. 6–7.

41 Schapiro, *The Origin of the Communist Autocracy*, pp. 306–7.

42 Paul Avrich, *Kronstadt 1921*, New York: W. W. Norton, 1974, pp 73–4.

43 Stephen M. Berk, 'The "Class Tragedy" of Izhevsk: Working-Class Opposition to Bolshevism in 1918', *Russian History*, vol. 2, no. 2, 1975, p. 180.

44 S. A. Smith, *Red Petrograd. Revolution in the Factories 1917–1918*, Cambridge, England: Cambridge University Press, 1983, p. 167.

45 Oliver Henry Radkey, *The Sickle under the Hammer. The Russian Socialist Revolutionaries in the Early Months of Soviet Rule*, New York: Columbia University Press, 1963, p. 157.

46 ibid., p. 154.

47 For materials on the Russian anarchists, see Paul Avrich, *The Russian Anarchists*, Princeton, NJ: Princeton University Press, 1967; Paul Avrich (ed.), *The Anarchists in the Russian Revolution*, Ithaca, NY: Cornell University Press, 1973; Anthony D'Agostino, *Marxism and the Russian Anarchists*, San Francisco, Calif.: Germinal Press, 1977. This last source is particularly useful in describing and analyzing in detail the many political differences that existed *within* the world of Russian anarchism after the October Revolution.

48 Avrich, *The Russian Anarchists*, pp. 190–1.

49 ibid.

50 Cited by Peter Sedgwick in the Introduction to Victor Serge's *Memoirs of a Revolutionary. 1901–1941*, London, England: Oxford University Press, 1963, pp. xv–xvi.

CHAPTER 7   LENIN'S NEP AS AN ALTERNATIVE (1921–1923)

1 From Trotsky's speech at the Tenth Party Congress, 14 March 1921 in James Bunyan, *The Origin of Forced Labor in the Soviet State. 1917–1921. Documents and Materials*, Baltimore, Md: Johns Hopkins Press, 1967, p. 251. There is a small discrepancy between Trotsky's citation of Zinoviev, where he quotes the latter as saying that 99 per cent of the workers opposed the regime, and Leonard Schapiro's version, quoted in an earlier chapter, where the figure is given as 90 per cent. I have not been able to establish which is the more accurate source.

2 Vladimir Brovkin, 'The Mensheviks and NEP Society in Russia', *Russian History*, vol. 9, parts 2–3, 1982, p. 349; Paul Avrich, *Kronstadt 1921*, New York: W. W. Norton, 1974, pp. 36–51. See also John B. Hatch, 'Working-Class Politics in Moscow during the Early NEP: Mensheviks and Workers' Organizations, 1921–1922', *Soviet Studies*, vol. 39, no. 4, October 1987.

For a useful overall summary of working-class protest in the early years of the Russian Revolution, see Thomas F. Remington, *Building Socialism in Bolshevik Russia. Ideology and Industrial Organization. 1917–1921*, Pittsburgh, Pa: University of Pittsburgh Press, 1984, pp. 101–17.

3   Hatch, 'Working-Class Politics in Moscow during the Early NEP', pp. 557, 561.
4   Avrich, *Kronstadt 1921*, pp. 125–6, 168.
5   ibid., pp. 51–4.
6   ibid., pp. 72–4.
7   Leon Trotsky, 'Hue and Cry over Kronstadt', *The New International*, vol. 4, no. 4, April 1938, p. 106; my emphasis.
8   Avrich, *Kronstadt 1921*, pp. 135–7.
9   George Katkov, 'The Kronstadt Rising', in David Footman (ed.), *Soviet Affairs. Number Two, St. Antony's Papers. Number 6*, London: Chatto & Windus, 1959, pp. 26–7, 56–7; and Trotsky, 'Hue and Cry over Kronstadt', p. 105.
10 Avrich, *Kronstadt 1921*, pp. 80–1, 181.
11 Katkov, 'The Kronstadt Rising', pp. 44–5.
12 Avrich, *Kronstadt 1921*, pp. 110–11.
13 ibid., p. 101.
14 Chris Harman, 'How the Revolution Was Lost', *International Socialism* (London, England), no. 30, Autumn 1967, p. 10. Harman is following a line of argumentation established by John G. Wright, 'The Truth about Kronstadt', *The New International*, vol. 4, no. 2, February 1938, and Trotsky's 'Hue and Cry over Kronstadt' cited above. See also the Trotskyist collection *Kronstadt* by V. I. Lenin and Leon Trotsky, New York: Monad Press, 1979.
15 Katkov, 'The Kronstadt Rising', p. 21.
16 Israel Getzler, *Kronstadt 1917–1921. The Fate of a Soviet Democracy*, Cambridge, England: Cambridge University Press, 1983, pp. 208–9.
17 Evan Mawdsley, 'The Baltic Fleet and the Kronstadt Mutiny', *Soviet Studies*, vol. 24, no. 4, April 1973, p. 509.
18 Getzler, *Kronstadt 1917–1921*, p. 211.
19 ibid., p. 191.
20 Avrich, *Kronstadt 1921*, p. 70.
21 Getzler, *Kronstadt 1917–1921*, p. 210.
22 Avrich, *Kronstadt 1921*, p. 171.
23 ibid., pp. 155, 178–80.
24 Katkov, 'The Kronstadt Rising', pp. 52, 50.
25 Stephen M. Berk, 'The "Class Tragedy" of Ishevsk: Working-Class Opposition to Bolshevism in 1918', *Russian History*, vol. 2, no. 2, 1975, pp. 178–9.
26 Getzler, *Kronstadt 1917–1921*, p. 179.
27 ibid., p. 183.
28 ibid., p. 186.

29   ibid., pp. 186–9.

30   Stephen F. Cohen, *Rethinking the Soviet Experience. Politics and History since 1917*, New York: Oxford University Press, 1985, p. 58.

31   Alec Nove, 'Lenin and the New Economic Policy', in Bernard W. Eissenstat (ed.), *Lenin and Leninism. State, Law and Society*, Lexington, Mass.: Lexington Books, D. C. Heath, 1971, p. 163; Nove's emphasis.

32   For details and examples see Stephen F. Cohen, *Bukharin and the Bolshevik Revolution, A Political Biography 1888–1938*, Oxford, England: Oxford University Press, 1980. See also Boris Kagarlitsky, *The Thinking Reed. Intellectuals and the Soviet State. 1917 to the Present*, London, New York: Verso, 1988, translated by Brian Pearce, pp. 51–5.

33   'Political Report of the Central Committee of the R.C.P. (B), March 27. Eleventh Congress of the R.C.P. (B), March 27–April 2, 1922'; in V. I. Lenin, *Collected Works*, vol. 33, August 1921 – March 1923, Moscow: Progress Publishers, 1965, pp. 281–2.

34   George Leggett, *The Cheka: Lenin's Political Police*, Oxford, England: Clarendon Press, 1981, p. 321.

35   For a detailed discussion of the similarities and differences between the Menshevik position and Lenin's NEP, see Simon Wolin, 'The Opposition to the NEP', in Leopold H. Haimson (ed.), *The Mensheviks. From the Revolution of 1917 to the Second World War*, Chicago and London: University of Chicago Press, 1974, pp. 243–9. See also Jane Burbank, *Intelligentsia and Revolution. Russian Views of Bolshevism, 1917–1922*, New York: Oxford University Press, 1986, p. 60.

36   V. I. Lenin, 'Political Report of the Central Committee of the R.C.P.(B)', p. 282.

37   Aileen Kelly, 'Leonard Schapiro's Russia', Review of *Russian Studies* in *New York Review of Books*, vol. 34, no. 14, 24 September 1987.

38   Leon Trotsky, 'The New Course', in *Trotsky: The New Course with a new introduction and The Struggle for the New Course by Max Shachtman*, Ann Arbor, Mich.: University of Michigan Press, 1965.

39   Fernando Claudin, *The Communist Movement. From Comintern to Cominform. Part One*, New York: Monthly Review Press, 1975, translated by Brian Pearce, pp. 250–2.

40   V. I. Lenin, 'Our Revolution. (Apropos of N. Sukhanov's Notes)'; in *Collected Works*, vol. 33, pp. 478–9; Lenin's emphasis. This review was published in *Pravda* (no. 117) on 30 May 1923.

41   V. I. Lenin, 'Better Fewer, But Better', in *Collected Works*, vol. 33, pp. 499–501; my emphasis.

42   Nove, 'Lenin and the New Economic Policy', pp. 165–6. For some of the legal aspects of the role of the cooperatives in the early years of the Russian Revolution, see Rudolf Schlesinger, *Soviet Legal Theory. Its Social Background and Development*, London, England: Routledge & Kegan Paul, 1951, pp. 90–1.

43   E. H. Carr, *The Bolshevik Revolution 1917–1923*, vol. 2, Middlesex,

England: Penguin Books, 1966, pp. 124–30. See also Vera Broido, *Lenin and the Mensheviks. The Persecution of Socialists under Bolshevism*, Aldershot, England: Gower/Maurice Temple Smith, 1987, pp. 72–4.

44 V. I. Lenin, 'On Co-Operation', in *Collected Works*, vol. 33, p. 470.

45 Moshe Lewin, *Lenin's Last Struggle*, New York: Vintage Books, 1970; Adam B. Ulam, 'Lenin's Last Phase', *Survey*, vol. 21, nos 1/2 (94/95), Winter/Spring 1975, pp. 148–59.

46 Ulam, 'Lenin's Last Phase', p. 154.

47 Lewin, *Lenin's Last Struggle*, pp. 117–20.

48 Ulam, 'Lenin's Last Phase', pp. 156–9.

49 Peter Kenez, *The Birth of the Propaganda State. Soviet Methods of Mass Mobilization 1917–1929*, Cambridge, England: Cambridge University Press, 1985, p. 70.

50 Carmen Claudin-Urondo, *Lenin and the Cultural Revolution*, New Jersey: Humanities Press, 1977, translated by Brian Pearce, pp. 19–20.

51 Robert C. Tucker, *Stalin as Revolutionary. 1879–1929*, New York: W. W. Norton, 1973, p. 203. For a detailed account of the Polish campaign in April–October 1920, see Evan Mawdsley, *The Russian Civil War*, Boston: Allen & Unwin, 1987, pp. 250–61.

52 Tucker, *Stalin as Revolutionary*, pp. 224–38.

53 Abraham Ascher (ed.), *The Mensheviks in the Russian Revolution*, Ithaca, NY: Cornell University Press, 1976, p. 39.

54 ibid., p. 40; Peter Kenez, *Civil War in South Russia, 1918*, Berkeley, Calif.: University of California Press, 1971, pp. 240–3; Richard Pipes, *The Formation of the Soviet Union*, New York: Atheneum, 1968, p. 212; Stephen Jones, 'The Establishment of Soviet Power in Transcaucasia: The Case of Georgia 1921–1928', *Soviet Studies*, vol. 40, no. 4, October 1988, pp. 620–2, 627, 629–30.

55 Ascher, *The Mensheviks and the Russian Revolution*, p. 41; Pipes, *The Formation of the Soviet Union*, p. 234.

56 V. I. Lenin, 'On Compromises', in *Collected Works*, vol. 25, June–September 1917, Moscow: Progress Publishers, 1964, pp. 305–10.

57 Quoted in Isaac Deutscher, *Soviet Trade Unions. Their Place in Soviet Labour Policy*, London and New York: Royal Institute of International Affairs, 1950, p. 55.

58 V. I. Lenin, *The Revolutionary Proletariat and the Right of Nations to Self-Determination*, in *Collected Works*, vol. 21, August 1914 – December 1915, Moscow: Progress Publishers, 1964, pp. 408–9; Lenin's emphases.

59 See especially the section entitled 'The Working Class as a Champion of Democracy', in *What is to be Done?* in *Collected Works*, vol. 5, May 1901 – February 1902, Moscow: Progress Publishers, 1961, pp. 421–36.

60 V. I. Lenin, 'The Rights of Nations to Self-Determination'; in *Collected Works*, vol. 20, December 1913 – August 1914, Moscow: Progress Publishers, 1964, pp. 393–454. See also V. I. Lenin, *The Nascent Trend of*

Imperialist Economism; in *Collected Works*, vol. 23, August 1916 – March 1917, Moscow: Progress Publishers, 1964, pp. 13–21.

61 See, among others, Roy Medvedev, *On Socialist Democracy*, New York: Alfred A. Knopf, translated and edited by Ellen de Kadt, 1975, and *Leninism and Western Socialism*, London, England: Verso, 1981, translated by A. D. P. Briggs.

62 Marcel Liebman, *Leninism under Lenin*, London, England: Jonathan Cape, 1975, translated by Brian Pearce.

63 Ralph Miliband, 'The State and the Revolution', in Paul Sweezy and Harry Magdoff (eds), *Lenin Today*, New York: Monthly Review Press, 1970.

64 Carmen Sirianni, *Workers' Control and Socialist Democracy. The Soviet Experience*, London, England: Verso Editions and New Left Books, 1982.

65 See, for example, Alfred B. Evans, 'Rereading Lenin's *State and Revolution*', *Slavic Review*, vol. 46, no. 1, Spring 1987; Richard Sakwa, 'The Commune State in Moscow in 1918', *Slavic Review*, vol. 46, nos 3/4, Fall/Winter 1987, pp. 431–2.

66 L. Martov in Ascher, *The Mensheviks and the Russian Revolution*, p. 119.

67 This is a formulation stimulated by reading the interesting article by Tim Wohlforth entitled 'The Two Souls of Leninism', *Against the Current* (Detroit), vol. 1, nos 4–5 (new series), September–October 1986, pp. 37–42.

68 Oskar Anweiler, *The Soviets: The Russian Workers', Peasants', and Soldiers' Councils, 1905–1921*, New York: Pantheon Books, 1974, translated from the German by Ruth Hein, pp. 160–1.

69 Hal Draper, *The 'Dictatorship of the Proletariat' from Marx to Lenin*, New York: Monthly Review Press, 1987; see, in particular, pp. 39–41, 46, 92–3.

70 See, for example, 'Can "Jacobinism" Frighten the Working Class?' published in *Pravda* on 7 July (24 June), 1917; in V. I. Lenin, *Collected Works*, vol. 25, June–September 1917, Moscow: Progress Publishers, 1964, pp. 121–2. Jean P. Joubert in his article 'Lenine et le Jacobinisme' (Paris: *Cahiers Leon Trotsky*, no. 30, June 1987) has shown how on many occasions Lenin distanced himself from Jacobinism. However, Joubert has failed to show a single instance where Lenin critically analyzed Jacobinism with anywhere near the severity to be found in the writings of Marx and Engels, the younger Trotsky, or Rosa Luxemburg. Particularly noteworthy was Leon Trotsky's 1904 critique of Jacobinism and Leninism in his pamphlet *Our Political Tasks*. While this pamphlet has not yet been translated into English, fragments are available in Isaac Deutscher's *The Prophet Armed. Trotsky: 1879–1921*, New York: Vintage Books, 1965, pp. 88–97.

71 Rosa Luxemburg, 'The Russian Revolution', in *The Russian Revolution and Leninism or Marxism?* Ann Arbor, Mich.: University of Michigan Press, 1961, p. 72.

72 Roger Scruton, *A Dictionary of Political Thought*, New York: Harper & Row, 1982, p. 237.

73 See Robert V. Daniels (ed.), *A Documentary History of Communism. From Lenin to Mao*, New York: Random House, 1960, pp. 223–5. See also Lewin, *Lenin's Last Struggle*, pp. 77–89.

74 At least in the case of Lenin, when I write about wanting to 'hold on to power' I do not mean this in a narrow personal sense. Lenin's personal modesty and selflessness are legendary.

EPILOGUE

1 Jeffrey W. Hahn, 'Power to the Soviets?' *Problems of Communism* (Washington, DC), January–February 1989, pp. 38–9.

2 'The Law on State Enterprises', *Soviet Labour Review* (London, England), vol. 5, no. 2, August 1987, p. 4.

3 For a rich and fascinating history of KOR, see Jan Josef Lipski, *KOR. Workers' Defense Committee in Poland. 1976–1981*, Berkeley, Calif.: University of California Press, 1985.

4 'Hungary in 1989: The Transition to a Post-Communist Society? An Interview with Miklos Haraszti,' *Uncaptive Minds* (New York City), vol. 2, no. 1 (5), January–February 1989, pp. 1–8; Daniel Singer, 'Solidarity's Victory. Partnership for Poland?' *The Nation* (New York), 26 June 1989, p. 880.

5 Timothy Garton Ash, 'Refolution: The Springtime of Two Nations', *New York Review of Books*, vol. 36, no 10, 15 June 1989, p. 3.

Bibliography

Articles and Reviews in Journals and Collections

Adelman, Jonathan R., 'The development of the Soviet party apparat in the Civil War: Center, localities, and nationality areas', *Russian History*, 9, pt 1 (1982).

Avrich, Paul, 'Bolshevik opposition to Lenin: G. T. Miasnikov and the Workers' Group', *The Russian Review*, 43, 1 (January 1984).

—— 'The Bolshevik Revolution and Workers' Control in Russian industry', *Slavic Review*, 22, 1 (March 1963).

Bailes, Kendall E., 'Alexei Gastev and the Soviet controversy over Taylorism, 1918–1924', *Soviet Studies*, 29, 3 (July 1977).

Barfield, Rodney, 'Lenin's utopianism: *State and Revolution*', *Slavic Review*, 30, 1 (March 1971).

Bell, Daniel, 'Ten theories in search of reality: The prediction of Soviet behavior', in *The End of Ideology. On the Exhaustion of Political Ideas in the Fifties*, New York: The Free Press, 1960.

Berk, Stephen M., 'The "class tragedy" of Izhevsk: working-class opposition to Bolshevism in 1918', *Russian History*, 2, 2 (1975).

Brandenburgskii, Ia., 'On the social composition of the Soviet judiciary', in Zigurds L. Zile, (ed.), *Ideas and Forces in Soviet Legal History: Statutes, Decisions and Other Materials in the Development and Processes of Soviet Law*, 2nd edn, Madison, Wisc.: College Printing and Publishing, 1970.

Brooks, Jeffrey, 'The breakdown in production and distribution of printed material, 1917–1927', in Abbot Gleason, Peter Kenez, and Richard Stites (eds), *Bolshevik Culture. Experiment and Order in the Russian Revolution*, Bloomington, Ind.: Indiana University Press, 1985.

—— 'Public and private values in the Soviet press, 1921–1928', *Slavic Review*, 48, 1 (Spring 1989).

Brovkin, Vladimir, 'The Mensheviks and NEP society in Russia', *Russian History*, 9, pts 2–3 (1982).

—— 'The Mensheviks' political comeback: The elections to the provincial city soviets in Spring 1918', *The Russian Review*, 42, 1 (January 1983).

—— 'Politics, not economics was the key', *Slavic Review*, 44, 2 (Summer 1985).
Brumberg, Abraham, 'Moscow: the struggle for reform', *New York Review of Books*, 36, 5 (30 March 1989).

Carr, E. H., 'The origin and status of the Cheka', *Soviet Studies*, 10, 1 (July 1958).
Chase, William, 'Voluntarism, mobilisation and coercion: *subbotniki* 1919–1921', *Soviet Studies*, 41, 1 (January 1989).
Claudin, Fernando, 'Democracy and dictatorship in Lenin and Kautsky', *New Left Review*, 106 (November–December 1977).
Cliff, Tony, 'Trotsky on substitionism,' in *Party and Class. Essays by Cliff, Hallas, Harman and Trotsky*, London, England: Pluto Press, n.d.
Cohen, Stephen F., 'Bolshevism and Stalinism', in Robert C. Tucker (ed.), *Stalinism. Essays in Historical Interpretation*, New York and London: W. W. Norton, 1977.
Colletti, Lucio, 'Lenin's *State and Revolution,*' in Lucio Colletti, *From Rousseau to Lenin*, tr. John Merrington and Judith White, London, England: New Left Books, 1972.

Davies, R. W., 'Soviet history in the Gorbachev Revolution: the first phase', in Ralph Miliband, Leo Panitch, and John Saville (eds), *Socialist Register 1988*, London, England: Merlin Press, 1988.
—— 'The Syrtsov–Lominadze affair', *Soviet Studies*, 33, 1 (January 1981).
Draper, Hal, 'The two souls of socialism', *New Politics* (New York), 5, 1 (Winter 1966).
Duval, Charles, 'Iakov Mikhailovich Sverdlov: founder of the Bolshevik party machine', in Ralph Carter Elwood (ed.), *Reconsiderations on the Russian Revolution*, Cambridge, Mass.: Slavica Publishers, 1976.

Evans, Alfred B., 'Rereading Lenin's *State and Revolution*', *Slavic Review*, 46, 1 (Spring 1987).
Evans Clements, Barbara, 'Kollontai's contribution to the Workers' Opposition', *Russian History*, 2, 2 (1975).
—— 'Working-class and peasant women in the Russian Revolution, 1917–1923', *Signs*, 8, 2 (Winter 1982).

Fang, Lizhi, 'China's despair and China's hope', *New York Review of Books*, 36, 1 (2 February 1989).
Farber, Samuel, 'Cuba: still stuck in the ABC's. . .', *Against the Current* (New York, Fall 1983).
—— 'The Cuban communists in the early stages of the Cuban Revolution: revolutionaries or reformists?' *Latin American Research Review*, 18, 1 (1983).
Ferro, Marc, 'The birth of the Soviet bureaucratic system', in Ralph Carter Elwood (ed), *Reconsiderations on the Russian Revolution*, Cambridge, Mass.: Slavica Publishers, 1976.

Figes, Orlando, 'The village and *volost* soviet elections of 1919', *Soviet Studies*, 40, 1 (Janaury 1988).

Fitzpatrick, Sheila, 'Cultural revolution as class war,' in Sheila Fitzpatrick (ed.), *Cultural Revolution in Russia, 1928–1931*, Bloomington, Ind.: Indiana University Press, 1978.

Frank, Pierre, Maitan, Livio, and Mandel, Ernest, 'In defense of the Portuguese Revolution', *Intercontinental Press*, 8 September 1975.

Garton Ash, Timothy, 'Revolution: the springtime of two nations', *New York Review of Books*, 36, 10 (15 June 1989).

Gouldner, Alvin W., 'Metaphysical pathos and the theory of bureaucracy', *American Political Science Review*, 49 (1955).

Hahn, Jeffrey W., 'Power to the Soviets?' *Problems of Communism* (Washington DC), January-February 1989.

Haimson, Leopold, 'The Mensheviks after the October Revolution. Part I', *Russian Review*, 38, 4 (October 1979).

—— 'The Mensheviks after the October Revolution. Part II', *Russian Review*, 39, 2 (April 1980).

Harman, Chris, 'How the revolution was lost', *International Socialism*, (London, England), 30 (Autumn 1967).

Hatch, John B., 'Working-class politics in Moscow during the early NEP: Mensheviks and workers' organizations, 1921–1922', *Soviet Studies*, 39, 4 (October 1987).

Holmes, Larry E., 'Soviet rewriting of 1917: the case of A. G. Shliapnikov', *Slavic Review*, 38, 2 (June 1979).

Holmstrom, Nancy, 'The morality of abortion', *Against the Current* (New York), 2, 2, (Spring 1983).

Holter, Howard R., 'The legacy of Lunacharsky and artistic freedom in the USSR', *Slavic Review*, 29, 2 (June 1970).

Huskey, Eugene, 'Vyshinskii, Krylenko and the shaping of the Soviet legal order', *Slavic Review*, 46, 3/4 (Fall/Winter 1987).

'The "Index" of the Soviet Inquisition', *Slavonic Review*, 4 (1926).

Jaggar, Alison, 'Abortion and a woman's right to decide', in Carol C. Gould and Marx W. Wartofsky (eds), *Women and Philosophy. Toward a Theory of Liberation*, New York: Capricorn Books, G. P. Putnam Sons, 1976.

Jones, Stephen, 'The establishment of Soviet power in Transcaucasia: the case of Georgia 1921–1928', *Soviet Studies*, 40, 4 (October 1988).

Joubert, Jean P., 'Lenine et le Jacobinisme', *Cahiers Leon Trotsky* (Paris, France), 30 (June 1987).

Katkov, George, 'The Kronstadt rising', in David Footman (ed.), *Soviet Affairs*.

Number Two, St. Antony's Papers. Number 6, London, England: Chatto & Windus, 1959.

Keep, John L. H., 'Lenin's letters as an historical source', in Bernard W. Eissenstat (ed.), *Lenin and Leninism. State, Law, and Society*, Lexington, Mass.: Lexington Books, 1971.

—— 'October in the provinces', in Richard Pipes (ed.), *Revolutionary Russia*, Cambridge, Mass.: Harvard University Press, 1968.

Kelly, Aileen, 'Leonard Schapiro's Russia', Review of *Russian Studies*, in *New York Review of Books*, 34, 14 (24 September 1987).

Kenez, Peter, 'Lenin and the freedom of the press', in Abbott Gleason, Peter Kenez, and Richard Stites (eds), *Bolshevik Culture. Experiment and Order in the Russian Revolution*, Bloomington, Ind.: Indiana University Press, 1985.

Kozlov, Nicholas N., 'Nikolai Ivanovich Bukharin: reconsiderations on a 'neo-Narodnik *litterateur*', *Review of Radical Political Economics*, 17, 4 (Winter 1985).

Lapenna, Ivo, 'Lenin, law and legality', in Leonard Schapiro and Peter Reddaway (eds), *Lenin. The Man, The Theorist, The Leader. A Reappraisal*, New York: Praeger, 1967.

Lenin, V. I., 'Can "Jacobinism" frighten the working class?' *Collected Works*, vol. 25, June–September 1917, Moscow: Progress Publishers, 1964.

—— 'Draft resolution on freedom of the press', *Collected Works*, vol. 26, September 1917 – February 1918, Moscow: Progress Publishers, 1964.

—— 'How to organise competition?' *Collected Works*, vol. 26, September 1917 – February 1918, Moscow: Progress Publishers, 1964.

—— 'Our revolution. (Apropos of N. Sukhanov's Notes)', *Collected Works*, vol. 33, August 1921 – March 1923, Moscow: Progress Publishers, 1965.

—— 'Our tasks and the Soviet of Workers' Deputies. A letter to the Editor', *Collected Works*, vol. 10, November 1905 – June 1906, Moscow: Foreign Languages Publishing House, 1962.

—— 'Rough theses of a decision on the strict observance of the laws', *Collected Works*, vol. 42, October 1917 – March 1923, Moscow: Progress Publishers, 1969.

—— 'Socialism and Anarchism', *Collected Works*, vol. 10, November 1905 – June 1906, Moscow: Foreign Languages Publishing House, 1962.

—— 'The Socialist Party and non-party revolutionism', *Collected Works*, vol. 10, November 1905 – June 1906, Moscow: Foreign Languages Publishing House, 1962.

Lewin, Moshe, 'More than one piece is missing in the puzzle', *Slavic Review*, 44, 2 (Summer 1985).

Lih, Lars T., 'Bolshevik *Razverstka* and War Communism', *Slavic Review*, 45, 4 (Winter 1986).

Mawdsley, Evan, 'The Baltic fleet and the Kronstadt mutiny', *Soviet Studies*, 24, 4 (April 1973).

Meijer, Jan M., 'Town and country in the Civil War', in Richard Pipes (ed.), *Revolutionary Russia*, Cambridge, Mass.: Harvard University Press, 1968.

Miliband, Ralph, 'Lenin's *The State and Revolution*', in Ralph Miliband and John Saville (eds), *The Socialist Register 1970*, London, England: Merlin Press, 1970.

Nove, Alec, 'Lenin and the New Economic Policy', in Bernard W. Eissenstat (ed.), *Lenin and Leninism. State, Law and Society*, Lexington, Mass.: Toronto and London, England: Lexington Books, D. C. Heath, 1971.

Oppenheim, Samuel A., 'The making of a Right Communist – A. I. Rykov to 1917', *Slavic Review*, 36, 3 (September 1977).

Pashukanis, E. B., *The General Theory of Law and Marxism* and *The Marxist Theory of Law and the Construction of Socialism*, reprinted in Piers Beirne and Robert Sharlet (eds), *Pashukanis. Selected Writings on Marxism and Law*, Tr. Peter B. Maggs, London: Academic Press, 1980.

Petchesky Pollack, Rosalind, 'Reproductive freedom: beyond "A Woman's Right to Choose"', *Signs*, 5, 4 (Summer 1980).

Pethybridge, R. W., 'Railways and press communications in Soviet Russia in the early NEP period', *Soviet Studies*, 38, 2 (April 1986).

Rabinowitch, Alexander, 'The evolution of local soviets in Petrograd, November 1917 – June 1918: the case of the first city district soviet', *Slavic Review*, 46, 1 (Spring 1987).

Rakovsky, Christian, 'The "professional dangers" of power', in Tariq Ali (ed.), *The Stalinist Legacy*, Middlesex, England: Penguin Books, 1984.

Reed, John, 'Soviets in action', *International Socialism* (London, England). 69, (May 1974). Reprinted from *The Liberator*, October 1918.

Reiman, Michael, 'Political trials of the Stalinist era', *Telos*, 54 (Winter 1982–3).

Resis, Albert, 'Lenin on freedom of the press', *The Russian Review*, 36, 3 (July 1977).

Rigby, T. H., 'Staffing USSR Incorporated: the origins of the nomenklatura system', *Soviet Studies*, 40, 4 (October 1988).

Roberts, Paul Craig, ' "War Communism": A Re-Examination', *Slavic Review*, 29, 2 (June 1970).

Rosenberg, William G., 'Reply', *Slavic Review*, 44, 2 (Summer 1985).

—— 'Russian labor and Bolshevik power after October', *Slavic Review*, 44, 2 (Summer 1985).

Rosenthal, A. M., 'Save the T. V. Giraffe', *New York Times*, 21 May 1987, p. A31.

Sabine, George, H., 'The two democratic traditons', *Philosophical Review*, 61 (October 1952).

Sakwa, Richard, 'The commune state in Moscow in 1918', *Slavic Review*, 46, 3/4 (Fall/Winter 1987).

Schapiro, Leonard, 'Bukharin's Way' and 'My Fifty Years of Social Science', in Leonard Schapiro, *Russian Studies*, ed. Ellen Dahrendorf with an Introduction by Harry Willetts, New York: Elisabeth Sifton Books, Viking Press, 1987.

Serge, Victor, 'Once more: Kronstadt', *The New International*, 4, 7 (July 1938).

—— 'Secrecy and revolution – a reply to Trotsky, Peter Sedgwick, *Peace News* (London, England), 27 December 1963.

Sharlet, Robert, 'Pashukanis and the withering away of the law in the USSR', in Sheila Fitzpatrick (ed.), *Cultural Revolution in Russia, 1928–1931*, Bloomington, Ind.: Indiana University Press, 1978.

—— 'Stalinism and Soviet legal culture', in Robert C. Tucker (ed.), *Stalinism. Essays in Historical Interpretation*, New York: W. W. Norton, 1977.

Singer, Daniel, 'Solidarity's victory. Partnership for Poland? *The Nation* (New York), 26 June 1989.

Singleton, Seth, 'The Tambov revolt (1920–1921),' *Slavic Review*, 25, 3 (September 1966).

Slavin, I., 'The judiciary and the New Economic Policy', in Zigurds L. Zile (ed.), *Ideas and Forces in Soviet Legal History: Statutes, Decisions and Other Materials in the Development and Processes of Soviet Law*, 2nd edn, Madison, Wisc.: College Printing and Publishing, 1970.

Smith, S. A., Review of Marc Ferro, *October 1917: A Social History of the Russian Revolution*, London: Routledge & Kegan Paul, 1980, in *Soviet Studies*, 33, 3 (July 1981), pp. 454–9.

Solomon, Peter H. Jr, 'Soviet penal policy, 1917–1934: A reinterpretation', *Slavic Review*, 39, 2 (June 1980).

Stuchka, P., 'Five years of revolution in law', in William G. Rosenberg (ed.), *Bolshevik Visions: First Phase of the Cultural Revolution in Soviet Russia*, Ann Arbor, Mich.: Ardis, 1984.

Trotsky, Leon, 'Hue and cry over Kronstadt', *The New International* 4, 4 (April 1938).

—— 'More on the suppression of Kronstadt', *The New International*, 4, 8 (August 1938).

Ulam, Adam B., 'Lenin's last phase', *Survey*, 21, 1/2 (Winter/Spring 1975).

Wade, Rex A., 'The rajonnye sovety of Petrograd: the role of local political bodies in the Russian Revolution', *Jahrbücher für Geschichte Osteuropas*, 20, 2 (June 1972).

Wohlforth, Tim, 'The two souls of Leninism', *Against the Current. New Series* (Detroit), 1, 4–5 (September–October 1986).

Wolfe, Bertram D., 'Krupskaya purges the people's liberaries', *Survey*, 72, (Summer 1969).

Wolin, Simon, 'The opposition to the NEP', in Leopold H. Haimson (ed.), *The Mensheviks. From the Revolution of 1917 to the Second World War*, tr. Getrude Vakar, Chicago and London: University of Chicago Press, 1974.

Wright, John G., 'The truth about Kronstadt', *The New International*, 4, 2 (February 1938).

Zhengtian, Li, 'Lawless laws and crimeless crimes,' in Anita Chan, Stanley Rosen, and Jonathan Unger (eds), *On Socialist Democracy and the Chinese Legal System. The Li Yizhe Debates*, Armonk, NY: M. E. Sharpe, 1985.

Books, Pamphlets, and Speeches

Abramovitch, Raphael R., *The Soviet Revolution 1917–1939*, New York: International Universities Press, 1962.

Ali, Tariq, *The Stalinist Legacy. Its Impact on 20th Century Politics*, Middlesex, England: Penguin Books, 1984.

Andreyev, A., *The Soviets of Workers' and Soldiers' Deputies on the Eve of the October Revolution*, Moscow: Progress Publishers, 1971.

Anweiler, Oskar, *The Soviets: The Russian Workers', Peasants', and Soldiers' Councils, 1905–1921*, tr. from the German by Ruth Hein, New York: Pantheon Books, 1974.

Ascher, Abraham (ed.), *The Mensheviks in the Russian Revolution*, Ithaca, NY: Cornell University Press, 1976.

Avrich, Paul (ed.), *The Anarchists in the Russian Revolution*, Ithaca, NY: Cornell University Press,1973.

—— *Kronstadt 1921*, New York: W. W. Norton 1974.

—— *The Russian Anarchists*, Princeton, NJ: Princeton University Press, 1967.

Avtorkhanov, Abdurakhman, *The Communist Party Apparatus*, Chicago, Ill.: Henry Regnery Company, 1966.

Balabanoff, Angelica, *Impression of Lenin*, tr. Isotta Cesari, Ann Arbor, Mich.: University of Michigan Press, 1964.

Barber, Benjamin, *Strong Democracy. Participatory Politics for a New Age*, Berkeley, Calif.: University of California Press, 1984.

Barron, Jerome A., *Freedom of the Press for Whom? The Right of Access to the Mass Media*, Bloomington and London: Indiana University Press, 1973.

Beirne, Piers and Sharlet, Robert (eds), *Pashukanis: Selected Writings on Marxism and Law*, tr. Peter B. Maggs, London, England: Academic Press, 1980.

Bettelheim, Charles, *Class Struggles in the USSR. First Period: 1917–1923*, tr. Brian Pearce, New York and London: Monthly Review Press, 1976.

Blobaum, Robert, *Feliks Dzierzynski and the SDKPiL: A Study of the Origins of Polish Communism*, Boulder, Colo., and New York: East European Monographs distributed by Columbia University Press, 1984.

Brinton, Clarence Crane, *The Jacobins. An Essay in the New History*, New York: Russell & Russell, 1961.

Brinton, Maurice, *The Bolsheviks and Workers' Control*, Montreal, Canada: Black Rose Books, 1975.

Broido, Vera, *Lenin and the Mensheviks. The Persecution of Socialists under Bolshevism*, Aldershot, England: Gower/Maurice Temple Smith, 1987.

Broue, Pierre, *Le Parti Bolshevique. Histoire du P.C. de l'URSS*, Paris, France: Les Editions de Minuit, 1963.

Brovkin, Vladimir N., *The Mensheviks after October. Socialist Opposition and the Rise of the Bolshevik Dictatorship*, Ithaca and London: Cornell University Press, 1987.

Brzezinski, Zbigniew, *The Grand Failure. The Birth and Death of Communism in the Twentieth Century*, New York: Charles Scribner's Sons, 1989.

Bunyan, James, *The Origin of Forced Labor in the Soviet State, 1917–1921. Documents and Materials*. Baltimore, Md: Johns Hopkins Press, 1967.

Bunyan, James (ed.), *Intervention, Civil War, and Communism in Russia. April–December 1918. Documents and Materials*. Balitmore, Md: Johns Hopkins Press, 1936.

Bunyan, James and H. H. Fisher (eds), *The Bolshevik Revolution 1917–1918. Documents and Materials*. Stanford, Calif.: Stanford University Press, 1934.

Burbank, Jane, *Intelligentsia and Revolution. Russian Views of Bolshevism, 1917–1922*, New York: Oxford University Press, 1986.

Campbell, Tom, *The Left and Rights. A Conceptual Analysis of the Idea of Socialist Rights*, London, England: Routledge & Kegan Paul, 1983.

Carr, E. H. , *The Bolshevik Revolution. 1917–1923*. 3 vols, Middlesex, England: Penguin Books, 1966.

Caute, David, *The Left in Europe since 1789*, New York and Toronto: World University Library, McGraw-Hill 1966.

Central Committee Minutes of the Russian Social-Democratic Labour Party (Bolsheviks) August 1917 – February 1918, *The Bolsheviks and the October Revolution*, tr. Ann Bone, London, England: Pluto Press, 1974.

Chamberlin, William Henry, *The Russian Revolution 1917–1921*, vol. 2 New York: Macmillan, 1935.

Chan, Anita, Rosen, Stanley, and Unger, Jonathan (eds), *On Socialist Democracy and the Chinese Legal System. The Li Yizhe Debates*, Armonk, NY: M. E. Sharpe, 1985.

Chase, William J., *Workers, Society, and the Soviet State. Labor and Life in Moscow, 1918–1929*, Urbana and Chicago, Ill.: University of Illinois Press, 1987.

Ciliga, Ante, *The Russian Enigma*, tr. Fernand G. Fernier and Anne Cliff (part I) and Margaret and Hugo Dewar (part II), London, England: Ink Links, 1979.

Clark, Ronald W., *Lenin. A Biography*. New York: Harper & Row, 1988.

Claudin, Fernando, *The Communist Movement. From Comintern to Cominform*, Part One, tr. Brian Pearce, New York: Monthly Review Press, 1975.

Claudin-Urondo, Carmen, *Lenin and the Cultural Revolution*, tr. Brian Pearce, New Jersey: Humanities Press, 1977.

Cohen, Stephen F., *Bukharin and the Bolshevik Revolution. A Political Biography 1888–1938*. Oxford, England: Oxford University Press, 1980.

—— *Rethinking the Soviet Experience. Politics and History since 1917*, New York and Oxford: Oxford University Press, 1985.

D'Agostino, Anthony, *Marxism and the Russian Anarchists*, San Francisco, Calif.: Germinal Press, 1977.

Dallin, David J. and Nicolaevsky, Boris I., *Forced Labor in Soviet Russia*, New Haven, Conn.: Yale University Press, 1947.

Daniels, Robert Vincent, *A Documentary History of Communism. From Lenin to Mao*, New York: Random House, 1960.

—— *The Conscience of the Revolution. Communist Opposition in Soviet Russia*, New York: A Clarion Book published by Simon & Schuster, 1960.

—— *Red October. The Bolshevik Revolution of 1917*, New York: Charles Scribiner's Sons, 1967.

Deutscher, Isaac, *The Prophet Armed. Trotsky: 1879–1921*, New York: Vintage Books, 1965.

—— *Russia in Transition and other essays*, New York: Coward-Mccann, 1957.

—— *Soviet Trade Unions. Their Place in Soviet Labour Policy*, London and New York: Royal Institute of International Affairs, 1950.

—— *Stalin. A Political Biography*, 2nd edn, New York: Oxford University Press, 1967.

—— *The Unfinished Revolution Russia 1917–1967*, New York: Oxford University Press, 1967.

Dobb, Maurice, *Soviet Economic Development sicne 1917*, London, England: Routledge & Kegan Paul, 1978.

Draper, Hal, *The 'Dictatorship of the Proletariat' from Marx to Lenin*, New York: Monthly Review Press, 1987.

—— *Karl Marx's Theory of Revolution. Volume III: The 'Dictatorship of the Proletariat'*, New York: Monthly Review Press, 1986.

Durkheim, Emile, *Socialism*, New York: Collier Books, 1962.

Dworkin, Ronald, *Taking Rights Seriously*, Cambridge, Mass.: Harvard University Press, 1977.

Dzerzhinsky, Felix, *Prison Diary and Letters*, Moscow: Foreign Languages Publishing House, 1959.

Emerson, Thomas I., *The System of Freedom of Expression*, New York: Random House, 1970.

Engels, Friedrich, *Socialism: Utopian and Scientific*, in Robert C. Tucker (ed.), *The Marx–Engels Reader*, 2nd edn New York: W. W. Norton, 1978.

Evans Clements, Barbara, *Bolshevik Feminist. The Life of Aleksandra Kollontai*, Bloomington and London: Indiana University Press, 1979.

Fagan, Gus (ed.), *Christian Rakovsky. Selected Writings on Opposition in the USSR 1923–30*, London and New York: Allison & Busby, 1980.

Farber, Samuel, *Revolution and Reaction in Cuba. 1933–1960*, Middletown, Conn.: Wesleyan University Press, 1976.

Ferro, Marc, *October 1917. A Social History of the Russian Revolution*, Norman Stone, London, Boston, and Henley: Routledge & Kegan Paul, 1980.

Filtzer, Donald, *Soviet Workers and Stalinist Industrialization. The Formation of Modern Soviet Production Relations, 1928–1941*, Armonk, NY: M. E. Sharpe, 1986.

Fitzpatrick, Sheila (ed.), *Cultural Revolution in Russia, 1928–1931*, Bloomington and London: Indiana University Press, 1978.

—— *The Russian Revolution*, Oxford and New York: Oxford University Press, 1982.

Gerson, Lennard, D., *The Secret Police in Lenin's Russia*, Philadelphia, Pa.: Temple University Press, 1976.

Getzler, Israel, *Kronstadt 1917–1921. The Fate of a Soviet Democracy*, Cambridge, England: Cambridge University Press, 1983.

—— *Martov. A Political Biography of a Russian Social Democrat*, Cambridge, England, and Melbourne, Australia: Cambridge University Press and Melbourne University Press, 1967.

Geyer, Dietrich, *The Russian Revolution. Historial Problems and Perspectives*, Bruce Little, Leamington Spa, England, Hamburg, and New York: Berg, distributed by St Martin's Press, 1987.

Gibson, Mary, *Workers' Rights*, Totowa, NJ: Rowman & Allanheld, 1983.

Gill, Graeme J., *Peasants and Government in the Russian Revolution*, London and Basingstoke, England: Macmillan, 1979.

Gorbachev, Mikhail, *Perestroika. New Thinking for Our Country and the World*, New York: Harper & Row, 1987.

Gorky, Maxim, *Days with Lenin*, New York: International Publishers, 1932.

—— *Untimely Thoughts. Essays on Revolution, Culture and the Bolsheviks 1917–1918*, tr. Herman Ermolaev, New York: Paul S. Eriksson, 1968.

Got'e, Iurii Vladimirovich, *Time of Troubles. The Diary of Iurii Vladimirovich Got'e. Moscow. July 8, 1917 to July 23, 1922*, translated, edited and introduced by Terence Emmons, Princeton, NJ: Princeton University Press, 1988.

Grigor Suny, Ronald, *The Baku Commune 1917–1918. Class and Nationality in the Russian Revolution*, Princeton, NJ: Princeton University Press, 1972.

Haimson, Leopold H. (ed.), *The Mensheviks. From the Revolution of 1917 to the Second World War*, tr. Getrude Vakar, Chicago and London: University of Chicago Press, 1974.

Harding, Neil, *Lenin's Political Thought. Vol. 2. Theory and Practice in the Socialist Revolution*, London and Basingstoke, England: Macmillan, 1981.

Harris, Marvin, *Cultural Materialism. The Struggle for a Science of Culture*, New York: Vintage Books, 1980.

Haupt, Georges and Marie, Jean-Jacques, *Makers of the Russian Revolution. Biographies of Bolshevik Leaders*, translated from the Russian by C. I. P. Ferdinand and commentaries translated from the French by D. M. Bellos, Ithaca, NY: Cornell University Press, 1974.

Hazard, John N., *Settling Disputes in Soviet Society. The Formative Years of Legal Institutions*, New York: Columbia University Press, 1960.

—— (ed.), *Soviet Legal Philosophy*, Cambridge, Mass.: Harvard University Press, 1951.

Hobsbawm, E. J., *The Age of Revolution. 1789–1848*, New York: Mentor Book, New American Library, 1964.

Hough, Jerry F. and Fainsod, Merle, *How the Soviet Union is Governed*, Cambridge, Mass., and London, England: Harvard University Press, 1979.

Huskey, Eugene, *Russian Lawyers and the Soviet State. The Origins and Development of the Soviet Bar, 1917–1939*, Princeton, NJ: Princeton University Press, 1986.

James C. L. R., *The Black Jacobins*, New York: Vintage Books, 1963.

Jansen, Marc. *A Show Trial under Lenin. The Trial of the Socialist Revolutionaries, Moscow 1922*, tr. from the Dutch by Jean Sanders, The Hague, Boston, and London: Martinus Nijhoff 1982.

Judson, C. Fred, *Cuba and the Revolutionary Myth. The Political Education of the Cuban Rebel Army, 1953–1963*, Boulder, Col.: Westview Press, 1984.

Juviler, Peter H., *Revolutionary Law and Order. Politics and Social Change in the USSR,* New York and London: The Free Press and Collier Macmillan, 1976.

Kagarlitsky, Boris, *The Thinking Reed. Intellectuals and the Soviet State, 1917 to the Present*, tr. Brian Pearce, London and New York: Verso, 1988.

Kaiser, Daniel H. (ed.), *The Workers' Revolution in Russia, 1917. The View from Below*, Cambridge, England: Cambridge University Press, 1987.

Kaplan, Frederick I., *Bolshevik Ideology and the Ethics of Soviet Labor. 1917–1920: The Formative Years*, New York: Philosophical Library, 1968.

Kautsky, Karl, *The Dictatorship of the Proletariat*, tr. H. J. Stenning, Manchester, London, and Leicester, England: National Labour Press, n.d.

—— *Terrorism and Communism. A Contribution to the Natural History of Revolution*, W. H. Kerridge, London, England: National Labour Press, 1920; reprinted by Hyperion Press, Westport, Conn., 1973.

Keep, John L. H., *The Russian Revolution. A Study in Mass Mobilization*, New York: W. W. Norton, 1976.

—— (ed. and transl.), *The Debate on Soviet Power. Minutes of the All-Russian Central Executive Committee of Soviets. Second Convocation, October 1917 – January 1918*, Oxford, England: Clarendon Press, 1979.

Kenez, Peter, *The Birth of the Propaganda State. Soviet Methods of Mass Mobilization, 1917–1929*, Cambridge, England: Cambridge University Press, 1985.
—— *Civil War in South Russia, 1918. The First Year of the Volunteer Army*. Berkeley, Los Angeles, and London: University of California Press, 1971.

Kingston-Mann, Esther, *Lenin and the Problem of Marxist Peasant Revolution*, New York and Oxford: Oxford University Press, 1983.

Koenker, Diane, *Moscow Workers and the 1917 Revolution*, Princeton, NJ: Princeton University Press, 1981.

Kollontai, Aleksandra, *The Workers' Opposition*, London, England: Solidarity Pamphlet no. 7, n.d.

Korsch, Boris, *The Permanent Purge of Soviet Libraries*, Research Paper no. 50, Jerusalem, Israel: The Hebrew University of Jerusalem, the Soviet and East European Research Centre, April 1983.

Krupskaya, Nadezhda, *Memories of Lenin*, London, England: Panther History, 1970.

Kucherov, Samuel, *The Organs of Soviet Administration of Justice: Their History and Operation*, Leiden, Holland: E. J. Brill, 1970.

Lane, David, *The Roots of Russian Communism. A Social and Historical Study of Russian Social-Democracy 1898–1907*, Assen, Holland: Van Gorcum – Dr H. J. Prakke & H. M. G. Prakke, 1969.

Laqueur, Walter, *The Fate of the Revolution. Interpretations of Soviet History*, New York: Macmillan, 1967.

Leggett, George, *The Cheka: Lenin's Political Police. The All-Russian Extraordinary Commission for Combatting Counter-Revolution and Sabotage (December 1917 to February 1922)*, Oxford, England: Clarendon Press, 1981.

Lenin, V. I., 'Better Fewer, But Better', *Collected Works*, vol. 33, August 1921 – March 1923, Moscow: Progress Publishers, 1965.
—— 'The Constituent Assembly elections and the dictatorship of the proletariat', *Collected Works*, vol. 30, September 1919 – April 1920, Moscow: Progress Publishers, 1965.
—— 'Deception of the people with slogans of freedom and equality', *Collected Works*, vol. 29, March–August 1919, Moscow: Progress Publishers, 1965.
—— 'How to guarantee the success of the Constituent Assembly', *Collected Works*, vol. 25, June–September 1917, Moscow: Progress Publishers, 1964.
—— *The Nascent Trend of Imperialist Economism*, *Collected Works*, vol. 23, August 1916 – March 1917, Moscow: Progress Publishers, 1964.
—— 'On compromises', *Collected Works*, vol. 25, June–September 1917, Moscow: Progress Publishers, 1964.
—— 'On co-operation', *Collected Works*, vol. 33, August 1921 – March 1923, Moscow: Progress Publishers, 1965.
—— 'On slogans', *Collected Works*, vol. 25, June–September 1917, Moscow: Progress Publishers, 1964.
—— *One Step Forward. Two Steps Back*, *Collected Works*, vol. 7, September 1903 – December 1904, Moscow: Progress Publishers, 1961.

—— 'Party organisation and party literature', *Collected Works*, vol. 10, November 1905 – June 1906, Moscow: Foreign Languages Publishing House, 1962.

—— 'Political report of the Central Committee of the R.C.P.(B), March 27. Eleventh Congress of the R.C.P.(B), March 27 – April 2, 1922', *Collected Works*, vol. 33, August 1921 – March 1923, Moscow: Progress Publishers, 1965.

—— *The Proletarian Revolution and Kautsky the Renegade, Collected Works*, vol. 28, July 1918 – March 1919, Moscow: Progress Publishers, 1965.

—— 'Remarks on Ryazanov's amendment to the resolution on party unity', *Collected Works*, vol. 32, December 1920 – August 1921, Moscow: Progress Publishers, 1965.

—— 'Report on the New Economic Policy', *Collected Works*, vol. 33, August 1921 – March 1923, Moscow: Progress Publishers, 1966.

—— *The Revolutionary Proletariat and the Right of Nations to Self-Determination, Collected Works*, vol. 21, August 1914 – December 1915, Moscow: Progress Publishers, 1964.

—— 'Speech at a joint meeting of the Petrograd Soviet of Workers' and Soldiers' Deputies and delegates from the fronts', *Collected Works*, vol. 26, September 1917 – February 1918, Moscow: Progress Publishers, 1964.

—— 'Speech at a rally and concert for the All-Russian Extraordinary Commission Staff', *Collected Works*, vol. 28, July 1918 – March 1919, Moscow: Progress Publishers, 1965.

—— *State and Revolution, Collected Works*, vol. 25, June–September 1917, Moscow: Progress Publishers, 1964.

—— 'The tasks of the revolution', *Collected Works*, vol. 26, September 1917 – February 1918, Moscow: Progress Publishers, 1964.

—— *What is to be Done?, Collected Works*, vol. 5, May 1901 – February 1902, Moscow: Progress Publishers, 1961.

Lewin, Moshe, *Lenin's Last Struggle*, New York: Vintage Books, 1970.

Liberman, Simon, *Building Lenin's Russia*, Chicago, Ill.: University of Chicago Press, 1945.

Liebman, Marcel, *Leninism under Lenin*, tr. Brian Pearce, London, England: Jonathan Cape, 1975.

Lipski, Jan Josef, *KOR. Workers' Defense Committee in Poland, 1976–1981*, Berkeley, Calif.: University of California Press, 1985.

Lovejoy, Arthur G., *The Great Chain of Being*, Cambridge, Mass.: Harvard University Press, 1948.

Lukes, Steven, *Marxism and Morality*, Oxford, England: Clarendon Press, 1985.

Luxemburg, Rosa, *The Russian Revolution and Leninism or Marxism?* Ann Arbor, Mich.: University of Michigan Press, 1961.

McCauley, Martin (ed.), *The Russian Revolution and the Soviet State 1917–1921, Documents*, New York: Barnes & Noble, 1975.

McNeal, Robert H., *Bride of the Revolution. Krupskaya and Lenin*, Ann Arbor, Mich.: University of Michigan Press, 1972.

Malle, Silvana, *The Economic Organization of War Communism, 1918–1921*, Cambridge, England: Cambridge University Press, 1985.

Mandel, David, *The Petrograd Workers and the Soviet Seizure of Power. From the July Days 1917 to July 1918*, New York: St Martin's Press, 1984.

Marx, Karl, *The Civil War in France*, New York: International Publishers, 1940.

—— 'Inaugural address of the Working Men's International Association', in Robert C. Tucker (ed.), *The Marx–Engels Reader*, 2nd edn, New York: W. W. Norton, 1978.

Mawdsley, Evan, *The Russian Civil War*, Boston: Allen & Unwin, 1987.

Medvedev, Roy A., *Leninism and Western Socialism*, tr. A. D. P. Briggs, London, England: Verso, 1981.

—— *Let History Judge. The Origins and Consequences of Stalinism*, tr. Colleen Taylor, David Joravsky and Georges Haupt, New York: Alfred A. Knopf, 1971.

—— *Nikolai Bukharin. The Last Years*, tr. D. P. Briggs, New York: W. W. Norton, 1980.

—— *The October Revolution*, tr. George Saunders, New York: Columbia University Press, 1979.

—— *On Socialist Democracy*, tr. and ed. Ellen de Kadt, New York: Alfred A. Knopf, 1975.

Meiklejohn, Alexander, *Political Freedom. The Constitutional Powers of the People*, New York: Harper & Brothers, 1960.

Melgounov, Sergey Petrovich, *The Red Terror in Russia*, London and Toronto: J. M. Dent and Sons, 1926, reprinted by Hyperion Press, Westport, Conn., 1975.

Michnik, Adam, *Letters from Prison and other Essays*, tr. Maya Latynski, Berkeley, Calif.: University of California Press, 1985.

Nettl, Peter, *Rosa Luxemburg*, abridged edn, London, England: Oxford University Press, 1969.

Nove, Alec, *An Economic History of the USSR*, London, England: Penguin Books, 1984.

Orwell, George, *The Lion and the Unicorn. Socialism and the British Genius*, London: Secker & Warburg, 1962.

Owen, Lancelot A., *The Russian Peasant Movement. 1906–1917*, New York: Russell & Russell, 1937.

Pipes, Richard, *The Formation of the Soviet Union*, revised edn, New York: Atheneum, 1968.

—— (ed.), *Revolutionary Russia*, Cambridge, Mass.: Harvard University Press, 1968.

Rabinowitch, Alexander, *The Bolsheviks Come to Power. The Revolution of 1917 in Petrograd*, New York and London: W. W. Norton, 1978.
—— *Prelude to Revolution. The Petrograd Bolsheviks and the July 1917 Uprising*, Bloomington and London: Indiana University Press, 1968.
Radkey, Oliver Henry, *The Election to the Russian Constituent Assembly of 1917*, Cambridge, Mas.: Harvard University Press, 1950.
—— *The Sickle under the Hammer. The Russian Socialist Revolutionaries in the Early Months of Soviet Rule*, New York and London: Columbia University Press, 1963.
—— *The Unknown Civil War in Soviet Russia. A Study of the Green Movement in the Tambov Region 1920–1921*, Stanford, Calif.: Hoover Institution Press, 1976.
Rakovsky, Christian, 'Declaration of August 1929' and 'Declaration of April 1930', in Gus Fagan (ed.), *Christian Rakovsky. Selected Writings on Opposition in the USSR 1923–1930*, London, England: Allison & Busby, 1980.
Raz, Joseph, *Practical Reason and Norms,*, London, England: Hutcheson, 1975.
Raymond, Boris, *Krupskaia and Soviet Russian Librarianship, 1917–1939*, Metuchen, NJ, and London: The Scarecrow Press, 1979.
Reed, John, *Ten Days That Shook the World*, New York: The Modern Library, 1935.
Reisner, M. A., *Law, Our Law, Foreign Law, General Law*, In John N. Hazard (ed.), *Soviet Legal Philosophy*, Cambridge, Mass.: Harvard University Press, 1951.
Remington, Thomas F., *Building Socialism in Bolshevik Russia. Ideology and Industrial Organization 1917–1921*, Pittsburgh, Pa.: University of Pittsburgh Press, 1984.
Resolutions of the Twelfth World Congress of the Fourth International (January 1985), in *International Viewpoint. Special Issue*, n.d.
Rigby, T. H., *Lenin's Government: Sovnarkom 1917–1922*, Cambridge, England: Cambridge University Press, 1979.
Rosenberg, William G., *Liberals in the Russian Revolution. The Constitutional Democratic Party, 1917–1921*, Princeton, NJ: Princeton University Press, 1974.
—— (ed.), *Bolshevik Visions: First Phase of the Cultural Revolution in Soviet Russia*, Ann Arbor, Mich.: Ardis, 1984.
Rousset, David, *The Legacy of the Bolshevik Revolution. Volume I of a Critical History of the USSR*, tr. Alan Freeman, New York: St Martin's Press, 1982.
The Russian Constitution. Adopted July 10, 1918, reprinted by *The Nation*, 4 January 1919.

Sakwa, Richard, *Soviet Communists in Power. A Study of Moscow during the Civil War, 1918–1921*, New York: St Martin's Press, 1988.
Schapiro, Leonard, *The Communist Party of the Soviet Union*, New York: Random House, 1960.

—— *The Origin of the Communist Autocracy. Political Opposition in the Soviet State. First Phase 1917–1922*, Cambridge, Mass.: Harvard University Press, 1956.

—— *The Russian Revolutions of 1917. The Origins of Modern Communism*, New York: Basic Books, 1984.

—— *Russian Studies*, New York: Elisabeth Sifton Books, Viking, 1987.

—— and Reddaway, Peter (eds), *Lenin. The Man, The Theorist, The Leader. A Reappraisal*, New York: Praeger, 1967.

Schlesinger, Rudolf, *Soviet Legal Theory. Its Social Background and Development*, London, England: Routledge & Kegan Paul, 1951.

Schumpeter, Joseph A., *Capitalism, Socialism and Demcoracy*, New York: Harper Torchbooks, 1962.

Schwarz, Solomon K., *The Russian Revolution of 1905: The Workers' Movement and the Formation of Bolshevism and Menshevism*, Chicago: University of Chicago Press, 1976.

Scruton, Roger, *A Dictionary of Political Thought*, New York: Harper & Row, 1982.

Serge, Victor, *Memoirs of a Revolutionary 1901–1941*, tr. ed., and Introduction Peter Sedgwick, London, England: Oxford University Press, 1963.

—— *Year One of the Russian Revolution*, tr. and ed. Peter Sedgwick, Chicago, New York, and San Francisco: Holt, Rinehart & Winston, 1972.

Service, Robert, *The Bolshevik Party in Revolution. A Study in Organisational Change*, London, England: Macmillan, 1979.

—— *Lenin: A Political Life. Vol. 1. The Strengths of Contradiction*, Bloomington, Ind.: Indiana University Press, 1985.

Shanin, Teodor, *The Awkward Class. Political Sociology of Peasantry in a Developing Society. Russia 1910–1925*, Oxford, England: Clarendon Press, 1972.

Shlyapnikov, Alexander, *On the Eve of 1917*, tr. Richard Chappell, London and New York: Allison & Busby, 1982.

Siebert, Fred S., Peterson, Theodore, and Schramm, Wilbur, *Four Theories of the Press*, Urbana, Ill.: University of Illinois Press, 1963.

Sirianni, Carmen, *Workers' Control and Socialist Democracy. The Soviet Experience*. London, England: Verso Editions and New Left Books, 1982.

Slusser, Robert M., *Stalin in October. The Man Who Missed the Revolution*, Baltimore and London: Johns Hopkins University Press, 1987.

Smith, S. A., *Red Petrograd. Revolution in the Factories 1917–1918*, Cambridge, England: Cambridge University Press, 1983.

Sorenson, Jay B., *The Life and Death of Soviet Trade Unionism 1917–1928*, New York: Atherton Press, 1969.

Souvarine, Boris, *Stalin. A Critical Survey of Bolshevism*, New York: Octagon Books, 1972.

Spirin, A. M., *Klassy i partii v grazhdankou'voine v Rossii (1917–1920 gg)*, Moscow: 'Mysl', 1968.

Steinberg, I. N., *In the Workshop of the Revolution*, New York and Toronto: Rinehart & Company, 1953.

Tedford, Thomas L., *Freedom of Speech in the United States*, New York: Random House, 1985.

Thompson, E. P., *Whigs and Hunters. The Origin of the Black Act*, New York: Pantheon Books, 1975.

Tiersky, Ronald, *Ordinary Stalinism. Democratic Centralism and the Question of Communist Political Development*, Boston, London, and Sydney: Allen & Unwin, 1985.

Treadgold, Donald W., *Lenin and His Rivals. The Struggle for Russia's Future, 1898–1906*, New York: Praeger, 1955.

Trotsky, Leon, *The Revolution Betrayed*, New York: Merit Publishers, 1965.

—— *The Transitional Program. The Death Agony of Capitalism and the Tasks of the Fourth International*, in *The Transitional Program for Socialist Revolution*, New York: Pathfinder Press, 1973.

—— *Trotsky: The New Course with a new introduction and The Struggle for the New Course by Max Shachtman*, Ann Arbor, Mich.: University of Michigan Press, 1965.

—— et al., *Their Morals and Ours. Marxist versus Liberal Views on Morality. Four Essays by Leon Trotsky, John Dewey, George Novack*, New York: Merit Publishers, 1966.

Tucker, Robert C., *Political Culture and Leadership in Soviet Russia. From Lenin to Gorbachev*, New York: W. W. Norton, 1987.

—— *Stalin as Revolutionary, 1879–1929*, New York: W. W. Norton, 1973.

Ulam, Adam, *The Bolsheviks*, New York: Collier Macmillan, 1965.

Volin, Lazar, *A Century of Russian Agriculture. From Alexander II to Khrushchev*, Cambridge, Mass.: Harvard University Press, 1970.

Wade, Rex A., *Red Guards and Workers' Militia in the Russian Revolution*, Stanford, Calif.: Stanford University Press, 1984.

Weeks, Albert L., *The First Bolshevik. A Political Biography of Peter Tkachev*, New York: New York University Press, and London: University of London Press, 1968.

Wildman, Allan K., *The Making of a Workers' Revolution. Russian Social Democracy, 1891–1903*, Chicago: University of Chicago Press, 1967.

Williams, Robert C., *The Other Bolsheviks. Lenin and His Critics 1904–1914*, Bloomington and London: Indiana University Press, 1986.

Wolin, Sheldon, *Politics and Vision. Continuity and Innovation in Western Political Thought*, Boston: Little, Brown & Company, 1960.

Wolin, Simon and Slusser, Robert M (eds), *The Soviet Secret Police*, New York: Praeger, 1957.

Wolfe, Bertram D., *The Bridge and the Abyss. The Troubled Friendship of Maxim Gorky and V. I. Lenin*, New York, Washington, and London: Praeger, 1967.

Zile, Zigurds L. (ed.), *Ideas and Forces in Soviet Legal History: Statutes, Decisions and Other Materials in the Development and Processes of Soviet Law*, 2nd edn, Madison, Wisc.: College Printing and Publishing, 1970.

Unpublished Material

Abrams, Robert, 'The local soviets of the RSFSR, 1918–1921', PhD diss., Columbia University, New York, 1966.

Helgesen, Malvin Magnus, 'The origins of the party-state monolith in Soviet Russia: relations between the soviets and party committees in the central provinces, October 1917 – March 1921', PhD diss., State University of New York at Stony Brook, 1980.

Lih, Lars Thomas, 'Bread and authority in Russia: food supply and revolutionary politics, 1914–1921', PhD diss., Princeton University, 1984.

Index

Index by Meg Davies